THE PSYCHOLOGY OF
ATTITUDES AND
ATTITUDE CHANGE

The Sydney Symposium of Social Psychology series

This book is Volume 12 in the *Sydney Symposium of Social Psychology* series. The aim of the Sydney Symposia of Social Psychology is to provide new, integrative insights into key areas of contemporary research. Held every year at the University of New South Wales, Sydney, each symposium deals with an important integrative theme in social psychology, and the invited participants are leading researchers in the field from around the world. Each contribution is extensively discussed during the symposium and is subsequently thoroughly revised into book chapters that are published in the volumes in this series. For further details see the website at www.sydneysymposium.unsw.edu.au

Previous Sydney Symposium of Social Psychology volumes:

SSSP 1. FEELING AND THINKING: THE ROLE OF AFFECT IN SOCIAL COGNITION** ISBN 0-521-64223-X (Edited by J.P. Forgas). *Contributors*: Robert Zajonc, Jim Blascovich, Wendy Berry Mendes, Craig Smith, Leslie Kirby, Eric Eich, Dawn Macauley, Len Berkowitz, Sara Jaffee, EunKyung Jo, Bartholomeu Troccoli, Leonard Martin, Daniel Gilbert, Timothy Wilson, Herbert Bless, Klaus Fiedler, Joseph Forgas, Carolin Showers, Anthony Greenwald, Mahzarin Banaji, Laurie Rudman, Shelly Farnham, Brian Nosek, Marshall Rosier, Mark Leary, Paula Niedenthal & Jamin Halberstadt.

SSSP 2. THE SOCIAL MIND: COGNITIVE AND MOTIVATIONAL ASPECTS OF INTERPERSONAL BEHAVIOR** ISBN 0-521-77092-0 (Edited by J.P. Forgas, K.D. Williams, & L. Wheeler). *Contributors*: William & Claire McGuire, Susan Andersen, Roy Baumeister, Joel Cooper, Bill Crano, Garth Fletcher, Joseph Forgas, Pascal Huguet, Mike Hogg, Martin Kaplan, Norb Kerr, John Nezlek, Fred Rhodewalt, Astrid Schuetz, Constantine Sedikides, Jeffry Simpson, Richard Sorrentino, Dianne Tice, Kip Williams, and Ladd Wheeler.

SSSP 3. SOCIAL INFLUENCE: DIRECT AND INDIRECT PROCESSES* ISBN 1-84169-038-4 (Edited by J.P. Forgas & K.D. Williams). *Contributors*: Robert Cialdini, Eric Knowles, Shannon Butler, Jay Linn, Bibb Latane, Martin Bourgeois, Mark Schaller, Ap Dijksterhuis, James Tedeschi, Richard Petty, Joseph Forgas, Herbert Bless, Fritz Strack, Eva Walther, Sik Hung Ng, Thomas Mussweiler, Kipling Williams, Lara Dolnik, Charles Stangor, Gretchen Sechrist, John Jost, Deborah Terry, Michael Hogg, Stephen Harkins, Barbara David, John Turner, Robin Martin, Miles Hewstone, Russell Spears, Tom Postmes, Martin Lea, Susan Watt.

SSSP 4. THE SOCIAL SELF: COGNITIVE, INTERPERSONAL, AND INTERGROUP PERSPECTIVES** ISBN 1-84169-062-7 (Edited by J.P. Forgas & K.D. Williams). *Contributors*: Eliot R. Smith, Thomas Gilovich, Monica Biernat, Joseph P. Forgas, Stephanie J. Moylan, Edward R. Hirt, Sean M. McCrea, Frederick Rhodewalt, Michael Tragakis, Mark Leary, Roy F. Baumeister, Jean M. Twenge, Natalie Ciarocco, Dianne M. Tice, Jean M. Twenge, Brandon J. Schmeichel, Bertram F. Malle, William Ickes, Marianne LaFrance, Yoshihisa Kashima, Emiko Kashima, Anna Clark, Marilynn B. Brewer, Cynthia L. Pickett, Sabine Otten, Christian S. Crandall, Diane M. Mackie, Joel Cooper, Michael Hogg, Stephen C. Wright, Art Aron, Linda R. Tropp, and Constantine Sedikides.

SSSP 5. SOCIAL JUDGMENTS: IMPLICIT AND EXPLICIT PROCESSES** ISBN 0-521-82248-3. (Edited by J.P. Forgas, K.D. Williams, & W. von Hippel). *Contributors*: Herbert Bless, Marilynn Brewer, David Buss, Tanya Chartrand, Klaus Fiedler, Joseph Forgas, David Funder, Adam Galinsky, Martie Haselton, Denis Hilton, Lucy Johnston, Arie Kruglanski, Matthew Lieberman, John McClure, Mario Mikulincer, Norbert Schwarz, Philip Shaver, Diederik Stapel, Jerry Suls, William von Hippel, Michaela Waenke, Ladd Wheeler, Kipling Williams, Michael Zarate.

SSSP 6. SOCIAL MOTIVATION: CONSCIOUS AND UNCONSCIOUS PROCESSES** ISBN 0-521-83254-3 (Edited by J.P. Forgas, K.D. Williams, & S.M. Laham). Contributors: Henk Aarts, Ran Hassin,Trish Devine, Joseph Forgas, Jens Forster, Nira Liberman, Judy Harackiewicz, Leanne Hing, Mark Zanna, Michael Kernis, Paul Lewicki, Steve Neuberg, Doug Kenrick, Mark Schaller, Tom Pyszczynski, Fred Rhodewalt, Jonathan Schooler, Steve Spencer, Fritz Strack, Roland Deutsch, Howard Weiss, Neal Ashkanasy, Kip Williams, Trevor Case, Wayne Warburton, Wendy Wood, Jeffrey Quinn, Rex Wright and Guido Gendolla.

SSSP 7. THE SOCIAL OUTCAST: OSTRACISM, SOCIAL EXCLUSION, REJECTION, AND BULLYING* ISBN 1-84169-424-X (Edited by K.D. Williams, J.P Forgas, & W. Von Hippel). *Contributors*: Kipling D. Williams, Joseph P. Forgas, William von Hippel, Lisa Zadro, Mark R. Leary, Roy F. Baumeister, and C. Nathan DeWall, Geoff MacDonald, Rachell Kingsbury, Stephanie Shaw, John T. Cacioppo, Louise C. Hawkley, Naomi I. Eisenberger Matthew D. Lieberman, Rainer Romero-Canyas, Geraldine Downey, Jaana Juvonen, Elisheva F. Gross, Kristin L. Sommer, Yonata Rubin, Susan T. Fiske, Mariko Yamamoto, Jean M. Twenge, Cynthia L. Pickett, Wendi L. Gardner, Megan Knowles, Michael A. Hogg, Julie Fitness, Jessica L. Lakin, Tanya L. Chartrand, Kathleen R. Catanese and Dianne M. Tice, Lowell Gaertner, Jonathan Iuzzini, Jaap W. Ouwerkerk, Norbert L. Kerr, Marcello Gallucci, Paul A. M. Van Lange, and Marilynn B. Brewer.

SSSP 8. AFFECT IN SOCIAL THINKING AND BEHAVIOR* ISBN 1-84169-454-2 (Edited by J.P. Forgas). *Contributors*: Joseph P. Forgas, Carrie Wyland, Simon M. Laham, Martie G. Haselton Timothy Ketelaar, Piotr Winkielman, John T. Cacioppo,

Herbert Bless, Klaus Fiedler, Craig A. Smith, Bieke David, Leslie D. Kirby, Eric Eich, Dawn Macaulay, Gerald L. Clore, Justin Storbeck, Roy F. Baumeister, Kathleen D. Vohs, Dianne M. Tice, Dacher Keltner, E.J. Horberg, Christopher Oveis, Elizabeth W. Dunn, Simon M. Laham, Constantine Sedikides, Tim Wildschut, Jamie Arndt, Clay Routledge, Yaacov Trope, Eric R. Igou, Chris Burke, Felicia A. Huppert, Ralph Erber, Susan Markunas, Joseph P. Forgas, Joseph Ciarrochi, John T. Blackledge, Janice R. Kelly, Jennifer R.Spoor, John G. Holmes, Danu B. Anthony.

SSSP 9. EVOLUTION AND THE SOCIAL MIND* ISBN 1-84169-458-0 (Edited by J.P. Forgas, M.G. Haselton, & W. von Hippel). *Contributors*: William von Hippel, Martie Haselton, Joseph P. Forgas, R.I.M. Dunbar, Steven W. Gangestad, Randy Thornhill, Douglas T. Kenrick, Andrew W. Delton, Theresa E. Robertson, D. Vaughn Becker, Steven L. Neuberg, Phoebe C. Ellsworth, Ross Buck, Joseph P. Forgas, Paul B.T. Badcock, Nicholas B. Allen, Peter M. Todd, Jeffry A. Simpson, Jonathon LaPaglia, Debra Lieberman, Garth J. O. Fletcher, Nickola C. Overall, Abraham P. Buunk, Karlijn Massar, Pieternel Dijkstra, Mark Van Vugt, Rob Kurzban, Jamin Halberstadt, Oscar Ybarra, Matthew C. Keller, Emily Chan, Andrew S. Baron, Jeffrey Hutsler, Stephen Garcia, Jeffrey Sanchez-Burks, Kimberly Rios Morrison, Jennifer R. Spoor, Kipling D. Williams, Mark Schaller, Lesley A. Duncan.

SSSP 10. SOCIAL RELATIONSHIPS: COGNITIVE, AFFECTIVE, AND MOTIVATIONAL PROCESSES* ISBN 978-1-84169-715-4 (Edited by J.P. Forgas & J. Fitness). *Contributors*: Joseph P. Forgas, Julie Fitness, Elaine Hatfield, Richard L. Rapson, Gian C. Gonzaga, Martie G. Haselton, Phillip R. Shaver, Mario Mikulincer, David P. Schmitt, Garth J.O. Fletcher, Alice D. Boyes, Linda K. Acitelli, Margaret S. Clark, Steven M. Graham, Erin Williams, Edward P. Lemay, Christopher R. Agnew, Ximena B. Arriaga, Juan E. Wilson, Marilynn B. Brewer, Jeffry A. Simpson, W. Andrew Collins, SiSi Tran, Katherine C. Haydon, Shelly L. Gable, Patricia Noller, Susan Conway, Anita Blakeley-Smith, Julie Peterson, Eli J. Finkel, Sandra L. Murray, Lisa Zadro, Kipling D. Williams, Rowland S. Miller.

SSSP 11. PSYCHOLOGY OF SELF-REGULATION: COGNITIVE, AFFEC-TIVE, AND MOTIVATIONAL PROCESSES* ISBN 978-1-84872-842-4 (Edited by J.P. Forgas, R. Baumeister, & D.M. Tice). *Contributors*: Joseph P. Forgas, Roy F. Baumeister, Dianne M. Tice, Jessica L. Alquist, Carol Sansone, Malte Friese, Michaela Wänke, Wilhelm Hofmann, Constantine Sedikides, Christian Unkelbach, Henning Plessner, Daniel Memmert, Charles S. Carver, Michael F. Scheier, Gabriele Oettingen, Peter M. Gollwitzer, Jens Förster, Nira Liberman, Ayelet Fishbach, Gráinne M. Fitzsimons, Justin Friesen, Edward Orehek, Arie W. Kruglanski, Sander L. Koole, Thomas F. Denson, Klaus Fiedler, Matthias Bluemke, Christian Unkelbach, Hart Blanton, Deborah L. Hall, Kathleen D. Vohs, Jannine D. Lasaleta, Bob Fennis, William von Hippel, Richard Ronay, Eli J. Finkel, Daniel C. Molden, Sarah E. Johnson, Paul W. Eastwick.

* Published by Psychology Press
**Published by Cambridge University Press

THE PSYCHOLOGY OF ATTITUDES AND ATTITUDE CHANGE

Edited by

Joseph P. Forgas
University of New South Wales

Joel Cooper
Princeton University

William D. Crano
Claremont Graduate University

Psychology Press
Taylor & Francis Group

New York   London

Psychology Press
Taylor & Francis Group
711 Third Avenue
New York, NY 10017

Psychology Press
Taylor & Francis Group
27 Church Road
Hove, East Sussex BN3 2FA

© 2010 by Taylor and Francis Group, LLC
Psychology Press is an imprint of Taylor & Francis Group, an Informa business

International Standard Book Number: 978-1-84872-908-7 (Hardback)

Visit the Taylor & Francis Web site at
http://www.taylorandfrancis.com

and the Psychology Press Web site at
http://www.psypress.com

Contents

List of Contributors

David M. Amodio
New York University
New York, New York, USA

Jim Blascovich
University of California, Santa Barbara
Santa Barbara, California, USA

Marcella H. Boynton
Duke University
Durham, North Carolina, USA

Zhansheng Chen
University of Hong Kong
Pokfulam, Hong Kong

Joel Cooper
Princeton University
Princeton, New Jersey, USA

William D. Crano
Claremont Graduate University
Claremont, California, USA

Klaus Fiedler
University of Heidelberg
Heidelberg, Germany

Joseph P. Forgas
University of New South Wales
Sydney, Australia

Cindy Harmon-Jones
Texas A&M University
College Station, Texas, USA

Eddie Harmon-Jones
Texas A&M University
College Station, Texas, USA

Allyson L. Holbrook
University of Illinois at Chicago
Chicago, Illinois, USA

Blair T. Johnson
University of Connecticut
Storrs, Connecticut, USA

Jon A. Krosnick
Stanford University
Stanford, California, USA

Tina Langer
University of Trier
Trier, Germany

Alison Ledgerwood
University of California, Davis
Davis, California, USA

Brenda Major
University of California, Santa Barbara
Santa Barbara, California, USA

Cade McCall
University of California, Santa Barbara
Santa Barbara, California, USA

Jennifer Peach
University of Waterloo
Waterloo, Ontario, Canada

Benjamin Peterson
University of Utah
Salt Lake City, Utah

Radmila Prislin
San Diego State University
San Diego, California, USA

Leonie Reutner
University of Basel
Basel, Switzerland

Frederick Rhodewalt
University of Utah
Salt Lake City, Utah, USA

Steven J. Spencer
University of Waterloo
Waterloo, Ontario, Canada

Sarah S. M. Townsend
University of California, Santa Barbara
Santa Barbara, California, USA

Yaacov Trope
New York University
New York, New York, USA

Eva Walther
University of Trier
Trier, Germany

Michaela Wänke
University of Basel
Basel, Switzerland

Duane Wegener
Purdue University
West Lafayette, Indiana, USA

Kipling D. Williams
Purdue University
West Lafayette, Indiana, USA

Emiko Yoshida
University of Waterloo
Waterloo, Ontario, Canada

Mark P. Zanna
University of Waterloo
Waterloo, Ontario, Canada

Section *I*

Introduction and Basic Issues

1

Attitudes and Attitude Change
An Introductory Review

WILLIAM D. CRANO, JOEL COOPER,
AND JOSEPH P. FORGAS

One of the most striking characteristics of human beings is our ability to effort-lessly and automatically construct elaborate plans and form predispositions and behavioral intentions based on our past experiences, media exposure, and other forms of socially supplied information. The concept of attitudes is central to under-standing how experience gives rise to predispositions, and psychologists have spent the best part of the past hundred years trying to understand the intricacies of this process. The main objective of this book is to review and integrate some of the most recent developments in research on attitudes and attitude change, presenting the work of eminent scholars in this field.

Despite decades of research, the question of how attitudes are created, main-tained, and changed, and how they eventually come to influence behavior, remain as intriguing as ever. What role do associative processes play in the formation of attitudes? How do attitudes function as global and local action guides? What is the function of implicit evaluations and vicarious experiences in producing attitude change? Are implicit associations really a useful way to measure attitudes? What are the respective roles played by affect, needs, and social interactions in attitude formation and change, and how effectively can persuasion be used in pragmatic and real-life contexts to change attitudes? What contribution can attitude research make to understanding prejudice, intergroup attitudes, and political attitudes? These are just some of the issues we intend to explore in this volume.

To answer questions such as these, we have divided this volume into four basic sections. The first section of the book, after this introductory chapter, addresses some of the *general issues* about the nature and characteristics of attitudes and the processes underlying their formation (chapters by Johnson & Boynton; Ledgerwood & Trope; Walther & Langer; Fiedler). In the second section, a number of contributors consider the *cognitive and affective processes* involved in attitude formation and change (Spencer, Peach, Yoshida, & Zanna; Holbrook & Krosnick; Cooper; Forgas). The third section of the book presents research that explores the processes, mechanisms, and applications of *attitude change and persuasion* (Harmon-Jones, Amodio, & Harmon-Jones; Wänke & Reutner; Williams, Chen, & Wegener; Prislin). Finally, in the fourth, concluding section of the book we focus on the *application, implications, and extensions* of attitude research to various applied and real-life domains (chapters by Crano; Major & Townsend; Rhodewalt & Peterson; Blascovich & McCall). We will begin, however, with a brief theoretical and historical review of attitude research in social psychology.

FROM EXPERIENCE TO PREDISPOSITION

It has long been recognized in social science theorizing that humans possess a unique symbolic capacity to distill their social experiences into stable mental representations that come to guide their future plans and behaviors. Several influential theories sought to deal with this proposition. The theories of Max Weber (1947), although rarely invoked in experimental social psychology, assume a direct relationship between an individual's beliefs and evaluations—their "attitudes"—and their subsequent social behavior in how larger social systems and structures are created and maintained. Weber's classic analysis linking the advent of capitalism with the spread of the protestant ethic is fundamentally a social psychological theory.

Weber suggests that the historical change to the attitudes and values of protestantism was the fundamental force that shaped large-scale social and economic processes, such as the advent of capitalist social organization (Weber, 1947). For Weber, mental representations—attitudes—are the key to understanding interpersonal and societal processes, still one of the key objectives of contemporary attitude research (see Crano, this volume; Major & Townsend, this volume). His work on bureaucracies is especially interesting, as he argued that understanding the attitudes and mind-set of the bureaucrat is the key to explaining how bureaucracies function. On the one hand, the rule systems that define bureaucracies play a critical role in shaping and maintaining the attitudes of the bureaucrat; in turn, such attitudes help to explain their behaviors toward their clients and coworkers.

Weber's methodologies also involved an innovative attempt to combine qualitative and quantitative data with the analysis of historical and cultural processes. Several of the chapters here report important progress in research on the interface of individual attitudes and social systems and behavior that has a distinctly Weberian flavor (e.g., Crano; Prislin; Ledgerwood & Trope; Wänke & Reutner). Indeed, one could make a plausible case that Max Weber was one of the precursors of modern social attitude research, and it is regrettable that his work and approach remain largely unrecognized by most social psychologists today.

Another important theoretical framework that is highly relevant to the concerns of the present book is symbolic interactionism, and the work of George Herbert Mead. Mead's "social behaviorism" was a comprehensive attempt to create a theory that links individual symbolic mental processes to the regulation of real-life social behaviors. Mead emphasized that interpersonal behavior is both the source and the product of the symbolic representations and expectations—in essence, attitudes—of social actors.

By symbolically distilling and representing social experiences, the individual acquires social expertise and attitudes, which lie at the core of the socialized "me." Attitudes and symbolic representations in turn regulate subsequent behaviors—although attitudes are not acted out in a simple determinate fashion in everyday life. It is the role of the unique, creative "I" to continuously reassess, monitor, and redefine attitudes as they are applied, injecting a sense of indeterminacy and openness into our social behaviors. Understanding the nature of this indeterminacy in the attitude-behavior relationship has remained one of the core concerns of attitude research to this day (see chapters by Johnson & Boynton; Spencer et al.; Prislin; Williams et al.; Crano).

Symbolic interactionism has not become a dominant theory within social psychology, most probably because the methodologies available at the time did not provide a suitable empirical means for studying individual mental representations. Yet contemporary attitude and social cognitive research often deals with the same kinds of questions that were of interest to Weber and Mead: How are individual thoughts, beliefs, representations, and attitudes derived from social experiences, and do they in turn influence interpersonal behavior (see also chapters by Cooper; Forgas; Wänke & Reutner; Major & Townsend; Rhodewalt & Peterson; Holbrook & Krosnick, this volume). The work of Weber and Mead thus provides a fascinating and largely untapped reservoir of intriguing theories and hypotheses about the ways that symbolic representations of past experiences give rise to attitudes and eventually influence real social behaviors.

ATTITUDES IN EMPIRICAL PSYCHOLOGY: HISTORY AND BACKGROUND

The study of attitudes, their measurement, formation, stability, change, and their causes and effects, has been a central preoccupation of social psychology from the field's earliest days. Although the science of social psychology is only a little more than a century old, Thomas and Znaniecki wrote in 1928 that social psychology was essentially the study of the attitude. The understanding of what constituted an attitude was broader then than it is today, and for Thomas and Znaniecki, the term *attitude* denoted a collective, cultural construct, rather than the now dominant conceptualization of attitude as an individualistic, intrapsychic characteristic.

The scientific study of attitudes was made possible by the development of methods to assess them. L. L. Thurstone (1928) and R. Likert (1932) developed sophisticated methods to develop scales that could be used to study attitudes. With the publication of attitude measurement techniques, the volume of empirical research in attitudes exploded. Gordon Allport (1935) declared the attitude to be "the most distinctive and indispensable concept in contemporary American social psychology" (p. 198). From the perspective of the 21st century, it is clear that Allport's assessment remains true, with the caveat that the qualifying term *American* is no longer required. A literature search using *attitude* as the search term yields approximately 50,000 articles, chapters, books, and dissertations (Visser & Cooper, 2007).

Indeed it is difficult to find much in the voluminous literature of social psychology that does not refer in some ways directly or indirectly to attitudes as a central construct. Only a few years after innovative attitude measurement techniques were introduced by Thurstone and Likert, attitude scaling and measurement became a defining preoccupation of social psychologists. We have developed additional distinctive and indispensible concepts and techniques since Allport's days, but it is fair to say that attitudes have always maintained their place at the head of social psychology's table.

This is not to suggest that it has been all smooth sailing. Social psychology's attitudes toward attitudes have waxed and waned. At times, other constructs have generated more excitement, but the place of attitudes in social psychology has never been supplanted. Perhaps the best historical perspective of the role of attitudes in social psychology was put, as might be expected, by Bill McGuire (1985), who observed, "The field has been a mosaic of heterogeneous pieces from the start, but attitudes have always been one of the central elements of the design" (p. 234). This measured appraisal reflects social psychology's romance with the attitude construct more fairly than Allport's more sanguine view. The relationship has not always been steady. There have been rifts and occasional dalliances but never a divorce.

Why this focus on a construct that has characterized an entire field of behavioral research for the past 80 years persists is explained in this volume. The intellectual scope of the work is vast, ranging from the apparently simple associative learning models of the evaluative conditioners (see Wänke & Reutner, this volume) to the more complex considerations of the implicit attitudes theorists (see Fiedler, this volume) to applied researchers' concern over the factors that impel a consumer to choose one product over another, or to initiate or resist using an illicit drug. The theories and methods underlying these varied operations are well developed, and still developing (see Spencer et al.; Williams et al.; Holbrook & Krosnick, this volume). The breadth of our studies speaks to the diversity and richness of the field, and to the potential for researchers in this area to contribute meaningfully to social progress and to solving practical problems. The work outlined in this volume is timely, exciting, and useful. However, before we begin to consider this rich fare, some background is necessary to fully appreciate this splendid table of intellectual treats set here for our readers.

THE PEAKS AND TROUGHS IN ATTITUDE RESEARCH

Research activity on attitudes has ebbed and flowed over the years. McGuire (1985) identified three peaks in interest in the intellectual progression of research on attitudes, to which Prislin and Crano (2008) added a fourth. The first peak (1920s–1930s) was concerned with the fundamental nature and consequent measurement of the construct. Here we find the giants of attitude measurement—Thurstone, Guttman, Likert, Osgood—whose ideas regarding the proper way to measure (i.e., operationalize) attitudes of necessity shaped the very ways we conceptualize the construct. Their work is honored in today's measurement approaches, none of which stray far from the bases laid down so many years ago, and in the emphasis on the evaluative nature of attitudes, a defining feature of most attitude measures from Thurstone onward.

An interregnum in the 1940s followed the first peak, when social psychology and the world at large focused on bigger game than attitudes. It is fair to say, however, that World War II also was a watershed time for the development of attitude theory, for during this period, Carl Hovland worked in the Information and Education Division of the U.S. War Department, where he designed and evaluated the training programs and films prepared for American troops. During this period, he assembled some of the most talented attitude researchers in North America to help in the war effort.

In the second peak (1950s and 1960s), Hovland brought many of his wartime colleagues to Yale, where he founded the Yale Communication and Attitude Change Program, which arguably set the stage for investigation of many of the phenomena with which attitude researchers today concern themselves. The basic laboratory experimental approach, coupled with issues of real-world relevance, characterized the Yale group's general investigative orientation. The field has preserved much of the experimental orientation of the Yale group, but over the years often failed to connect its work with issues of social importance, a guiding principle of Hovland and his colleagues.

During this same peak period, important developments in attitude research and theory also were being made on the country's other coast, at Stanford University. There, blessed with a stable of some of the country's most talented students, Leon Festinger was researching an audacious theory that was to turn the standard attitude → behavior chain on its head. Of his three seminal contributions—the theories of social communication, social comparison, and cognitive dissonance—dissonance has had the most widespread effect, though social comparison, with its periodic renewals of popularity, has obvious staying power as well (Festinger, 1950, 1954, 1957; Stapel & Suls, 2007).

Dissonance has been a central feature of much research in social psychology (see Cooper; Harmon-Jones et al., this volume). The theory has been cited more than 2,000 times, and the count rises with every passing day as dissonance researchers continue to unravel the mysteries of this uniquely human phenomenon. The relevance and importance of dissonance for attitudes is immediately apparent, because a primary source of dissonance is the lack of fit between competing cognitions (read, attitudes) and between cognitions and behaviors. The attitude-behavior link has come in for the most scrutiny in dissonance research, because dissonance researchers have been so ingenious in fabricating situations in which behaviors inconsistent with beliefs are induced and cannot be undone. Under these circumstances, the theory leads us to expect a change of cognition (attitude), and the theory is more often right than wrong. This reconceptualization of the attitude-behavior link was critically important in facilitating social psychologists' more complete understanding of the role of attitudes on actions, and the role of actions on attitudes and attitude change.

However, an even more important contribution of the dissonance movement was the effect it had on freeing social psychology from the tight constraints of learning theory, which largely ruled the attitude roost until Festinger. His willingness to speak of, and research, social cognitions was not always appreciated by other psychologists, who were tied to a more strict operationism (e.g., see Bem, 1972; Chapanis & Chapanis, 1964; Rosenberg, 1965; but see Crano & Messé, 1970; Zanna & Cooper, 1974). Debates over the proper understanding of dissonance phenomena continue to this day, but they rarely seem as lively as those seen in the second peak.

Research in the third peak (1980s and, as McGuire predicted, into the 1990s) was concerned with structural factors, the fundamental nature of attitudes, and the change models built on these understandings. To be sure, there was a considerable effort to differentiate attitudes along a weak-strong continuum (Petty & Krosnick, 1995), but this facet of attitudes was largely overshadowed by the burgeoning research on the dual process models (Chaiken, 1980; Petty & Cacioppo, 1986). The dual process approach captured research on attitude change and set the agenda for much of the research of the third peak.

Some of McGuire's predictions missed—the expected rise in the influence of consistency models did not materialize. They seemed to have reached their zenith with Abelson et al. (1968), though a general preference for consistency is axiomatic in much of the work of attitude researchers in general, and dissonance theorists in particular. Another unconfirmed prediction was McGuire's guess that functionalist approaches would come to play a greater role in contemporary attitude research. Although there were some interesting starts in this direction (e.g., Breckler & Wiggins, 1991, 1993), as a whole the more formal functional models did not make much of a comeback from the 1950s and 1960s (Katz, 1960; Smith, Bruner, & White, 1956).

We are in now the fourth peak, which we see as starting from the year 2000 onward. This phase, which Prislin and Crano (2008) labeled the contemporary period, extends the third peak with the development of a more varied diet of process models, including, among others:

- Kruglanski's unimodel (Kruglanski et al., 2003; Kruglanski & Thompson, 1999), which argues for the functional equivalence of source cues and message arguments (Erb, Pierro, Mannetti, Kruglanski, & Spiegel, 2007),
- The reflective/impulsive model of Strack and Deutsch (2004, 2005), a dual process model that posits two different but interacting modes of information integration in coming to a behavior, including a reflective mode in which decisions are based on facts and values, and an impulsive system, in which associations and motivational variations determine responses, and
- The quad model (Conrey, Sherman, Gawronski, Hugenberg, & Groom, 2005), which holds that consideration of four or more distinct and interacting processes provides a more accurate prediction of decisions, most of the time, than the more limited numbers available in the dual process and uniprocess models (Sherman, 2006).

In addition to the more extensive development and elaboration of uniprocess, dual process, and multiprocess models, the contemporary period also has seen a greater focus on the measurement implicit motives, associations, and attitudes, and their associations with behavior. At the level of measurement, the Implicit Association Test (IAT; Greenwald, McGhee, & Schwartz, 1998) has engulfed the field and has become a popular—albeit much criticized (see Fiedler, this volume)— methodology of assessing attitudes and dispositions of which its holders appear largely unaware. This approach has spawned a mini-industry of implicit measurements of just about everything, from implicit racial bias (Amodio & Devine, 2006) to brand awareness (Maison, Greenwald, & Bruin, 2004) to alcohol use (Houben, Rothermund, & Weiss, 2009) to self-esteem (Greenwald et al., 2002). Not all are persuaded that the implicit measure is as useful as its proponents and its popularity suggest (see Blanton & Jaccard, 2006; De Houwer, Beckers, & Moors, 2007; Fiedler, Messner, & Bluemke, 2006), and the critiques of the approach are well taken. The measurement approach should not be simply pulled off the shelf—or the computer—and used without care and concern for its construct validity.

Even given growing disquiet over the implicit attitude measurement approaches, there is more openness to the unconscious end of the cognitive spectrum in attitude research than was evident in the earlier peaks. In some ways, this was to be expected, as the field gradually moved from the behaviorist to the more cognitive models that characterize the field. Also, openness has been encouraged by the movement of emotion researchers into the realm of attitudes (Forgas, 2008, this volume), and surprisingly, by research on evaluative conditioning (Walther & Langer, 2008; see also Walther & Langer, this volume), which suggests that at least sometimes, behaviors may be motivated by conditioned responses quite beyond the awareness of the actor. Paradoxically, this reemerging area of research, with ties to the ancient behaviorist traditions of Pavlov, Watson, and Hull, has encouraged social psychologists to develop mentalistic constructs that would have been anathema to these seminal figures.

Another noteworthy trend in the fourth peak of social psychology's intellectual romance with attitudes is evident in today's at least tepid linkage of basic theory with applications. This association, which Campbell (1969) challenged the field to adopt in his classic *Reforms as Experiments*, has been prompted in no small measure by federal agencies that require a clear return on their investments in the field's practitioners. The movement has strengthened the quality of work in a host of areas in which the application of principles of attitude formation, structure, and change is critical (see also Crano, this volume). More than in merely creating a better mousetrap—or, better yet, selling the mousetrap to more people—this move in the direction of application is important as it feeds the growing requirements of social marketers, whose work for the betterment of society sorely needs the best insights the field has to offer.

Research as wide ranging as preventing cancer-causing behavior, attenuating risky sex and drunk driving, and delaying onset of illicit drug use in young adolescents have all been facilitated by applications of basic principles of attitude formation and change. These applications in part answer Campbell's call to return the investments society has made in the training and development of those whose training was largely sustained by the society they now serve. The field has come to the conclusion, perhaps, that there is no free lunch, an insight that is as welcome as it is overdue.

ATTITUDE CHANGE

As we have seen from this brief review, attitudes really do matter. They express our evaluations, influence our perceptions, and guide our behavior. A matter of great practical and theoretical concern is how to alter them. Political candidates know that people's attitudes toward them, and possibly the issues they represent, predict their voting behavior. Commercial marketers know that people's attitudes toward a product predict their purchasing behavior. Finding the principles that govern the creation and change of attitudes has been the focus of a healthy proportion of those 50,000 entries in the psychological literature.

Research on attitudes diverged on two different paths. One major tradition studied the structure, function, and assessment of attitudes. The other developed to study how attitudes change, focusing on the situational contexts that cause people to be persuaded. Ironically, those traditions often ran on parallel tracks with only sparse and infrequent intersections.

Understanding persuasion has been central to the political process and to rhetoric in social discourse. And so it was that a political dilemma in the midst of a world war prompted the government of the United States to facilitate the study of persuasion. In the early 1940s, the U.S. War Department anticipated a problem convincing U.S. citizens to continue their sacrifice and determination to support military action in the Pacific following the successful conclusion of World War II on the European continent. The War Department knew the difficulty in terms of resources, casualties, and time that it would take to defeat the Japanese and needed to convince the population of the length and difficulty of such a war.

As discussed, Yale University psychologist Carl Hovland was asked to head this new research program at the U.S. Army's Information and Education Division, analyzing and developing indoctrination films that could successfully change attitudes and boost morale. What were the principles that science had determined were key to changing attitudes toward the war? The state of the science of social psychology at that time had very few suggestions in its arsenal.

Hovland set about the task of developing a series of techniques that would serve not only as the basis for indoctrination films but also for understanding the basic principles governing changes of attitudes. He joined with several colleagues to found the Yale Communication and Attitude Change Program—the first systematic investigation of the principles of attitude change (Hovland, Janis, & Kelley, 1953; Hovland, Lumsdaine, & Sheffield, 1949).

The Yale group took as their challenge the identification of as many of the variables as possible that affect attitude change. To be systematic, they needed a framework, and they found one in the writings of the Greek master of rhetoric, Aristotle. In *The Rhetoric*, Aristotle wrote, "Of the modes of persuasion furnished by the spoken word, there are three kinds. The first depends on the personal character of the speaker; the second on putting the audience in a certain frame of mind; the third on the proof...provided by the words of the speech itself." Despite the spread of centuries, Aristotle had provided the way to organize the study of persuasion. Methodically, Hovland and his colleagues divided the landscape into the study of the communicator, the audience, and the communication.

Having parsed the persuasion process into the study of the three Aristotelian components, the next major issue involved what predictions to make about each of the factors involved in attitude change. Some predictions seemed apparent and obvious, but the Hovland group sought to confirm empirically the obvious as well as the non-obvious. Communicator credibility was one of the first notions to be tested: Is a credible communicator more influential in producing attitude change than a non-credible communicator (Hovland & Weiss, 1951)? How long lasting are such effects (Kelman & Hovland, 1953)? The message also received attention: Should a message contain weak or strong arguments, be one-sided or two-sided (Hovland, 1957)? Do the audience's attitudes matter (Hovland, Harvey, & Sherif, 1957)? Some of the findings confirmed the obvious: For example, credible communicators are more persuasive than non-credible communicators. Other findings showed surprising evidence for the non-obvious. Perhaps the most memorable of these findings was the sleeper effect: the observation that the persuasive effect of a communicator who is low in credibility increases over time whereas the persuasiveness of a highly credible communicator decreases over time. And so, as most social psychologists know, the early days of attitude change research were filled with systematic application of social psychological methods to establish a compendium of research results to ascertain the fundamental aspects of how and why people change their attitudes.

What was less apparent about the contributions of the Yale Communication and Attitude Change program was its theoretical foundation. Arguably, the theoretical underpinnings of the work were influential for two categories of reasons. First, the conceptual basis of the work was barely noticed because it seemed as uncontroversial as, for example, the law of effect. And second, when results began to accumulate that seemed difficult to understand through the broad theoretical lens of the original program, it gave urgent impetus to finding alternative theoretical foundations for persuasion. That search created an explosion of research in attitude change that has continued through the present day.

The underlying theoretical mechanism for Hovland and colleagues was learning theory. It was hardly noticed as the underlying mechanism because in the era in which the work was conceived, one form of learning theory or another was at the heart of most of psychology. For Hovland et al., persuasion *was* learning. People needed to learn the content of a persuasive message. If they successfully learned the message, then attitudes changed. Any factor that impacted the learning of a message was considered to be grist for the mill of attitude change. In order to learn a message, people must attend to it, so the role of attention was studied. In order for the message to produce persuasion, it needed to be convincing, so the message was studied. Incentives and disincentives to learning were studied. A credible source was predicted to be more persuasive than a non-credible source because it was thought to be more rewarding to agree with someone who is correct. An attractive source was predicted to be more persuasive than a less attractive source because it was considered more rewarding to agree with someone whom you like. The use of incentives and rewards as a theoretical guidepost was taken for granted in the decades of early attitude change research so that the theoretical tenets were rarely examined in detail.

As research on attitude change progressed, it was apparent that something was very wrong with the conceptual approach. The mystery for researchers was to understand the many anomalies that were appearing. Persuasive communications were not always based on strong arguments. Communicators whose credibility was suspect in terms of their knowledge of an issue or their expertise about a product were, in the right circumstances, more persuasive than credible experts in changing attitudes. At first, such phenomena were intriguing exceptions to the general rules of learning. However, as such interesting exceptions continued to grow, new and exciting theories emerged to explain them. When theory battles theory in the research laboratory, new scholars are drawn into the field, more data are collected, and our knowledge expands exponentially. That was the story of attitude change research in the decade of the 1960s and beyond.

The most prominent new theory to explain how persuasion works was cognitive response theory (e.g., Brock, 1967; Greenwald, 1968). In the wake of evidence showing very little correlation between learning the content of a message and the degree of persuasion that is engendered, the cognitive response model proposed that attitude change is driven by the generation and retention of one's own idiosyncratic cognitive reaction to a persuasive message, and not the learning of the message per se. Arguing from a different set of traditions, dissonance theory (Festinger, 1957) showed that people can be persuaded by generating their own arguments and that the degree of attitude change was an inverse function of the degree of incentive people had to generate their arguments (Cohen, 1962; Linder, Cooper, & Jones, 1967). The assumption that attitude change was shackled to the theoretical structure of rewards, reinforcements, and learning was broken. Attitude research was freed to search for multiple causes and contextual specificities for adopting and changing attitudes.

The theoretical innovation that probably was most influential in changing the modern face of attitude change research was the promulgation of dual factor theories of persuasion. Petty and Cacioppo (1986) and Chaiken (1987) advanced the argument that persuasion consists of two potentially independent processes that account for attitude change. One was a thoughtful, deliberate, and effortful process that Petty and Cacioppo called central route processing and that Chaiken called systematic processing. The other was a less effortful, quicker and less deliberate process called peripheral route or heuristic processing. For two decades, the literature on attitude change has been infused with myriad empirical and theoretical contributions seeking to extend, refine, or limit the impact of dual processes of persuasion.

One ironic aspect of the research on attitude change is that it has not consistently relied on the research on attitudes. Despite the long-standing tradition of scholarly work on the concept, definition, and measurement of an attitude, the research on attitude change rarely paused to consider what was meant by an attitude. While it may be overly glib to say that an attitude is whatever an attitude scale measures, research on attitude change has not often been more sophisticated than that. Hovland et al.'s classic work on source credibility assessed what they called opinions. For example, people were asked whether they held the opinion that the Soviet Union would build a nuclear submarine. The percentage of agreement following the communication was compared to the percentage of agreement prior to the communication. Attitude change was simply the change in the percentage of participants who held that opinion. Through the ensuing decades, a consensus emerged that an attitude was at least characterized by an evaluation of an object. Discussions of whether that evaluation was necessarily emotional or affective, whether it subsumed beliefs and behaviors, were dulled by the operations "on the ground," that is, in our studies and experiments. "Likert-like" scales asked people their agreement or disagreement with a particular position on a topic, and that seemed sufficient to assess attitude change. The fact that Rensis Likert would likely have been disappointed by the modification of his technique notwithstanding, the "Likert-like" scale seemed to do the job adequately for understanding how particular messages influenced people to change their attitudes.

At the current moment, there is a rare opportunity to meld together the study of attitude change and the study of the structure and meaning of the attitude. The creation of implicit measures of attitudes (Fazio & Olson, 2003; Greenwald & Banaji, 1995) has forced persuasion researchers to be clearer about what they mean by an attitude (see also Fiedler, this volume). The old saw that attitudes are whatever an attitude scale measures is not helpful when implicit and explicit measures of attitudes differ. Is the IAT a measure of *real* attitudes relative to explicit measures? If a message persuades someone to change his or her attitude on an explicit measure but not on an implicit measure, which measure has assessed the *real* attitude? If two implicit measures show different responses to a communication, which one is the true measure of an attitude?

To begin to resolve this question, attitude change researchers have begun to grapple with what attitude researchers have traditionally focused on. What do we mean by *attitude*? How do experiences give rise to attitudes, and how do such attitudes in turn influence subsequent behaviors? This are the very same questions that early theories by Max Weber and George Herbert Mead sought to answer. The coming together of research in structure and assessment of the attitude with the long-standing research on attitude change may be the most exciting challenge of the coming decades.

OVERVIEW OF THE BOOK

This book seeks to contribute to this process by surveying some of the most important recent developments in research on attitudes and attitude change. The content of the book is organized into four sections.

Section I, after this introductory review, looks at some basic issues in attitude research. *Johnson and Boynton* consider the thorny issue of why attitude-behavior links remain as difficult to demonstrate as ever and suggest reliably measuring behaviors may be just as problematic as measuring attitudes that supposed to predict them. *Ledgerwood and Trope* propose that attitudes have a dual function, guiding action in the current social context and also influencing planning and behavior in the distant future, and it is this dual nature that accounts for some of the difficulties in identifying robust attitude-behavior correspondences. In the next chapter, *Walther and Langer* discuss the role of associative processes and evaluative conditioning in attitude formation and suggests a close link between Pavlovian learning and these mechanisms. *Fiedler* offers a thoughtful review and criticism of the burgeoning literature on implicit attitude measurement and identifies a number of serious conceptual and methodological problems with this approach.

Section II of the book explores the role of *cognitive and affective processes* in attitude formation and change. *Spencer, Peach, Yoshida, and Zanna* examine how implicit normative evaluations can be quite different from implicit attitudes and can predict important behaviors above and beyond implicit attitudes in areas such as stereotyping, prejudice, stereotype threat, and identity protection. *Holbrook and Krosnick* explore the relationship between attitude accessibility and attitude functioning and suggest that greater accessibility is associated with resistance to attitude change. *Cooper* describes the role that vicarious processes play in attitude change—when the observed pains and pleasures of others influence our own attitudes. In the last chapter in this section, *Forgas* describes a series of experiments demonstrating the important role that temporary affective states and moods can play in the formation, expression, and change of social attitudes.

Section III of the book focuses on *attitude change and persuasion*. *Harmon-Jones, Amodio, and Harmon-Jones* review research and theoretical developments on the theory of cognitive dissonance and present an action-based model of dissonance that extends the original theory by specifying *why* cognitive inconsistency prompts dissonance and dissonance reduction. *Wänke and Reutner* look at pragmatic processes in persuasion and suggest that conversational norms (the expectation of persuasion) can improve the effectiveness of persuasive attempts. *Williams, Chen, and Wegener* present new theory and data showing that people are especially vulnerable to persuasion when their needs for belonging and self-esteem are threatened, and the persuasive message is cloaked in language that replenishes this deficiency. *Prislin* proposes a conceptualization of persuasion as social interaction involving bidirectional exchanges over a period of time and describes a series of studies supporting such a model.

In Section IV of the book, *applications, implications, and extensions* of attitude research are considered. In the first chapter in this section, *Crano* reviews past and present work on applied, mass media persuasion campaigns and argues that applying evidence gained from scientific research could make such campaigns much more effective. *Major and Townsend* describe a series of experiments showing that status ideologies—attitudes about the fairness and legitimacy of status relations in society—shape perceptions of and reactions to prejudice. *Rhodewalt and Peterson* review and integrate research on the fragile and narcissistic self and suggest that intergroup attitudes may be influenced by personal goals as a means for defensive self-regulation. Finally, *Blascovich and McCall* describe existing research and the fascinating potential uses of virtual reality techniques for the study of attitude formation and change.

CONCLUSIONS

Understanding the way that social experiences are mentally represented and give rise to attitudes and predispositions that guide subsequent behavior is in a sense the core question of social psychology. As the introductory review shows, interest in this issue has never been far from the center of social psychological inquiry. For the past three decades or so, the social cognitive paradigm has been in ascendancy in our discipline, and we have discovered much about the cognitive, affective, and motivational mechanisms that influence attitude formation and change. Our main purpose with this volume is to survey the latest developments in this exciting field. The chapters included here, in their various ways, all make the point that the study of attitude formation, maintenance, and change is a thriving, productive field today. We hope that readers will find this book an informative and interesting overview of the current status of this fascinating area of inquiry.

REFERENCES

Abelson, R. P., et al. (Eds.). (1968). *Theories of cognitive consistency: A sourcebook*. Chicago: Rand McNally.

Allport, G. W. (1935). Attitudes. In C. Murcheson (Ed.), *Handbook of social psychology* (pp. 794–884). Worcester, MA: Clark University Press.

Amodio, D. M., & Devine, P. G. (2006). Stereotyping and evaluation in implicit race bias: Evidence for independent constructs and unique effects on behavior. *Journal of Personality and Social Psychology, 91*, 652–661.

Bem, D. J. (1972). Self-perception theory. In L. Berkowitz (Ed.), *Advances in experimental social psychology* (Vol. 6, pp. 1–62). New York: Academic Press.

Blanton, H., & Jaccard, J. (2006). Arbitrary metrics in psychology. *American Psychologist, 61*, 27–41.

Breckler, S. J., & Wiggins, E. C. (1991). Cognitive responses in persuasion: Affective and evaluative determinants. *Journal of Experimental Social Psychology, 27*, 180–200.

Breckler, S. J., & Wiggins, E. C. (1993). Emotional responses and the affective component of attitude. *Journal of Social Behavior and Personality, 8*, 281–296.

Brock, T. C. (1967). Communication discrepancy and intent to persuade as determinants of counterargument production. *Journal of Experimental Social Psychology, 3*, 296–309.

Campbell, D. T. (1969). Reforms as experiments. *American Psychologist, 24*, 409–429.

Chaiken, S. (1980). Heuristic versus systematic information processing and the use of source versus message cues in persuasion. *Journal of Personality and Social Psychology, 39*, 752–766.

Chaiken, S. (1987). The heuristic model of persuasion. In M. P. Zanna, J. M. Olson, & C. P. Herman (Eds.), *Social influence: The Ontario symposium* (Vol. 5, pp. 3–39). Hillsdale, NJ: Erlbaum.

Chapanis, N. P., & Chapanis, A. (1964). Cognitive dissonance. *Psychological Bulletin, 61*, 1–22.

Cohen, A. R. (1962). An experiment on small rewards for discrepant compliance and attitude change. In J. W. Brehm & A. R. Cohen (Eds.), *Explorations in cognitive dissonance* (pp. 73–78). New York: Wiley.

Conrey, F. R., Sherman, J. W., Gawronski, B., Hugenberg, K., & Groom, C. (2005). Separating multiple processes in implicit social cognition: The quad-model of implicit task performance. *Journal of Personality and Social Psychology, 89*, 469–487.

Crano, W. D., & Messé, L. A. (1970). When does dissonance fail? The time dimension in attitude measurement. *Journal of Personality, 38*, 493–508.

De Houwer, J., Beckers, T., & Moors, A. (2007). Novel attitudes can be faked on the Implicit Association Test. *Journal of Experimental Social Psychology, 43*, 972–978.

Erb, H.-P., Pierro, A., Mannetti, L., Kruglanski, A. W., & Spiegel, S. (2007). Biassed processing of persuasive information: On the functional equivalence of cues and message arguments. *European Journal of Social Psychology, 37,* 1057–1075.

Fazio, R. H., & Olson, M. A. (2003). Implicit measures in social cognition research. Their meaning and use. *Annual Review of Psychology, 54,* 297–327.

Festinger, L. (1950). Informal social communication. *Psychological Review, 57,* 271–282.

Festinger, L. (1954). A theory of social comparison processes. *Human Relations, 7,* 117–140.

Festinger, L. (1957). *A theory of cognitive dissonance.* Stanford, CA: Stanford University Press.

Fiedler, K., Messner, C., & Bluemke, M. (2006). Unresolved problems with the "I," the "A," and the "T": A logical and psychometric critique of the Implicit Association Test (IAT). *European Review of Social Psychology, 17,* 74–147.

Forgas, J. P. (2008). The role of affect in attitudes and attitude change. In W. D. Crano & R. Prislin (Eds.), *Attitudes and attitude change* (pp. 131–158). New York: Psychology Press.

Greenwald, A. G. (1968). Cognitive learning, cognitive response to persuasion and attitude change. In A. G. Greenwald, T. C. Brock, & T. M. Ostrom (Eds.), *Psychological foundations of attitudes* (pp. 147–170). San Diego, CA: Academic Press.

Greenwald, A. G., & Banaji, M. (1995). Implicit social cognitions. Attitudes, self-esteem and stereotypes. *Psychological Review, 102,* 4–27.

Greenwald, A. G., McGhee, D. E., & Schwartz, J. L. K. (1998). Measuring individual differences in implicit cognition: The Implicit Association Test. *Journal of Personality and Social Psychology, 74,* 1464–1480.

Greenwald, A. G., Rudman, L. A., Nosek, B. A., Banaji, M. R., Farnham, S. D., & Mellott, D. S. (2002). A unified theory of implicit attitudes, stereotypes, self-esteem, and self-concept. *Psychological Review, 109,* 3–25.

Houben, K., Rothermund, K., & Wiers, R. W. (2009). Predicting alcohol use with a recoding-free variant of the Implicit Association Test. *Addictive Behaviors, 34,* 487–489.

Hovland, C. I. (1957). *The order of presentation in persuasion.* New Haven, CT: Yale University Press.

Hovland, C. I., Harvey, O., & Sherif, M. (1957). Assimilation and contrast effects in communication and attitude change. *Journal of Abnormal and Social Psychology, 55,* 242–252.

Hovland, C. I., Janis, I. L., & Kelley, H. H. (1953). *Communication and persuasion: Psychological studies of opinion change.* New Haven, CT: Yale University Press.

Hovland, C. I., Lumsdaine, A., & Sheffield, F. (1949). *Experiments on mass communication.* Princeton, NJ: Princeton University Press.

Hovland, C. I., & Weiss, W. (1951). The influence of source credibility on communication effectiveness. *Public Opinion Quarterly, 15,* 635–650.

Katz, D. (1960). The functional approach to the study of attitudes. *Public Opinion Quarterly, 24*(2), 163–204.

Kelman, H. C., & Hovland, C. I. (1953). Reinstatement of the communicator in delayed measurement of opinion change. *Journal of Abnormal and Social Psychology, 48,* 326–335.

Kruglanski, A. W., Chun, W. Y., Erb, H. P., Mannetti, L., Spiegel, S., & Pierro, A. (2003). A parametric unimodel of human judgment: Integrating dual-process frameworks in social cognition from a single-mode perspective. In J. P. Forgas, K. D. Williams, & W. von Hippel (Eds.), *Social judgments: Implicit and explicit processes* (pp. 137–161). New York: Cambridge University Press.

Kruglanski, A. W., & Thompson, E. P. (1999). The illusory second mode or, the cue is the message. *Psychological Inquiry, 10,* 182–193.

Likert, R. A. (1932). A technique for the measurement of attitudes. *Archives of Psychology* (Whole No. 140).

Linder, D. E., Cooper, J., & Jones, E. E. (1967). Decision freedom as a determinant of the role of incentive magnitude in attitude change. *Journal of Personality and Social Psychology, 6,* 254–245.

Maison, D., Greenwald, A. G., & Bruin, R. H. (2004). Predictive validity of the Implicit Association Test in studies of brands, consumer attitudes, and behavior. *Journal of Consumer Psychology, 14*, 405–415.

McGuire, W. J. (1985). Attitudes and attitude change. In G. Lindzey & E. Aronson (Eds.) *The handbook of social psychology* (3rd Ed., Vol. 2, pp. 233–346). New York: Random House.

Petty, R. E., & Cacioppo, J. T. (1986). *Communication and persuasion: Central and peripheral routes to attitude change.* New York: Springer-Verlag.

Petty, R. E., & Cacioppo, J. T. (1986). The elaboration likelihood model of persuasion. In: L. Berkowitz (Ed.). *Advances in Experimental Social Psychology*, Vol. 19, pp. 123–205, San Diego, CA: academic Press.

Petty, R. E., & Krosnick, J. A. (Eds.). (1995). *Attitude strength: Antecedents and consequences.* Mahwah, NJ: Erlbaum.

Prislin, R., & Crano, W. D. (2008). Attitudes and attitude change: The fourth peak. In W. D. Crano & R. Prislin (Eds.), *Attitudes and attitude change* (pp. 3–15). New York: Psychology Press.

Rosenberg, M. J. (1965). When dissonance fails: On eliminating evaluation apprehension from attitude measurement. *Journal of Personality and Social Psychology, 1*, 28–42.

Sherman, J. W. (2006). On building a better process model: It's not only how many, but which ones and by which means? *Psychological Inquiry, 17*, 173–184.

Smith, M. B., Bruner, J. S., & White, R. W. (1956). *Opinions and personality.* Oxford, England: Wiley.

Stapel, D. A., & Suls, J. (Eds.). (2007). *Assimilation and contrast in social psychology.* New York: Psychology Press.

Strack, F., & Deutsch, R. (2004). Reflective and impulsive determinants of social behavior. *Personality and Social Psychology Review, 8*, 220–247.

Strack, F., & Deutsch, R. (2005). Reflection and impulse as determinants of conscious and unconscious motivation. In J. P. Forgas, K. D. Williams, & S. M. Laham (Eds.), *Social motivation: Conscious and unconscious processes* (pp. 91–112). New York: Cambridge University Press.

Thomas, W. I., & Znaniecki, F. (1928). *The Polish peasant in Europe and America.* Boston: Badger.

Thurstone, L. L. (1928). Attitudes can be measured. *American Journal of Sociology, 33*, 529–554.

Visser, P., & Cooper, J. (2007). Attitude change. In M. H. Hogg & J. Cooper (Eds.), *The Sage handbook of social psychology* (pp. 197–218). London: Sage.

Walther, E., & Langer, T. (2008). Attitude formation and change through association: An evaluative conditioning account. In W. D. Crano & R. Prislin (Eds.), *Attitudes and attitude change* (pp. 87–109). New York: Psychology Press.

Weber, M. (1947). *The theory of social and economic organisation* (T. Parsons, Ed.). Glencoe, IL: The Free Press.

Zanna, M. P., & Cooper, J. (1974). Dissonance and the pill: An attribution approach to studying the arousal properties of dissonance. *Journal of Personality and Social Psychology, 29*, 703–709.

2

Putting Attitudes in Their Place
Behavioral Prediction in the Face of Competing Variables

BLAIR T. JOHNSON AND MARCELLA H. BOYNTON

The greatest discovery of our generation is that human beings can alter their lives by altering their attitudes of mind. As you think, so shall you be.

—William James

As James's words imply, our lives and the courses of our lives often appear to hinge on our preferences. What foods we eat, where we choose to work or go to school, who we marry—to the average person, much of our behavior seems to be driven by our likes and dislikes. *Attitude* is the term that psychologists use to denote these differing preferences for objects, ideas, behaviors, and people. A more formalized and conventional version is that an attitude "is a psychological tendency that is expressed by evaluating a particular entity with some degree of favor or disfavor" (Eagly & Chaiken, 1993, p. 1). Over the more than 80 years of attitude research history, opinions have varied about the degree of influence that attitudes have on our behavior. Many early social psychologists were compelled by the notion that an individual attitude could significantly impact behavior. Perhaps most prominent among them, Gordon W. Allport (1935) asserted that attitudes exert a direct and dynamic impact upon behavior, whereas his contemporary Richard LaPiere (1934) contended that attitudes may only minimally predict behavior.

Even today the attitude-behavior debate continues, although discourse has often centered more on the precise etiology and role of attitudes. Many have contended attitudes really do underlie and cause behaviors (e.g., Ajzen & Fishbein, 2005), whereas others have demonstrated that behavior often impacts attitudes (Festinger & Carlsmith, 1959; Zimbardo, 1971), especially when attitudes are weak

(Bem, 1972; Wells & Petty, 1980). More recently, some researchers have argued that attitudes are generated on the spot to guide and sometimes rationalize actions (e.g., Schwarz, 2000), that attitudes are either open to awareness or are subconscious (e.g., Greenwald & Banaji, 1995), and that attitudes can even impact what beliefs people hold (Marsh & Wallace, 2005). In summary, researchers continue to strive to further define the nature and role of attitudes in everyday life.

In this chapter, we offer a brief history of the main streams of theory and research that have addressed attitude-behavior relations. We discuss variables both conceptual and methodological that have been shown to impact the attitude-behavior relation. Additionally, we point out that past research on attitude-behavior relations has largely focused on the nature of the attitude under question and of variables allied to attitude, all but ignoring the nature of the behavior being predicted. Studies on attitude-behavior relations have operationalized behavior in myriad ways, often with little thought to mundane realism or external validity. Although the behaviors being studied might often be convenient choices and offer face validity, they leave the impression that attitude scholars believe that attitudes are complex and variable but that behaviors are simple and static. We conclude that behaviors are often just as complex as attitudes—if not more so—and that when studying the attitude-behavior relation, much can be learned by focusing on the criterion instead of solely on the predictor.

A BRIEF HISTORY OF ATTITUDE-BEHAVIOR RESEARCH

Early Doubts About the Attitude Construct

Although our opening paragraphs may have implied that the field is unified behind the sort of definition that Eagly and Chaiken have provided, in fact there have been considerable differences across the history of the attitude research (cf., Eagly & Chaiken, 2007; Johnson, Maio, & Smith-McLallen, 2005). These variations in the definition of attitude have resulted in varied operationalizations of the attitude construct, partially explaining the dramatic variation in attitude-behavior results that have accrued in the literature. Whereas some early definitions of attitude defined it very globally or even omitted evaluation (G. W. Allport, 1935), others gave it a primarily affective tone (Thurstone, 1931). Others were broader; in the tripartite model of attitudes (e.g., Breckler, 1984; Katz & Stotland, 1959; Ostrom, 1969; Rosenberg & Hovland, 1960), affective components of attitudes are the pleasurable or unpleasurable emotions or feelings associated with an attitude object, cognitive components are beliefs about an attitude object, and behavioral components are conations or actions toward the attitude object. Unfortunately, different studies on the attitude-behavior relation have employed widely varying measures to personify these conceptual differences. Coupled with other methodological factors, such as Hovland's (1959) comparison of laboratory to naturalistic field studies, it is no surprise that the literature on attitude-behavior linkages is marked by widely conflicting results. Wicker's (1969) rudimentary meta-analysis of the literature also revealed correlation coefficients rarely above .30 and often near zero. With Wicker, attitude scholars began to doubt whether the attitude concept maintained any validity at all. Indeed, by the 1970s, attitude research was on the wane within the field of social psychology (Eagly, 1992; McGuire, 1986).

Attitudes Return to Power

Key among those who reinvigorated the field of attitude research was Martin Fishbein. In his early work, Fishbein (e.g., 1963) had defined the structure of attitudes as based on beliefs, and although he maintained this theoretical structure in his subsequent work, the measures of attitude that he used were purely evaluative and permitted input from any source, be it cognitive, affective, behavioral, or other. Along with his colleagues, Fishbein commenced on a series of studies and reviews that established a veritable canon for the psychometrics of attitude measurement. According to Fishbein and Ajzen (1974), distinguishing between attitudes toward *objects* and attitudes toward *behaviors* is essential. Prior measures had often assessed attitudes toward this entity or that, without asking about the respondents' attitudes toward *action* with regard to the entity in question. For most people at most times in most places, it is one thing to measure an attitude toward an object (attitude$_{object}$), say an international social psychology conference in Sydney, Australia, but quite another to measure an attitude toward a behavior (attitude$_{behavior}$), such as attending said conference (Fishbein & Ajzen, 1974). The beauty of defining attitudes and behaviors following this conceptualization was that it forced respondents to construe the behavior more narrowly than measures had previously done. More specifically, Fishbein and colleagues (Azjen & Fishbein, 1977; Fishbein & Jaccard, 1973) maintained that behaviors are composed of four elements: (a) a target (a cigar), (b) an action (e.g., smoking), (c) context (at a conference in Sydney), and (d) time (after the keynote address). These elements are commonly referred to as TACT.

As part of their *principle of compatibility* (also popularly called the *correspondence principle*), attitude-behavior relations are limited to the extent that the measures of attitude and of behavior match in terms of the stated elements in those measures. Thus, for example, a measure of attitude that merely asks for ratings of the desirability of "smoking" will usually fare very poorly in predicting the behavior of smoking a cigar at a conference in Sydney after the keynote address. By the same token, attitude toward smoking a cigar at a conference in Sydney after the keynote address will likely fare very poorly in predicting smoking behavior defined more generally. Thus, it is not necessary that attitude and behavior measures be highly specific, only that they correspond to each other in terms of their level of specificity. Attitudes and behavior can correspond just as highly when both measures are specific as when both measures are general. Substantiating Ajzen and Fishbein's (1977) narrative review, Kraus's (1995) meta-analysis of the attitude-behavior literature confirmed that studies had much larger attitude-behavior correlations when they used compatible measures than when they did not.

Perhaps an even more significant contribution to the attitude-behavior field than Fishbein's measurement canon was the theory of attitude-behavior relations that Fishbein and Ajzen originated: the theory of reasoned action (TRA; Fishbein, 1980; Fishbein & Ajzen, 1975). Instead of attitude being the direct cause of behavior, the TRA postulates that human behavior is primarily driven by behavioral intention, which is a person's readiness or desire to perform a given behavior. Intention, in turn, is driven by attitudes—defined as we have described—and subjective norms, which are a person's view of how important others would like him or her to behave. If a person accepts that their close others would regard a specific behavior in a negative light, then it is less likely he or she will perform that behavior. In this traditional TRA model, the influence of attitudes and subjective norms are entirely mediated by behavioral intention, without any direct impact on behavior. Fishbein and Ajzen proposed that all other influences on behavior are mediated through their impact on the beliefs that underlie attitudes and subjective norms. Aspects as widely varied as gender, ethnicity, culture, and past behavior were elegantly assumed to have their impacts in this fashion, without directly impacting behavior. Finally, Fishbein and Ajzen advocated measures that defined each element of the model with compatible elements. To the extent that the measures lacked compatibility, the relations between variables were likely to be low.

Ajzen (1991) later augmented the TRA by adding a third exogenous variable, perceived behavioral control (PBC), and termed this revised model the theory of planned behavior (TPB). Parallel to the concept of behavioral self-efficacy (Bandura, 1997), PBC taps perceptions of control over performing a given behavior. In the TPB model, PBC affects behavior directly as well as though the mediating variable of intentions. To the extent that an individual perceives control over a behavior, he or she will be more likely to enact it. According to both the TRA and the TPB, the influence both of subjective norm and of attitude on behavior is mediated by intention, with no direct impacts of these variables on behavior. The impact of perceived behavioral control on behavior is typically mediated through intention, but, when perceived control reflects actual control, a direct relation to behavior may emerge, independent of intentions.[*]

If published citations are any gauge of success, the TRA and the TPB are two of the most successful theories that the social sciences have ever produced, with tens of thousands of scholarly citations; hundreds of studies have explored their relations and there have been numerous reviews of this work. As an example, Albarracín, Johnson, Fishbein, and Muellerleile (2001) conducted a meta-analysis of TRA/TPB studies examining condom use, a focus justified because correctly used condoms are an important protection against the spread of human immunodeficiency virus (HIV) and other sexually transmitted infections (STIs), not to mention such other outcomes as unwanted pregnancy. Albarracín and colleagues collected and analyzed 96 independent data sets ($N = 22,594$) examining linkages between the variables implied by the TRA and/or the TPB, focusing on prospective studies in which the measures were taken at an initial point and then the amount of condom use that occurred by a later point was used as the criterion variable. It is also notable that these studies tended to sample from non-university-student populations, drawing instead from populations at higher risk for HIV and other STIs.

---

[*] Importantly, Armitage and Conner's (2001) review developed the logic that perceived behavioral control ought to interact with intention to affect behavior, and their meta-analysis had results supportive of this conclusion.

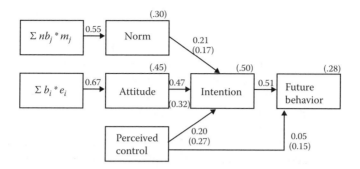

Figure 2.1.   Theory of planned behavior path model based on an entire literature ($k = 96$ studies) related to a single behavior, condom use.

Albarracín et al. submitted the matrix of mean correlations of these variables to path analyses and found that both the TRA and the TPB were good-fitting models of this relation. This good fit generalized across a wide array of methodological and sample variations in the source studies, ranging from statistical concerns (studies with completely reported matrices) to forms of condom use (e.g., vaginal vs. nonvaginal) to samples of higher or lower risk for infection with HIV.

By the logic of structural equation modeling, having "good fit" essentially means that the correlations among attitude, intention, subjective norm, perceived behavioral control, and behavior can be modeled well by knowing the path coefficients for the relations specified by the TRA and the TPB. It does not necessarily imply that other pathways to behavior do not exist. It also does not necessarily imply that there is a high degree of explanation in the ultimate endogenous behavior. Indeed, although tests of the model typically showed that all elements relate significantly in the pattern that the TRA and the TPB predict (Figure 2.1), the overall variance explained (R^2) for prediction of condom use was .30 for studies assessing the TRA and .28 for studies assessing the TPB.* Armitage and Conner (2001) compiled the most comprehensive sample of TPB studies to date and found a similar overall number, .27 for prediction of behavior. In meta-analyses focusing on different behaviors, prediction of behavior has also varied. For example, Hagger, Chatzisarantis, and Biddle's (2002) meta-analysis examined physical activity as the criterion and found a mean R^2 of .26. As another example, Sheppard, Hartwick, and Warshaw's (1988) cross-behavior review found studies with R^2s as low as .01 (for being absent from work) and as high as .92 (for having an abortion).

In sum, the TRA/TPB conceptualization of the attitude-behavior relation was a major step forward in attitude-behavior research, particularly when coupled with the Fishbeinian canon of measurement, and these reinvigorated the attitude field. If attitudes, subjective norms, and perceived behavioral control weigh heavily

---

* Because slightly different studies entered into these comparisons, one should not conclude that including perceived behavioral control negatively impacts behavioral prediction. Instead, other differences among the two groups of studies (e.g., time between intention and behavior measures) are the likely cause. Indeed, Armitage and Conner's (2001) meta-analysis found that adding PBC increased prediction of behavior, over and above intention, by 2%.

toward enacting a behavior, then it is likely the resulting intention would be to perform that behavior, and for many actions, as we have reviewed, this relation appears to be genuine (see also Ledgerwood & Trope, this volume). The application of the TRA or TPB has helped to illuminate many phenomena and to guide intervention efforts (e.g., Ajzen, Albarracín, & Hornik, 2007). Although neither the TRA nor the TPB is a theory of attitude *change* per se, the pattern of results has important implications for change. For instance, if attitudes relate more markedly to intentions than do either subjective norms or PBC, as is the case with condom use, then a focus on changing attitudes is indicated. Indeed, Albarracín and colleagues' (2005) meta-analysis of literature related to sexual risk reduction against HIV suggested that provision of attitudinal arguments enhanced condom use (see also Webb & Sheeran, 2006).

Limitations and Criticisms

Although the TRA and the TPB have been supported across numerous disciplines and different behaviors, there are critics and alternative perspectives. First, the assessment of attitudes and behaviors with explicit measures at one point in time may inflate observed relations. For example, by asking an individual to express an attitude explicitly, we may be in fact changing the attitude in some way, or we may influence the cognitive processes underlying the action in question. Perhaps another way to think about it is that the TACT style of measurement forces respondents out of their natural ways of thinking about attitudes. Meta-cognitively, that is, TACT style of measurement comes off rather artificially for most people. One explanation is that the measures themselves are stilted toward deliberate rather than spontaneous attitudes and behaviors. For example, asking a group of researchers to RSVP whether they intend to smoke a cigar in the designated smoking room after the keynote address may push a decision that would have previously been an impulsive decision (i.e., nondeliberative) to one that is planned (i.e., intentional). The implication is that the variation in attitude-behavior relations is probably not completely explained by differences in measurement of the constructs of interest. Rather, there are likely several reasons, in addition to measurement variability, that can help to explain the wide range in attitude behavior relation coefficients.

As already alluded, in addition to the observer effect and the correspondence principle, there are other issues associated with attitude measurement that may also influence its expression. Note that in the tradition of research we have reviewed in this section, attitudes are nearly always assessed using bipolar scales. The advantage of a bipolar scale is that it is a relatively simple and face-valid way of measuring an attitude. The use of bipolar scales assumes a bipolar structure and does not permit the assessment of ambivalent attitudes (e.g., Cacioppo & Berntson, 1994). An alternative conception is that attitudes can have a unipolar structure (e.g., neutral-very good; neutral-very bad) and that, while often correlated, unipolar measures of an attitude are at times in conflict (e.g., Scott-Sheldon & Johnson, 2009). In theory, unipolar scales should be more predictive than the bipolar scales for all except the strongest attitudes (see Holbrook & Krosnick, this

volume; Rhodewalt & Peterson, this volume). Work on attitudinal ambivalence further suggests that a given attitude object likely has not just a single attitude associated with it, but rather, a network of attitudes. Take the earlier example of smoking
a cigar at a conference in Sydney after the keynote address. An individual might
have, on one hand, positive attitudes toward the social and professional network-
ing elements of the behavior, but on the other hand, negative attitudes toward the
smoking element. Such attitudinal nuances would be lost using a bipolar scale.
In contrast, one or more unipolar scales could pick up on these subtleties, potentially identifying which attitudinal component is most predictive of the behavior in
question. Research on moral attitudes also is consonant with this perspective (e.g.,
Godin, Conner, & Sheeran, 2005).

Another argument, consonant with the preceding paragraph, is that people
are often minimally rational, relying on heuristics and basic cues as the driving
force behind much of their behavior (e.g., Baumeister, 2005; Sheeran, 2002). Thus,
structuring a behavioral prediction model around intentionality may not be universally appropriate. Finally, and importantly, other critics argue that attitudes toward
targets can be important forces in and of themselves (e.g., Fazio, 1990). We develop
these themes in the next section.

RECENT DEVELOPMENTS IN
ATTITUDE-BEHAVIOR RESEARCH

Are Psychometric Factors the Prime Determinant of
Attitude-Behavior Relations?

The discussion of psychometric factors may leave the impression that measurement
factors are the sole explanation for variation in the attitude-behavior relation, as
well as the intention-behavior relation. Yet, even when measurement accords with
the Fishbein-Ajzen psychometric prescriptions, the amount of behavior explained
by these models varies quite widely from study to study and from behavior to
behavior (see Ajzen & Fishbein, 2005; Sheppard et al., 1988). As a case in point,
Albarracín, Kumkale, and Johnson (2004) conducted a meta-analysis of an updated
literature related to condom use (k = 129 databases and N = 30,270 participants)
and showed that when the intention and behavior measures are compatible, the
intention-behavior relation is much larger, as compared to when they lack compatibility. Yet measurement compatibility could not explain all of the variation
in intention-behavior correlations. Among other study differences that related to
the magnitude of the intention-behavior relation was the amount of time elapsed
between the attitude and behavior measures, consistent with Ajzen and Fishbein's
(e.g., 2005) position that larger gaps of time give more opportunities for individuals to change their intentions, a pattern also confirmed in primary-level studies
(e.g., Sheeran & Abraham, 2003; Sheeran, Orbell, & Trafimow, 1999).

Albarracín et al.'s (2004) report focused on those relations key to the TRA and
TPB predictions, as conventionally construed. Although their meta-analysis evaluated the bivariate linkages between compatibility and the lag between the intention and behavior measures, it did not evaluate the joint effects of these variables

TABLE 2.1   Measurement Factors as Incomplete Moderators of Both Attitude-Behavior and Intention-Behavior Relations

Moderator or Statistic	Level	Attitude-Behavior rs		Intention-Behavior rs	
		r_+ (95% CI)[a]	β	r_+ (95% CI)[a]	β
Measurement compatibility			0.04		0.56°°°
	Complete	.38 (.35, .41)		.55 (.53, .58)	
	Partial	.36 (.30, .41)		.33 (.30, .35)	
Time lag between measures			−0.22°°		−0.44°°°
	30 days	.41 (.38, .44)		.60 (.57, .62)	
	365 days	.21 (.074, .34)		.12 (.026, .21)	
Homogeneity of rs before moderators[b]		$I^2 = 73.79$°°°		$I^2 = 90.32$°°°	
Variance explained by moderators		$R^2 = .053$°		$R^2 = .45$°°°	
Homogeneity of rs after moderators[b]		$I^2 = 73.71$°°°		$I^2 = 84.90$°°°	
k of studies		$k = 44$		$k = 41$	
N of participants		$N = 8,098$		$N = 8,076$	

Note: Positive correlations (r or r_+) imply stronger linkages between the respective variables. The two moderator variables were entered simultaneously as predictors in a fixed-effects regression analysis with weights equivalent to the sampling error of each correlation, where the correlations were represented as Fisher's z values and transformed back to r for display purposes.
[a] Tabled r_+ values control for the presence of the other moderator.
[b] Significance implies a rejection of the hypothesis of homogeneity and the presence of more variability than expected by sampling error alone.
°$p < .05$. °°$p < .01$. °°°$p < .001$.
From Albarracín, Kumkale, and Johnson's (2004) Meta-Analytic Database Related to Condom Use.

and did not examine whether these factors relate to variations in attitude-behavior correlations. We provide this analysis, summarized in Table 2.1. The varying magnitude of the intention-behavior relation (right-most columns) clearly illustrates the importance of compatibility and time lag between the measures in determining the predictive validity of the TRA/TPB. That is, compatibility and time lag between measures each pick up significant variation in the intention-behavior relation. The intention-behavior relation can be quite large when the measures have complete compatibility or when the behavior measures are taken relatively close to the measure of intention. In contrast, the intention-behavior links drop dramatically as compatibility decreases or time lag increases. Indeed, at a year from the intention measures, the intention-behavior correlation is nearly nonsignificant.

Surprisingly, these two measurement factors had a much smaller role with regard to the attitude-behavior relation, shown in the left columns of the table. Measurement compatibility did not relate to attitude-behavior relations, and time related in a similar though smaller pattern than it did with intention-behavior relations. Of note, the intention-behavior relationship decayed more rapidly than did the attitude-behavior relation. Indeed, at the 1-year measurement point, the relation of intention to behavior was actually smaller than the relation of attitude to behavior. Given that the behavior is kept fairly constant in these analyses, it appears that attitudes are more stable than intentions, at least in the domain of condom use. Finally, for both sets of correlations, these measurement factors left significant variability remaining; indeed, the homogeneity values,° which can range from 0 to 100, are relatively high prior to any explanation from the moderators, and the values remain high after their application. These analyses illuminate the point that although psychometric dimensions have a clear effect on the intention-behavior relation, they may not always have an equivalent impact on the attitude-behavior link. In short, even after one accounts for measurement-related variables, there may still be significant variability left to explain in the intention-behavior relation and especially the attitude-behavior relation. To our knowledge, ours is the first such demonstration of this point.

Toward a More Spontaneous View of Attitude

The TRA and TPB view of the relation between attitude and behavior is a primarily deliberative one. Although Fishbein and Ajzen (e.g., 1975) have said their models are *reasoned* rather than *rational,* it seems fair to conclude that these models construe beliefs, attitudes, and their other variables as consciously accessible and as psychological elements that can serve as deliberative input into intentions and behavior. The TRA and TPB assume that behaviors involve at least some level of deliberation. Other social psychologists have taken the sharply contrasting view that behavior is usually relatively spontaneous. These scholars contend that intentionality can be important, but that the lion's share of behavior is dictated by automatic processes, independent of intention (Bargh, 1994; Baumeister, 2005; Schwartz, 2000; Wegner & Bargh, 1998). Models of behavior have in recent years tended to emphasize deliberate processes on the one hand and spontaneous processes on the other (for reviews, see Chaiken & Trope, 1999; Smith & DeCoster, 2000). For instance, Strack and Deutsch's (2004) reflective-impulsive model assumes that these two systems interact but operate differently. Like the TRA and TPB, the reflective system bases behavioral decisions on knowledge about facts and values. In contrast, the impulsive system bases behavior on associative links and motivational orientations. Thus, although the TRA and TPB are likely to be useful models for deliberative behavior, their utility is likely to be diminished for more spontaneous behaviors.

Although the notion that the influence of attitude on behavior is completely mediated by intention is quite popular, some researchers have been more open to the concept that attitudes may directly impact behaviors. Of particular note is conceptual work by Fazio (1990) that made the case that the relation between attitudes and behavior can be relatively automatic in spontaneous contexts, whereas it can be relatively deliberative in other contexts. Dubbed the motivation and opportunity as determinants (MODE) model, the approach is based on an accuracy motivation, and the basic premise is that when motivation and opportunity are

---

° In the I^2 index, values that differ significantly from zero are interpreted as rejecting the hypothesis of homogeneity. In other words, significant values imply that greater variation is exhibited across the studies than would be expected based on sampling error alone (Huedo-Medina, Sánchez-Meca, Marín-Martínez, & Botella, 2006).

high, the influence of attitudes on behavior is due to effortful reflection. In contrast, when motivation or opportunity is low, the influence of attitudes on behavior is relatively spontaneous (i.e., nondeliberative), which has seen empirical support (e.g., Sanbonmatsu & Fazio, 1990).

A closer examination of two seemingly disparate lines of research allows us to more closely evaluate the utility of the MODE model approach: aversive racism and condom use with casual and steady partners. First, Dovidio and colleagues' (e.g., Dovidio, Brigham, Johnson, & Gaertner, 1996; Dovidio, Kawakami, & Gaertner, 2002; Dovidio, Kawakami, Johnson, & Johnson, 1997) work on the aversive racism framework largely squares with the MODE model perspective. Intergroup relation studies provide an important context to evaluate attitudinal phenomena because they so often involve individuals from real-world groups that possess differential status. According to the framework, aversive racists harbor hidden—perhaps unconscious—prejudice against ethnic or racial minority members; these individuals act without prejudice when social norms are clearly egalitarian, but with prejudice when circumstances are more ambiguous. Indeed, Dovidio et al.'s (1996) meta-analysis revealed a smaller link between explicit measures of prejudice and the negativity of interracial behavior when the behavior had a spontaneous nature (e.g., the distance at which someone sat from a minority target) than when it had a deliberate nature (e.g., judging candidates for a position). These predictions were directly confirmed in Dovidio et al.'s (2002) laboratory simulation, with the augmentation that implicit measures of prejudice were employed as well (see Fiedler, this volume). Implicit prejudice predicted spontaneous behavior (e.g., nonverbal behavior such as physical distancing and eye blinks) more markedly than explicit prejudice. Explicit measures of prejudice did not predict spontaneous behavior but did predict deliberate behavior. These studies suggest that implicit attitudes will pick up variation in behavior that explicit attitudes miss, and that it is important, once again, to consider the nature of the behavior under consideration.

The second area of research relevant to examining the notion that attitudes can directly impact more spontaneous behaviors is work conducted with the Albarracín et al. condom use database. Although there is much to recommend the position that the best measure of attitude is attitude$_{behavior}$, some scholars have maintained an interest in predicting behaviors from attitudes toward targets (viz., attitude$_{object}$). Many studies evaluating the TPB or TRA also include measures of attitude$_{object}$ in addition to attitude$_{behavior}$;[*] therefore, we coded these variables in the condom studies database. The TPB and TRA predict that measures of attitude$_{object}$ should negligibly predict behavior or intention, yet the literature has seldom evaluated these possibilities. In parallel, studies that focus on attitude$_{behavior}$ rarely examine whether intentions explain away the observed attitude$_{object}$-behavior correlations. We evaluated these hypotheses in our meta-analytic database focusing on condom use ($k = 58$).

---

[*] Similarly, some studies have used attitude toward the object measures instead of attitude toward the behavior measures, but these are omitted from the analyses summarized in our Table 2.1 and kept separate in the analyses we describe in the next paragraph.

We theorized that condom use (or nonuse) in committed, steady partner relationships is more routinized and deliberate than condom use (or nonuse) in new or casual relationships. If so, we should see that direct linkages of $attitude_{behavior}$ and $attitude_{object}$ to behavior should be greater for casual partners than for steady partners. We calculated matrices of mean correlations separately for the two types of partners and then fit TRA structural equation models to these correlations, evaluating models in which behavior is regressed on intention, $attitude_{behavior}$, and $attitude_{object}$. Unfortunately, no study that assessed $attitude_{object}$ also assessed perceived behavioral control (PBC), so the TPB could not be evaluated in this analysis. Results were largely consistent with our hypotheses: Variance explained for condom use for main partners was much greater (R^2 = .13) than for casual partners (R^2 = .070). Further, intentions were a much better predictor for main partners (β = .31) than for casual partners (β = .19), although each relation achieved significance. More interesting is that $attitude_{behavior}$ and $attitude_{object}$ each picked up significant variation in condom use that intention did not, and this pattern emerged for each partner type. For main partners, $attitude_{behavior}$'s and $attitude_{object}$'s relations were smaller than the impact of intention (βs = .17 and .08, respectively); with casual partners, the attitudinal influences rivaled that of intention (βs = .13 and .13, respectively). Taken as a whole, these results are supportive not only of the notion that there can be multiple related attitudes predictive of behavior, but also of the idea that attitudes may be especially influential for spontaneous behaviors.

These results suggest that even relatively subtle differences between behaviors can have important consequences for the variables that relate to them. Moreover, attitudes—both specific and general—can play a more powerful role in predicting behavior than most studies have reported. Of note, these studies have tended to take the TRA and TPB predictions at face value and have *not* assessed the fully saturated models. Consequently, their models could *not* show direct relations of attitude to behavior that might exist but would remain hidden. Our conclusion that attitudes play a more powerful role than past studies have shown is even more impressive given that we have used data collected to evaluate the TRA in order to examine a competing hypothesis and shown that measurement artefacts do not adequately explain the $attitude_{object}$-behavior relation. Our results thus create new conclusions from previously underanalyzed data. One might therefore predict that a review of non-TRA research would prove even more supportive of the role that attitudes play in behavior enactment and that intentions to act are unlikely to explain away observed $attitude_{object}$-behavior correlations. The finding that attitudes toward objects can relate directly to behavior is consonant with the finding that implicit attitudes can also relate directly to behavior. We discuss additional relevant research later in the chapter (see "Other Perspectives on Behavior").

A Better Focus on Behavior

Research on the nature and structure of attitudes is copious and complex and the subject of rather large tomes (e.g., Albarracín, Johnson, & Zanna, 2005; Eagly & Chaiken, 1993). Yet, other than the focus on the elements of behavior that Fishbein and colleagues initiated, the subject of *behavior* has been given short shrift in social psychology. Even a casual observer of behavior will realize that some behaviors are more easily predicted than others. Similarly, the results we presented earlier reveal the same pattern. Might a focus on the nature of the behavior enhance an understanding of attitude-behavior relations?

If not all behaviors are the same, then attitude-behavior relations ought to hinge on important features of the behaviors in question. Indeed, the research we reviewed in the prior section strongly suggests that the nature of the behavior matters. Condom use with steady partners appears to differ importantly from condom use with new or casual partners. In interracial interactions, nonverbal behaviors such as smiling are far different than judging an applicant's potential worth in a particular professional post. Starting smoking is far different than stopping the habit.

As Eagly and Chaiken (1993) reviewed, the complexity of attitudinal beliefs has proven a useful tool in the attitude research field (e.g., they have been associated with greater attitude strength when beliefs are correlated; Scott, 1963; Tetlock, 1989; Zajonc, 1960). Attitudinal complexity has been conceptualized in a number of ways and has operated under names such as differentiation (Zajonc, 1960), dimensionality (Scott, 1963), cognitive complexity (Bieri, 1966; Harvey, Hunt, & Schroder, 1961; Schroder, Driver, & Streufert, 1967), and integrative complexity. At its most basic, attitudinal complexity is the number of distinct beliefs associated with an attitude (Tetlock, 1989).

Recent research has extended this concept to include complexity of behavior (Boynton & Johnson, 2009). Just as attitudinal complexity gauges the sophistication of the structure of an attitude (Bieri, 1966; Scott, 1963; Tetlock, 1989; Zajonc, 1960), the idea of behavioral complexity refers to the sophistication of the structure of a behavior. Because attitudes are intangible constructs, the degree of complexity of an attitude for a given attitude object can vary widely. In contrast, whereas there is likely to be a degree of variability among people's assessments of a given behavior's complexity, it is overall prone to function at a similarly complex way for a specific population, although there will certainly be variability in perceptions of behavior's complexity between individuals.

In order to test whether the attitude-behavior relation varies as a function of attitude, behavior, and behavioral complexity measures for 46 unique behaviors were administered to 461 undergraduate students (Boynton & Johnson, 2009). The behaviors were sampled from the broader attitude-behavior literature to represent a wide range of complexity, and our participants' judgments confirmed that they do differ considerably. Smiling back at someone and smoking a cigarette are examples of relatively simple behaviors, whereas applying for a promotion and quitting smoking are examples of relatively complex behaviors. Repeated-observations multi-level modeling (MLM) permitted the examination of the idea that behavioral complexity predicts the strength of the attitude-behavior relation.[*] The results of

---

[*] The main and interaction effects for attitudes and the M complexity scores (linear and quadratic effects) were calculated. Variables were initially tested as random effects, and because the resulting slopes were nonsignificant, were subsequently treated as fixed effects. Further, model fit was assessed with the addition of each new variable, and variables were only kept if they significantly improved model fit using the χ^2 difference test for the -2 log likelihood statistic.

the analyses show that both the main and interaction effects of attitudes and complexity predict behavior (*ps* < .001). Specifically, as complexity increases, the predictive power of attitudes decreases, with more strongly held attitudes showing the greatest drop. In other words, complex behaviors show a weaker attitude-behavior link than simple behaviors. Given that simpler behaviors are more likely to be nondeliberative, this finding supports the notion that attitudes most directly impact spontaneous behaviors. Another interpretation is that complex behaviors are more difficult to control. As the behaviors grow in complexity, multiple factors are logically implicated. If there are many sub-behaviors necessary to enact some behavior, then attitudes, norms, and control over the sub-behaviors are more likely to vary. To the extent these conflict, execution of the penultimate behavior will be less likely. The research we presented regarding attitude$_{behavior}$ and attitude$_{object}$ is supportive of this interpretation. No matter the mediation of the effects, this research supports the conclusion that not all behaviors are the same and that the nature of the behavior under consideration can be key.

Other Perspectives on Behavior

Evolutionary perspectives assert that human beings never start life as perfectly blank slates (Pinker, 2002; Tesser, 1993), but it is clear that attitudes are quite elastic (Schwarz, 2000), so if anything, attitudinal flexibility is merely evolutionarily advantageous, facilitating spontaneous and functional adjustment to widely varying ecological milieus. The review of research previously presented highlights how attitude-behavior relations are subject to measurement aspects (e.g., compatibility, time lag between measures) as well as competing variables and processes (e.g., intentions, automatic cognitive processes). In this final subsection, we consider alternative conceptions of behavior. A first aspect is implied by our demonstration that attitude-behavior relations vary for different behaviors. Attitudes toward using condoms relate differently to condom use depending on the target of the action (steady vs. casual partners). In this instance, different attitudes may well be at work, but so also is an interaction of the individual with different people who may co-act. The implication of present knowledge is that the individual attitudes are insular, separate from each other, but the reality is that they are usually correlated. Unfortunately, past research has seldom considered intra-attitudinal structures. Condom use is once again a case in point. An instance of condom use can be modeled as we have shown in this chapter, but these efforts almost always consider only a single attitude. Also relevant would be attitudes and subjective norms toward having sex with a particular partner, attitudes toward pregnancy, attitudes toward STIs, and attitudes toward purchases of prophylactics (and alternatives), to name but a few. Related is the fact that research has tended to focus on a single person, when in fact sexual behaviors such as condom use are by definition co-acted. Almost no research has examined these interdependencies (for an exception, see Etcheverry & Agnew 2004). Finally, elicited attitudes may well be tapping allied attitudes within the cognitive system. Smith-McLallen, Johnson, Dovidio, and Pearson (2006) examined the often-replicated finding that Whites express implicit attitudes in favor of Whites and against Blacks but do not hold differential explicit attitudes toward these two groups. In three studies, they found that Whites' implicit preferences for the colors black versus white explained nearly all of the variation in their implicit preferences for the races Black versus White (see also Fiedler, this volume). Remaining to be answered is whether these implicit attitudes toward colors actually relate to intergroup relations, controlling for variables such as we have reviewed in this chapter. We predict that they will prove predictive of spontaneous interracial behaviors such as Dovidio and colleagues have examined.

A hallmark of social psychology since its origination (e.g., F. H. Allport, 1924; Triplett, 1898) that has continued to the present day (e.g., Reis, 2008; Ross & Nisbett, 1991; Zimbardo, 2007) has been its emphasis on social situational factors that shape behavior. For instance, Bargh and his colleagues' (Bargh, Chen, & Burrows, 1996) "chameleon effect" studies demonstrated that people will act more rudely, walk more slowly, and respond with more hostility when they are primed with rude, elderly, and African American stereotypes, respectively. More recently, Williams and Bargh (2008) demonstrated that experiencing physical warmth promotes interpersonal warmth with regard to a target other: Participants who had held a hot (vs. cold) drink (or a "therapeutic pad") were more likely to take a gift for a friend than a personal reward in exchange for participating in the study. The mediation of such effects is typically understood as activating perception-action links, overlearned tendencies that are triggered by situational cues. Another possibility that is consistent with perception-action links is priming of attitudes, which Bargh, Chaiken, Govender, and Pratto (1992) have shown can occur even for weakly held attitudes. It is ironic and a loss for the field that the literature on perception (e.g., Ross & Nisbett, 1991) so rarely mentions the attitude concept. Many studies' assessments of "perception" (e.g., an impression of friendliness) are essentially attitudes by another name (e.g., liking of a target person). The same omission occurs in the literature on attitudes, routinely omitting consideration of perception. Indeed, the study of attitude change is literally the study of how social situations dynamically afford and adjust individuals' attitudes (Johnson et al., 2005). The attitude and perception literatures would profit from a knowledge exchange, and the result would be better integration of social psychological knowledge.

The concept of overlearned perception-action (*and* attitude-behavior) linkages tacitly acknowledges that past experiences are important, even crucial, to understand behavior. In turn, the mechanism of automaticity underlying behaviors may be considered highly adaptive because it frees up other cognitive resources that can be utilized for other purposes (Bargh & Chartrand, 1999). In short, habits would appear to underlie much human behavior, but contemporary habit perspectives are more sophisticated than this statement would imply. Past behavior alone is not necessarily sufficient to produce future behavior, despite the tired adage that "the best predictor of behavior is past behavior."

The most prominent contemporary perspective on habit builds on the auto-motives perspective (Bargh, 1994) mentioned earlier. Specifically, Ouellette and Wood (1998) contended that although numerous behaviors can be intentionally driven, they are, in some cases, habitual and therefore operating independent of behavioral intentions. Using this framework, it is reasonable to posit that one overarching intention can set into motion a whole series of sub-behaviors that result in the desired end being met. Instead of defining habits as a function of repetition, this framework maintains that when a behavior is performed frequently enough in a stable context, the environmental cues that are present in that context become sufficient to elicit that behavior, independent of a process involving intention. The implication is that past behavior can directly influence future behavior when contextual cues are constant. For instance, it could be that whereas a person might initially form the intention to put on a seatbelt after entering a motor vehicle, after repeated times enacting this behavior, the simple act of entering a motor vehicle is enough to cause the buckling of a seatbelt, even when this action is not necessary (e.g., the vehicle is only going to be driven a few feet). Wood and her colleagues (e.g., Ouellette & Wood, 1998; Verplanken & Wood, 2006; Wood, Quinn, & Kashy, 2002; Wood, Tam, & Witt, 2005) present a great deal of evidence from meta-analyses and original studies that squares with the theory. Past behaviors that are repeated appear to lead to future behaviors when contexts remain relatively stable, whereas apparent "habits" are broken when contexts change. Finally, the influence of past behaviors appears to emerge even without conscious thought (Wood, Quinn, & Kashy, 2002).

Like Wood and her colleagues, Marsh, Scott-Sheldon, Johnson, and colleagues (under review) also investigated the role of past behavior on future behavior, examining condom use in two prospective studies of college undergraduates, using traditional (i.e., explicit) measures of attitude, but adding implicit attitudes toward condoms. As previously mentioned, condom use with main partners constitutes a relatively constant situation, whereas casual, new partners implies novelty. Consistent with the habit-perceptive, for main partners but not casual partners, past condom use related significantly to future condom use. For casual but not main partners, implicit attitudes significantly related to condom use. Both of these patterns were present controlling for intentions. Consequently, implicit attitudes could be the underlying mediator of habitual behavioral patterns.

It is also worth noting that researchers in the auto-motives tradition often select relatively simple behaviors to demonstrate situation-cued, spontaneous phenomena and largely excluded complex behaviors.° This approach makes sense given that complex behaviors are unlikely ever to be a simple function of a situational trigger. In contrast, such behaviors as eye blinking and smiling would seem chronically triggered by situations and rarely intentional. In the face of this perspective, it is tempting to conclude that researchers in the reasoned action tradition have chosen relatively complex, deliberative behaviors. Yet, our survey found that they have selected a fairly wide array of behaviors (Boynton & Johnson, 2009). Given that our data demonstrate that the predictive utility of the TPB (as measured by model fit) decreases as behavioral complexity decreases, the TRA/TPB may not be a universally appropriate model of behavior.

° One exception is performing well at an intellectual task (Bargh et al., 2001), but given that this research examined college undergraduates, who have a chronic goal of performing well at intellectual tasks, it seems reasonable that, for this population, the behavior is relatively simple and overlearned.

CONCLUSIONS

After nearly a century of research investigating measures of attitude, it is clear that social scientists understand them very well. It is also evident that attitudes often impact behaviors, either directly or indirectly. The field has also successfully identified some key attitudinal dimensions that mediate attitude-behavior linkages (e.g., behavioral intentions). Measurement issues such as the observer effect, scale structure, time lag, and measures correspondence all have important roles in influencing the size of the attitude-behavior link. Additionally, recent work on automatic cognitive processes, habits, and implicit attitudes strongly suggests that the effect of attitude on behavior is not solely an explicit process but often a spontaneous, implicit one.

Perhaps most importantly, past attitude-behavior reviews have left many inconsistencies unexplained. One possible avenue of inquiry for resolving these mysteries is by better understanding the dimensions of behavior. Behavioral complexity offers itself as one potentially meaningful way to categorize behavior. In brief, behaviors vary in their complexity, and as complexity increases, the utility of attitude-like variables decreases and the importance of other factors increases. Behavioral complexity may one day help scholars pick the attitudinal dimensions that are most relevant to explaining variation in different behaviors. As William James asserted in our opening epigraph, as you think, so shall you be, and it can change your life. The twist is that our experiences in life also change how we think.

REFERENCES

Ajzen, I. (1991). The theory of planned behavior. *Organizational Behavior and Human Decision Processes, 50*, 179–211.

Ajzen, I., Albarracín, D., & Hornik, R. (Eds.). (2007). *Prediction and change of health behavior: Applying the reasoned action approach.* Mahwah, NJ: Erlbaum.

Ajzen, I., & Fishbein, M. (1977). Attitude-behavior relations: A theoretical analysis and review of empirical research. *Psychological Bulletin, 84*, 888–918.

Ajzen, I., & Fishbein, M. (2005). The influence of attitudes on behavior. In D. Albarracín, B. T. Johnson, & M. P. Zanna (Eds.), *The handbook of attitudes* (pp. 173–221). Mahwah, NJ: Erlbaum.

Albarracín, D., Johnson, B. T., Fishbein, M., & Muellerleile, P. A. (2001). Theories of reasoned action and planned behavior as models of condom use: A meta-analysis. *Psychological Bulletin, 127*, 142–161.

Albarracín, D., Johnson, B. T., & Zanna, M. P. (Eds.). (2005). *The handbook of attitudes.* Mahwah, NJ: Erlbaum.

Albarracín, D., Kumkale, G. T., & Johnson, B. T. (2004). Influences of social power and normative support on condom use decisions: A research synthesis. *AIDS Care, 16*, 700–723.

Allport, F. H. (1924). *Social psychology.* Boston: Houghton Mifflin.

Allport, G. W. (1935). Attitudes. In C. Murchison (Ed.), *Handbook of social psychology* (pp. 798–844). Worchester, MA: Clark University Press.

Armitage, C. J., & Conner, M. (2001). Efficacy of the theory of planned behavior: A meta-analytic review. *British Journal of Social Psychology, 40*, 471–499.

Bandura, A. (1977). Self-efficacy: Toward a unifying theory of behavioral change. *Psychological Review, 84*, 191–215.

Bargh, J. A. (1994). The four horsemen of automaticity: Awareness, intention, efficiency, and control in social cognition. In: R. S. Wyer, & T. K. Srull (Eds.), *Handbook of social cognition: Basic processes* (Vol. 1., pp. 1–40). Hillsdale, NJ: Erlbaum.

Bargh, J. A., Chaiken, S., Govender, R., & Pratto, F. (1992). The generality of the automatic attitude activation effect. *Journal of Personality and Social Psychology, 62,* 893–912.

Bargh, J. A., & Chartrand, T. L. (1999). The unbearable automaticity of being. *American Psychologist, 54,* 462–479.

Bargh, J. A., Chen, M., & Burrows, L. (1996). Automaticity of social behavior: Direct effects of trait construct and stereotype activation on action. *Journal of Personality and Social Psychology, 71,* 230–244.

Bargh, J. A., Gollwitzer, P. M., Lee-Chai, A., Barndollar, K., & Trötschel, R. (1996). The automated will: Nonconscious activation and pursuit of behavioral goals. *Journal of Personality and Social Psychology, 81,* 1014–1027.

Baumeister, R. F. (2005). The cultural animal: Human nature, meaning, and social life. New York, NY: Oxford University Press.

Bem, D. J. (1972). Self-perception theory. In L. Berkowitz (Ed.), *Advances in experimental social psychology* (Vol. 6, pp. 1–62). New York: Academic Press.

Boynton, M. H., & Johnson, B. T. (2009). *Bridging the divide between automatic and deliberative models of behavior: The behavioral complexity scale.* Manuscript submitted for publication and under review.

Breckler, S. J. (1984). Empirical validation of affect, behavior, and cognition as distinct components of attitude. *Journal of Personality and Social Psychology, 47,* 1191–1205.

Cacioppo, J. T., & Berntson, G. G. (1994). Relationships between attitudes and evaluative space: A critical review with emphasis on the separability of positive and negative substrates. *Psychological Bulletin, 115,* 401–423.

Chaiken S., & Trope, Y. (1999). *Dual-process theories in social psychology.* New York: Guilford Press.

Dovidio, J. F., Brigham, J. C., Johnson, B. T., & Gaertner, S. L. (1996). Stereotyping, prejudice, and discrimination: Another look. In N. Macrae, C. Stangor, & M. Hewstone (Eds.), *Stereotypes and stereotyping* (pp. 276–319). New York: Guilford Press.

Dovidio, J. F., Kawakami, K., & Gaertner, S. L. (2002). Implicit and explicit prejudice and interracial interaction. *Journal of Personality and Social Psychology, 82,* 62–68.

Dovidio, J. F., Kawakami, K., Johnson, C., & Johnson, B. (1997). On the nature of prejudice: Automatic and controlled processes. *Journal of Experimental Social Psychology, 33,* 510–540.

Eagly, A. H. (1992). Uneven progress: Social psychology and the study of attitudes. *Journal of Personality and Social Psychology, 63,* 693–710.

Eagly, A. H., & Chaiken, S. (1993). *The psychology of attitudes.* New York: Harcourt, Brace.

Eagly, A. H., & Chaiken, S. (2007). The advantages of an inclusive definition of attitude. *Social Cognition, 25,* 582–602.

Etcheverry, P. E., & Agnew, C. R. (2004). Subjective norms and the prediction of romantic relationship state and fate. *Personal Relationships, 11,* 409–428.

Fazio, R. H. (1990). Multiple processes by which attitudes guide behavior: The MODE model as an integrative framework. In: M. P. Zanna (Ed.), *Advances in experimental social psychology* (Vol. 23, pp.75–109). San Diego, CA: Academic Press, Inc.

Festinger, L., & Carlsmith, J. M. (1959). Cognitive consequences of forced compliance. *The Journal of Abnormal and Social Psychology, 58,* 203–210.

Fishbein, M. (1963). An investigation of the relationships between beliefs about an object and the attitude toward that object. *Human Relations, 16,* 233–240.

Fishbein, M. (1980). A theory of reasoned action: Some applications and implications. In: Howe, H.E., and Page, M.M. (Eds.), *Nebraska Symposium on Motivation,* 1979. Lincoln, NE: University of Nebraska Press, 1980. pp. 65–116.

Fishbein, M., & Ajzen, I. (1974). Attitudes toward objects as predictors of single and multiple behavioral criteria. *Psychological Review, 81*, 59–74.

Fishbein, M., & Ajzen, I. (1975). *Belief, attitude, intention, and behavior: An introduction to theory and research*. Reading, MA: Addison-Wesley.

Fishbein, M., & Jaccard, J. (1973). Theoretical and methodological issues in the prediction of family planning intentions and behaviors. *Representative Research in Social Psychology, 4*, 37–52.

Godin, G., Connere, M., & Sheeran, P. (2005). Bridging the intention-behavior "gap": The role of moral norm. *British Journal of Social Psychology, 44*, 497–512.

Greenwald, A. G., & Banaji, M. R. (1995). Implicit social cognition: Attitudes, self-esteem, and stereotypes. *Psychological Review, 102*, 4–27.

Hagger, M. S., Chatzisarantis, N. L. D., & Biddle, S. J. H. (2002). A meta-analytic review of the theories of reasoned action and planned behavior in physical activity: Predictive validity and the contribution of additional variables. *Journal of Sport and Exercise Psychology, 24*, 3–32.

Harvey, O. J., Hunt, D., & Schroder, H. M. (1961). *Conceptual systems and personality organization*. New York: Wiley.

Hovland, C. I. (1959). Reconciling conflicting results derived from experimental and survey studies of attitude change. *American Psychologist, 14*, 8–17.

Huedo-Medina, T. B., Sánchez-Meca, J., Marín-Martínez, F., & Botella, J. (2006). Assessing heterogeneity in meta-analysis: I2 or Q statistic? *Psychological Methods, 11*, 193–206.

Johnson, B. T., Maio, G. R., & Smith-McLallen, A. (2005). Communication and attitude change: Causes, processes, and effects. In D. Albarracín, B. T. Johnson, & M. P. Zanna (Eds.), *The handbook of attitudes* (pp. 617–669). Mahwah, NJ: Erlbaum.

Katz, D., & Stotland, E. (1959). A preliminary statement to a theory of attitude structure and change. In S. Koch (Ed.), *Psychology: A study of a science* (Vol. 3, pp. 423–475). New York: McGraw-Hill.

Kraus, S. J. (1995). Attitudes and the prediction of behavior: A meta-analysis of the empirical literature. *Personality and Social Psychology Bulletin, 21*, 58–75.

LaPiere, R. T. (1934). Attitudes vs. actions. *Social Forces, 13*, 230–237.

Marsh, K. L., Johnson, B. T., & Scott-Sheldon, L. A. J. (2001). Heart versus reason in condom use. *Zeitschrift für Experimentelle Psychologie, 48*, 161–175.

McGuire, W. J. (1986). The vicissitudes of attitudes and similar representational constructs in twentieth century psychology. *European Journal of Social Psychology, 16*, 89–130.

Ostrom, T. M. (1969). The relationship between the affective, behavioral, and cognitive components of attitude. *Journal of Experimental Social Psychology, 5*, 12–30.

Ouellette, J. A., & Wood, W. (1998). Habit and intention in everyday life: The multiple processes by which past behavior predicts future behavior. *Psychological Bulletin, 124*, 54–74.

Pinker, S. (2002). *The blank slate: The denial of human nature in modern intellectual life*. New York: Penguin.

Reis, H. T. (2008). Reinvigorating the concept of situation in social psychology. *Personality and Social Psychology Review, 12*, 311–329.

Rosenberg, M. J., & Hovland, C. I. (1960). Cognitive, affective, and behavioral components of attitudes. In M. J. Rosenberg, C. I. Hovland, W. J. McGuire, R. P. Abelson, & J. W. Brehm (Eds.), *Attitude organization and change: An analysis of consistency among attitude change* (pp. 1–14). New Haven, CT: Yale University Press.

Ross, L., & Nisbett, R. E. (1991). *The person and the situation: Perspectives of social psychology*. New York: McGraw-Hill.

Sanbonmatsu, D. M., & Fazio, R. H. (1990). The role of attitudes in memory-based decision making. *Journal of Personality and Social Psychology, 59*, 614–622.

Schroder, H. M., Driver, J. J., & Streufert, S. (1967). *Human information processing*. New York: Holt, Rinehart & Winston.

Schwarz, N. (2000). Social judgment and attitudes: Warmer, more social, and less conscious. *European Journal of Social Psychology, 30*, 149–176.

Scott, W. A. (1963). Cognitive complexity and cognitive balance. *Sociometry, 26*, 66–74.

Scott-Sheldon, L. A. J., & Johnson, B. T. (2009). [Evaluative tension and marijuana use: Examining the moderating role of ambivalent marijuana attitudes]. Unpublished raw data.

Sheeran, P. (2002). Intention-behavior relations: A conceptual and empirical review. In: W. Stroebe, M. Hewstone (Eds.), *European review of social psychology* (Vol. 12, pp. 2–36). London: Psychology Press.

Sheeran, P., & Abraham, C. (2003). Mediator of moderators: Temporal stability of intention and the intention-behavior relation. *Personality and Social Psychology Bulletin, 29*, 205–215.

Sheeran, P., Orbell, S., & Trafimow, D. (1999). Does the temporal stability of behavioral intentions moderate intention-behavior and past behavior-future behavior relations? *Personality and Social Psychology Bulletin, 25*, 724–730.

Sheppard, B. H., Hartwick, J., & Warshaw, P. R. (1988). The theory of reasoned action: A meta-analysis of past research with recommendations for modifications and future research. *Journal of Consumer Research, 15*, 325–343.

Smith, E. R., & DeCoster, J. (2000). Dual process models in social and cognitive psychology: Conceptual integration and links to underlying memory systems. *Personality and Social Psychology Review, 4*, 108–131.

Smith-McLallen, A., Johnson, B. T., Dovidio, J. F., & Pearson, A. R. (2006). Black and white: The role of color bias in implicit race bias. *Social Cognition, 24*, 42–69.

Strack, F., & Deutsch, R. (2004). Reflective and impulsive determinants of social behavior. *Personality and Social Psychology Review, 8*, 220–247.

Tesser, A. (1993). On the importance of heritability in psychological research: The case of attitudes. *Psychological Review, 100*, 129–142.

Tetlock, P. E. (1989). Structure and function in political belief systems. In: A. R. Pratkanis, S. J. Breckler, & A. G. Greenwald (Eds.), *Attitude structure and function* (pp. 129–151). Hillsdale, NJ: Erlbaum.

Thurstone, L. L. (1931). The measurement of social attitudes. *Journal of Abnormal and Social Psychology, 26*, 249–269.

Triplett, N. (1898). The dynamogenic factors in pacemaking and competition. *American Journal of Psychology, 9*, 507–533.

Verplanken, B., & Wood, W. (2006). Interventions to break and create consumer habits. *Journal of Public Policy & Marketing, 25*, 90–103.

Webb, T. L., & Sheeran, P. (2006). Does changing behavioral intentions engender behavior change? A meta-analysis of the experimental evidence. *Psychological Bulletin, 132*, 249–268.

Wegner, D. M., & Bargh, J. A. (1998). Control and automaticity in social life. In D. T. Gilbert, S. T. Fiske, & G. Lindzey (Eds.), *The handbook of social psychology* (Vols. 1–2, 446–496). New York, NY: McGraw-Hill.

Wells, G. L., & Petty, R. E. (1980). The effects of overt head-movements on persuasion: Compatibility and incompatibility of responses. *Basic and Applied Social Psychology, 1*, 219–230.

Wicker, A. W. (1969). Attitude versus actions: The relationship of verbal and overt behavioral responses to attitude objects. *Journal of Social Issues, 25*, 41–78.

Williams, L. E., & Bargh, J. A. (2008). Experiencing physical warmth promotes interpersonal warmth. *Science, 322*, 606–607.

Wood, W., Quinn, J. M., & Kashy, D. A. (2002). Habits in everyday life: Thought, emotion, and action. *Journal of Personality and Social Psychology, 83*, 1281–1297.

Wood, W., Tam, L., & Witt, M. G. (2005). Changing circumstances, disrupting habits. *Journal of Personality and Social Psychology, 88*, 918–933.

Zajonc, R. B. (1960). The concepts of balance, congruity, and dissonance. *Public Opinion Quarterly, 24*, 280–296.

Zimbardo, P. G. (1971). The power and pathology of imprisonment. *Congressional Record*(Serial No. 15, Oct. 25, 1971). U.S. Governmental Printing Office.

Zimbardo, P. G. (2007). *The Lucifer effect: Understanding how good people turn evil.* New York: Random House.

AUTHOR NOTE

The preparation of this chapter was facilitated by U.S. Public Health Service Grants R01-MH58563 to Blair T. Johnson and F31-MH079759 to Marcella H. Boynton.

Address correspondence to Blair T. Johnson, Department of Psychology, 406 Babbidge Road Unit 1020, University of Connecticut, Storrs, CT 06269-1020, USA. E-mail: blair.t.johnson@uconn.edu.

3

Attitudes as Global and Local Action Guides*

ALISON LEDGERWOOD AND YAACOV TROPE

We often think of our attitudes and beliefs as stable personality characteristics—when asked to describe ourselves, we might cite our love of a particular composer, our support for a long-preferred political party, or perhaps a deep and abiding hatred of Oreo cookies. Echoing this assumption, attitudes have historically been considered relatively stable individual differences that remain consistent across time and contexts, unless or until an overt persuasion attempt is encountered. However, more recently, a far more malleable picture of attitudes has emerged from research suggesting that evaluations can shift quite flexibly in response to the immediate social environment (e.g., Baldwin & Holmes, 1987; Kawakami, Dovidio, & Dijksterhuis, 2003; Ledgerwood & Chaiken, 2007; Lowery, Hardin, & Sinclair, 2001).

In this chapter, we propose that these competing conceptualizations of attitudes as stable versus shifting may reflect two different roles that attitudes play in regulating evaluative responding. On the one hand, attitudes can function to guide action with respect to the current social context. In order to act effectively and efficiently in the here and now, individuals need quick summaries of pertinent information to guide their interactions with objects and people in the present situation. On the other hand, attitudes can function to guide action at a distance. When planning behavior in the distant future or making decisions about a faraway location, individuals need to be able to efficiently abstract across the particularities of any one experience to extract evaluation-relevant information that is stable across time, contexts, and relationships.

We begin this chapter by providing some background on how attitudes are typically characterized in the literature. Next, we describe in more detail our

* Preparation of this chapter was supported in part by a National Science Foundation Graduate Research Fellowship to Alison Ledgerwood and by the National Institute of Mental Health Grant R01 MH59030-06A1 to Yaacov Trope.

global-local perspective on evaluation, which distinguishes between two different forms of evaluations that serve two different regulatory functions. We propose that distance will play a key role in determining which form of evaluation is used to guide responding, and we draw on construal level theory to delineate the cognitive process by which this could occur. After describing a series of empirical studies that provide support for several of our hypotheses, we discuss points of interface with other attitudinal theories and highlight some implications of our perspective for understanding related areas such as attitude-behavior correspondence, ideology, and conformity.

CONCEPTUALIZING ATTITUDES

Attitudes have long been assumed to play a key role in the regulation of behavior. One important function that they serve is to provide a quick summary of whether an attitude object is positive or negative, in order to facilitate approach or avoidance of that object (Eagly & Chaiken, 1998; Fazio, 1986; Greenwald, 1989; Katz, 1960; Shavitt, 1990; Smith, Bruner, & White, 1956; Wilson, Lindsey, & Schooler, 2000). Furthermore, attitudes can function to coordinate social action and interaction by summarizing information from the social environment, such as other people's opinions, that helps individuals create and maintain a shared view of the world with those around them (Hardin & Higgins, 1996; Jost, Ledgerwood, & Hardin, 2008; Smith et al., 1956; Williams, Chen, & Wegener, this volume). Thus, attitudes help to guide both action and interaction by providing efficient, valenced summaries of information that would simply be too overwhelming and complex to consider piece by piece before each behavior we undertake in everyday life.

Although few researchers would dispute that attitudes can be functional, there is far less agreement about what they should look like. Traditionally, attitudes have often been conceptualized as dispositional evaluative tendencies toward a given attitude object that remain relatively consistent across situations, unless (or until) a successful persuasion attempt changes the first attitude into a new one (e.g., Ajzen, 1988; Allport, 1935; Campbell, 1950; Krech & Crutchfield, 1948; Tourangeau & Rasinski, 1988). Extensive research on attitude stability has demonstrated that individuals often selectively attend to, think about, and remember information in ways that support their prior attitudes (e.g., Eagly, Kulesa, Chen, & Chaiken, 2001; Giner-Sorolla & Chaiken, 1997; Lord, Ross, & Lepper, 1979; Pomerantz, Chaiken, & Tordesillas, 1995; Sweeney & Gruber, 1984). Meanwhile, research on attitude structure suggests that substantial attitudinal consistency can be predicted by aspects of intra-attitudinal structure, such as the consistency between an overall evaluation and the evaluative meaning of supporting cognitions or affect, as well as inter-attitudinal structure, such as an attitude's connectedness to other beliefs and values (see, e.g., Chaiken, Pomerantz, & Giner-Sorolla, 1995; Ostrom & Brock, 1968). Consistency pressures can also arise at the interpersonal level: For example, publicly committing to an attitudinal position increases subsequent resistance to change (Hovland, Campbell, & Brock, 1957). Thus, there is good evidence to suggest that attitudes can be consistent across contexts.

Furthermore, the very idea that one can predict a person's behavior from her attitudes rests on the assumption that an attitude measured now will predict a later attitude and subsequent behavior. Research suggests this relationship can sometimes be quite strong (see, e.g., Schuman & Johnson, 1976; Wallace, Paulson, Lord, & Bond, 2005): For instance, attitudes toward political candidates are excellent predictors of voting behavior (e.g., Campbell, Converse, Miller, & Stokes, 1960). Evidence of attitudinal stability can even be found in studies of attitude change, when the postmanipulation attitude is measured repeatedly over time and shown to be consistent (e.g., Freedman, 1965; Higgins & Rholes, 1978; Peterson & Thurstone, 1933; Rokeach, 1975; Rokeach & Cochrane, 1972).

Meanwhile, however, other research has painted a far more malleable picture of attitudes, suggesting that they fluidly shift in response to the immediate social context. In line with this view, some of the earliest studies on social influence demonstrated that people's attitudes and judgments conform to the views of others (e.g., Asch, 1955; Deutsch & Gerard, 1955; Sherif, 1935; see Eagly & Chaiken, 1993; Turner, 1991, for reviews). More recent research has revealed that attitudes shift, often outside of awareness, in response to other people in the local social context, including salient social categories, significant others, communication partners, and even complete strangers (Baldwin & Holmes, 1987; Blanchard, Lilly, & Vaughn, 1991; Cooper, this volume; Davis & Rusbult, 2001; Higgins & Rholes, 1978; Kawakami et al., 2003; Ledgerwood & Chaiken, 2007; Lowery et al., 2001). Even implicit attitudes can shift to align with the presumed attitudes of other people in the local social situation (see Blair, 2002, for a review). For example, Lowery et al. (2001) found that when White participants were motivated to get along with an experimenter, implicit racial bias decreased when the experimenter was Black (and therefore presumably possessed more positive attitudes toward Blacks) versus White. Likewise, Sinclair, Lowery, Hardin, and Colangelo (2005) demonstrated that when participants liked an experimenter, their implicit racial attitudes shifted to align with the presumed attitudes of the experimenter.

The growing literature on attitude malleability in response to the presumed attitudes of others reflects an overall shift in the field of social psychology, as researchers move beyond classic assumptions of stable, schematic representations to recognize malleability in a wide range of phenomena (see Blair, 2002; Smith & Semin, 2004, 2007, for reviews). For instance, stereotypes have historically been conceptualized as stable knowledge structures that are inevitably activated when a person encounters a relevant group or group member (e.g., Devine, 1989; Hamilton & Trolier, 1986; Katz & Braly, 1935; Kunda & Oleson, 1995). However, recent research increasingly suggests that stereotypes are far more malleable and context-dependent than once assumed (e.g., Blair, Ma, & Lenton, 2001; Garcia-Marques, Santos, & Mackie, 2006; Sechrist & Stangor, 2001; Sinclair & Kunda, 1999; Stangor, Sechrist, & Jost, 2001). Likewise, research on self-worth, attributional tendencies, self stereotyping, and even nonsocial concepts such as pianos and kites indicates that a host of psychological constructs may be far more flexible and context-dependent than previously believed (e.g., Crocker, Karpinsky, Quinn, & Chase, 2003; Norenzayan & Schwarz, 1999; Sinclair, Huntsinger, Skorinko, & Hardin, 2005; Yeh & Barsalou, 2006).

GLOBAL AND LOCAL ACTION GUIDES

Former assumptions of attitude stability are thus called into question by a size-able body of recent evidence emerging from both within and beyond the attitude domain. Nonetheless, the extensive literature on attitude stability summarized in the previous paragraphs empirically documents that attitudes can also at least appear to be fairly stable and resistant to momentary contextual influences. We propose that these seemingly contradictory characterizations reflect two different forms that evaluations may take.[*]

First, an attitude could take the form of a local evaluation. Such an evaluation could provide a relatively flexible guide for action by incorporating information that is unique to a specific situation. It would therefore be shaped by details of the current context, including the presumed attitudes of another person who just happens to be in the present situation, as well as other (social or nonsocial) aspects of the context itself, short-term concerns, and unique details of a particular instantiation of the attitude object.

Second, an attitude could take the form of a global evaluation. This type of evaluation could provide a relatively stable summary guide for engaging with an attitude object by taking into account general information from multiple contexts. It would therefore be shaped by what is consistently relevant for action toward an attitude object across different situations, including broad principles and values, long-term goals, normative societal standards, the views and values of important relationship partners or groups, and central and enduring features of the attitude object.

From a functional perspective, both forms of evaluation could be useful for guiding action. On the one hand, one can argue that a malleable evaluative response that allows a person to flexibly adapt to the demands of his current social environment should be helpful in facilitating approach or avoidance of an attitude object (see, e.g., Schwarz, 2007). Different contexts call for different responses (if someone needs to slice an apple, for example, he might approach a paring knife if it is sitting peacefully on the counter, but jump away if it slides off and clatters to the floor). Moreover, malleable evaluative responses facilitate the creation of socially shared viewpoints, which are a necessary basis of communication, relation-ships, and the regulation of social action (see, e.g., Brennan & Clark, 1996; Clark, 1996; Festinger, 1950; Hardin & Higgins, 1996; Isaacs & Clark, 1987; Rokeach & Mezei, 1966; Turner, 1991). From this perspective, local evaluations that flexibly tune to the current situation might be optimal for guiding action.

---

[*] Ours is of course not the first attempt to integrate these competing conceptualizations. For instance, Wilson's dual attitudes model suggested that individuals can possess both a stable and habitual implicit attitude, as well as one or more context-dependent, actively constructed, explicit attitudes (Wilson, Lindsey, & Schooler, 2000). However, in light of accumulating evidence suggesting that implicit attitudes are at least as malleable and context-dependent as their explicit cousins (Dasgupta & Greenwald, 2001; Lowery et al., 2001; Richeson & Ambady, 2001; Wittenbrink, Judd, & Park, 2001; see Blair, 2002; Ferguson & Bargh, 2007; Gawronski, LeBel, & Peters, 2007, for reviews), the implicit-explicit distinction seems unlikely to successfully reconcile evidence of stability and malleability.

On the other hand, local information often seems irrelevant for evaluative responding. If someone is voting for the next president, for instance, it does not seem particularly functional for variations in the weather or who happens to be standing outside the polling station that day to influence her evaluative responses toward the candidates. Furthermore, stable evaluative responses could serve an important social function by facilitating the maintenance of existing shared perspectives with important relationship partners or groups (see, e.g., Asch, 1952; Hardin & Conley, 2001; Hardin & Higgins, 1996; Ledgerwood & Liviatan, in press; McGuire, 1969). For example, if a group of friends all prefer a particular political candidate, stability in their evaluative responses across contexts will help protect the shared view of reality that has been formed within the group. From this perspective, action would ideally be based on a summary guide of whether a person, object, or event tends to be positive or negative across situations. Thus, a global evaluative response that remains stable in the face of contextual fluctuation would seem particularly functional in some cases.

Given that both types of evaluations seem functional, we propose that both should exist. In the here and now, people must be able to flexibly adapt their actions to serve their immediate goals, coordinate with others around them, and interact effectively with their present surroundings. Local evaluations can facilitate approach/avoidance responding within the current situation, because they are sensitive to specific contextual information. However, humans are also able to transcend their immediate situation to plan for the future, coordinate action at a distance, predict other people's behavior, and generate counterfactual alternatives. Thus, they must be able to regulate their behavior not only for the here and now, but also for the there and then. Global evaluations can serve to guide action outside of the immediate situation by drawing on evaluation-relevant information that is consistent across contexts.

This functional analysis suggests that the proximity of an attitude object will play a critical role in determining which form of evaluation is used to guide responding. More specifically, we suspect that information about distance sets into motion a self-regulatory evaluative system geared toward guiding action either within the current context or outside of it. Whereas proximal objects should trigger local evaluations, tuned to the present context, distal objects should trigger more global evaluations, tuned to what is invariant across contexts.

How exactly might such a process work? In order to better delineate both the construct of distance as well as the cognitive process by which it could influence evaluative responding, we turn to construal level theory.

CONSTRUAL LEVEL THEORY

Construal level theory (Liberman & Trope, 2008; Liberman, Trope, & Stephan, 2007; Trope & Liberman, 2003; Trope, Liberman, & Wakslak, 2007) suggests that psychological distance plays a critical role in how we mentally construe the world around us. The concept of psychological distance refers to any dimension along which an object or event can be removed from me, here, and now, and thus dovetails nicely with the current perspective. Psychological distance is defined as perceived or experienced (rather than actual) distance, and can include various dimensions (e.g., time, space, social distance, and hypotheticality).

According to construal level theory, we think about objects or events that are psychologically removed from us in terms of their high-level, abstract, and enduring characteristics. Thus, as psychological distance increases, our mental representations become more coherent and structured; they extract gist information and screen out irrelevant details. When the same objects or events are psychologically closer to us, we think about them in terms of low-level, detailed, and contextualized features. That is, with proximity, our mental representations become more concrete and lose the structure that separates important from peripheral and irrelevant features.

Considerable evidence for the impact of psychological distance on construal level exists. For example, research on temporal distance has shown that participants place greater importance on an object or event's central features (e.g., the sound quality of a radio) versus peripheral features (e.g., the clarity of the radio's clock display) when considering a decision for the distant future rather than the near future (Trope & Liberman, 2000, Study 3). Likewise, people tend to describe distant future activities in terms of abstract ends and near future activities in terms of concrete means (Liberman & Trope, 1998, Study 1; see also Vallacher & Wegner, 1985, 1989). Temporal distance has also been shown to influence individuals' judgments about other people: In one study, participants predicted that a target person would behave more consistently across different situations when imagining the person in the distant (vs. near) future (Nussbaum, Trope, & Liberman, 2003, Study 2). In other words, in the distant future, the target's behaviors were construed more abstractly than in the near future, and were thus seen as less contextualized and more stable.

Recent research suggests that various dimensions of psychological distance, including spatial distance, social distance, and hypotheticality, all have a similar impact on mental representation (e.g., Fujita, Henderson, Eng, Trope, & Liberman, 2006; Henderson, Fujita, Trope, & Liberman, 2006; Libby & Eibach, 2002; Todorov, Goren, & Trope, 2007; Wakslak, Trope, Liberman, & Alony, 2006; see Liberman & Trope, 2008, for a review). For example, participants who viewed a cartoon film depicting a scene at a summer camp located in a spatially distant (vs. near) location perceived the film as being composed of a few large behavioral chunks, rather than many small ones, presumably because they formed more abstract representations of the behaviors rather than focusing on each specific action (Henderson et al., 2006, Study 1). Similarly, research on hypotheticality as a dimension of psychological distance showed that participants gave relatively greater weight to abstract desirability (vs. concrete feasibility) concerns when choosing to enter lotteries that involved low probabilities (i.e., distant chances) versus high probabilities (i.e., near certainties; Todorov et al., 2007, Study 2).

Furthermore, the impact of psychological distance on mental representation tends to generalize beyond the specific object or event whose proximity is manipulated. In one study, participants who imagined their lives a year from now (distant future) versus tomorrow (near future) showed a heightened ability to creatively generate abstract solutions on a subsequent and unrelated task (Förster, Friedman, & Liberman, 2004, Study 5). In fact, simply priming words associated with distance (vs. closeness) can impact construal: For example, this task can increase participants' relative preferences for describing activities in terms of abstract ends rather than concrete means (Smith & Trope, 2006, Study 2; Wakslak et al., 2006, Study 7). Moreover, research using the Implicit Association Test has suggested that an automatic association exists between various dimensions of psychological distance and words related to high- or low-level construals (Bar-Anan, Liberman, & Trope, 2006).

CONSTRUING THE ATTITUDE OBJECT

The impact of psychological distance on level of construal suggests a key mechanism by which distance could influence evaluative action guides. By focusing attention on the central and defining features of an attitude object, high-level construals enable global evaluations that draw on what is consistent about the object across contexts. Thus, evaluations of distal attitude objects can be based on information relevant for evaluating the object's enduring, core features and will appear relatively stable in the face of contextual fluctuation. In contrast, by including the concrete, contextual aspects of an attitude object, low-level construals enable local evaluations that draw on the unique particularities of the present situation. Attitudinal responses toward such objects can therefore incorporate evaluative information from specific contextual details and will therefore appear relatively malleable.

Thus, we postulate that distance directs the self-regulatory system via its impact on the mental representation of an attitude object, which determines the basis or form of an evaluative response. This pattern should therefore generalize beyond any one particular dimension of distance. Any variable that influences the level at which an attitude object is construed should be sufficient to trigger these self-regulatory effects.

EMPIRICAL SUPPORT

Conceptualizing evaluations as local and global action guides suggests a number of predictions about how psychological distance should influence evaluative responding. We chose to begin to test our model by focusing on two in particular. First, we thought our perspective could help elucidate when people will be susceptible versus resistant to incidental social influences. As guides to action and interaction in the current situation, local evaluations should flexibly adapt to the immediate social context. Therefore, evaluations of psychologically proximal (vs. distal) attitude objects should show greater malleability in response to the incidental attitudes of a stranger.

Second, we suspected that our model could help shed light on an ongoing debate in the political psychology literature and beyond as to whether ideology can be meaningfully said to exist, or whether ideological values are instead relatively useless as predictors of evaluative responding (see, e.g., Converse, 1964; Jost, 2006; McGuire, 1999). As guides to action and interaction that must transcend the present situation, global evaluations should reflect a person's core ideological values: that is, those broad principles that relate to judgments and actions across situations (Rokeach, 1968, p. 160) and that tend to be shared within important and long-term dyadic and group relationships (Conover & Feldman, 1981; Jost et al., 2008; Kitt & Gleicher, 1950; Major & Townsend, this volume; Stillman, Guthrie, & Becker, 1960). Thus, our perspective suggests that responses to distant (vs. near) attitude objects might be more "ideological" in that they could more strongly reflect a person's basic values (see also Eyal, Sagristano, Trope, Liberman, & Chaiken, 2009).

Here, we highlight three of the studies we conducted to test these predictions. The first study focused on temporal distance and examined whether attitude alignment with an incidental stranger would be greater when a political policy was to be implemented in the near (vs. distant) future. In Study 2, we used a more direct manipulation of level of construal in order to determine whether our hypothesized mechanism was really responsible for the differential malleability observed in Study 1. Our third study sought to shed additional light on the lack of malleability observed in the previous studies' distant or high-level construal conditions, given that the absence of a partner effect on evaluative responding could reflect either attitudinal stability or simple apathy. We therefore examined whether inducing participants to adopt a high (vs. low) level of construal would decrease the extent to which contextual factors predicted evaluative responding, while leaving unchanged—or even increasing—the extent to which participants' evaluations were consistent with their previously reported ideological values.

Temporal Distance and Social Alignment

Our first study was designed to test the basic notion that evaluative responses toward psychologically near objects would indeed show greater context dependence than evaluative responses toward psychologically distant objects. Based on our theoretical perspective, we hypothesized that participants would align their attitudes with those of an incidental stranger when contemplating an attitude object that was temporally close, but not one that was temporally distant. Participants took part in an anticipated interaction paradigm (Chen, Schechter, & Chaiken, 1996), in which they expected to discuss a proposed policy on deporting illegal immigrants with another student in the study. They learned that the policy would be implemented either next week (near future condition) or next year (distant future condition), and that their discussion partner was either in favor of or against deporting illegal immigrants. Distance to the partner, as well as time until the ostensible conversation, was always held constant; thus, the only difference between conditions was whether the attitude object was close or distant in time. Participants then reported how likely they would be to vote for the described policy, as part of a set of pre-discussion questions that they answered privately (rather than expecting their responses to be shared with their partner). In actuality, this attitude measure was our variable of interest, and no discussion took place. The experimenter provided a full debriefing after carefully probing participants for suspicion.

Consistent with our hypothesis, results showed that participants' voting intentions aligned with those of their discussion partner when the policy was going to be implemented in the near future. When the partner supported deporting illegal immigrants, participants were slightly in favor of the policy; when the partner was anti-deportation, participants were against the policy. In contrast, participants were unaffected by their partners' views when the policy was going to be implemented in the distant future. Moreover, these findings obtained despite participants in the two conditions reporting equal motivation to get along with their discussion partner, suggesting that the distance manipulation was not simply changing participants' affiliative goals. These findings thus support the idea that responses to near attitude objects are guided by a local evaluative summary that incorporates information from the current social context, whereas responses to distant attitude objects are guided by a global summary that is less context-dependent.

Construal Level and Social Alignment

A global-local model of attitudes suggests that this pattern of results is not an effect of time per se, but rather a more general process that has to do with how an attitude object is mentally construed. In other words, the results of our first study presumably reflected a process in which increasing psychological distance led participants to mentally represent an attitude object in terms of its central and enduring features, which in turn caused them to rely on global, context-independent guides for action. Our next study zeroed in on this hypothesized process to directly manipulate level of construal. We predicted that individuals would be more influenced by an incidental stranger's attitudes when they construed an attitude object concretely than when they construed an attitude object abstractly.

An important aspect of construal is whether one focuses on the superordinate, goal-related aspects of activities, or rather the more subordinate, concrete means. Adapting a mind-set prime developed by Freitas, Gollwitzer, and Trope (2004), we induced participants to either adopt an abstract focus by asking them a series of "Why" questions (e.g., Why would you do well in school?), or a concrete focus by asking them a series of "How" questions (e.g., How would you do well in school?). After completing the mind-set prime, participants learned that an anticipated interaction partner was either in favor of or against physician-assisted suicide. Finally, they completed a 7-item measure of their own attitudes toward physician-assisted suicide.

The results again supported our model. Consistent with the notion that individuals rely on local action guides when responding to a concretely construed attitude object, but on global action guides when responding to an abstractly construed attitude object, social alignment was moderated by level of construal. Participants shifted their attitudes to align with those of their partner when they had been led to think concretely, but not when they had been led to think abstractly.

Construal Level and Ideological Values

Importantly, our perspective predicts not only that local action guides will tune to a particular situation, but also that global action guides will show stability across time and contexts. Although the studies reported thus far provide important support for the global-local model, it is unclear whether the lack of a social alignment effect in the distant future or abstract construal condition truly reflects attitude stability. For example, it is possible that this apparent "stability" resulted from apathy engendered by time discounting or the priming of superordinate goals (which could perhaps make certain political issues seem relatively unimportant). If evaluative responding at a distance is truly directed by global action guides that summarize context-independent information, then responses to distant attitude objects should be predicted by people's overarching, decontextualized ideological values. Follow-up analyses on a subset of our initial study's participants provided preliminary support for this prediction, demonstrating that a measure of individuals' ideological values assessed at the beginning of the semester predicted their voting intentions toward the distant future (but not near future) policy.

A subsequent study extended these findings to a more general manipulation of construal level. Participants reported their ideological support for the status quo (one of the two key components of left-right ideologies; see Jost, Banaji, & Nosek, 2004; Jost, Glaser, Kruglanski, & Sulloway, 2003) at the beginning of the semester in a mass-testing session and were brought into the lab several weeks later as part of an ostensibly unrelated study. Once there, they were assigned to either the "Why" or the "How" mind-set prime used in our second study to promote either an abstract or a concrete processing orientation. Next, participants took part in the anticipated interaction paradigm, learning their partner's attitude (this time toward universal health care) and then privately reporting their own.

The results showed that when participants were led to think concretely, their attitudes were predicted by their partner's attitude and not by their previously reported ideological values. Individuals' evaluative responses toward changing the health care system were more positive when their partner was in favor of rather than against universal health care, regardless of their previously reported ideological values. However, after being led to think abstractly, participants' attitudes were predicted by their ideological values rather than by their partners' opinions. The greater their support was for preserving the societal status quo at Time 1, the more they opposed radically revamping the health care system at Time 2, regardless of an incidental stranger's views. These results suggest that when people have been led to focus on concrete, low-level means and therefore construe an attitude object concretely, their evaluative response toward an attitude object is context-dependent. However, when they construe the same attitude object abstractly because they have been led to focus on high-level, superordinate goals, responding is based on global, decontextualized action guides that reflect previously reported ideological values.

CONNECTIONS AND IMPLICATIONS

The notion that attitudes can be either stable or malleable depending on a person's subjective construal of the attitude object may help to shed light on the frequently observed tension between these two characterizations of evaluative responding across multiple domains. In this section, we discuss several ways in which the global-local model of evaluation proposed here builds on existing theory and research in a number of areas, including attitude-behavior correspondence, political ideology, conformity, and connectionist models of attitude representation.

Attitude-Behavior Correspondence

The current model's distinction between global and local evaluations both complements and extends prior work on the relationship between attitudes and behavior,
which was spurred by criticism of attitudes research in the 1960s over low correlations between attitudes and action (e.g., DeFleur & Westie, 1958; McGuire, 1969;
Wicker, 1969). In an attempt to shed light on issues of measurement that could
be obscuring a stronger relationship between attitudes and behavior, Fishbein
and Ajzen (1974, 1975; Ajzen & Fishbein, 1977) took a psychometric perspective,
suggesting that attitudes and behaviors can be more or less strongly correlated
depending on the extent to which an attitude object is specified during measurement. According to Fishbein and Ajzen, an attitude object can be specified (or not)
with regard to action, target, context, and time. Low correlations between attitudes
and behavior frequently arise because an attitude toward a general (i.e., relatively
unspecified) object is used to predict a highly specified behavior. For example,
a person's attitude toward recycling (unspecified in terms of target, context, and
time) might be used to predict a highly specified behavior, such as whether she
recycles (action) her water bottle (target) in the lunchroom (context) today (time).
Fishbein and Ajzen suggest that such a highly specified behavior is best predicted
by measuring a person's attitude toward an equally specified attitude object,
whereas an attitude toward a more general attitude object will better predict an
index comprising many different specific behaviors.

This *compatibility principle* (Ajzen, 1988) provided key insight into the problem
of how to increase attitude-behavior correlations by highlighting the importance
of measurement techniques and mapping out when different attitude or behavior
criteria would be most appropriate. In this sense, it represents an important theory
of measurement, rather than a theory of psychological process: It does not speak
to how or why a more specified attitude now better predicts a highly specified
behavior later (see Eagly & Chaiken, 1993, pp. 165–166, for a similar observation).
The global-local model of evaluation proposed here *is* concerned with process and
can therefore potentially help to refine and extend the principle of compatibility
in multiple ways.

First, a global-local model suggests that an attitude object is not only objectively
defined by the researcher, but subjectively construed by the participant (see also
Lord & Lepper, 1999). Thus, even the same, equally specified attitude object can
be mentally represented in different ways, and the level of this *subjective* mental
construal enables either a local or global evaluation of the attitude object. To return
to our previous example, a person might represent the highly specified attitude
object "recycling a water bottle in the lunchroom today" in terms of its abstract
ends and value-related qualities (e.g., promoting environmentalism) or in terms
of its concrete means (e.g., walking across the lunchroom to the recycling bin),
and this subjective representation should determine whether the individual uses a
global or local evaluation to guide behavior.

This analysis suggests that measuring attitudes toward a highly specified attitude object tends to improve prediction of later specific behaviors because a specified attitude object will often include dimensions of distance that influence level

of construal, as well as important contextual features that can be incorporated into a local evaluation. Consider a researcher who measures participants' attitudes toward recycling a water bottle in the lunchroom today. The specified near point in time (today) should lead participants to construe the attitude object in a low-level, concrete way, and their response should therefore reflect a local evaluation that incorporates available contextual information (such as the attitude of a coworker who often eats lunch at the same time). Because people often focus on the here and now, they are likely to also construe the attitude object concretely later that day when they actually enter the lunchroom, and thus will also use a local evaluation (which draws on the same contextual details that influenced the previously measured attitude) to guide their recycling behavior.

However, a global-local model of evaluation also suggests situations in which the principle of compatibility might not apply. For instance, a researcher might measure participants' attitudes toward voting for a particular presidential candidate in next year's election. The specified distant point in time (next year) should lead participants to construe the attitude object in a high-level, abstract way, and their response should therefore reflect a global evaluation of the political candidate. When people are actually voting in the here and now, however, they may construe the political candidate concretely and vote based on a local, contextualized evaluation that does not match their previously reported global evaluation. Conversely, a researcher might measure participants' attitudes in a way that elicits a low-level construal and local evaluation of the candidate (e.g., by specifying a proximal context: participants will vote in the nearby polling station down the street), but aspects of the actual voting situation may elicit a high-level construal and global evaluation (perhaps the individual has a conversation with a friend on the way to the voting booth about *why* they prefer a particular candidate, or perhaps it is particularly salient that the next president will not be sworn in until the following year, which may seem relatively distant in time). Here again, an incongruity between measurements with respect to the level at which an attitude object is *subjectively* construed, rather than the extent to which an attitude object is objectively specified, could lead to inconsistencies between the measured attitudes and behaviors.

A global-local model of evaluation also suggests that instability in attitudinal responding is not simply an issue of compatibility (in objective specification of the attitude object, or even subjective level of construal). According to the present perspective, local evaluations of an attitude object tend to shift in response to incidental details of the current social context. This approach therefore makes predictions about susceptibility to incidental social influence that lie beyond the scope of even a broadly interpreted compatibility principle. An evaluation of a highly specified and concretely construed attitude object in one situation may differ substantially from an evaluation of the same specific and concretely construed object in another situation. For example, participants' evaluations of the same presidential candidate in two different contexts might differ even when the measures are compatible in degree of specificity and when the participants adopt the same low level of construal, if their local evaluations in the two contexts incorporate incidental details with different evaluative implications.

Ideology

The studies described here may also help to shed light on questions of whether and when ideological values can be expected to guide evaluative responding—a question that has caused considerable controversy in the literature (see Eagly & Chaiken, 1993; Feldman, 2003; Jost, 2006; McGuire, 1985, for reviews). Whereas some researchers have argued that ideological principles often guide evaluative responses to social and political issues, and can display considerable stability across time and contexts (e.g., Jost, 2006; Judd, Krosnick, & Milburn, 1981; Judd & Milburn, 1980; Kerlinger, 1984; Stern, Dietz, Kalof, & Guagnano, 1995), others question whether ideologies can be meaningfully said to exist for the majority of the population, citing evidence suggesting that most people's attitudes toward specific policy issues show considerable fluctuation over time and rarely seem to consistently reflect core ideological values (Campbell et al., 1960; Converse, 1964; Tedin, 1987; Zaller, 1992).

The present studies suggest that ideology may be more likely to predict evaluative responding when an issue or policy is construed abstractly rather than concretely. Thus, voting behavior may tend to more strongly reflect people's ideological values when a policy or issue is psychologically distant rather than proximal (e.g., when a policy will be implemented next year rather than next week, or when someone is voting by absentee ballot from a spatially distant location, rather than in person at the voting booth). Such a notion would be consistent with past research (e.g., Converse, 1964) suggesting that individuals' here-and-now evaluations of particular political policies may often bear little relation to their ideological values. On the other hand, it would suggest that in the distance (or more generally, when a person is thinking abstractly), ideology may guide evaluative responding in a predictable and meaningful way.

Interestingly, such a link between abstraction and ideological consistency to some extent echoes Converse's (1964) classification of voters into five categories reflecting their "level of conceptualization" of politics, ranging from those at lowest level, who reported no knowledge of issue content or policy significance, to those at the highest level, whose political attitudes reflected "a relatively abstract and far reaching conceptual dimension" (p. 216). While Converse viewed differences in abstraction as a between-persons variable, the present perspective in some ways simply extends his analysis to consider the possibility that the same individual may view a given issue at varying levels of abstraction. Thus, ideological consistency may vary not only from person to person, but also for the same person across different situations, depending on the level at which he or she subjectively construes an attitude object at that particular moment.

Conformity

A global-local model of evaluation can also be used to make predictions about when individuals will conform to group norms. Importantly, information about normative behavior can influence global or local evaluations, depending on whether the norms relate to an important and enduring cultural setting or social group, or rather to an incidental and temporary social context. On the one hand, long-standing social norms should often inform global evaluations, because they extend across time and contexts and therefore provide information that is relevant for evaluating an attitude object across different situations. However, social norms can at times constitute an aspect of the local social situation. For instance, if one were judging the physical length of a line and happened to be in a room with some strangers, the strangers' perceptions of the line's length would be a local (and objectively irrelevant) concern for one's own judgment.

In the latter case, we would predict that conformity to an incorrect and incidental majority (as in the Asch line paradigm; Asch, 1955) would decrease as psychological distance increases (for instance, when the lines were projected on a spatially near vs. distant wall). Of course, this prediction is somewhat counterintuitive: When an object of judgment is close rather than far away, one should if anything be more certain that one is seeing it clearly and thus be more confident in the accuracy of one's own judgment. However, at the same time, the proximity of the judged object should lead people to construe it more concretely. In turn, this should lead them to rely on local (vs. global) guides, which will be more susceptible to the incidental social influence of the incorrect majority in the present situation.

Distributed Connectionist Network Models

Although our global-local perspective does not necessarily rely on a specific cognitive model of memory, it is worth noting its particular congruence with a distributed connectionist network model of attitude representation (Conrey & Smith, 2007; Ferguson & Bargh, 2007; Smith & Conrey, 2007). Distributed connectionist systems view mental representation as patterns of activation that occur across large numbers of processing units in response to a range of inputs (rather than as discrete "files" of information that are stored, static, in the mind until they are retrieved). Such models suggest that malleability in evaluative responding naturally arises from variability in pattern activation in response to attitude objects in various contexts. However, distributed connectionist networks can also easily account for evaluative stability, which should occur when the same pattern is activated in multiple situations. According to Conrey and Smith (2007), this can explain why domain expertise is associated with attitudinal stability:

> given sufficient experience with a domain, someone may learn to activate roughly the same pattern in many different contexts. This is accomplished by focusing on the key inputs that trigger that particular attractor [i.e., pattern of activation]...while ignoring other inputs, even highly salient ones, as irrelevant...and this ability to focus is precisely what constitutes domain expertise. (p. 721)

For example, whereas someone who knows little about computers might evaluate a given laptop differently depending on a range of superficial inputs (e.g., the color, the case, the opinion of another customer), a computer expert would be likely to focus on the most important and essential characteristics of the computer (inputs that would not vary with the context). In a similar manner, level of construal may influence the range of inputs to which people attend, so that abstract construals screen out incidental information and facilitate stability in evaluative responding, whereas concrete construals include these inputs and facilitate evaluative flexibility in response to the immediate context. Integrating a distributed connectionist approach with a global-local model of evaluation therefore has the potential to unite a number of predictors of attitude stability (including expertise, abstraction, and perhaps also attitude importance) via their common impact on the extent to which incidental inputs are included in, or screened out of, one's subjective construal of an attitude object.

CONCLUSION

In summary, we have suggested that individuals must be able to regulate their behavior both within and outside the present context. To do so, they use two forms of evaluative action guides. Local evaluations serve to guide behavior in the here and now by incorporating specific details of the present context; they can therefore shift flexibly to align with the views of incidental others and tend to look relatively malleable. Global evaluations, meanwhile, enable individuals to transcend the here and now to act on the "there and then." They draw on what is invariant about an attitude object across contexts, and therefore tend to reflect people's core values and ideals and appear relatively stable in the face of changing contextual details.

REFERENCES

Ajzen, I. (1988). *Attitudes, personality, and behavior*. Buckingham, England: Open University Press.

Ajzen, I., & Fishbein, M. (1977). Attitude-behavior relations: A theoretical analysis and review of empirical research. *Psychological Bulletin, 84*, 888–918.

Allport, G. W. (1935). Attitudes. In C. Murchison (Ed.), *A handbook of social psychology* (pp. 798–844). Worcester, MA: Clark University Press.

Asch, S. E. (1955). Opinions and social pressure. *Scientific American, 193*, 31–35.

Baldwin, M. W., & Holmes, J. G. (1987). Salient private audiences and awareness of the self. *Journal of Personality and Social Psychology, 52*, 1087–1098.

Bar-Anan, Y., Liberman, N., & Trope, Y. (2006). The association between psychological distance and construal level: Evidence from an implicit association test. *Journal of Experimental Psychology: General, 135*, 609–622.

Blair, I. V. (2002). The malleability of automatic stereotypes and prejudice. *Personality and Social Psychology Review, 6*, 242–261.

Blair, I. V., Ma, J. E., & Lenton, A. P. (2001). Imagining stereotypes away: The moderation of implicit stereotypes through mental imagery. *Journal of Personality and Social Psychology, 81*, 828–841.

Blanchard, F. A., Lilly, T., & Vaughn, L. A. (1991). Reducing the expression of racial prejudice. *Psychological Science, 2*, 101–105.

Brennan, S., & Clark, H. H. (1996). Conceptual pacts and lexical choice in conversation. *Journal of Experimental Psychology: Learning, Memory, & Cognition, 22*, 1482–1493.

Campbell, A., Converse, P. E., Miller, W. E., & Stokes, D. E. (1960). *The American voter.* Oxford, England: Wiley.

Campbell, D. T. (1950). The indirect assessment of social attitudes. *Psychological Bulletin, 47*, 15–38.

Chaiken, S., Pomerantz, E. M., & Giner-Sorolla, R. (1995). Structural consistency and attitude strength. In R. E. Petty & J. A. Krosnick (Eds.), *Attitude strength: Antecedents and consequences* (pp. 387–412). Hillsdale, NJ: Erlbaum.

Chen, S., Shechter, D., & Chaiken, S. (1996). Getting at the truth or getting along: Accuracy- versus impression-motivated heuristic and systematic processing. *Journal of Personality and Social Psychology, 71*, 262–275.

Clark, H. H. (1996). *Using language*. Cambridge: Cambridge University Press.

Conover, P. J., & Feldman, S. (1981). The origins and meaning of liberal/conservative self identification. *American Journal of Political Science, 25*, 617–645.

Conrey, F. R., & Smith, E. R. (2007). Attitude representation: Attitudes as patterns in a distributed, connectionist representational system. *Social Cognition, 25*, 718–735.

Converse, P. E. (1964). The nature of belief systems in mass publics. In D. E. Apter (Ed.), *Ideology and discontent*. New York: Free Press.

Crocker, J., Karpinski, A., Quinn, D. M., & Chase, S. (2003). When grades determine self-worth: Consequences of contingent self-worth for male and female engineering and psychology majors. *Journal of Personality and Social Psychology, 85*, 507–516.

Dasgupta, N., & Greenwald, A. G. On the malleability of automatic attitudes: Combating automatic prejudice with images of admired and disliked individuals. *Journal of Personality and Social Psychology, 81*, 800–814.

Davis, J. L., & Rusbult, C. E. (2001). Attitude alignment in close relationships. *Journal of Personality and Social Psychology, 18,* 65–84.

DeFleur, M. L., & Westie, F. R. (1958). Verbal attitudes and overt acts: An experiment on the salience of attitudes. *American Sociological Review, 23*, 667–673.

Deutsch, M., & Gerard, H. B. (1955). A study of normative and informational social influences upon individual judgment. *Journal of Abnormal and Social Psychology, 51*, 629–636.

Devine, P. G. (1989). Stereotypes and prejudice: Their automatic and controlled components. *Journal of Personality and Social Psychology, 56*, 5–18.

Eagly, A. H., & Chaiken, S. C. (1993). *The psychology of attitudes*. Belmont, CA: Wadsworth.

Eagly, A. H., Kulesa, P., Chen, S., & Chaiken, S. (2001). Do attitudes affect memory? Tests of the congeniality hypothesis. *Current Directions in Psychological Science, 10*, 5–9.

Eyal, T., Sagristano, M. D., Trope, Y., Liberman, N., & Chaiken, S. (2009). When values matter: Expressing values in behavioral intentions for the near vs. distant future. *Journal of Experimental Social Psychology, 45*, 35–43.

Fazio, R. H. (1986). How do attitudes guide behavior? In R. M. Sorrentino & E. T. Higgins (Eds.), *The handbook of motivation and cognition: Foundations of social behavior* (pp. 204–243). New York: Guilford Press.

Feldman, S. (2003). Values, ideology, and the structure of political attitudes. In D. O. Sears, L. Huddy, & R. Jervis (Eds.), *Oxford handbook of political psychology* (pp. 477–508). New York: Oxford University Press.

Ferguson, M. J., & Bargh, J. A. (2007). Beyond the attitude object: Implicit attitudes spring from object-centered contexts. In B. Wittenbrink & N. Schwarz (Eds.), *Implicit measures of attitudes: Progress and controversies* (pp. 216–246). New York: Guilford Press.

Festinger, L. (1950). Informal social communication. *Psychological Review, 57*, 271–282.

Fishbein, M., & Ajzen, I. (1974). Attitudes toward objects as predictors of single and multiple behavioral criteria. *Psychological Review, 81*, 59–74.

Fishbein, M., & Ajzen, I. (1975). *Belief, attitude, intention, and behavior: An introduction to theory and research*. Reading, MA: Addison-Wesley.

Förster, J., Friedman, R. S., & Liberman, N. (2004). Temporal construal effects on abstract and concrete thinking: Consequences for insight and creative cognition. *Journal of Personality and Social Psychology, 87,* 177–189.

Freedman, J. (1965). Long-term behavioral effects of cognitive dissonance. *Journal of Experimental Social Psychology, 1,* 145–155.

Freitas, A. L., Gollwitzer, P. M., & Trope, Y. (2004). The influence of abstract and concrete mindsets on anticipating and guiding others' self regulatory efforts. *Journal of Experimental Social Psychology, 40,* 739–752.

Fujita, K., Henderson, M., Eng, J., Trope, Y., & Liberman, N. (2006). Spatial distance and mental construal of social events. *Psychological Science, 17,* 278–282.

Fujita, K., Trope, Y., & Liberman, N. (2006). The role of mental construal in self-control. In D. DeCremer, M. Zeelenberg, & J. K. Murnighan (Eds.), *Social psychology and economics* (pp. 193–211). New York: Sage.

Garcia-Marques, L., Santos, A. S. C., & Mackie, D. M. (2006). Stereotypes: Static abstractions or dynamic knowledge structures? *Journal of Personality and Social Psychology, 91,* 814–831.

Gawronski, B., LeBel, E. P., & Peters, K. R. (2007). What do implicit measures tell us?: Scrutinizing the validity of three common assumptions. *Perspectives on Psychological Science, 2,* 181–193.

Giner-Sorolla, R., & Chaiken, S. (1997). Selective use of heuristic and systematic processing under defense motivation. *Personality and Social Psychology Bulletin, 23,* 84–97.

Greenwald, A. G. (1989). Why attitudes are important: Defining attitude and attitude theory 20 years later. In A. R. Pratkanis, S. J. Breckler, & A. G. Greenwald (Eds.), *Attitude structure and function* (pp. 429–440). Hillsdale, NJ: Erlbaum.

Hamilton, D. L., & Trolier, T. K. (1986). Stereotypes and stereotyping: An overview of the cognitive approach. In J. Dovidio & S. L. Gaertner (Eds.), *Prejudice, discrimination, and racism* (pp. 127–163). New York: Academic Press.

Hardin, C. D., & Conley, T. D. (2001). A relational approach to cognition: Shared experience and relationship affirmation in social cognition. In G. B. Moskowitz (Ed.), *Cognitive social psychology: The Princeton symposium on the legacy and future of social cognition* (pp. 3–17). Mahwah, NJ: Lawrence Erlbaum Associates Publishers.

Hardin, C. D., & Higgins, E. T. (1996). Shared reality: How social verification makes the subjective objective. In R. M. Sorrentino & E. T. Higgins (Eds.), *Handbook of motivation and cognition: Vol. 3. The interpersonal context* (pp. 28–84). New York: Guilford Press.

Henderson, M. D., Fujita, K., Trope, Y., & Liberman, N. (2006). Transcending the "here": The effect of spatial distance on social judgment. *Journal of Personality and Social Psychology, 91,* 845–856.

Higgins, E. T., & Rholes, W. S. (1978). "Saying is believing": Effects of message modification on memory and liking for the person described. *Journal of Experimental Social Psychology, 14,* 363–378.

Hovland, C. I., Campbell, E. H., & Brock, T. (1957). The effects of "commitment" on opinion change following communication. In C. I. Hovland et al. (Eds.), *The order of presentation in persuasion.* New Haven, CT: Yale University Press.

Isaacs, E., & Clark, H. H. (1987). References in conversation between experts and novices. *Journal of Experimental Psychology: General, 116,* 26–37.

Jost, J. T. (2006). The end of the end of ideology. *American Psychologist, 61,* 651–670.

Jost, J. T., Banaji, M. R., & Nosek, B. A. (2004). A decade of system justification theory: Accumulated evidence of conscious and unconscious bolstering of the status quo. *Political Psychology, 25,* 881–919.

Jost, J. T., Glaser, J., Kruglanski, A. W., & Sulloway, F. (2003). Exceptions that prove the rule: Using a theory of motivated social cognition to account for ideological incongruities and political anomalies. *Psychological Bulletin, 129*, 383–393.

Jost, J. T., Ledgerwood, A., & Hardin, C. D. (2008). Shared reality, system justification, and the relational basis of ideological beliefs. *Social and Personality Psychology Compass, 2*, 171–186.

Judd, C. M., Krosnick, J. A., & Milburn, M. A. (1981). Political involvement in attitude structure in the general public. *American Sociological Review, 46*, 660–669.

Judd, C. M., & Milburn, M. A. (1980). The structure of attitude systems in the general public: Comparisons of a structural equation model. *American Sociological Review, 45*, 627–643.

Katz, D. (1960). The functional approach to the study of attitudes. *Public Opinion Quarterly, 24*, 163–204.

Katz, D., & Braly, K. (1935). Racial prejudice and racial stereotypes. *Journal of Abnormal and Social Psychology, 30*, 175–193.

Kawakami, K., Dovidio, J. F., & Dijksterhuis, A. (2003). Effect of social category priming on personal attitudes. *Psychological Science, 14*, 315–319.

Kerlinger, F. N. (1984). *Liberalism and conservatism: The nature and structure of social attitudes.* Hillsdale, NJ: Erlbaum.

Kitt, A. S., & Gleicher, D. B. (1950). Determinants of voting behavior. *Public Opinion Quarterly, 14*, 393–412.

Krech, D., & Crutchfield, R. S. (1948). *Theory and problems of social psychology.* New York: McGraw-Hill.

Kunda, Z., & Oleson, K. C. (1995). Maintaining stereotypes in the face of disconfirmation: Constructing grounds for subtyping deviants. *Journal of Personality and Social Psychology, 68*, 565–579.

Ledgerwood, A., & Chaiken, S. (2007). Priming us and them: Automatic assimilation and contrast in group attitudes. *Journal of Personality and Social Psychology, 93*, 940–956.

Ledgerwood, A., & Liviatan, I. (in press). The price of a shared vision: Group identity goals and the social creation of value. *Social Cognition.*

Liberman, N., & Trope, Y. (1998). The role of feasibility and desirability considerations in near and distant future decisions: A test of temporal construal theory. *Journal of Personality and Social Psychology, 75*, 5–18.

Liberman, N., & Trope, Y. (2008). The psychology of transcending the here and now. *Science, 322*, 1201–1205.

Liberman, N., Trope, Y., & Stephan, E. (2007). Psychological distance. In A. W. Kruglanski & E. T. Higgins (Eds.), *Social psychology: Handbook of basic principles* (Vol. 2, pp. 353–383). New York: Guilford Press.

Libby, L. K., & Eibach, R. P. (2002). Looking back in time: Self-concept change affects visual perspective in autobiographical memory. *Journal of Personality and Social Psychology, 82*, 167–179.

Lord, C. G., & Lepper, M. (1999). Attitude representation theory. In M. Zanna (Ed.), *Advances in experimental social psychology* (Vol. 31, pp. 265–343). San Diego, CA: Academic Press.

Lord, C. G., Ross, L., & Lepper, M. R. (1979). Biased assimilation and attitude polarization: The effects of prior theories on subsequently considered evidence. *Journal of Personality and Social Psychology, 37*, 2098–2109.

Lowery, B. S., Hardin, C. D., & Sinclair, S. (2001). Social influence effects on automatic racial prejudice. *Journal of Personality and Social Psychology, 81*, 842–855.

McGuire, W. J. (1969). The nature of attitudes and attitude change. In G. Lindzey & E. Aronson (Eds.), *The handbook of social psychology* (Vol. 3, pp. 136–314). Reading, MA: Addison-Wesley.

McGuire, W. J. (1985). Attitudes and attitude change. In G. Lindzey & E. Aronson (Eds.), *Handbook of social psychology* (3rd ed., Vol. 2, pp. 233–346). New York: McGraw-Hill.

McGuire, W. J. (1999). The vicissitudes of attitudes in social psychology. In W. J. McGuire (Ed.), *Constructing social psychology: Creative and critical processes* (pp. 325–347). Cambridge, England: Cambridge University Press. (Original work published 1986)

Norenzayan, A., & Schwarz, N. (1999). Telling what they want to know: Participants tailor causal attributions to researchers' interests. *European Journal of Social Psychology, 29,* 1011–1020.

Nussbaum, S., Trope, Y., & Liberman, N. (2003). Creeping dispositionism: The temporal dynamics of behavior prediction. *Journal of Personality and Social Psychology, 84,* 485–497.

Ostrom, T. M., & Brock, T. C. (1968). A cognitive model of attitudinal involvement. In R. P. Abelson, E. Aronson, W. J. McGuire, T. M. Newcombe, M. J. Rosenberg, & P. H. Tannenbaum (Eds.), *Theories of cognitive consistency: A sourcebook* (pp. 373–383). Chicago: Rand McNally.

Peterson, R. C., & Thurstone, L. L. (1932). *The effect of motion pictures on the social attitudes of high school children.* Ann Arbor, MI: Edwards Bros.

Pomerantz, E. M., Chaiken, S., & Tordesillas, R. S. (1995). Attitude strength and resistance processes. *Journal of Personality and Social Psychology, 69,* 408–419.

Richeson, J. A., & Ambady, N. (2003). Effects of situational power on automatic racial prejudice. *Journal of Experimental Social Psychology, 39,* 177–183.

Rokeach, M. (1968). *Beliefs, attitudes, and values: A theory of organization and change.* San Francisco: Jossey-Bass.

Rokeach, M. (1975). Long-term value changes initiated by computer feedback. *Journal of Personality and Social Psychology, 32,* 467–476.

Rokeach, M., & Cochrane, R. (1972). Self-confrontation and confrontation with another as determinants of long-term value change. *Journal of Applied Social Psychology, 2,* 283–292.

Rokeach, M., & Mezei, L. (1966). Race and shared beliefs as factors in social choice. *Science, 151,* 167–172.

Schuman, H., & Johnson, M. P. (1976). Attitudes and behavior. *Annual Review of Sociology, 2,* 161–207.

Sechrist, G. B., & Stangor, C. (2001). Perceived consensus influences intergroup behavior and stereotype accessibility. *Journal of Personality and Social Psychology, 80,* 645–654.

Shavitt, S. (1990). The role of attitude objects in attitude functions. *Journal of Experimental Social Psychology, 26,* 124–148.

Sherif, M. (1935). A study of some social factors in perception. *Archives of Psychology,* No. 187.

Sinclair, L., & Kunda, Z. (1999). Reactions to a Black professional: Motivated inhibition and activation of conflicting stereotypes. *Journal of Personality and Social Psychology, 77,* 885–904.

Sinclair, S., Huntsinger, J., Skorinko, J., & Hardin, C. D. (2005). Social tuning of the self: Consequences for the self-evaluations of stereotype targets. *Journal of Personality and Social Psychology, 89,* 160–175.

Sinclair, S., Lowery, B. S., Hardin, C. D., & Colangelo, A. (2005). Social tuning of automatic racial attitudes: The role of affiliative motivation. *Journal of Personality and Social Psychology, 89,* 583–592.

Smith, E. R., & Conrey, F. R. (2007). Mental representations as states not things: Implications for implicit and explicit measurement. In B. Wittenbrink & N. Schwarz (Eds.), *Implicit measures of attitudes* (pp. 247–264). New York: Guilford Press.

Smith, E. R., & Semin, G. R. (2004). Socially situated cognition: Cognition in its social context. In M. P. Zanna (Ed.), *Advances in experimental social psychology* (Vol. 36, pp. 53–117). San Diego, CA: Academic Press.

Smith, E. R., & Semin, G. R. (2007). Situated social cognition. *Current Directions in Psychological Science, 16,* 132–135.

Smith, M. B., Bruner, J. S., & White, R. W. (1956). *Opinions and personality.* New York: Wiley.

Smith, P. K., & Trope, Y. (2006). You focus on the forest when you're in charge of the trees: Power priming and abstract information processing. *Journal of Personality and Social Psychology, 90,* 578–596.

Stangor, C., Sechrist, G. B., & Jost, J. T. (2001). Changing racial beliefs by providing consensus information. *Personality and Social Psychology Bulletin, 27,* 486–496.

Stern, P. C., Dietz, T., Kalof, L., & Guagnano, G. A. (1995). Values, beliefs, and pro-environmental action: Attitude formation toward emergent attitude objects. *Journal of Applied Social Psychology, 26,* 1611–1636.

Stillman, J. G., Guthrie, G. M., & Becker, S. W. (1960). Determinants of political party preference. *Journal of Social Psychology, 51,* 165–171

Sweeney, P. D., & Gruber, K. L. (1984). Selective exposure: Voter information preferences and the Watergate affair. *Journal of Personality and Social Psychology, 46,* 1208–1221.

Tedin, K. L. (1987). Political ideology and the vote. *Research in Micropolitics, 2,* 63–94.

Todorov, A., Goren, A., & Trope, Y. (2007). Probability as a psychological distance: Construal and preference. *Journal of Experimental Social Psychology, 43,* 473–482.

Tourangeau, R., & Rasinski, K. A. (1988). Cognitive processes underlying context effects in attitude measurement. *Psychological Bulletin, 103,* 299–314.

Trope, Y., & Liberman N. (2000). Temporal construal and time-dependent changes in preference. *Journal of Personality and Social Psychology, 79,* 876–889.

Trope, Y., & Liberman, N. (2003). Temporal construal. *Psychological Review, 110,* 403–421.

Trope, Y., Liberman, N., & Wakslak, C. (2007). Construal levels and psychological distance: Effects on representation, prediction, evaluation, and behavior. *Journal of Consumer Psychology, 17,* 83–95.

Turner, J. C. (1991). *Social influence. Mapping social psychology series.* Belmont, CA: Brooks/Cole.

Vallacher, R. R., & Wegner, D. M. (1985). *A theory of action identification.* Hillsdale, NJ: Erlbaum.

Vallacher, R. R., & Wegner, D. M. (1989). Levels of personal agency: Individual variations in action identification. *Journal of Personality and Social Psychology, 57,* 660–671.

Wakslak, C. J., Trope, Y., Liberman, N., & Aloni, R. (2006). Seeing the forest when entry is unlikely: Probability and the mental representation of events. *Journal of Experimental Psychology: General, 135,* 641–653.

Wallace, D. S., Paulson, R. M., Lord, C. G., & Bond, C. F. (2005). Which behaviors do attitudes predict? Meta-analyzing the effects of social pressure and perceived difficulty. *Review of General Psychology, 9,* 214–227.

Wicker, A. W. (1969). Attitudes versus actions: The relationship of verbal and overt behavioral responses to altitude objects. *Journal of Social Issues, 25,* 41–78.

Wilson, T. D., Lindsey, S., and Schooler, T. Y. (2000). A model of dual attitudes. *Psychological Review, 107,* 101–126.

Wittenbrink, B., Judd, C. M., & Park, B. (2001). Spontaneous prejudice in context: Variability in automatically activated attitudes. *Journal of Personality and Social Psychology, 81,* 815–827.

Yeh, W., & Barsalou, L. W. (2006). The situated nature of concepts. *American Journal of Psychology, 119,* 349–384.

Zaller, J. R. (1992). *The nature and origins of mass opinion.* Cambridge, England: Cambridge University Press.

4

For Whom Pavlov's Bell Tolls
Processes Underlying Evaluative Conditioning

EVA WALTHER AND TINA LANGER

INTRODUCTION: ATTITUDE FORMATION AND CHANGE THROUGH EVALUATIVE CONDITIONING

Human behavior is governed to a large extent by our likes and dislikes. Whereas some attitudinal reactions seem to be almost universal (e.g., many people like ice cream better than spiders), many other attitudes appear to reflect individual learning history. After all, social psychology relies to a large extent on the assumption that negative attitudes (e.g., prejudice) as well as positive attitudes (e.g., preferences) can be acquired by and cured with individual learning experiences (see Crano, this volume). However, the question remains of how learning must be designed in order to form and change attitudes.

One experimental answer to this question comes from so-called evaluative conditioning (EC) research (for reviews, see De Houwer, Thomas, & Baeyens, 2001; Walther, Nagengast, & Trasselli, 2005). EC refers to changes in (dis-) liking that are due to the pairing of stimuli (De Houwer, 2007). In a prototypical EC study, a subjectively neutral picture of a human face (conditioned stimulus [CS]) is repeatedly presented with a subjectively liked or disliked human face (unconditioned stimulus [US]). The common result is a substantial shift in the valence of the formerly neutral CS, such that it acquires the evaluative quality of the US. This is presumably different from signal or Pavlovian learning, in which the CS acquires a *predictive value*. In an EC paradigm the CS merely attains the *affective quality* of the US, which is usually explained by the formation of an association between the cognitive representation of the CS and the US

(De Houwer et al., 2001). As such, subsequent activation of the CS in memory may associatively spread to the US, which in turn activates the evaluation of the US. The result is an evaluative response to the CS that directly corresponds to the one toward the US.

EXAMPLES OF EC IN SOCIAL PSYCHOLOGY

EC is a relatively simple effect that helps to explain many phenomena in social psychology. For instance, EC is involved in illusory correlations in which observers acquire an association between a group of individuals and a certain positive or negative evaluation (Chapman & Chapman, 1967; Fiedler, Russer, & Gramm, 1993; Hamilton & Gifford, 1976). Even more obvious is the influence of EC in the famous "kill-the-messenger effect," which describes the phenomenon whereby transmitters are inevitably associated with the valence of the message they have conveyed (Manis, Cornell, Moore, & Jeffrey, 1974). Whereas in persuasion a neutral message (CS) usually experiences a revaluation through its co-occurrence with an evaluated communicator (US), the opposite mechanism occurs in the kill-the-messenger effect: The messenger (CS) experiences a revaluation by being associated with bad news (US).

Similar effects were obtained in a series of studies by Skowronski, Carlston, Mae, and Crawford (1998), who demonstrated that communicators become involuntarily associated with their verbal description (i.e., traits) of others. Although descriptions of other people are logically independent of the communicator, simple associative processes nevertheless link these two events together and produce such boomerang-like phenomena. Recently, Gawronski and Walther (2008) found that these transference effects are not confined to traits, but that the overall evaluation affects the attitude toward the person who endorsed the evaluation. Gawronski and Walther (2008) called this the TAR effect (transfer of attitudes recursively), which refers to the recursive influence of an observed evaluation on the formation of a corresponding attitude toward the source of that evaluation.

EC also plays a crucial role when it comes to the evaluation of the self (see Rhodewalt & Peterson, this volume). There are several demonstrations that the (normally positive) evaluation of the self also influences the evaluation of other objects and events. The mere ownership effect (Feys, 1991, 1995), for instance, states that people have a preference for objects belonging to the self. Giving people an object (e.g., a pen) leads to a more favorable attitude toward this object compared to a not-owned object (Beggan, 1992). That people exhibit a preference for aspects associated with the self is also supported by the name letter effect, which describes the phenomenon that people like letters that are part of their own names better than other letters (Nuttin, 1985; see also Koole, Dijksterhuis, & van Knippenberg, 2001). In terms of EC, self-evaluation can be conceptualized as a US and other individuals or objects as CSs. Thus, people can use themselves to evaluate others. According to evaluative learning theory (De Houwer et al., 2001), the mere spatio-temporal CS-US co-occurrence is a sufficient condition for the transfer of valence from the US to the CS (Martin & Levey, 1978). Given that self-evaluation is predominantly positive, associating an object or event with the self may therefore lead to a favorable attitude toward this object or event (Gawronski, Bodenhausen, & Becker, 2007; Walther & Trasselli, 2003). However, self-evaluation can serve not only as a source (US), but also as an object (CS) of attitude formation (Dijksterhuis, 2004).

EC in social psychology is probably most apparent in the area of persuasion, indicating that EC is not confined to attitude formation, but can also produce attitude change. It is well documented in persuasion research how simple evaluative features of the source, such as attractiveness (Petty & Cacioppo, 1984), credibility, or likeability of the communicator (Petty, Cacioppo, & Goldman, 1981), serve as potent persuasion cues especially when participants are distracted or low in motivation (see also Crano, this volume). In terms of EC, the persuasion message can be considered the CS, and the characteristics of the communicator the US. Similar to EC effects, the transfer of valence from the US to the CS can occur unconsciously; that is, the audience usually does not know why they suddenly like one message better than the other. It is also typical for EC-like phenomena that these communicator effects are not reduced, but, if anything, enhanced when people are distracted or not motivated to deeply process the information. Moreover, research on the US-revaluation effect demonstrates that peripheral persuasion cues, such as source attractiveness, may influence attitudes even when the original message is not available anymore. If an originally likeable source acquires a negative valence, this change in source valence can affect attitudes toward the object without any additional contact to the original message. However, it is also well known in persuasion literature that attitudes elicited by evaluative persuasion cues are weaker, less resistant to counterevidence, and less predicting of behavior than attitudes based on deep cognitive elaboration. (Petty, Haugtwedt, & Smith, 1995). It is not clear if this is also true for conditioned attitudes because studies addressing the structural nature of conditioned attitudes and their predictive quality on behavior do not yet exist. Thus, more research is necessary in order to address the specific similarities and differences between persuasion and EC.

HOW TO EXPLAIN EC? AN UNSOLVED ISSUE

Notwithstanding the significance of EC in many areas of psychology, EC research from the outset experienced vigorous debates concerning the explanation of the effect. Up to now there is no doubt that EC exists. EC has been demonstrated within the picture-picture paradigm (Baeyens, Eelen, van den Bergh, & Crombez, 1989; Pleyers, Corneille, Luminet, & Yzerbyt, 2007; Walther & Grigoriadis, 2004), with haptic stimuli (Hammerl & Grabitz, 2000), and even cross-modally (Todrank, Byrnes, Wrzesniewski, & Rozin, 1995) and vicariously (see also Cooper, this volume).

However, it is widely debated whether EC is fundamentally different from signal learning or just a much simpler version of the same basic principle. Why is this question important for attitude research? If EC could be identified as a variety of signal learning, this would suggest that attitude formation and change are confined to cognitive processes as suggested by Fishbein and Ajzen (1975) and related models, because signal learning is generally considered a cognitive rule-based process (e.g., De Houwer & Beckers, 2002). Thus, showing that EC is different from signal learning provides a strong reason to doubt the general notion of merely cognitively based attitudes.

Differences and Similarities Between EC and Signal Learning

The procedural similarities between EC and signal learning (i.e., CSs acquire meaning through pairing with USs) suggest that they are based on similar mechanisms. However, early EC researchers Martin and Levey (1978) inferred from their own findings that EC and signal learning were fundamentally different. This claim was supported by a number of observations that did not fit into the signal learning schema and that could not be explained by signal learning theory (e.g., Rescorla & Wagner, 1972). The first attribute that seems to be different in signal learning and EC is the dependency on contingency. As a logical consequence of defining signal learning as the formation of an expectancy that the US is going to occur when the CS is presented, the contingency (i.e., statistical correlation) between the CS and US is a crucial determinant of signal learning. Predictions can only be formed when there is a negative or positive correlation between the CS and the US, but not when USs and CSs co-occur on a random basis. Present research, however, indicates that EC appears not to be dependent on the CS-US correlation, which suggests that predictability of the US is not a major ingredient in the EC learning process. This assumption is also supported by the lack of blocking effects in EC (Kamin, 1968). In an intriguing set of studies, Kamin (1968) demonstrated that the association between a CS1 and a US prevents the subsequent association of another CS2 and the same US, although both stimuli perfectly predicted the occurrence of the US. For example, if a person is repeatedly presented with a picture of an icy bridge followed by an accident in an insurance commercial, the individual will form an association between these events. However, if the observer then experiences the icy street along with fog, and both precede the accident, the person will exhibit no reactions toward the fog because the already acquired icy street–accident association appears to "block" learning about the fog and the accident. The reason observers do not learn about the fog is that they already have learned that the icy street predicts the accident. Thus, the fog becomes redundant and no associations are formed. Blocking experiments were highly influential in animal conditioning, but also in human causal learning because they highlight the importance of the "informational value" of one cue (e.g., CS1) relative to another cue (e.g., CS2) in associative learning situations (Rescorla & Wagner, 1972). Although blocking was extensively investigated in classical conditioning as well as in human causal learning (e.g., Baker, Mercier, Vallée-Tourangeau, Frank, & Pan, 1993; Chapman & Robbins, 1990; Dickinson & Shanks, 1985; van Osselaer & Alba, 2000), to our knowledge there is no evidence for blocking in EC (Walther, Weil, & Langer, 2009; Walther, Ebert, & Meinerling, 2010).

A further attribute that distinguishes signal learning from EC is the resistance to extinction. After an evaluative response is established in the CS, CS-alone presentations do not alter the valence of the stimulus; that is, EC is not impaired by extinction (Baeyens, Crombez, van den Bergh, & Eelen, 1988). EC is stable over time, which means that the affective meaning of an individual or object, once acquired, is not impaired if the person is presented in different settings after conditioning. This is, again, because EC is not based on an expectancy that the US is going to occur if the CS is presented. In view of its resistance to extinction, EC is more plausibly explained with a transfer of valence such that the CS acquires some affective attributes of the US (De Houwer et al., 2001; Hammerl & Grabitz, 1996).

Beside these two differences, the most debated topic is the question of whether EC is dependent on contingency awareness. As mentioned, people in some EC experiments do not know why they started to like a particular CS. Thus, in contrast to signal learning, EC seems to be independent of contingency awareness. However, there are also studies in which only participants aware of the contingencies exhibited EC effects (Allen & Janiszewski, 1989; Fulcher & Cocks, 1997; Ghuman & Bar, 2006; Pleyers et al., 2007; Shimp, Stuart, & Engle, 1991). On the one hand, this contradictory finding may be the result of the fact that there is no standardized EC paradigm and EC studies differ with respect to nearly all learning parameters that are involved. For example, the typical picture-picture study uses rather mild USs (e.g., liked faces). However, some EC studies use highly arousing aversive or appetitive USs, which may increase the organism's need to predict these events in order to approach or avoid them. This evoked need for prediction in turn renders these particular EC studies more similar to the prototypical signal learning paradigm in which almost always strong aversive USs (e.g., electric shock, white noise) are applied.

On the other hand, there is no agreement on how awareness should be assessed (Baeyens, Hermans, & Eelen, 1993; Dawson & Reardon, 1973; Field, 2000, 2001; Field & Moore, 2005; Hammerl, 2000; Lovibond & Shanks, 2002). However, it is clear that the way contingency awareness is measured strongly determines whether an individual is categorized as aware or unaware (see Walther & Nagengast, 2006). The debate over whether likes and dislikes can actually be formed without contingency awareness is important, because a growing body of evidence suggests that conscious awareness of the contingencies between CS and US is a necessary precondition for signal learning to occur (Brewer, 1974; Dawson, 1973; Dawson & Schell, 1987). If EC can be demonstrated without awareness, this would encourage the view of EC as an effect qualitatively different from signal learning.

Beside these differences, there are also similarities between EC and signal learning that motivated the assumption in some researchers that both paradigms are based on the same learning mechanisms. These similarities are obvious in the word use and the constituents of the paradigms. In both paradigms, a former neutral CS gains meaning through the co-occurrence with an already meaningful stimulus, the US. Both paradigms are sensitive to sensory preconditioning, which means that the affective value of the CS is transferred to objects or events that are preassociated with this stimulus due to prior learning (Barnet, Grahame, & Miller, 1991; Hammerl & Grabitz, 1996; Rizley & Rescorla, 1972; Walther, 2002). Furthermore, there is evidence in both paradigms for the US-revaluation effect (Baeyens, Eelen, van den Bergh, & Crombez, 1992; Delamater & Lolordo, 1991; Hosoba, Iwanaga, & Seiwa, 2001; Walther, Gawronski, Blank, & Langer, 2009) and second-order conditioning (Barnet et al., 1991; Rizley & Rescorla, 1972; Walther, 2002). Second-order conditioning means that the CS itself attains the power of a

US through conditioning. In other words, the CS is first made affectively meaning-ful through signal learning before it is used as a US in a subsequent phase of the experiment. Evidence for the similarity between EC and signal learning comes also from the signal learning front: Whereas signal learning was traditionally con-fined mostly to aversive USs, there have been some recent examples of appetitive conditioning in the area of animal learning (Jennings & Kirkpatrick, 2006).

Taken together, there is mixed and controversial evidence for the assumption that EC is an effect different from signal learning. There are indeed some char-acteristics of EC that clearly separate EC effects from signal learning effects. The most important differences seem to be that EC is not dependent on contingency awareness and is resistant to extinction. On the other hand, phenomena like sen-sory preconditioning, the US-revaluation effect, and second-order conditioning that appear in EC, as well as in signal learning, cast doubt on the assumption that EC is indeed a learning mechanism distinct from signal learning.

MECHANISMS UNDERLYING EC AND SIGNAL LEARNING

Although EC has been investigated for almost 30 years now, the processes underly-ing evaluative learning are still not sufficiently well understood (De Houwer et al., 2001). As already mentioned, it is not clear whether EC can be explained within the same theoretical framework as signal learning, or whether different theoretical assumptions are needed to explain EC. Given the previously mentioned empirical differences between EC and signal learning with respect to awareness, extinc-tion, and dependency on contingency, the conclusion suggests that two different learning principles may be at work in these paradigms. Within the "dissimilarity approach" group, however, there are still many different ideas about which pro-cesses may underlie signal learning and EC.

Dissimilarity Approaches

Martin and Levey (1994): Holistic Versus Associative   Early EC theo-rists Martin and Levey (1987) explained EC's difference from associative learning as the result of a "holistic representation," established during conditioning, which comprises elements of the CS as well as the evaluative nature of the US. This fusion process during conditioning is considered an automatic and very basic form of learning. The holistic account implies that perceptual characteristics of the CS are changed during the conditioning procedure in a way that they become more similar to the US. The holistic model accounts for many characteristic of evalua-tive conditioned attitudes, for instance, the resistance to extinction: Because every presentation of the CS evokes elements of the US, the CS "brings about its own reinforcement" (Martin & Levey, 1994, p. 301). While the holistic account can also explain EC's independence of the contingency between the CS and the US, it is hard to explain sensory preconditioning within this framework (Hammerl & Grabitz, 1996; Walther, 2002).

Field and Davey (1999): Conceptual Versus Associative An account similar to the holistic account has been proposed by Davey (1994) and Field and Davey (1999), who suggested that EC represents an instance of conceptual categorization. The idea is that during the pairing of CS and US, the common features of the stimuli become more and more salient, which increases the perceived similarity between them. Field and Davey more specifically argued that EC does not reflect "real" associative learning, but is the result of an experimental artifact in which CSs and USs are paired with respect to their preexperimental similarity. Although this critique was applicable to a particular subgroup of early EC experiments (Baeyens, Eelen, & Van den Bergh, 1990; Baeyens et al., 1989), it has been demonstrated in the meantime that EC effects occur even when CSs and USs are randomly paired, and there are also demonstrations of cross-modal EC (Todrank et al., 1995), which could not be explained by Field and Davey's account.

Baeyens, Eelen, Crombez, and van den Bergh (1992): Referential Versus Signal Learning In signal learning literature there is consensus that individuals acquire an if-then relationship between the US and the CS during conditioning. Thus, the CS signals the occurrence of the US after successful learning. This is why the correlation between the CS and the US is of critical importance. As several studies indicate, however, EC is not restricted to a contingency between the CS and the US; rather, it depends on the mere co-occurrence (i.e., contiguity) of these stimuli. To illustrate, consider the conditioning of a neutral individual "Peter" with a liked person "George." In EC, the acquired positive evaluation of Peter is not diminished when the observer meets Peter in a different context in which George is not present. Baeyens, Eelen, Crombez, and van den Bergh (1992) hypothesized that this insensitivity of evaluative learning to violations of the contingency rule exists because EC may be a kind of "referential learning" in which the CS acquires the capacity to activate the US representation. They argue that signal learning as well as EC present instances of associative learning. However, they assume that EC represents a simpler form in which a given CS activates the US representation without generating the expectancy that the US is going to occur in the presence of the CS. This is different from signal learning in which the CS elicits the expectancy that the US appears after successful conditioning. However, in EC, social observers would not, for instance, expect George (US) to appear in the presence of Peter (CS).

The referential account can explain many phenomena in the EC literature. However, it should be noted that the referential account only refers to the simple transfer of valence and does not cover the conditioning of attributes different from valence. This is at odds with results from the area of odor conditioning, which suggest that attributes like "sour" or "sweet" can be acquired during conditioning (Stevenson, Boakes, & Prescott, 1998). Moreover, the referential account is silent with respect to the exact mechanisms that underlie EC.

Gawronski and Bodenhausen (2006): Associative Versus Propositional Learning Whereas all accounts reported so far are rooted in basic learning psychology, dual process accounts like Gawronski and Bodenhausen's

(2006) associative-propositional evaluation (APE) approach are much broader and refer to a wide array of social psychological phenomena such as stereotyping, attitude formation, judgment, and decision making. Similar to other contemporary dual process models, the APE model postulates that two qualitatively distinct processes underlie the attitudinal judgment: associative and propositional processes. According to the authors, associative processes involve the activation of associative networks and are independent of the assignment of truth values. Gawronski and Bodenhausen (2006) consider EC a prototypical example of this kind of learning. According to the APE model, EC can be characterized as an automatic affective reaction that results from the activation and spreading of evaluations associated with the relevant stimulus (e.g., De Houwer et al., 2001; Walther et al., 2005). In contrast to associative processes, propositional processes are defined as validation processes that do depend on the assignment of truth values. Although it should be noted that the APE model is mainly applied to EC, it can be assumed that propositional reasoning is involved in signal learning in which contingency based rules are acquired. This dual process perspective of conditioning is supported by the finding that EC effects sometimes decreases under awareness, whereas signal learning effects apparently benefits from conscious awareness (Dawson & Schell, 1987; Lovibond & Shanks, 2002). Further support for this view comes from Olson and Fazio (2001), who successfully used an implicit learning paradigm to produce evaluative conditioned attitudes. If conditioned attitudes can be acquired implicitly, this speaks to the notion that EC is different from signal learning in which learning occurs on an explicit level.

However, in both EC and signal learning, there are studies that contradict this EC = associative = implicit versus signal learning = propositional = explicit perspective. For instance, Schienle, Schäfer, Walter, Stark, and Vaitl (2005) found that disgust was conditioned in phobic individuals only when people were aware of the contingencies. Likewise, there is evidence in signal learning that conditioning occurs without awareness under certain conditions (Öhman, Esteves, & Soares, 1995; Öhman & Soares, 1998; Schell, Dawson, & Marinkovic, 1991).

Similar Process Approaches

Although the idea of two different processes underlying EC and signal learning is intuitively plausible and has received some empirical support, there are also arguments that speak against the dual process assumption. To begin with, there are epistemic arguments. First, how different must phenomena be before they are explained by different processes? Like any science, psychology should be prudent and conservative before new processes are invented just because two effects appear dissimilar. Second, what constitutes the differences between phenomena? In other words, how do we know that different processes are at work producing an effect?

One heuristic that is often applied to solve this problem is the distinction between implicit and explicit attitude measurements (Greenwald & Banaji, 1995; Petty, Fazio, & Briñol, 2009; Wilson, Lindsey, & Schooler, 2000; Wittenbrink & Schwarz, 2007). Although it is very tempting to use this heuristic, empirical data often contradict the clear-cut dissociation between implicit and explicit processes (see also Fiedler, this volume). For instance, there are many cases in which evidence for so-called explicit processes can be found in implicit measurements and vice versa (De Houwer, Teige-Mocigemba, Spruyt, & Moors, 2009; Gawronski, Walther, & Blank, 2005). With respect to signal learning and EC, the question could be raised whether their similarities or their dissimilarities should receive more weight. Third, dual process models are often postulated in order to explain seemingly inconsistent data. For example, approximately 90% of human behavior can be explained by the simple operant learning theory of avoiding pain and approaching pleasure. But what happened before this basic principle was recognized? People may have postulated many different subtheories in order to explain human behavior. Thus, it could be the case that one theory is simply not broad enough to explain a wide array of human behavior (see Holbrook & Krosnick, this volume). Besides these epistemological arguments, there are empirical as well as theoretical arguments that speak for a uniprocess perspective.

Associative Processes   There is a long tradition in learning theory to explain conditioning effects by means of associative models: The assumption is that during conditioning, an association is established between the CS and the US. The popularity of this view has gone so far that signal learning is considered a synonym of associative learning. One of the most prominent associative models designed to explain signal learning is the Rescorla-Wagner model (RW model, 1972). According to the RW model, associations are only learned when a surprising event in the environment occurs that goes along with the occurrence of a CS. The RW model expresses the subsequent changes in associative strength between a CS and a US based on conditioning trials. Although the RW model was criticized from the beginning because it could not explain several empirical effects, such as conditioned inhibition and backward blocking, it is nevertheless seen as providing the best explanation of most signal learning phenomena (Shanks, 1985).

Within the group of associative models there are two competing assumptions of how classical conditioning works, referring to the two distinct possible effects of the repeated co-occurrence of CS and US on the representational level. The first is the development of a connection between the CS and the US at the response level. According to this account, the CS acquires its own response that mimics the unconditioned response (UR) elicited by the US (S-R learning). The second possibility is that EC reflects a link between the cognitive representations of the CS and the US. Thus, exposure to the CS after repeated pairings with a US will activate the representation of the US, which in turn activates its corresponding response (S-S learning). Rescorla (1974) suggested an experimental paradigm, the US-revaluation paradigm, which provides a straightforward test of these two possibilities. If postconditional changes in the valence of a US lead to corresponding changes in the valence of preassociated conditioned stimuli (CS), this would support the notion of S-S learning. Evidence for US-revaluation and therefore for the S-S account has been provided by Rescorla in signal learning as well as by Walther et al. (2009) in the EC area.

Beyond these experimental examples that help to distinguish theoretical accounts on the CS-US representational level, the question remains what exactly is meant by an association within these approaches. An association refers to connections between events in memory (Carr, 1930). However, it is important to note that the term *association* is merely descriptive in nature and refers neither to the substance of this link, nor to a particular theory of how this link is formed or maintained. What the content of associations is and how they are expressed in the organism's behavior has not been sufficiently addressed in learning theory so far. Because of this lack of theorizing within associative approaches, a distinction between, for instance, associative versus propositional learning is misleading (see also Fiedler, this volume). This is because propositional learning (e.g., the learning of an if-then relation) is naturally an instance of associative learning as long as the formation of a connection between stimuli is assumed.

The Unimodel of EC—An Integrative Approach   Rather than focusing on the common dual process distinction, the unimodel (Kruglanski & Thompson, 1999) is an integrative approach, which assumes that a single (not dual) cognitive process underlies all types of (rule-based and associative) judgments. Differences in the unimodel are a function of several orthogonal parameter values that are represented in any judgmental response. "It is the particular constellation of these values that determines whether the information given would impact an individual's judgment" (Kruglanski, Erb, Pierro, Mannetti, & Chun, 2006, p. 156). Parameters of the unimodel are cognitive resources, task demands, motivation, and relevance. Applying the unimodel to EC research, it could be assumed that relevant parameters of cognitive resources refer to the accessibility of the conditioned evaluation, time pressure or load, and the time the organism has to express the judgment. The number of trials, the intertrial interval, and the interstimulus interval could be considered relevant task demand parameters. The motivation parameters could be given as the salience or surprisingness of the US, and relevance may refer to the valence and the intensity of the US.

Based on the unimodel, it can be suggested that EC and signal learning are not qualitatively different effects, but that the particular composition of the parameters given in the respective learning context constitutes outcome differences. Thus, differences on the phenomenological level presumably can be explained by differences in parameters and can be considered an epiphenomenon of the same basic (rule-based) process. This process might refer to the acquisition of a primitive if-then rule. For instance, in attitude formation this rule could be: If I feel positively in the context of this stimulus, I like it. On a representational level, however, there are many possibilities of how this rule is represented. One of these possibilities is that if an object O (i.e., the US) is presented with neutral object X (i.e., the CS), then a compound between O and X is formed. A compound is a holistic mental representation consisting of two elemental stimuli. For instance, two single stimuli, a man and a woman, may be cognitively represented as a couple. Likewise, two visual stimuli, X and O, can be stored within the same figural representation. Thus, a subsequent presentation of X necessarily activates a presentation of O, which can explain the resistance to extinction and the independence of contingencies in EC. However, depending on the composition of the parameters, other, more sophisticated rules may be acquired. For instance, in the case of strong appetitive or aversive events, the individual's need to control those events may result in the prediction rule: If X occurs, then O will happen. According to common learning approaches (Dickinson, 2001), nonexpected events result in stronger associations than predicted events. Thus, in the case of a surprising US, a more sophisticated if-then rule, the prediction rule, may be acquired. Depending on parameters like motivation (i.e., surprisingness), the if-then rule therefore graduates from very basic similarity to more sophisticated causal inferences. Applying this logic to the distinction between EC and signal learning, it is not implausible to assume that the relevance (intensity) of the US determines the degree of awareness. Contingency awareness in turn might be necessary in order to predict the US. Thus, with increasing intensity of the US, EC becomes more and more similar to signal learning, which could explain why EC can be found in aware as well as in unaware individuals (Pleyers et al., 2007; Walther & Nagengast, 2006).

Evidence for a single rule-based process that underlies all types of conditioning has come from recent animal research. Beckers, Miller, De Houwer, and Urishihara (2006) addressed blocking in the conditioning of rats and found that causal inferential reasoning is involved in this learning process. This result not only challenges the view that causal reasoning is the key operation that differentiates humans from other animals, but it also supports the unimodel approach claiming that the same process underlies all kinds of judgments (see also Blaisdell, Sawa, Leising, & Waldmann, 2006). In the area of attitude research, De Houwer and Vandorpe (in press) recently showed that the IAT (Greenwald, McGhee, & Schwartz, 1998), which is usually considered a prototypical test for nonpropositional implicit processes, is sensitive to causal learning. Furthermore, there are studies by Deutsch and colleagues indicating that negation processes are much less dependent on controlled processes than hitherto assumed (Deutsch, Kordts-Freudinger, Gawronski, & Strack, 2009).

CONCLUSION

This chapter addresses the mechanisms underlying attitude formation and change. While it is stated that EC plays a central role in these attitudinal processes, it should also be noted that mechanisms underlying EC are not well understood yet. For instance, it is not clear whether EC and signal learning refer to similar or different processes. We have discussed similarities and dissimilarities between both learning effects and presented theoretical accounts explaining them. An integral unimodel perspective is suggested, in which it is assumed that EC and signal learning both refer to a similar rule-based learning mechanism.

REFERENCES

Allen, C. T., & Janiszewski, C. A. (1989). Assessing the role of contingency awareness in attitudinal conditioning with implications for advertising research. *Journal of Marketing and Research, 26,* 30–43.

Allport, G. W. (1954). *The nature of prejudice*. Cambridge, MA: Addison-Wesley.

Baeyens, F., Crombez, G., van den Bergh, O., & Eelen, P. (1988). Once in contact always in contact: Evaluative conditioning is resistant to extinction. *Advances in Behaviour Research and Therapy, 10,* 179–199.

Baeyens, F., Eelen, P., Crombez, G., & van den Bergh., O. (1992). Human evaluative conditioning: Acquisition trials, presentation schedule, evaluative style and contingency awareness. *Behavior Research and Therapy, 30,* 133–142.

Baeyens, F., Eelen, P., & van den Bergh, O. (1990). Contingency awareness in evaluative conditioning: A case for unaware affective-evaluative learning. *Cognition and Emotion, 4,* 3–18.

Baeyens, F., Eelen, P., van den Bergh, O., & Crombez, G. (1989). Acquired affective-evaluative value. Conservative but not unchangeable. *Behaviour Research and Therapy, 27,* 279–287.

Baeyens, F., Eelen, P., van den Bergh., O., & Crombez, G. (1992). The content of learning in human evaluative conditioning: Acquired valence is sensitive to US revaluation. *Learning and Motivation, 23,* 200–224.

Baeyens, F., Hermans, R., & Eelen, P. (1993). The role of CS-US contingency in human evaluative conditioning. *Behaviour Research and Therapy, 31,* 731–737.

Baker, A. G., Mercier, P., Vallée-Tourangeau, F., Frank, R., & Pan, M. (1993). Selective associations and causality judgments: Presence of a strong causal factor may reduce judgments of a weaker one. *Journal of Experimental Psychology: Learning, Memory, and Cognition, 19,* 414–432.

Barnet, R. C., Grahame, N. J., & Miller, R. E. (1991). Comparing the magnitude of second-order conditioning and sensory preconditioning effects. *Bulletin of the Psychonomic Society, 29,* 133–135.

Beckers, T., Miller, R. R., De Houwer, J., & Urushihara, K. (2006). Reasoning rats: Forward blocking in Pavlovian animal conditioning is sensitive to constraints of causal inference. *Journal of Experimental Psychology: General, 135,* 92–102.

Beggan, J. K. (1992). On the social nature of nonsocial perception: The mere ownership effect. *Journal of Personality and Social Psychology, 62,* 229–237.

Blaisdell, A. P., Sawa, K., Leising, K. J., & Waldmann, M. R. (2006). Causal reasoning in rats. *Science, 311,* 1020–1022.

Brewer, W. F. (1974). There is no convincing evidence for operant or classical conditioning in adult humans. In W. B. Weimer & D. S. Palermo (Eds.), *Cognition and the symbolic process.* Hillsdale, NJ: Erlbaum.

Carr, H. (1930). Functionalism. In C. Murchison (Ed.), *Psychologies of 1930* (pp. 59–78). Worchester, MA: Clark University Press.

Chapman, G. B., & Robbins, S. J. (1990). Cue interaction in human contingency judgment. *Memory & Cognition, 18,* 537–545.

Chapman, L. J., & Chapman, J. P. (1967). Genesis of popular but erroneous psychodiagnostic observations. *Journal of Abnormal Psychology, 72,* 193–204.

Davey, G. C. L. (1994). Is evaluative conditioning a qualitatively distinct form of classical conditioning? *Behaviour Research and Therapy, 32,* 291–299.

Dawson, M. E. (1973). Can classical conditioning occur without contingency learning? A review and evaluation of the evidence. *Psychophysiology, 10,* 82–86.

Dawson, M. E., & Reardon, P. (1973). Construct validity of recall and recognition postconditioning measures of awareness. *Journal of Experimental Psychology, 98,* 308–315.

Dawson, M. E., & Schell, A. (1987). Human autonomic and skeletal classical conditioning: The role of conscious cognitive factors. In G. Davey (Ed.), *Cognitive processes and Pavlovian conditioning in humans* (pp. 27–55). Chichester, England: Wiley.

De Houwer, J. (2007). A conceptual and theoretical analysis of evaluative conditioning. *Spanish Journal of Psychology, 10,* 230–241.

De Houwer, J., & Beckers, T. (2002). A review of recent developments in research and theories on human contingency learning. *Quarterly Journal of Experimental Psychology, 55B*, 289–310.

De Houwer, J., Teige-Mocigemba, S., Spruyt, A., & Moors, A. (2009). Implicit measures: A normative analysis and review. *Psychological Bulletin, 135*, 347–368.

De Houwer, J., Thomas, S., & Baeyens, F. (2001). Associative learning of likes and dislikes: A review of 25 years of research on human evaluative conditioning. *Psychological Bulletin, 127*, 853–869.

De Houwer, J., & Vandorpe, S. (in press). Using the Implicit Association Test as a measure of causal learning does not eliminate effects of rule learning. *Experimental Psychology.*

Delamater, A. R., & Lolordo, V. M. (1991). Event revaluation procedures and associative structures in Pavlovian conditioning. In L. Dachowski & C. Flaherty (Eds.), *Current topics in animal learning: Brain, emotion, and cognition* (pp. 55–94). Hillsdale, NJ: Erlbaum.

Deutsch, R., Kordts-Freudinger, R., Gawronski, B., & Strack, F. (2009). Fast and fragile: A new look at the automaticity of negation processing. *Experimental Psychology, 56, 434–446.*

Dickinson, A. (2001). Causal learning: Association versus computation. *Current Directions in Psychological Science, 10*, 127–132.

Dickinson, A., & Shanks, D. (1985). Animal conditioning and human causality judgment. In L.-G. Nilsson & T. Archer (Eds.), *Perspectives on learning and memory* (pp. 167–191). Hillsdale, NJ: Erlbaum.

Dijksterhuis, A. (2004). I like myself but I don't know why: Enhancing implicit self-esteem by subliminal evaluative conditioning. *Journal of Personality and Social Psychology, 86*, 345–355.

Eagly, A. H., & Chaiken, S. (1993). *The psychology of attitudes.* Fort Worth, TX: Harcourt Brace Jovanovich.

Feys, J. (1991). Briefly induced belongingness to self and preference. *European Journal of Social Psychology, 21*, 547–552.

Feys, J. (1995). Mere ownership: Affective self-bias or evaluative conditioning? *European Journal of Social Psychology, 25*, 559–575.

Fiedler, K., Russer, S., & Gramm, K. (1993). Illusory correlations and memory performance. *Journal of Experimental Social Psychology, 29*, 111–136.

Field, A. P. (2000). Evaluative conditioning is Pavlovian conditioning: Issues of definition, measurement, and the theoretical importance of contingency awareness. *Consciousness and Cognition, 9*, 41–49.

Field, A. P. (2001). When all is still concealed: Are we closer to understanding the mechanisms underlying evaluative conditioning? *Consciousness and Cognition, 10*, 559–566.

Field, A. P., & Davey, G. C. L. (1999). Reevaluating evaluative conditioning: A nonassociative explanation of conditioning effects in the visual evaluative conditioning *paradigm. Journal of Experimental Psychology: Animal Behavior Processes, 25*, 211–224.

Field, A. P., & Moore, A. C. (2005). Dissociating the effects of attention and contingency awareness on evaluative conditioning effects in the visual paradigm. *Cognition and Emotion, 19*, 217–243.

Fishbein, M., & Ajzen, I. (1975). *Belief, attitude, intention, and behavior.* Reading, MA: Addison-Wesley.

Fulcher, E. P., & Cocks, P. (1997). Dissociative storage systems in human evaluative conditioning. *Behaviour Research and Therapy, 35*, 1–10.

Gawronski, B. (2007). Attitudes can be measured! But what is an attitude? *Social Cognition, 25*, 573–581.

Gawronski, B., & Bodenhausen, G. V. (2006). Associative and propositional processes in evaluation: An integrative review of implicit and explicit attitude change. *Psychological Bulletin, 132,* 692–731.

Gawronski, B., Bodenhausen, G. V., & Becker, A. P. (2007). I like it, because I like myself: Associative self-anchoring and post-decisional change of implicit evaluations. *Journal of Experimental Social Psychology, 43,* 221–232.

Gawronski, B., & Walther, E. (2008). The TAR effect: When the ones who dislike become the ones who are disliked. *Personality and Social Psychology Bulletin, 34,* 1276–1289.

Gawronski, B., Walther, E., & Blank, H. (2005). Cognitive consistency and the formation of interpersonal attitudes: Cognitive balance affects the encoding of social information. *Journal of Experimental Social Psychology, 41,* 618–626.

Ghuman, A. S., & Bar, M. (2006). The influence of nonremembered affective associations on preference. *Emotion, 6,* 215–223.

Greenwald, A. G., & Banaji, M. R. (1995). Implicit social cognition: Attitudes, self-esteem, and stereotypes. *Psychological Review, 102,* 4–27.

Greenwald, A. G., McGhee, D. E., & Schwartz, J. L. (1998). Measuring individual differences in implicit cognition: The Implicit Association Test. *Journal of Personality and Social Psychology, 74,* 1464–1480.

Hamilton, D. L., & Gifford, R. K. (1976). Illusory correlation in interpersonal perception: A cognitive basis of stereotypic judgments. *Journal of Experimental Social Psychology, 12,* 392–407.

Hammerl, M. (2000). I like it, but only when I'm not sure why: Evaluative conditioning and the awareness issue. *Consciousness and Cognition, 9,* 37–40.

Hammerl, M., & Grabitz, H.-J. (1996). Human evaluative conditioning without experiencing a valued event. *Learning and Motivation, 27,* 278–293.

Hammerl, M., & Grabitz, H.-J. (2000). Affective-evaluative learning in humans: A form of associative learning or only an artifact? *Learning and Motivation, 31,* 345–363.

Hosoba, T., Iwanaga, M., & Seiwa, H. (2001). The effect of UCS inflation and deflation procedures on fear conditioning. *Behaviour Research and Therapy, 39,* 465–475.

Jennings, D., & Kirkpatrick, K. (2006). Interval duration effects on blocking in appetitive conditioning. *Behavioural Processes, 71,* 318–329.

Kamin, L. J. (1968). Attention-like processes in classical conditioning. In M. R. Jones (Ed.), *Miami symposium on the prediction of behavior: Aversive stimuli* (pp. 9–32). Coral Gables, FL: University of Miami Press.

Koole, S. L., Dijksterhuis, A., & van Knippenberg, A. (2001). What's in a name: Implicit self-esteem and the automatic self. *Journal of Personality and Social Psychology, 80,* 669–685.

Kruglanski, A. W., Erb, H.-P., Pierro, A., Mannetti, L., & Chun, W. Y. (2006). On parametric continuities in the world of binary either ors. *Psychological Inquiry, 17,* 153–165.

Kruglanski, A. W., & Thompson, E. P. (1999). Persuasion by a single route: A view from the unimodel. *Psychological Inquiry, 10,* 83–109.

Lovibond, P. F., & Shanks, D. R. (2002). The role of awareness in Pavlovian conditioning: Empirical evidence and theoretical implications. *Journal of Experimental Psychology: Animal Behavior Processes, 28,* 3–26.

Manis, M., Cornell, S. D., Moore, J. C., & Jeffrey, C. (1974). Transmission of attitude relevant information through a communication chain. *Journal of Personality and Social Psychology, 30,* 81–94.

Martin, I., & Levey, A. B. (1978). Evaluative conditioning. *Advances in Behaviour Research and Therapy, 1,* 57–101.

Martin, I., & Levey, A. B. (1987). Learning what will happen next: Conditioning, evaluation, and cognitive processes. In G. Davey (Ed.), *Cognitive processes and Pavlovian conditioning in humans* (pp. 57–81). Chichester, England: Wiley.

Martin, I., & Levey, A. B. (1994). The evaluative response: Primitive but necessary. *Behaviour Research and Therapy, 32*, 301–305.

Nuttin, J. M. (1985). Narcissism beyond Gestalt and awareness: The name letter effect. *European Journal of Social Psychology, 15*, 353–361.

Öhman, A., Esteves, F., & Soares, J. J. F. (1995). Preparedness and preattentive associative learning: Electrodermal conditioning to masked stimuli. *Journal of Psychophysiology, 9*, 99–108.

Öhman, A., & Soares, J. J. F. (1998). Emotional conditioning to masked stimuli: Expectancies for aversive outcomes following nonrecognized fear-relevant stimuli. *Journal of Experimental Psychology: General, 127*, 69–82.

Olson, M. A., & Fazio, R. H. (2001). Implicit attitude formation through classical conditioning. *Psychological Science, 12*, 413–417.

Petty, R. E., & Cacioppo, J. T. (1984). The effects of involvement on responses to argument quantity and quality: Central and peripheral routes to persuasion. *Journal of Personality and Social Psychology, 46*, 69–81.

Petty, R. E., Cacioppo, J. T., & Goldman, R. (1981). Personal involvement as a determinant of argument-based persuasion. *Journal of Personality and Social Psychology, 41*, 847–855.

Petty, R. E., Fazio, R. H., & Briñol, P. (Eds.). (2009). *Attitudes: Insights from the new implicit measures*. New York: Psychology Press.

Petty, R. E., Haugtvedt, C., & Smith, S. M. (1995). Elaboration as a determinant of attitude strength: Creating attitudes that are persistent, resistant, and predictive of behavior. In R. E. Petty & J. A. Krosnick (Eds.), *Attitude strength: Antecedents and consequences* (pp. 93–130). Mahwah, NJ: Erlbaum.

Pleyers, G., Corneille, O., Luminet, O., & Yzerbyt, V. (2007). Aware and (dis)liking: Item-based analyses reveal that valence acquisition via evaluative conditioning emerges only when there is contingency awareness. *Journal of Experimental Psychology: Learning, Memory, and Cognition, 33*, 130–144.

Rescorla, R. A. (1974). Effect of inflation of the unconditioned stimulus value following conditioning. *Journal of Comparative and Physiological Psychology, 86*, 101–106.

Rescorla, R. A., & Wagner, A. R. (1972). A theory of Pavlovian conditioning: Variations in the effectiveness of reinforcement and nonreinforcement. In A. H. Black & W. F. Prokasy (Eds.), *Classical conditioning: II. Current research and theory* (pp. 64–99). New York: Appleton.

Rizley, R. C., & Rescorla, R. A. (1972). Associations in second-order conditioning and sensory preconditioning. *Journal of Comparative and Physiological Psychology, 81*, 1–11.

Schell, A. M., Dawson, M. E., & Marinkovic, K. (1991). Effects of potentially phobic conditioned stimuli on retention, reconditioning, and extinction of the conditioned skin conductance response. *Psychophysiology, 28*, 140–153.

Schienle, A., Schaefer, A., Walter, B., Stark, R., & Vaitl, D. (2005). Elevated disgust sensitivity in blood phobia. *Cognition and Emotion, 19*, 1229–1241.

Shanks, D. R. (1985). Forward and backward blocking in human contingency judgement. *Quarterly Journal of Experimental Psychology, 37*, 1–21.

Shimp, T. A., Stuart, E. W., & Engle, R. W. (1991). A program of classical conditioning experiments testing variations in the conditioned stimulus and context. *Journal of Consumer Research, 18*, 1–12.

Skowronski, J. J., Carlston, D. E., Mae, L., & Crawford, M. T. (1998). Spontaneous trait transference: Communicators take on the qualities they describe in others. *Journal of Personality and Social Psychology, 74*, 837–848.

Stevenson, R. J., Boakes, R. A., & Prescott, J. (1998). Changes in odor sweetness resulting from implicit learning of a simultaneous odor-sweetness association: An example of learned synesthesia. *Learning and Motivation, 29*, 113–132.

Todrank, J., Byrnes, D., Wrzesniewski, A., & Rozin, P. (1995). Odors can change preferences for people in photographs: A cross-modal evaluative conditioning study with olfactory USs and visual CSs. *Learning and Motivation, 26,* 116–140.

van Osselaer, S. M. J., & Alba, J. W. (2000). Consumer learning and brand equity. *Journal of Consumer Research, 27,* 1–16.

Walther, E. (2002). Guilty by mere association: Evaluative conditioning and the spreading attitude effect. *Journal of Personality and Social Psychology, 82,* 919–934.

Walther, E., Ebert, I., & Meinerling, K. (under review). Does cue competition reduce conditioned liking of brand and products? Psychology & Marketing.

Walther, E., Gawronski, B., Blank, H., & Langer, T. (2009). Changing likes and dislikes through the back door: The US-revaluation effect. *Cognition and Emotion, 23,* 889–919.

Walther, E., & Grigoriadis, S. (2004). Why sad people like shoes better: The influence of mood on the evaluative conditioning of consumer attitudes. *Psychology and Marketing, 21,* 755–773.

Walther, E., & Nagengast, B. (2006). Evaluative conditioning and the awareness issue: Assessing contingency awareness with the four-picture recognition test. *Journal of Experimental Psychology: Animal Behavior Processes, 32,* 454–459.

Walther, E., Nagengast, B., & Trasselli, C. (2005). Evaluative conditioning in social psychology: Facts and speculations. *Cognition and Emotion, 19,* 175–196.

Walther, E., & Trasselli, C. (2003). I like her, because I like myself: Self-evaluation as a source of interpersonal attitudes. *Experimental Psychology, 50,* 239–246.

Walther, E., Weil, R., & Langer, T. (2009). There is no evidence for blocking in EC. Unpublished manuscript, University of Trier.

Wilson, T. D., Lindsey, S., & Schooler, T. Y. (2000). A model of dual attitudes. *Psychological Review, 107,* 101–126.

Wittenbrink, B., & Schwarz, N. (Eds.). (2007). *Implicit measures of attitudes: Procedures and controversies.* New York: Guilford Press.

5

The Asymmetry of Causal and Diagnostic Inferences
A Challenge for the Study of Implicit Attitudes

KLAUS FIEDLER

Imagine a sports fan, who is perfectly convinced to be free of any nationalist attitudes and who has developed a really international identity. Yet, when watching a soccer match, the same person feels a strong preference for his own national team, which elicits positive emotions as strong as hardly any other object in daily life. In contemporary research on social cognition, one might attribute this phenomenon to an implicit nationalist attitude that diverges from the person's explicit anti-nationalist attitude. Likewise, a full-hearted vegetarian who has not eaten fish for 10 years discovers herself developing a salivation response at the sight of delicious grilled monk fish in a Pacific Ocean tavern. Again, an implicit pro-fish attitude might be postulated that leaks through the explicit-attitude facade.

INTRODUCTION: FROM TRADITIONAL ATTITUDES TO MODERN IMPLICIT ATTITUDES

Both examples are typical of the phenomenon that recent research (cf. Nosek, 2007; Wittenbrink & Schwarz, 2007) has termed *implicit attitudes*. The most prominent types pertain to ethnic and racist targets, elderly and handicapped people, political parties, and consumer attitudes toward brands and products (for an overview, see Nosek, Greenwald, & Banaji, 2006). The construct of an implicit attitude has been adopted so readily that there is hardly any serious debate about its theoretical status. How else should one account for covert reactions and affective tendencies that are obviously incompatible with a person's overt questionnaire responses or introspective self-reports, if not by implicit attitudes?

Upon some reflection, though, one has to admit that the old attitude research program, prior to the advent of the implicit-attitude idea, already had a number of theoretical degrees of freedom. With regard to the soccer fan example, one could have assumed that the cognitive, affective, and conative attitude components (Harmon-Jones, Amodio, & Harmon-Jones, this volume; Rosenberg and Hovland, 1966) diverge. Somebody may, at the cognitive level, believe that nationality does not matter and, yet, the affective component may be biased toward one's own national soccer team. The vegetarian's autonomic reaction to fish could similarly reflect a normal discrepancy between behavior and attitudes (Ajzen, 1991; Johnson & Boynton, this volume; Snyder & Swann, 1976) conceived as a relatively stable disposition that need not be visible in each and every manifest behavior.

Changing Definition

Given the flexibility of a three-component attitude model, there was indeed little need to postulate an extra explanatory construct, *implicit attitudes*, to deal with phenomena provided at the outset. However, notably, the new research program came along with a minimalist definition. Even when the useful definition as a stable behavioral disposition was not given up explicitly (Olson & Fazio, 2008), proponents of the implicit-cognition research program decided to define implicit attitudes as mere associations between attitude target and evaluative meaning (Fazio, 2001; Fazio, Chen, McDonel, & Sherman, 1982; Greenwald et al., 2002). This minimalist definition as a mere association, which must not be equated with genuinely affective conceptions, leads to an inflation of attitudes diagnosed in so-called implicit measurement procedures. This problem is at the heart of the present critique.

If each and every association constitutes an attitude, regardless of its temporal stability, person specificity, and its relation to other attitudes or components, this amounts to a dramatic increase in the number of attitudes a person holds. The vegetarian no longer has one generic, pro-vegetarian attitude, but in addition, she has another implicit anti-vegetarian attitude for every forbidden association. If she only participates in an evaluative conditioning experiment with food as conditioned stimulus, or if she is exposed to food along with attractive persons or feelings during advertising, a new (implicit) attitude is created on the spot. As a consequence of this inflation of minimal attitudes at the level of mere associations, a number of theoretical constraints are given up: (a) An attitude no longer requires a plastic configuration of three components. (b) It need not represent a stable personality disposition. (c) It is irrelevant whether an attitudinal association reflects something about the person or the stimuli, which may elicit similar associations in every person. (d) And it does not matter if the association is genuine or spurious, that is, whether the association of the soccer fan's national team with positive valence is directly or indirectly mediated by other attributes, such as the own national team's familiarity or the normative belief that friends and colleagues also like the national team.

Chapter Preview

The remainder of this chapter is devoted to a critical discussion of theoretical and empirical consequences of this basic inflation. Starting from a discussion of different rationales for attitude measurement, I will first outline a taxonomy of pertinent procedures. From this taxonomy, it will be evident that the distinction between implicit and explicit measures is largely a matter of convention rather than well-defined test or task features (cf. De Houwer, 2006; Fazio & Olson, 2003). It will also be apparent that a variety of potentially very useful attitude measures have been largely neglected. Instead, the greatest part of current research revolves around a few latency-based measures, which mostly fit the definition of an attitude as a mere association in semantic memory. Because the Implicit Association Test (IAT) and the evaluative priming (EP) task are by far the most frequently cited procedures, my critique will refer to these two most prominent measures. I will show that, as a consequence of the inflation of attitudes defined as mere associations, the well-known asymmetry of causal and diagnostic inference is amplified, making diagnostic inferences from test scores to underlying attitudes extremely prone to false alarms. In other words, the inflated rate of significant IAT and EP scores may reflect many attitude-independent influences. I will finally discuss some implications and potential remedies to this fundamental problem of diagnostic inference.

THEORETICAL FOUNDATIONS OF ATTITUDE MEASUREMENT

What rationale justifies the assumption that certain responses capture latent person attributes, such as attitudes? When diagnosing intelligence, the rationale is based on content validity. Each intelligence test item constitutes an elementary sample of the very construct to be measured. When error variance is minimized by aggregating over many items, test performance affords a representative sample of intelligence proper.

When testing attitudes in a traditional Likert-scale questionnaire, the situation is similar but slightly different. Each item also refers to an elementary sample of content pertaining to the same attitude, which is assumed to express itself on the test. However, whether an individual endorses the statement "I never discriminate against members of foreign ethnic groups" is not fully determined by the attitude proper. It also depends on the willingness to reveal that attitude, on social-desirability and self-presentation concerns (Snyder & Swann, 1976). The test rationale also relies on nontrivial assumptions about the verbal comprehension of test items, intact autobiographical memory, and introspective capacity.

Rationales for Attitude Assessment

Let us use the term *auto-expression* for content-valid samples of attitude-related elementary behaviors (i.e., items), on which the attitude is assumed to express itself (see upper part of Table 5.1). This rationale applies to many questionnaires, but

TABLE 5.1   Taxonomy of Existing Procedures for Attitude Assessment

	Scaling Method	
	Direct	
Rationale for Attitude Inference	**(Measurement Function Presupposed)**	**Indirect (Testable Measurement Model)**
Auto-expression	Likert-scaled attitude *questionnaires* [18110] *Observation techniques* [5] Analysis of *facial expression* [121]	*Thurstone*-scaled measurement [17] *Guttman* scalogram analysis [32] *Rasch* scaling [109]
Approach-avoidance	*Arm movement* [4] *Immediacy* [89] Linguistic *abstractness* [13] *Eye-tracking* [12] *Binocular rivalry* & attitude [6] *Dichotic listening* [3] *Polygraph* [9]	*Perceptual defense* [1]
Representation in associative memory	*Projective tests* [18] *Incomplete sentence blank* [3] *Implicit Association Test* [325] *Evaluative* or *affective priming* [62]	

Note: PsychInfo inquiries were always based on the italicized keywords in conjunction with the term *attitude*. The number of references found in PsychInfo (after 2000) for each procedure is indicated in brackets.

also holds for attitude inferences from facial expressions or manifest behaviors. Common to all these procedures is the assumption that attitude-relevant stimuli (e.g., attitude items, attitude objects) have the power to elicit diagnostically useful expressive behaviors. Both verbal and nonverbal expressions are assumed to be consistent with the latent attitude. This consistency rule may override other motives and distracters, such as shame, distrust, privacy, or display rules that prevent individuals from revealing their attitudes. Yet, auto-expression is a complex function of the attitude itself and a complex set of social motives, affective states (Forgas, this volume), and introspective abilities to retrieve information from memory.

A second rationale that has been widely accepted as a basis for the straightforward assessment of attitudes relies on *approach versus avoidance responses* (middle part in Table 5.1). It is commonly presupposed that organisms approach pleasant and avoid unpleasant stimuli (Brendl, Markman, & Messner, 2005). Reversing this rule, positive and negative attitudes are inferred from approach and avoidance responses, respectively. Examples include behavioral observations of approach and avoidance behavior in real settings (Weaver, 2008), reflexive versus extractive arm movements (Förster & Strack, 1997), perceptual defense against unwanted stimuli (Gackenbach, 1978), immediacy (Mehrabian, 1966), abstractness of language use (Pennebaker, Mehl, & Niederhoffer, 2003), eye-tracking assessment of attended stimuli (Balcetis & Dunning, 2006), preferences in dichotic listening (Schotte, McNally, & Turner, 1990) or dichoptic viewing (Gumpper, 1972), and analyses of the implications of thematic associations in projective tests (Lilienfeld,

Wood, & Garp, 2000). Blascovich and McCall's (this volume) procedures for virtual realities might be added.

Whereas verbal attitude measures are commonly called explicit, most approach-avoidance measures are considered implicit, although the approach-avoidance rationale is very similar to the auto-expression rationale. Approach-avoidance can be understood as a special case of auto-expression on a relative-distance scale; positive and negative attitudes are assumed to express themselves in decreasing and increasing distance, respectively. Both rationales share the assumption that attitudes tend to express themselves in attitude-consistent behaviors, thereby overriding other conscious and unconscious factors, display rules, controlled and strategic influences, and regulatory motives, which might obscure the manifestation of the attitude. Although it is commonly taken for granted that the consistency of attitudes and expressive behaviors is stronger for approach-avoidance movements than for verbal measures, systematic evidence for this claim is missing.

A third rationale, which underlies the new definition, draws on the diagnostic value of *representations in associative memory* (bottom part in Table 5.1). Clearly, this rationale underlies the most popular IAT and EP procedures. The inference of an attitude from response latencies in an IAT or EP does not rely on auto-expression or approach-avoidance impulses. Rather, it relies on response speed as a reflection of the association of attitude target and evaluation in memory. Both IAT and EP are consensually called implicit, although both IAT and EP are susceptible to strategic influences and explicit instructions to exhibit or suppress an attitude (De Houwer, 2001; Fiedler, Bluemke, & Unkelbach, 2009).

Clarifying the Explicit-Implicit Distinction

To quote from Nosek (2007), "variation in controllability, intentionality, awareness, or efficiency is thought to differentiate implicit and explicit attitudes" (p. 65). These are the "four horsemen" of automaticity (Bargh, 1994) supposed to discriminate automatic tasks like IAT and EP from other, non-automatic tasks. However, as we shall see, all three methods—corresponding to auto-expression, approach-avoidance, and associative distance—involve a complex mix of conscious and unconscious mental processes, controlled and automatic responses, revealed and concealed attitude targets. No task or test can be said to be detached from strategic, motivational, and conscious volitional influences. What is classified as implicit or explicit appears to be mainly a matter of arbitrary convention.

Automaticity is indeed an unrealistically strong criterion. Neither IATs nor most EPs conceal the attitude target. They have been repeatedly shown to be subject to intentional and volitional influence, faking, self-instruction, and amenable to strategic control (Blair, 2002; Fiedler, Bluemke, & Unkelbach, 2010; Teige-Mocigemba & Klauer, 2008). Given this evidence, which is growing rapidly as more researchers are interested in critical tests of automaticity, the conjunction of all four horsemen—lack of awareness, control, intention, and efficiency—can be hardly upheld as a defining feature of implicit attitude measurement.

In the absence of clear-cut defining features, we are thus facing a problem of circularity: Those attitude measures that are supposed to assess implicit attitudes are called implicit and, vice versa, those attitudes that are diagnosed by implicit measures are called implicit. However, neither the cause (i.e., the attitude) nor the effect (the measure) is determined independently. Regardless of how an attitude is acquired—through argumentation, observation, imitation, conditioning, or instruction—it is a candidate for implicit measurement if it creates an association. Likewise, no theory imposes constraints on the type of latency (or approach-avoidance) data that can be used for implicit measurement.

One sensible alternative to the ill-defined implicit-explicit distinction is the distinction of direct and indirect scaling methods (De Houwer, 2006; Vargas, 2008). Direct (e.g., Likert-type) scaling methods are based on raw data that are already supposed to reflect the same dimension as the attitude to be assessed (e.g., responses to attitude statements). Indirect (e.g., Thurstonian) attitude scaling, in contrast, is derived from attitude-independent data (e.g., latencies or confusion probabilities), which are then translated onto an attitude scale using an explicitly spelled-out, testable model. This model does not guarantee a solution; it may not be applicable when the premises are falsified. From a scientific point of view, transparency and falsifiability give an obvious advantage to indirect over direct scaling methods.°

Taxonomy of Attitude Measurement Procedures

Unfortunately, this potential advantage of indirect scaling is not exploited in IAT and EP methods, because no testable and falsifiable psychometric model is offered to translate latency data into attitudes. Rather, it is presupposed that every IAT or EP score automatically reflect an attitude. No limiting conditions are identified under which the psychometric model fails. In the taxonomy of Table 5.1, IAT and EP are therefore classified as direct rather than indirect measures, because the latency data are conceived as direct measures of an attitude redefined as mere association.

Table 5.1 reveals a whole variety of attitudinal measures, distributed across all six cells. Most of these originally quite promising procedures have been met with little research interest, as evident from the number of literature references encountered in the PsychInfo database [in brackets], using the italicized phrases in Table 5.1 as search prompts.

Why is it the case that fascinating methods, like eye-tracking, linguistic content analysis, or binocular rivalry, received so much less attention than IAT and EP? Two speculative answers may be considered. First, consistent with the influence of instrumentation on the growth of science (Gigerenzer, 1991), the availability and shareability of inexpensive hardware and software tools has rendered chronometric measurement easy and convenient. Other methods (e.g., eye-tracking) are more expensive, laborious, and difficult to handle. Second, the minimal attitude definition as mere associations makes IAT and EP likely to yield many significant findings, pointing to unconscious, repressed, "implicit" secrets of the mind.

° It should be noted, though, that Likert scaling also involves a test of one testable premise: internal consistency.

ASYMMETRY OF CAUSAL AND DIAGNOSTIC INFERENCES: A MAJOR PROBLEM FOR IMPLICIT MEASURES

Whatever historical interpretation is correct, the likelihood ratio of diagnosed attitudes D to really existing attitudes A is exaggerated as a consequence of the inflated number of attitudes diagnosed in IAT and EP research (Figure 5.1). The inflation effect is vividly evident in findings of p(D) = 90% White Americans having a significant score in a race IAT, and a similar huge base rate of Germans diagnosed as prejudiced against Turks. Although the true base rate p(A) is unknown, behavioral data (such as the number of Americans voting for Obama, or the number of colored friendships and partnerships) strongly suggest that p(A) is clearly lower than p(D). To be sure, one might reify p(D) using the circularity of implicit measurement, arguing that whenever test persons exhibit an implicit association on an IAT or EP task, they *do hold* a corresponding attitude. However, logically, this argument implies that significant IAT or EP scores must always reflect an attitudinal association in the individual's memory. To the extent that test scores may originate in different causes, independent of an attitude, it can be proven that p(D) exceeds the true base rate p(A). The remainder of this chapter is devoted to a review of false alarms in IAT and EP research, which may account for the inflation of p(D) in Figure 5.1.

It should be noted in passing that the asymmetry of p(D) and p(A) has been recognized as a major problem in many other areas of diagnostic inference, including medicine (Gigerenzer & Hoffrage, 1995), legal decisions (Fiedler, Kaczor, Haarmann, Stegmüller, & Maloney, 2009; Wells & Olson, 2003), and risk assessment (Swets, Dawes, & Monahan, 2000). For example, the rate of p(positive HIV test) is roughly 7 times higher than the actual p(HIV) rate. The same ratio can be shown to hold for the asymmetry of causal and diagnostic inference. Thus, although the causal probability for a positive HIV test given the presence of the HIV virus is virtually perfect, p(positive test|HIV) = 100%, the reverse diagnostic probability that

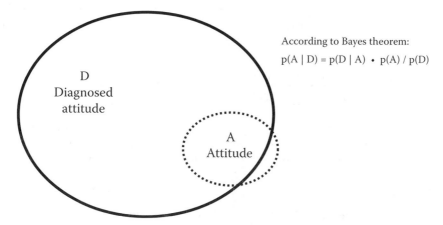

According to Bayes theorem:

$$p(A \mid D) = p(D \mid A) \cdot p(A) / p(D)$$

D
Diagnosed
attitude

A
Attitude

Figure 5.1.   If the base rate p(D) of a diagnosed attitude is higher than the base rate p(A) of the attitude proper, diagnostic inferences of D from A are less likely to be true than causal inferences of A from D.

someone who is tested positively actually has the HIV virus is only p(HIV|positive test) = 15% (i.e., roughly one seventh of the causal probability; Swets et al., 2000).

The same Bayesian rule holds for attitude measurement. To the extent that p(D) is inflated relative to p(A), diagnostic inferences from D to A are less likely than causal inferences from A to D (cf. Figure 5.1). For example, if the actual rate of racist attitudes is 30%, whereas the prevalence of racist IAT scores is 90% (giving a base rate ratio of 1/3), a significant IAT score will very likely (i.e., in two thirds of the cases) reflect something different from an attitude. Even when an IAT experiment in which A has been manipulated (e.g., through conditioning) yields an ideal causal probability of p(IAT|A) = 100%, the asymmetry implies that the same ideal IAT may inform only 33% correct diagnostic inferences from individuals' IAT score to a latent attitude. If the base rate ratio is more extreme than one third, the diagnostic accuracy rate may further shrink to 20%, 10%, or below.

This scenario is not derived from a fallible theory; it is an analytical truth derived from Bayesian calculus. If something as mundane as an association is sufficient proof for an attitude, then it is very likely that p(D) will be inflated relative to p(A). Causes other than A may also produce D. This universal problem of all diagnostic inference is not peculiar to IAT or EP. It rather arises from asymmetric base rates, when an inflated p(D) exceeds p(A).

One intriguing (though certainly unpopular) implication of this basic insight is that symmetric correlation coefficients provide misleading estimates of criterion validity, despite the fact that their use has been customary. However, if the purpose is to predict a criterion, then the asymmetry of causal and diagnostic (or prognostic) inferences must not be ignored.

Psychometricians did not ignore but actively avoided this problem by normalizing test scores. Intelligence scores, for instance, are calibrated such that roughly one half of the population receives a score above and below the average, respectively, yielding a balanced ratio of p(intelligent) to p(diagnosed as intelligent). After appropriate normalization, symmetric correlations can be trusted, to be sure. However, the failure to normalize an inflated test breeds low diagnostic accuracy, for the reasons summarized in Figure 5.1.

EMPIRICAL EVIDENCE FOR THE INFLATION OF IMPLICIT ATTITUDES

Thus, the crucial question to be pursued in the remainder of this chapter is whether IAT and EP outcomes may reflect nonattitudinal causes. What evidence is there for false alarms in implicit-attitude measurement, or spurious influences that let p(D) exceed p(A)?

Deliberate Strategies Mimicking Implicit Attitudes

There is compelling evidence that IAT and EP effects can be reduced, eliminated, reversed, simulated, or controlled strategically. Although these strategic influences on allegedly automatic performance can serve both to inflate (simulate) and to deflate (dissimulate) IAT and EP effects, they highlight the operation of non-attitudinal causes of test outcomes that are supposed to be cogent evidence for an attitude. Let us first examine the impact of overt intentions to produce certain IAT and EP outcomes before we turn to evidence on unconscious strategies.

A growing number of findings show that self-instruction or mental imagination moderate IAT or EP performance. Blair's (2002) insightful review describes several studies in which participants were asked to mentally generate or imagine positive experiences with members of ethnic groups (e.g., Blacks) prior to an IAT. Convergent results demonstrated that IAT attitudes are malleable, suggesting that there is considerable latitude for self-induced test outcomes. In a similar vein, it has been shown that both IAT-experienced and IAT-inexperienced respondents can fake their IAT scores. Successful faking is relatively independent of training and assisting instructions (Fiedler & Bluemke, 2005), the only premise being at least one prior exposure to an IAT task. Recent evidence by Teige-Mocigemba and Klauer (2008) shows that EP performance is subject to similar intentional or volitional influences.

Thus, an unknown proportion of diagnosed attitudes may reflect short-term associations induced through deliberate instruction or self-instruction. If it is possible to undo a racist IAT score by simply letting a randomized group of participants think of Black celebrities, the question arises whether experimenters can solicit any "attitude" that they want from a participant. More generally, the question is whether the experimental task reveals something about the respondent's personality or, if most participants exhibit the same response, whether the task reveals something about the task or the stimuli used for the IAT or EP task.

With regard to the latter possibility, Bluemke and Friese (2006) have provided impressive evidence that subtle changes in the stimuli used for an IAT can induce dramatic changes. In a German-Turk IAT, they manipulated cross-category associations between target labels and valence stimuli. That is, they varied the extent to which the words representing Germans and Turks also carried slightly different valence, and the extent to which the positive and negative valence terms also had slightly different affinity to Germans or Turks. This kind of semantic overlap is hardly ever controlled in IAT research (Fiedler, Messner, & Bluemke, 2006). Bluemke and Friese (2006) showed that a "normal" IAT effect (i.e., roughly 80% Germans seemingly prejudiced against Turks) can be reversed (i.e., most Germans favoring Turks) just by giving slightly more positive (negative) meaning to Turkish (German) labels and by giving slightly Turkish (German) connotations to positive (negative) attributes.*

A similar problem with EP as a measure of prejudice against Blacks was already noted by Lepore and Brown (1997), who pointed out that the specific stimuli used to prime the concept of Black people in Devine's (1989) seminal priming study had been biased toward negative valence.

A third possibility, besides person and stimulus attribution, is to attribute IAT and EP findings to the test situation. Thus, even when the stimuli used to

---

* By analogy, including positive insects (bee, butterfly) along with negative flowers (Venus flytrap, poison ivy) in an IAT will likely produce many pro-insect attitudes (cf. Govan & Williams, 2004).

represent Germans and Turks, or positive and negative valence, are unbiased and not confounded, they may take on different meaning as soon as they are juxtaposed in a task that pits Germans against Turks. In such a "minimal-group" setting (Tajfel, Flament, Billig, & Bundy, 1971), the meaning of neutral Turkish concepts may move in the direction of an out-group, whereas the meaning of originally neutral German concepts may become valenced in-group labels. Such a meaning shift—which may generalize to all participants—may account for an inflated p(D), reflecting situation-specific states rather than enduring personality attributes. The same individuals who can give an emergent negative meaning to Turkish labels in this minimal intergroup context may be able to generate a positive emergent meaning for Turks in another comparative context (cf. Bluemke & Friese, 2006).

An intriguing question in this regard is whether IAT effects may be prone to stereotype threat (Steele, 1997). Just as a Black respondent's performance on an intelligence test may deteriorate when he or she is reminded of the existence of the stereotype that being Black is associated with low intelligence, alerting IAT participants to the fact that their prejudice is being tested can worsen the IAT effect (Frantz, Cuddy, Burnett, Ray, & Hart, 2004). Any compulsive attempt to speed up on incompatible trials (i.e., when Black and positive stimuli have to be mapped onto the same response keys) may only amplify the impairment on such trials, reflecting an unsuccessful attempt to suppress an apparent prejudice.

Han, Olson, and Fazio (2006) have pointed out that IAT effects may be due to "extra-personal" associations, as distinguished from genuine attitudes. This alternative account refers to consensual knowledge that most people, or the society as a whole, associate an attitude target (e.g., Blacks) with negative evaluation (e.g., low intelligence), as distinguished from the respondent's own evaluation. If the valence-target association reflects only vicarious rather than self-referent knowledge, it can hardly be an attitude. Otherwise, a lonely lover and admirer of Blacks, who lives among a majority of White racists, could be called a racist.

In summary, there are various ways in which goals, self-instructions, and malleable stimulus meanings can induce and moderate IAT and EP effects, in the absence of a genuine attitude. However, the full spectrum of false alarms or attitude-independent IAT and EP effects becomes only visible when more primitive, unconscious response strategies are taken into account. Elaborating on this idea will disclose an extended class of strategic false alarms.

Simplifying Response Strategies

Many primitive response strategies need not be planned consciously. The brain has a built-in capacity to exploit stimulus redundancy by using simplifying strategies, which are independent of conscious awareness. For an illustration, consider maximizing and probability matching (cf. Shanks, Tunney, & McCarthy, 2002). When an organism (e.g., a pigeon motivated to find food) is exposed to a discrimination learning task involving two paths, A and B, leading to food with reinforcement rates of 70% and 50%, respectively, the organism may always choose the better alternative A (maximizing), or choose A with a probability that matches the success rate (i.e., 70%). A primitive organism need not be aware of its strategy. Countless experiments testify to such simple response strategies (e.g., to continue doing what led to success).

Human participants follow similar strategies in speeded discrimination tasks, developing a bias toward more likely stimuli. Imagine an IAT respondent who is to classify, under speed instructions, an extended series of stimuli as either White or Black. If the prevalence of White stimuli is markedly higher, a simple but useful strategy would be to expect, by default, a White stimulus on every trial (or on most trials). Now imagine that positive stimuli are also more frequent than negative stimuli. This will induce a similar bias toward "positive," as shown in a recent study by Bluemke and Fiedler (2009).

Given such a double-response bias, toward the more prevalent target and valence labels, what happens in a double classification task involving alternating presentations of target and valence stimuli? On a congruent trial block of an IAT, when the two frequent categories, White and positive, have to be mapped onto the same response key, the coexistence of two biases toward the same motor response must be helpful. The alignment of two simultaneous biases onto the same motor response will facilitate the IAT performance. In contrast, on incongruent trials, when White and negative stimuli have to be mapped onto one response key while Black and positive stimuli call for the other key, the two response tendencies will be in conflict and latencies will be retarded. Thus, the mere coexistence of two primitive response biases can produce an IAT effect. No real attitude is involved in this scenario. It is sufficient to assume that organisms find strategies of making a straining task easier and more efficient.

To demonstrate empirically that simple response biases, induced by unequal stimulus frequencies, can attenuate or boost IAT effects, we (Bluemke & Fiedler, 2009) manipulated the base rates of IAT stimuli systematically. When the test included 75% West German (along with 25% East German) stimuli along with 75% positive (and 25% negative) stimuli, a normal IAT effect was obtained, suggesting a more positive attitude of West German participants toward the West German majority than toward the East German minority. The same effect was obtained when most targets were East Germans and most valence stimuli were negative, for the two response biases in this condition should also support the joint mapping of East Germans and negative stimuli (and by complement, of West Germans and positive stimuli) onto the same response keys. However, the other two base rate conditions, involving 75% West and 75% negative, or 75% East and 75% positive, resulted in a significant reduction of the apparently prejudiced attitude of West German participants.

As the base rate manipulation only reduced but did not reverse, the "normal" IAT effect might suggest that frequency-driven response biases do not seem to account for the entire IAT effect. Even when the prevalent categories driving the response strategies were West German and negative, or East German and positive, there was still a trend to respond faster on congruent than on incongruent trials. However, the strategic account can be easily extended to assimilate this residual bias. After all, the virtual stimulus base rates, which drive strategic responding, depend not merely on the frequency of stimuli in the experiment but also on stimuli in the participants' social environment. As there are many more West Germans than East Germans in their environment, and positive stimuli are indeed more frequent in the stimulus environment than negative stimuli (Parducci, 1968; Unkelbach, Fiedler, Bayer, Stegmüller, & Danner, 2008), it is not surprising to find a basic pro–West German IAT score, due to the coexistence of two environmental biases that facilitate fluent processing of West German and positive stimuli.

Extending the response-bias notion, biases may originate in many other factors, besides intra-experimental and extra-experimental stimulus frequencies. Rothermund and Wentura's (2004) figure-ground approach assumes that the two poles of dichotomous stimulus attributes are often asymmetric, bearing a figure-ground relation. From a West German's point of view, an East German is a figure against the ground of a West German environment. On the valence dimension, negative stimuli are the figure while positive stimuli are the ground. This structural aspect can be used to simplify speeded-classification tasks. Rather than switching the dimension (targets or valence) on every trial, participants can sort all stimuli on the same dimension, as either "figure" or "ground." Given such a simplifying strategy, congruent IAT trials (West German/positive vs. East/negative) are clearly easier than incongruent trials (East Germans/positive vs. West/negative), because the response keys in the former are aligned with the figure-ground strategy. Across eight experiments, Rothermund and Wentura (2004) demonstrated that this strategic principle can account for a plethora of IAT effects.

Proctor and Cho (2006) have shown the figure-ground principle to be but a special case of a much broader class of response strategies. They use the term *polarity correspondence* to denote a variety of compatibility relations between dichotomous distinctions. For instance, it is easier to pair "Yes" responses with unmarked variable poles and "No " responses with marked poles (e.g., using the prefix *un*; Clark, 1969) than vice versa, or it is easier to align "Go" than "No go" responses with marked variables, negative valence, or figure levels on the figure-ground dimension. All these structural compatibility effects afford candidates for non-attitudinal influences on speeded-classification tasks.

Suffice it to mention briefly that very similar response biases can mimic false attitudes on EP tasks as well. In a recent experiment, we (Freytag, Bluemke, & Fiedler, 2009) orthogonally manipulated the base rates of positive and negative primes and of positive and negative targets in an EP experiment. We expected that a double bias toward the more frequent prime valence and toward the more frequent target valence would facilitate the speeded-classification task. Guessing the more prevalent target valence should produce many quick and correct responses whenever the correct response does not come to mind smoothly. This facilitation effect should increase when the more prevalent prime valence supports the same bias. As expected, when there were 75% positive primes and 75% positive targets, the usual congruity effect was obtained; apparently, a congruent response bias facilitated responses on same-valence prime-target pairs. In contrast, given 75% negative primes but 75% positive targets so that the double response bias supported incongruent trials, the normal congruity effect turned into an incongruity effect (i.e., faster responding to targets following primes of the opposite valence). This pattern was most pronounced when participants were explicitly instructed to not only evaluate the target stimuli but also to judge or guess the primes' valence, which apparently made the double bias most salient. The sensitivity of EP to stimulus frequencies was also demonstrated by Chan, Ybarra, and Schwarz (2006).

In other EP experiments (Fiedler, Bluemke, et al., 2010), we manipulated the correlation of prime valence and target valence across all trials. In different conditions, the likelihood of positive targets was higher either when the preceding prime was positive or when the prime was negative. A normal congruity effect was obtained when the correlation of prime and target valence was positive, but a reversal was obtained when the correlation was negative, especially when participants were instructed to respond to both primes and targets. Similar findings were reported by Spruyt, Hermans, De Houwer, Vandromme, and Eelen (2007) with pictorial rather than verbal primes, and by Klauer, Roßnagel, and Musch (1997) for very short prime-target intervals.

In summary, these findings highlight the fact that strategic influences can moderate, eliminate, and even reverse allegedly automatic IAT and EP effects. There are many reasons for false alarms, in which significant test scores do not originate in an attitude but in any kind of response strategy, in deliberate attempts to fake or modify one's test result, in self-induced states, or in attempts to simplify the taxing speeded-classification task. Moreover, the conditions that produce these false alarms are typical of ordinary IAT and EP test situations. It is obvious that White is more prevalent in White respondents' stimulus world and that the "adaptive brain" invents strategies to reduce the load of an extended reaction time task.

HOW TO OVERCOME THE SHORTCOMINGS OF IMPLICIT ATTITUDE RESEARCH

Clearly, no single type of false alarm must explain all available evidence. The purpose of the preceding section was only to point out that diverse sources of attitude-independent IAT and EP effects can be found, which together account for a considerable inflation of p(D). Interestingly, the inflation of p(D) relative to p(A) can also be used to predict under what conditions diagnostic inferences from IAT or EP scores to criterion behaviors should be strongest. Apparently, this should be the case whenever p(A) is not too small. Thus, when a study sample is deliberately selected to include a reasonable proportion of racists, psychopaths, or gender-stereotyped people, the base rate p(A) and the ratio of p(A) to p(D) will not be too low. Consequently, inferences of attitudes from conspicuous test scores will not be as inflated as when a random sample is drawn from a population with a very low p(A) base rate. Indeed, a relatively high validity has been found for IAT and EP in study designs that warrant a reasonably high p(A) rate (cf. Fiedler et al., 2006). However, in diagnostic settings involving rare attributes like psychopathic or criminal personality with a p(A) of 5%, 1%, or less, a high inequality p(D) > p(A) will produce many false alarms.

Our discussion of the asymmetry problem has a number of implications for future research, which ought to be tackled to improve the diagnostic assessment of implicit attitudes.

First and foremost, studies of predictive validity must be aware of the asymmetry of causal and diagnostic inference. However familiar and customary the practice is to use correlation coefficients as indices of validity, the predictive probability p(attitude|test) can differ radically from the hit rate p(test|attitude). To the extent that an attitude is more likely diagnosed than encountered in reality, the causal hit rate p(test|attitude) can greatly overestimate the diagnostic likelihood p(attitude|test).

Second, it should now be obvious that asymmetry arises as a consequence of the way in which attitudes are defined. In science, definitions must be taken serious. The minimal definition that is widely adopted in the recent literature—considering a mere target-valence association as a sufficient condition of an implicit attitude—is hardly consistent with the social psychological definition of an attitude as a cognitive-affective structure that constitutes a behavioral disposition. The altered definition is much weaker, covering many associations that would not have been qualified as an attitude conceived as a triple-component behavioral disposition. This weak criterion for diagnosing attitudes amplifies the asymmetry problem by inflating the prevalence of diagnosed attitudes relative to the actual rate of attitude and corresponding behavior. Changing a basic concept is unfortunate in a cumulative science striving for coherence and precision. If the new "implicit attitudes" differ fundamentally from the old "explicit attitudes" not only in their implicitness but also in referring to a new attitude concept, this creates an unwanted source of confusion and misunderstanding.

Third, even when researchers consider it useful and necessary to add another attitude concept, the viability of the new definition must be examined critically. Rather than uncritically adopting and reifying the concept, it should be put to empirical test. For instance, a glance at the cognitive association literature suggests a rather complex and tricky architecture of associative memory, as expressed in the following quotation from Maki and Buchanan (2008):

> Semantic similarity determined from lexicographic measures is shown to be separable from the associative strength determined from word *association* norms, and these semantic and associative measures are in turn separable from abstract representations derived from computational analyses of large bodies of text. The three-factor structure is at odds with traditional views of word knowledge. (p. 598)

Attitude research must not ignore the state of the art in the cognitive psychology of associations. It is well known that strong associates not only include synonyms and words of related and similar meaning but also antonyms and concepts of opposite meaning. How can we exclude that an association of Black and negative valence represents an antonym rather than a synonym? How do we know which of the three dimensions distinguished by Maki and Buchanan (2008) is tapped by an associative measure? How do we know that an association reflects an individual's own valuation rather than cultural knowledge about others' valuation, or semantic knowledge?

Fourth, this reminder of the state of the art in fundamental cognitive psychology leads us to another desideratum, namely, the need to formulate clearly spelled out psychometric models, the assumption of which can be falsified, rather than assuming uncritically that every instance of an IAT or EP effect will automatically yield an attitude (Blanton, Jaccard, Gonzales, & Christie, 2006). What precise algorithm can translate a latency difference into an attitude? What psychometric model implies that an average latency difference obtained on an IAT or EP task reflects an association between attitude target and valence?

An IAT model must explain why a target category and a valence category, which can be easily sorted onto the same response keys, implies an association between target and valence (i.e., why does T → Key and V → Key imply T → V?). Similarly, an EP model would have to rule out the possibility that causes other than associative knowledge—for example, compound retrieval cues (Ratcliff & McKoon, 1988) or integrative priming (Estes & Jones, 2009)—can provide attitude-independent alternative explanations.

Last but not least, an informed analysis of attitude assessment should not be confined to a few chronometric measures. Rather, the research program should be open to all kinds of measurement (as shown in Table 5.1), and it should allow for a critical debate of the attitude itself. Maybe social behavior is often not determined by stable internal person dispositions, but by the external influence of culture, social ecologies, task affordances, or the power of eliciting stimuli. It would be a category mistake to call such external determinants attitudes. Ironically, the most widely used instruments for measuring (implicit) attitudes, IAT and EP, may turn out to play a major role in an attempt to cope with the fundamental attribution bias underlying the search for attitudes rather than situational causes of behavior.

REFERENCES

Ajzen, I. (1991). The theory of planned behavior. *Organizational Behavior and Human Decision Processes, 50*, 179–211.

Balcetis, E., & Dunning, D. (2006). See what you want to see: Motivational influences on visual perception. *Journal of Personality and Social Psychology, 91*, 612–625.

Bargh, J. A. (1994). The four horsemen of automaticity. In R. S. Wyer & T. K. Srull (Eds.), *Handbook of social cognition* (pp. 1–40). Hillsdale, NJ: Erlbaum.

Blair, I. V. (2002). The malleability of automatic stereotypes and prejudice. *Personality and Social Psychology Review, 6*(3), 242–261.

Blanton, H., Jaccard, J., Gonzales, P. M., & Christie, C. (2006). Decoding the Implicit Association Test: Implications for criterion prediction. *Journal of Experimental Social Psychology, 42*, 192–212.

Bluemke, M., & Fiedler, K. (2009). *Base rate effects on the IAT. Consciousness and Cognition, 18*, 1029–1038.

Bluemke, M., & Friese, M. (2006). Do features of stimuli influence IAT effects? *Journal of Experimental Social Psychology, 42*, 163–176.

Brendl, C. M., Markman, A. B., & Messner, C. (2005). Indirectly measuring evaluations of several attitude objects in relation to a neutral reference point. *Journal of Experimental Social Psychology, 41*, 346–368.

Chan, E., Ybarra, O., & Schwarz, N. (2006). Reversing the affective congruency effect: The role of target word frequency of occurrence. *Journal of Experimental Social Psychology, 42*, 365–372.

Clark, H., & Card, S. (1969). Role of semantics in remembering comparative sentences. *Journal of Experimental Psychology, 82*, 545–553.

De Houwer, J. (2001). A structural and process analysis of the Implicit Association Test. *Journal of Experimental Social Psychology, 37*, 443–451.

De Houwer, J. (2006). What are implicit measures and why are we using them? In R. Wiers & A. W. Stacy (Eds.), *Handbook of implicit cognition and addiction* (pp. 11–28). Thousand Oaks, CA: Sage.

Devine, P. G. (1989). Stereotypes and prejudice: Their automatic and controlled components. *Journal of Personality and Social Psychology, 56*, 5–18.

Estes, Z., & Jones, L. (2009). Integrative priming occurs rapidly and uncontrollably during lexical processing. *Journal of Experimental Psychology: General, 138*, 112–130.

Fazio, R. H. (2001). On the automatic activation of associated evaluations: An overview. *Cognition and Emotion, 15*, 115–141.

Fazio, R. H., Chen, J., McDonel, E. C., & Sherman, S. J. (1982). Attitude accessibility, attitude-behavior consistency, and the strength of the object-evaluation association. *Journal of Experimental Social Psychology, 18*, 339–357.

Fazio, R. H., & Olson, M. A. (2003). Implicit measures in social cognition research: Their meaning and use. *Annual Review of Psychology, 54*, 297–327.

Fiedler, K., & Bluemke, M. (2005). Faking the IAT: Aided and unaided response control on the Implicit Association Tests. *Basic and Applied Social Psychology, 27*, 307–316.

Fiedler, K., Bluemke, M., & Unkelbach, C. (2009). Exerting control over allegedly automatic associative processes. In J. P. Forgas, R. F. Baumeister, & D. M. Tice (Eds.), *Psychology of self-regulation: Cognitive, affective, and motivational processes* (pp. 249–269). New York: Psychology Press.

Fiedler, K., Bluemke, M., & Unkelbach, C. (2010). *Flexible cue utilization in evaluative priming*. Manuscript submitted for publication.

Fiedler, K., Kaczor, K., Haarmann, S., Stegmüller, M., & Maloney, J. (2009). Impression formation advantage in memory for faces: When eyewitnesses are interested in targets' likeability, rather than their identity. *European Journal of Social Psychology, 39*, 793–807.

Fiedler, K., Messner, C., & Bluemke, M. (2006). Unresolved problems with the "I," the "A," and the "T": A logical and psychometric critique of the Implicit Association Test (IAT). *European Review of Social Psychology, 17*, 74–147.

Förster, J., & Strack, F. (1997). Motor actions in retrieval of valenced information: A motor congruence effect. *Perceptual and Motor Skills, 85*, 1419–1427.

Frantz, C. M., Cuddy, A. J. C., Burnett, M., Ray, H., & Hart, A. (2004). A threat in the computer: The race Implicit Association Test as a stereotype threat experience. *Personality and Social Psychology Bulletin, 30*, 1611–1624.

Freytag, P., Bluemke, M., & Fiedler, K., (2009). *Stimulus and response baserates in evaluative priming*. Manuscript in preparation, University of Heidelberg.

Gackenbach, J. I. (1978). A perceptual defense approach to the study of gender sex related traits, stereotypes, and attitudes. *Journal of Personality, 46*, 645–676.

Gigerenzer, G. (1991). From tools to theories: A heuristic of discovery in cognitive psychology. *Psychological Review, 98*, 254–267.

Gigerenzer, G., & Hoffrage, U. (1995). How to improve Bayesian reasoning without instructions: Frequency formats. *Psychological Review, 102*, 684–704.

Govan, C. L., & Williams, K. D. (2004). Changing the affective valence of the stimulus items influences the IAT by re-defining the category labels. *Journal of Experimental Social Psychology, 40*, 357–365.

Greenwald, A. G., Banaji, M. R., Rudman, L. A., Farnham, S. D., Nosek, B. A., & Mellot, D. S. (2002). A unified theory of implicit attitudes, stereotypes, self-esteem, and self-concept. *Psychological Review, 109*(1), 3–25.

Gumpper, D. (1972). Convergence between own-categories and binocular-rivalry measures of attitudinal direction. *Psychological Reports, 31,* 111–117.

Han, H. A., Olson, M. A., & Fazio, R. H. (2006). The influence of experimentally created extrapersonal associations on the Implicit Association Test. *Journal of Experimental Social Psychology, 42,* 259–272.

Klauer, K. C., Roßnagel, C., & Musch, J. (1997). List-context effects in evaluative priming. *Journal of Experimental Psychology: Learning, Memory, and Cognition, 23,* 246–255.

Lepore, L., & Brown, R. (1997). Category and stereotype activation: Is prejudice inevitable? *Journal of Personality and Social Psychology, 72,* 275—287.

Lilienfeld, S. O., Wood, J. M., & Garp, H. O. (2000). The scientific status of projective techniques. *Psychological Science in the Public Interest, 1,* 27–66.

Maki, W. S., & Buchanan, E. (2008). Latent structure in measures of associative, semantic, and thematic knowledge. *Psychonomic Bulletin & Review, 15,* 598–603.

Mehrabian, A. (1966). Immediacy: An indicator of attitudes in linguistic communication. *Journal of Personality, 34,* 26–34.

Nosek, B. A. (2007). Implicit-explicit relations. *Current Directions in Psychological Science, 16,* 65–69.

Nosek, B. A., Greenwald, A. G., & Banaji, M. R. (2006). The Implicit Association Test at age 7: A methodological and conceptual review. In J. A. Bargh (Ed.), *Automatic Processes in Social Thinking and Behavior* (pp. 265–292). New York: Psychology Press.

Olson, M., & Fazio, R. (2008). Implicit and explicit measures of attitudes: The perspective of the MODE model. *Attitudes: Insights from the new implicit measures* (pp. 19–63). New York: Psychology Press.

Parducci, A. (1968). The relativism of absolute judgment. *Scientific American, 19,* 84–90.

Pennebaker, J. W., Mehl, M. R., & Niederhoffer, K. (2003). Psychological aspects of natural language use: Our words, our selves. *Annual Review of Psychology, 54,* 547–577.

Proctor, R. W., & Cho, Y. S. (2006). Polarity correspondence: A general principle for performance of speeded binary classification tasks. *Psychological Bulletin, 132,* 416–442.

Ratcliff, R., & McKoon, G. (1988). A retrieval theory of priming in memory. *Psychological Review, 95,* 385–408.

Rosenberg, M. J., & Hovland, C. I. (1966). *Attitude organization and change: An analysis of consistency among attitude components.* Oxford, England: Yale University Press.

Rothermund, K., & Wentura, D. (2004). Underlying processes in the Implicit Association Test (IAT): Dissociating salience from associations. *Journal of Experimental Psychology: General, 133,* 139–165.

Schotte, D. E., McNally, R. J., & Turner, M. L. (1990). A dichotic listening analysis of body weight concern in bulimia nervosa. *International Journal of Eating Disorders, 9,* 109–113.

Shanks, D. R., Tunney, R. J., & McCarthy, J. D. (2002). A reexamination of probability matching and rational choice. *Journal of Behavioral Decision Making, 15,* 233–250.

Snyder, M., & Swann, W.B. (1976). When actions reflect attitudes: The politics of impression management. *Journal of Personality and Social Psychology, 34,* 1034–1042.

Spruyt, A., Hermans, D., De Houwer, J., Vandromme, H., & Eelen, P. (2007). On the nature of the affective priming effect: Effects of stimulus onset asynchrony and congruency proportion in naming and evaluative categorization. *Memory and Cognition, 35,* 95–106.

Swets, J. A., Dawes, R. M., & Monahan, J. (2000). Psychological science can improve diagnostic decisions. *Psychological Science in the Public Interest, 1,* 1–26.

Steele, C. M. (1997). A threat in the air: How stereotypes shape intellectual identity and performance. *American Psychologist, 52,* 613–629.

Tajfel, H., Flament, C., Billig, M. G., & Bundy, R. P. (1971). Social categorization and intergroup behaviour. *European Journal of Social Psychology, 1,* 149–178.

Teige-Mocigemba, S., & Klauer, K. C. (2008). "Automatic" evaluation? Strategic effects on affective priming. *Journal of Experimental Social Psychology, 44,* 1414–1417.

Unkelbach, C., Fiedler, K., Bayer, M., Stegmüller, M., & Danner, D. (2008). Why positive information is processed faster: The density hypothesis. *Journal of Personality and Social Psychology, 95,* 36–49.

Vargas, P. (2008). Implicit consumer cognition. In C. P. Haugtvedt, P. M. Herr, & F. R. Kardes (Eds.), *Handbook of consumer psychology* (pp. 477–504). New York: Psychology Press.

Weaver, C. N. (2008). Social distance as a measure of prejudice among ethnic groups in the United States. *Journal of Applied Social Psychology, 38,* 779–795.

Wells, G. L., & Olson, E. A. (2003). Eyewitness testimony. *Annual Review of Psychology, 54,* 277–295.

Wittenbrink, B., & Schwarz, N. (2007). *Implicit measures of attitudes.* New York: Guilford Press.

AUTHOR'S NOTE

Please send correspondence concerning this chapter to kf@psychologie. uni-heidelberg.de. Helpful comments on the chapter by Matthias Bluemke and by Joel Cooper are gratefully acknowledged.

Section *II*

Attitudes: Cognitive and Affective Processes

6

Learning What Most People Like
How Implicit Attitudes and Normative Evaluations Shape Prejudice and Stereotype Threat and Are Shaped by Social Identity Protection and Culture

STEVEN J. SPENCER, JENNIFER PEACH,
EMIKO YOSHIDA, AND MARK P. ZANNA

As people interact with their social environment they face two fundamental tasks. On one hand, people need to understand how their world works and need to know what objects to approach and what objects to avoid. That is, they need to know what sort of objects in their environment will allow them to cope effectively and what objects impede their success. Such understanding should arise from personal experience and should form the basis of attitudes. On the other hand, however, people also live within social groups—they are social animals. Because of this basic social reality they need to not only understand what objects they want to approach and what objects they want to avoid, they also need to understand how people in their social environment react to the objects they encounter. They need to know what sort of objects in their environment will allow them to fit in with their social groups and what objects may impair their sense of belonging in their groups. Such understanding should arise from observing how objects are treated and depicted by the group and should form the basis of group norms.

We argue that these two basic tasks that people are likely to enact repeatedly can eventually lead to two very different types of automatic evaluative associations.

Interacting with an object repeatedly and judging whether one likes or does not like that object can lead to automatic associations between the object and liking— what has been described as automatic attitudes or personal associations (Olson & Fazio, 2004). Observing how others depict and treat an object, however, can lead to a different sort of automatic association in our view. When people repeatedly see an object treated or depicted in a particular way, we argue they are likely to form an automatic association between the object and how people evaluate the object. We call these automatic associations implicit normative evaluations.

In this chapter we highlight how implicit normative evaluations can be quite different from implicit attitudes and when implicit normative evaluations can predict important behaviors above and beyond implicit attitudes. We examine these questions in four domains: (1) stereotyping and prejudice, (2) stereotype threat, (3) social identity protection, and (4) culture.

IMPLICIT NORMATIVE EVALUATIONS AND STEREOTYPING AND PREJUDICE

People often do not endorse blatant forms of racism nor believe that they are prejudiced, yet they are likely to engage in discrimination in ambiguous situations (Dovidio & Gaertner, 1998, 2000). In such ambiguous situations the salience of norms tends to influence the expression of prejudice or discrimination. For example, when norms suggest that prejudice or discrimination against racial minorities is inappropriate, people tend to inhibit expression of negative attitudes toward racial minorities (Crandall, Eshleman, & O'Brien, 2002). As we have argued, implicit normative evaluations are expected to be shaped by exposure to people's evaluations of an object or group. When people express their preferences or beliefs about racial minorities in subtle ways, these expressions are expected to affect implicit normative evaluations.

Therefore, to examine how other people's reactions will affect implicit normative evaluations and discriminatory behavior, we manipulated norms toward racial minorities by changing the audience's reactions to racist jokes about people from the Middle East. We expected when the audience laughed at the racist jokes, implicit normative evaluations of people from the Middle East will become more negative, and people will be more likely to engage in discriminatory behavior than when the audience remains silent indicating their displeasure with the jokes.

To test this hypothesis, White participants were asked to watch a series of standup comedy clips. One of the comedy clips included offensive racist jokes against people from the Middle East. Participants were led to believe that the audience was from the same country as the participants. In one condition, the audience reacted to the racist jokes with laughter and cheers, subtly conveying that the audience evaluates people from the Middle East negatively. In another condition, the audience's reactions were removed. Thus, there was an awkward moment in which the comedian stood in front of the silent audience. These audience's reactions conveyed a clear norm that the racist jokes were not acceptable. Then, participants completed an Implicit Association Test (IAT) that measured implicit normative evaluations (by measuring the association between "most people like" and "Middle Easterner"). Finally, participants were told that the experiment was over but before they left a White experimenter explained that she wanted them to complete a survey from the Federation of Students that would be used to cut the budget for student organizations in the next year. Participants were asked to fill out a ballot (which forced budget cuts) and indicate how much money each student organization should receive (Son Hing, Li, & Zanna, 2002). One of the student organizations was the Muslim Student Association, and the amount of the money that participants allocated to the Muslim Student Association was our main dependent variable. Because a budget is one of the most important factors enabling student organizations to function, the budget reduction exercise provides a legitimate excuse to subtly discriminate against Muslim students.

Consistent with the hypothesis, participants who were exposed to the audience who laughed at the racist jokes exhibited more negative implicit normative evaluations of people from the Middle East than those who were exposed to the audience who did not laugh at the racist jokes. And, the more negative their implicit normative evaluations became, the more they cut down the budget for the Muslim Student Association, supporting the notion that the discriminatory behavior occurred through implicit normative evaluations.

It is important to note that implicit attitudes were not affected by the audience's reactions nor did they affect the amount of money that participants allocated to the Muslim Student Association. Implicit attitudes are presumably developed through direct interaction with social groups; therefore, when people are exposed to other people's evaluations of people from the Middle East, the exposure affected implicit normative evaluations but not implicit attitudes.

If implicit attitudes and normative evaluations develop through different processes, then implicit attitudes and normative evaluations will predict behavior in different contexts. Particularly, people's personal experience with Black people may diverge from societal views of them. We have argued that implicit normative evaluations are formed by exposure to other people's evaluations, beliefs, or behavior. These culturally shared beliefs or evaluations are reinforced through media depictions of Black people as involved in gang violence, robberies, or drive-by shootings, or by observing how other people subtly avoid Black people. Therefore, implicit normative evaluations of Black people may reflect consensual beliefs about Black people being more violent or dangerous than they actually are. By living in a society, people are exposed to these negative beliefs or evaluations of Black people in the context of violence, and implicit normative evaluations of Black people are expected to predict behavior in this context.

In contrast, most people have not encountered a situation where they have to make a decision about whether Black people are armed or not. Instead, they are likely to interact with Black people in everyday contexts such as school, work, or a grocery store. Given that implicit attitudes are well-practiced constructs that have been developed through early life experiences (Powell & Fazio, 1984; Rudman, 2004), implicit attitudes toward Black people are expected to be formed through experience with them or interacting with them in an everyday context. Indeed, research has shown that implicit attitudes predict everyday life behavior such as interracial interactions (Dovidio, Kawakami, & Gaertner, 2002; Dovidio, Kawakami, Johnson, Johnson, & Howard, 1997).

Given this reasoning we predicted that implicit normative evaluations would predict the tendency to shoot an unarmed Black target, whereas implicit attitudes would be less like to predict responses in this situation. Correll and his colleagues created a computer simulation of a police officer's task of shooting someone with a gun and not shooting an unarmed civilian (Correll, Park, Judd, & Wittenbrink, 2002; Correll et al., 2007). This research found participants responded more quickly to a target holding a gun when the target was African American than when the target was European American. More importantly, people reacted more slowly to a target holding a harmless object (e.g., cell phone) when the target was African American than when the target was European American. When people were under time pressure, they were more likely to shoot an unarmed target when the target was African American than when the target was European American. This bias is called the "shooter bias" (Correll et al., 2002).

Past research has shown that the shooter bias is not related to implicit attitudes, explicit attitudes, and the motivation to control prejudice (Correll et al., 2002). We predict, however, that implicit normative evaluations will predict the shooter bias.

To test this hypothesis, we asked participants to complete an implicit normative evaluation measure about Blacks and then 4 days later complete Correll et al.'s (2002) computer simulation. Replicating previous studies (Correll et al., 2002, 2007), participants were slower in reacting to an unarmed target when the target was Black than when the target was White, and were faster reacting to a target who was holding a gun when the target was Black than when the target was White. Also replicating past research, implicit attitudes and explicit attitudes were not correlated with the shooter bias. More importantly from our perspective, however, implicit normative evaluations about Black people were correlated with the shooter bias.

IMPLICIT NORMATIVE EVALUATIONS AND STEREOTYPE THREAT

Theorizing on stereotype threat has argued that when members of a stereotyped group perform in a domain in which they are negatively stereotyped, they are affected by a "threat in the air" that can harm their performance (Steele, 1997). Does this threat in the air reflect stereotyped groups' evaluations of their group, or does it reflect their knowledge of how others evaluate their group? We suggest that, instead of reflecting attitudes, a threat in the air is best captured by normative evaluations of a stereotyped group. That is, even if members of stereotyped groups do not believe the negative stereotypes about their group—as is often the case—the mere knowledge that others hold these stereotypes and evaluate their group negatively may be enough to negatively impact their performance. If this is the case, then situations that elicit stereotype threat should elicit negative normative evaluations of the stereotyped group in question, but should not elicit negative attitudes toward the stereotyped group. Because of the insidious nature of stereotype threat, it is likely that these normative evaluations function implicitly.

We sought to test this possibility by assessing whether the same situations that have reduced women's performance on math tests in the past lead to more negative implicit normative evaluations but not more negative implicit attitudes. We selected men and women from the University of Waterloo who were not math majors but who identified with math (Spencer, Steele, & Quinn, 1999). We randomly assigned them to a stereotype threat condition (in which they were told the test they would take was diagnostic of mathematical aptitude) or to a no stereotype threat condition (in which they were told the test they would take was not diagnostic, therefore eliminating women's concerns that they might be stereotyped to perform negatively on the test) (Quinn & Spencer, 2001). After reading the instructions for the upcoming math test, participants were then randomly assigned to an IAT that assessed either their implicit attitudes or their implicit normative evaluations of women.

Did the stereotype threat condition influence implicit normative evaluations of women? Compared to participants in the no stereotype threat condition, participants in the stereotype threat condition had more negative implicit normative evaluations of women. This occurred for both women and men, suggesting that in a stereotype threat situation, negative implicit evaluations of women are primed for both the targets of stereotype threat and those who are not targets. Were implicit attitudes similarly influenced? The implicit attitudes of participants in the stereotype threat and the no stereotype threat condition did not differ for either women or men. Interestingly, women had more positive implicit attitudes toward women compared to men (a finding we will see again in the next section of this chapter) regardless of whether they were under stereotype threat or not.

This research suggests that the same conditions that decrease women's performance on a test also call up negative implicit normative evaluations for both women and men, but do not influence their implicit attitudes toward women. Thus, this research does support the notion that a "threat in the air" can be captured on an implicit measure, and it is the knowledge of how a group is viewed in society that elicits this effect, not individuals' own attitudes toward their group.

The previous study suggests that when a situation is high in stereotype threat negative implicit normative evaluations are activated, but what happens when these situations are repeatedly encountered? Will chronic negative implicit normative evaluations develop? To address these questions, we assessed the implicit normative evaluations of incoming male and female engineering students during their first and second semester at University.

There are several ways that norms may form among this group. There are significantly less women than men in engineering, as they make up roughly 20% of undergraduate programs, and only 9% of professional engineers (Engineers Canada, 2007). This may form a strong descriptive norm about the gender composition of engineering. There is also research suggesting that women in engineering may be exposed to a "chilly climate" (Pascarella, Whitt, Edison, & Nora, 1997). This chilly climate may reflect women's negative experiences when exposed to local negative norms toward women in engineering. Indeed, research suggests that this "threat in the air" (Steele, 1997) can harm female engineering students' performance (Bell, Spencer, Iserman, & Logel, 2003). These negative norms may be communicated in more subtle ways during day-to-day interactions. One of these subtle cues may be the behavior of female engineers' male peers. Indeed, subtle, sexist behavior of male peers can harm female engineers' performance on math tests (Logel et al., 2009).

In this study, we wished to assess what factors of the situation influence the development of implicit normative evaluations of female engineers. First, we predicted that exposure to engineering (an environment in which women are underrepresented) would lead to more negative implicit normative evaluations of female engineers for both male and female engineering students. Second, we predicted that men and women's implicit normative evaluations would be sensitive to the specific ratio of male to female engineering students within each section of engineering, such that the fewer female engineers there were in a specific section of engineering (such as mechanical or nanotechnology), the more men and women would implicitly believe that most people do not like female engineers. Third, we predicted that the implicit normative evaluations of men within each section of engineering would impact women's implicit normative evaluations. Fourth, we predicted that a chilly climate (as captured by negative implicit normative evaluations of female engineers) would lead these female engineers to consider dropping out of engineering.

Participants for this study were recruited from engineering over 3 years. In the first year, participants were recruited via e-mail in June and August. In the second and third years, participants were recruited as members of a larger study (Walton, Logel, Peach, Spencer, & Zanna, 2010). We assessed participants' implicit normative evaluations in the first semester and the second semester and assessed whether they planned to stay in engineering (with the response options of yes/maybe/no) in the second semester.

What influenced male and female engineers' implicit normative evaluation of female engineers? First, we found that implicit normative evaluations of female engineers became more negative in the second semester than in the first semester, and this decrease did not vary based on gender, suggesting both men and women take on negative norms toward female engineers over time. Second, we found that implicit normative evaluations were indeed sensitive to the local norms within each type of engineering. Participants who were in sections of engineering with fewer women (e.g., mechanical engineering, where roughly 7% of the first-year class was female) came to have more negative implicit normative evaluations of female engineers than did participants who were in sections of engineering with more women (e.g., civil engineering, where roughly 45% of the first-year class was female). Again, the relation between percentage of women in engineering and implicit normative evaluations did not vary based on gender. To determine whether men's implicit normative evaluations were related to women's implicit normative evaluations, we calculated the mean implicit normative evaluations for men within each section of engineering, and let this predict the implicit normative evaluations of women in those same sections of engineering at the end of the first semester. We found that the more negative men's implicit normative evaluations of female engineers were within each section of engineering, the more negative were the implicit normative evaluations of their female peers.

Thus, we have seen that both men and women's implicit normative evaluations become more negative over time, that the percentage of women in each section of engineering influences these implicit normative evaluations, and that the implicit normative evaluations of men in each section of engineering are related to their female peers' implicit normative evaluations. But what impact do these negative implicit normative evaluations have on women? The more negative women's implicit normative evaluations of female engineers, the more likely they were to be considering dropping out of engineering. Clearly, these negative implicit normative evaluations do indeed adversely impact female engineers. Thus, these two studies suggest that implicit normative evaluations may capture the "threat in the air" that members of stereotyped groups are exposed to, and they can predict disengagement from a field in general. Will members of stereotyped and devalued groups always take on the negative views of the group they are exposed to in their environment? We suspect that at times they will not and now extend our reasoning to address why members of stereotyped and devalued groups may develop positive implicit normative evaluations of their group.

IMPLICIT NORMATIVE EVALUATION AND SOCIAL IDENTITY PROTECTION

Although the situation can cause people to develop negative normative evaluations of their group, as we have just seen, we believe that people will also be motivated to develop positive implicit normative evaluations of their group. Based on social identity research (Tajfel & Turner, 1979), we argue that members of devalued groups are motivated to have a positive social identity, and this motivation can lead to the development of both positive implicit attitudes and implicit normative evaluations. Specifically, in order to maintain a positive social identity, as compared to members of the majority, members of devalued groups may both implicitly like their own group and believe that others like their group as well. If these group differences are indeed due to a motivation to maintain a positive social identity, when this motivation is met through other means these group differences may disappear.

Do members of devalued groups indeed have more positive implicit attitudes and implicit normative evaluations of their group than do members of the majority? To test this possibility we selected African-Canadian and European-Canadian participants, and assessed their implicit attitudes toward and normative evaluations of Blacks versus Whites online in two separate sessions. We also assessed their explicit attitudes and normative evaluations in the same sessions (i.e., we assessed explicit attitudes at the same time as implicit attitudes). We found that, as we had predicted, African-Canadian participants had more positive implicit attitudes toward Blacks than did European-Canadian participants. They also had more positive implicit normative evaluations of Blacks than did European-Canadian participants. Was this the case for their explicit attitudes and normative evaluations as well? African-Canadians did have more positive explicit attitudes toward Blacks versus Whites than did European-Canadian participants, but contrary to their implicit normative evaluations and explicit attitudes, African-Canadians' explicit norms were more negative, and they were much more likely to say that visible minorities are the targets of discrimination than were European-Canadian participants, providing discriminant validity between implicit and explicit measures of normative evaluations. Thus, members of this devalued group showed evidence that their motivation to maintain a positive social identity may have influenced their implicit responses.

We replicated these findings with two other groups—feminists and Asian-Canadians—but how do we know that the findings are caused by people's motivation to maintain a positive social identity? To address this question, we selected Muslim and non-Muslim students, and randomly assigned them to a group-based affirmation or a control condition. In the group-based affirmation condition, participants were asked to think about a social group that was most important to them (Luhtanen & Crocker, 1992), and then to think about a value that was most important to their group. They could choose from: business/economics, relationships, art/music/theatre, science/pursuit of knowledge, or helping those in need (Fein & Spencer, 1997). Next, participants were asked to come up with three reasons why this value was important to their group, and an example of how their group has demonstrated this value (Sherman, Kinias, Major, Kim, & Prenovost, 2007). In the control condition, they were merely asked to choose the value that was least important to them and write three reasons why it might be important to someone else, as well as provide an example of how someone else might demonstrate this value. After completing the affirmation manipulation, we assessed participants' implicit normative evaluations of Muslims. We also assessed their explicit normative evaluations of Muslims.

Consistent with our previous findings, when participants were not affirmed, Muslim participants had more positive implicit normative evaluations of Muslims than did non-Muslims. In line with our hypothesis that the difference in the control condition was due to motivation, when participants were affirmed, Muslim and non-Muslim participants no longer had differing implicit normative evaluations of Muslims.

We found the opposite pattern of results for explicit normative evaluations. When Muslim participants were not affirmed, they believed most people do not like Muslims more than did non-Muslim participants. When participants were affirmed, this pattern actually reversed, such that Muslim participants thought most people like Muslims more than did non-Muslim participants. These results suggest that the positive implicit normative evaluations of devalued groups is indeed motivated, because when this motivation is met through other means (such as through affirming their group identity) group differences in implicit normative evaluations are not evident.

In the next study we sought to examine how implicit normative evaluations would affect collective action. For devalued groups, maintaining positive implicit attitudes and positive implicit normative evaluations may both serve to protect their social identity. When considering collective action, however, we reason that implicit attitudes and implicit normative evaluation may predict behavior in different ways. If one has positive implicit attitudes toward one's group this should if anything lead one to engage in more collective action for his or her group. In contrast, if one has positive implicit normative evaluations this signals that his or her group is viewed positively by others and that collective action may not be necessary. In this way, positive implicit normative evaluations might be expected to predict less collective action. Thus, we predict that implicit attitudes will be, if anything, positively related to collective action, whereas implicit normative evaluations will be negatively related to collective action.

To test this reasoning, we assessed whether implicit attitudes and normative evaluations of feminists predicted their intentions to engage in collective action. We assessed women's identification with feminism and selected women who both identified and did not identify with feminism for this study. We assessed implicit attitudes and normative evaluations online, as well as participants' general tendency to engage in collective action and their explicit normative evaluations of feminists. We then randomly assigned participants to volunteer for a cause that was framed as advancing the interests of feminists (i.e., a cause that was relevant to the social identity of feminists) or students (i.e., a cause that was irrelevant to the social identity of feminists). We then assessed their intention to volunteer for the cause (e.g., whether they were willing to sign a petition for the group, go to rallies, even march to parliament with the group).

We expected implicit normative evaluations to predict volunteering behavior for a relevant cause (i.e., a cause that benefits feminists) but not for an unrelated cause. Thus, we expected only women who are high in identification with feminism, who have relatively negative implicit normative evaluations of feminists, and who are asked to volunteer for a feminist cause to show greater collective action.

As we predicted, women who identified with feminism were willing to volunteer for a feminist cause when they implicitly believed most people do not like feminists (or, had negative implicit normative evaluations of feminists). This occurred over and above their general tendency toward activism, and their implicit attitudes and explicit normative evaluations. Implicit normative evaluations about feminists did not predict willingness to volunteer for an unrelated cause, or for women who did not identify with feminism. Thus, it appears that positive implicit normative evaluations of one's group and collective action to help that group are alternate ways to fulfill the goal to be part of a high-status group. These findings support our contention that positive implicit normative evaluations allow members of devalued groups to fulfill the goal of maintaining their groups' status and protect their social identity. Ironically then, feminists had to have *negative* implicit normative evaluations about feminists before they were motivated to engage in collective action, meaning that identity protection may reduce the efforts of members of devalued groups to improve the status of their group.

Thus, in this line of research we have found that members of devalued groups have more positive implicit attitudes toward their group than do members of the majority, and they implicitly believe that most people like their group to a greater extent than do members of the majority. We have found evidence suggesting these positive implicit normative evaluations are motivated; when affirmed, members of devalued groups and members of the majority no longer differ in their normative evaluations. Moreover, we have found more discriminant evidence between implicit attitudes and implicit normative evaluations, because implicit normative evaluations predicted collective action (a strongly social behavior), but implicit attitudes did not.

We have found evidence that groups can differ in their implicit attitudes and normative evaluations. But can groups differ in these constructs even when they may not differ in motivation? Specifically, can broad cultural differences be reflected in differing normative evaluations? Do implicit normative evaluations predict behavior differently depending on one's cultural background? We turn to these questions next.

CULTURE AND IMPLICIT NORMATIVE EVALUATIONS

People from different cultures are exposed to different normative evaluations of objects or social groups. When these people emigrate to a new country, they are exposed to new cultural norms or values. For example, East Asian cultures emphasize respect for older people and parents because of the influence of Confucianism. They tend to associate older people with wisdom or experience (Sung, 2001). In contrast, in North America negative stereotypes or normative evaluations, such as of frailty or forgetfulness, of older people are prevalent (Nelson, 2005).

Among people from East Asian cultures how will their implicit normative evaluations toward older people change if they have been exposed to Canadian culture over a prolonged period of time? If implicit normative evaluations are formed through exposure to most people's beliefs or preferences, then we expect Asian-Canadians' implicit normative evaluations of older people to become more negative over time. In contrast, implicit attitudes reflect well-practiced personal evaluations (Powell & Fazio, 1984); therefore, exposure to new cultural norms is not expected to affect implicit attitudes.

To test this reasoning, Asian-Canadian and European-Canadian participants completed an implicit attitude measure and implicit normative evaluation measure to assess their evaluations of older people. Consistent with our hypothesis, the longer Asian-Canadians stay in Canada, the more negative their implicit normative evaluation became. In contrast, implicit attitudes were not affected by exposure to Canadian culture. This pattern of results suggests that implicit attitudes and normative evaluations are formed in a different way. In addition, this study provides evidence of further discriminatory validity between implicit attitudes and normative evaluations by showing that exposure to Canadian culture predicted implicit normative evaluations but not implicit attitudes.

We also examined how cultures define appropriate behavior and how these norms affect behavior. For example, in our society (and in Asian society as well) people believe that they should eat vegetables and avoid eating fatty foods (e.g., chips) because vegetables are healthy. Individuals' preferences, however, for chips versus vegetables may not always be consistent with what the culture prescribes.

When determining what to eat, do people follow their own attitudes or cultural norms? Theorizing on culture and self-construal (Fiske, Kitayama, Markus, & Nisbett, 1998; Lehman, Chiu, & Schaller, 2004; Markus & Kitayama, 1991, 1994) has shown that the type of culture that one is exposed to determines the importance of attitudes versus normative evaluations in predicting behavior. Specifically, individualist cultures emphasize autonomy and uniqueness. Thus, internal attributes, such as one's goals, values, or attitudes have a strong influence in guiding behavior. In contrast, collectivist cultures emphasize relationships with others. Therefore, social roles, expectations, or cultural norms have a stronger influence in guiding behavior (Fiske et al., 1998; Lehman, Chiu, & Schaller, 2004; Markus & Kitayama, 1994). Based on this research, we expected that attitudes would be a stronger predictor of behavior for European-Canadians than for Asian-Canadians. In contrast, normative evaluations would be a stronger predictor for Asian-Canadians than for European-Canadians. To test this reasoning with implicit attitudes and implicit normative evaluations we conducted a study in which we examined people's food choices while they had limited cognitive resources.

We first had Asian-Canadian and European-Canadian participants complete an implicit attitude measure and an implicit normative evaluation measure about chips and vegetables before coming to the lab. The order of the measures was counterbalanced and separated by at least 4 days. When participants came to the lab they were told that the purpose of the study was to examine the relation between typing speed and hand strength. Therefore, they were asked to complete a typing task and squeeze a handgrip as long as they could, repeating this exercise twice with each hand. The typing task was bogus for the purpose of the cover story to get participants to do the handgrip exercise. After participants squeezed the handgrip, presumably they were in an ego-depleted mental state (i.e., mentally fatigued). Research on automaticity shows that automatic processes predict behavior better than deliberative processes when one's cognitive resources are limited (Bargh, 1994). To limit cognitive resources, we tired out participants by having them squeeze a handgrip (Muraven, Tice, & Baumeister, 1998).

Finally, participants were asked to taste "new dip products" using chips and vegetables in a supposedly unrelated "marketing research." Our dependent variable was the amount of chips or vegetables that participants ate. Consistent with our hypothesis, implicit attitudes were a stronger predictor of eating behavior for European-Canadians than for Asian-Canadians. For both groups, the more positive their implicit attitudes toward vegetables were, the more vegetables they ate in the lab. Similarly, implicit normative evaluations predicted eating behavior for Asian-Canadians such that the more positive their implicit normative evaluations of vegetables were, the more vegetables they ate. Interestingly, implicit normative evaluations predicted eating behavior for European-Canadians in the opposite direction. Specifically, the more positive their implicit normative evaluations of vegetables were, the less vegetables they ate.

This pattern of results is consistent with cross-cultural differences in independent and interdependent self-construals. In individualist cultures, people are concerned about expressing their own ideas and behaving consistently with their intentions; therefore, they are less likely to be influenced by what other people think (Markus & Kitayama, 1994). In contrast, in collectivist cultures, collective goals and group harmony are valued; therefore, in these cultures, people are more likely to conform to cultural norms (Markus & Kitayama, 1991, 1994; Triandis, 1989). Furthermore, conformity has different meanings or implications in individualist cultures and in collectivist cultures. Nonconformity is interpreted as uniqueness in individualist cultures, whereas in collectivist cultures, the same behavior is interpreted as deviation (Kim & Markus, 1999). Therefore, in individualist cultures, conformity is not perceived as positively as in collectivist cultures. The differences in the influence of implicit cultural norms on behavior may reflect these differences in cultural ideals and self-construals.

SUMMARY AND REMAINING QUESTIONS

Together the results of the studies described in this chapter provide compelling evidence that although implicit attitudes and implicit normative evaluations are both important constructs and predict meaningful behaviors, they are different constructs and predict behaviors in different situations. Both implicit attitudes and implicit normative evaluations are most likely to affect behavior when cognitive resources are scarce and/or when conscious deliberation is at a minimum. Implicit attitudes, however, are most likely to affect behavior when actions are taken individually and are focused on the individual self. In contrast, implicit normative evaluations are most likely to affect behavior when concerns about the group are high and the current research has shown that implicit normative evaluations can have important effects on discrimination, career aspirations, collective action, and health behaviors, and these affects are over and above the effects of implicit attitudes and explicit norms.

Despite the progress in understanding implicit normative evaluations described above a number of questions remain about the construct. First, when members of stereotyped or devalued groups develop implicit normative evaluations about their group, when will they be positive and when will they take on the negative evaluations of society? In the studies we report a number of groups had positive implicit normative evaluations of their group, but others developed more negative implicit normative evaluations. Why the discrepancy? We reason that although people are motivated to protect their social identity and this motivation often influences their implicit normative evaluations of their group, it is a motivation that is still subject to the constraints of reality. If people are isolated from other group members and persistently face negative evaluations from others in their environment—as is the case for the female engineers we studied—then it seems likely that the motivation to maintain a positive social identity will not be enough to lead to positive implicit normative evaluations about one's group. Consistent with this reasoning we find in a separate sample of Muslim students on the campus that the fewer Muslim friends they have the more negative are their implicit normative evaluations about Muslims.

Second, how do implicit attitudes and implicit normative evaluations affect one another? In our research we consistently find a small but reliable relation between implicit attitudes and implicit normative evaluations. Does one construct affect the other, perhaps in certain situations? We believe this is an interesting question for future research.

Third, how do discrepancies in implicit attitudes and implicit normative evaluations affect behavior? If someone has a positive implicit attitude about their group, but a negative implicit normative evaluation, what would be the consequences?

We suspect that such persons might be particularly threatened by negative evaluations from members of other groups and may be particularly motivated to improve the circumstances of their group.

Despite, and perhaps because of, these unanswered questions we believe that the constructs of implicit attitudes and implicit normative evaluations hold great promise in capturing how important thoughts become automatic. We believe they represent the evaluative associations that develop as people take on two fundamental tasks—understanding their world, and fitting in with their group. As such, it is not surprising that both constructs powerfully predict meaningful behaviors.

REFERENCES

Bargh, J. A. (1994). The four horsemen of automaticity: Awareness, intention, efficiency, and control in social cognition. In R. S. Wyer Jr. & T. K. Srull (Eds.), *Handbook of social cognition* (2nd ed., pp. 1–40). Hillsdale, NJ: Erlbaum.

Bell, A. E., Spencer, S. J., Iserman, E., & Logel, C. E. R. (2003). Stereotype threat and women's performance in engineering. *Journal of Engineering Education, 92*(4), 307–312.

Correll, J., Park, B., Judd, C. M., & Wittenbrink, B. (2002). The police officer's dilemma: Using ethnicity to disambiguate potentially threatening individuals. *Journal of Personality and Social Psychology, 83*(6), 1314–1329.

Correll, J., Park, B., Judd, C. M., Wittenbrink, B., Sadler, M. S., & Keesee, T. (2007). Across the thin blue line: Police officers and racial bias in the decision to shoot. *Journal of Personality and Social Psychology, 92*(6), 1006–1023.

Crandall, C. S., Eshleman, A., & O'Brien, L. (2002). Social norms and the expression and suppression of prejudice: The struggle for internalization. *Journal of Personality and Social Psychology, 82*(3), 359–378.

Dovidio, J. F., & Gaertner, S. L. (1998). On the nature of contemporary prejudice: The causes, consequences, and challenges of aversive racism. In J. L. Eberhardt & S. T. Fiske (Eds.), *Confronting racism: The problem and the response* (pp. 3–32). Thousand Oaks, CA: Sage.

Dovidio, J. F., & Gaertner, S. L. (2000). Aversive racism and selection decisions: 1989 and 1999. *Psychological Science, 11*(4), 315–319.

Dovidio, J. F., Kawakami, K., & Gaertner, S. L. (2002). Implicit and explicit prejudice and interracial interaction. *Journal of Personality and Social Psychology, 82*(1), 62–68.

Dovidio, J. F., Kawakami, K., Johnson, C., Johnson, B., & Howard, A. (1997). On the nature of prejudice: Automatic and controlled processes. *Journal of Experimental Social Psychology, 33*(5), 510–540.

Engineers Canada. (2007). *Women in engineering*. Retrieved August 22, 2007, from http://www.engineerscanada.ca/e/pr_women.cfm

Fein, S., & Spencer, S. J. (1997). Prejudice as self-image maintenance: Affirming the self through derogating others. *Journal of Personality and Social Psychology, 73*, 31–44.

Fiske, A. P., Kitayama, S., Markus, H. R., & Nisbett, R. E. (1998). *The cultural matrix of social psychology*. New York: McGraw-Hill.

Kim, H., & Markus, H. R. (1999). Deviance or uniqueness, harmony or conformity? A cultural analysis. *Journal of Personality and Social Psychology, 77*, 785–800.

Lehman, D. R., Chiu, C., & Schaller, M. (2004). Psychology and culture. *Annual Review of Psychology, 55*, 689–714.

Logel, C., Walton, G. M., Spencer, S. J., Iserman, E. C., von Hippel, W., & Bell, A. (2009). Interacting with sexist men triggers social identity threat among female engineers. *Journal of Personality and Social Psychology, 96*, 1089–1103.

Luhtanen R., & Crocker, J. (1992). A collective self-esteem scale: Self-evaluation of one's social identity. *Personality and Social Psychology Bulletin, 18*, 302–318.

Markus, H. R., & Kitayama, S. (1991). Culture and the self: Implications for cognition, emotion, and motivation. *Psychological Review, 98*, 224–253.

Markus, H. R., & Kitayama, S. (1994). A collective fear of the collective: Implications for selves and theories of selves. *Personality and Social Psychology Bulletin, 20*, 568–579.

Muraven, M., Tice, D. M., & Baumeister, R. F. (1998). Self-control as a limited resource: Regulatory depletion patterns. *Journal of Personality and Social Psychology, 74*, 774–789.

Nelson, T. D. (2005). Ageism: Prejudice against our feared future self. *Journal of Social Issues, 61*, 207–221.

Olson, M. A., & Fazio, R. H. (2004). Reducing the influence of extrapersonal associations on the Implicit Association Test: Personalizing the IAT. *Journal of Personality and Social Psychology, 86*, 653–667.

Pascarella, E. T., Whitt, E. J., Edison, M. I., & Nora, A. (1997). Women's perceptions of a "chilly climate" and their cognitive outcomes during the first year of college. *Journal of College Student Development, 38*(2), 109–124.

Powell, M. C., & Fazio, R. H. (1984). Attitude accessibility as a function of repeated attitudinal expression. *Personality and Social Psychology Bulletin, 10*(1), 139–148.

Quinn, D. M., & Spencer, S. J. (2001). The interference of stereotype threat with women's generation of mathematical problem-solving strategies. *Journal of Social Issues, 57*, 55–71.

Rudman, L. A. (2004). Sources of implicit attitudes. *Current Directions in Psychological Science, 13*(2), 79–82.

Sherman, D. K., Kinias, Z., Major, B., Kim, H. S., & Prenovost, M. (2007). The group as a resource: Reducing biased attributions for group success and failure via group affirmation. *Personality and Social Psychology Bulletin, 33*, 1100–1112.

Son Hing, L. S., Li, W., & Zanna, M. P. (2002). Inducing hypocrisy to reduce prejudicial responses among aversive racists. *Journal of Experimental Social Psychology, 38*(1), 71–78.

Spencer, S. J., Steele, C. M., & Quinn, D. M. (1999). Stereotype threat and women's math performance. *Journal of Experimental Social Psychology, 35*, 4–28.

Steele, C. M. (1997). A threat in the air: How stereotypes shape intellectual identity and performance. *American Psychologist, 52*, 613–629.

Sung, K. (2001). Elder respect: Exploration of ideals and forms in East Asia. *Journal of Aging Studies, 15*, 13–26.

Tajfel, H., & Turner, J. C. (1979). An integrative theory of intergroup conflict. In W. G. Austin & S. Worchel (Eds.), *The social psychology of intergroup relations*. Monterey, CA: Brooks/Cole.

Triandis, H. C. (1989). The self and social behavior in differing cultural contexts. *Psychological Review, 96*, 506–520.

Walton, G. M., Logel, C., Peach, J., Spencer, S. J., & Zanna, M. P. (2010) [An intervention to reduce stereotype threat in first-year engineering students]. Unpublished data, University of Waterloo.

7

Operative and Meta-Attitudinal Manifestations of Attitude Accessibility
Two Different Constructs, Not Two Measures of the Same Construct

ALLYSON L. HOLBROOK AND JON A. KROSNICK

Psychology has a long history of studying the workings of the human mind by asking research participants to describe their thoughts, feelings, and preferences. In the arena of attitude research, the most popular measures have relied on participants to describe their evaluations of objects via explicit measures (e.g., Likert, 1932; Osgood, Suci, & Tanenbaum, 1957; Thurstone, 1927a, 1927b). In contrast, researchers in many areas of psychology have gauged psychological processes and constructs indirectly, often by observing behaviors in a controlled environment (e.g., Bargh, Chen, & Burrows, 1996; Lieberman, Solomon, Greenberg, & McGregor, 1999). In the attitude domain, recent years have seen a surge of interest in implicit measures, such as the Implicit Association Test (Greenwald, McGhee, & Schwartz, 1998), Payne, Cheng, Govorun, and Stewart's (2005) affect misattribution paradigm, and Fazio's (1995) affective priming paradigm. These measures typically involve assessing aspects of task performance that are not under conscious control and that do not make participants overtly aware that their attitudes are being measured. Researchers interested in assessing attitudes have studied this distinction extensively (e.g., Fazio, Jackson, Dunton, & Williams, 1995; Greenwald & Banaji, 1995; Greenwald et al., 2002).

Paralleling the distinction between explicit and implicit measures of attitudes is a similar distinction in the attitude strength arena of "meta-attitudinal" (MA) versus "operative" (OP) indices. MA measures have been defined as people's "impressions of their own attitudes," whereas OP measures are measures that are "linked to the judgment processes responsible for attitude responses" (Bassili,

1996, p. 638). Our goal in this chapter is to broaden the implicit/explicit literature by exploring the operative/meta-level distinction with regard to the accessibility of attitudes. Specifically, we gauged whether meta-accessibility and operative accessibility reflect a single underlying construct or two distinct constructs and whether they have different impact in regulating the influence of attitudes on judgment and behavior.

CONSCIOUS EXPERIENCE

Throughout the history of psychology, beliefs about the role of conscious experience have varied widely. One perspective proposes that conscious experience is the most important aspect of psychology: "The question is not what you look at, but what you see" (Thoreau, 1993). Indeed, the earliest empirical research in experimental psychology relied heavily on introspection: Research participants described their conscious experiences in response to stimuli that were controlled by the researcher (e.g., Titchener, 1912; Wundt, 1897/1987).

This view did not survive unchallenged. Philosophers and psychologists alike questioned the notion that a person could be both observer and the object of observation (Comte, 1830–1842), and the pendulum swung far in the opposite direction when behaviorists argued that "what the psychologists have hitherto called thought is in short nothing but talking to ourselves" (Watson, 1924, p. 8) and that "mental life and the world in which it is lived are inventions" (Skinner, 1974, p. 36).

Currently, psychology thinks about mental processes and people's conscious awareness of these processes as related, parallel systems. For example, when asked to make a judgment or evaluate an object, people not only retrieve relevant information from memory, but they also have thoughts about the process of retrieval and about the information they have retrieved, or thoughts about their own thoughts. An example of a theory that takes consciousness into account is the meta-cognition model (Nelson, 1996), which makes a distinction between "object-level" cognitions about an outside object or stimulus and "meta-level" cognitions, which are thoughts about object level cognitions. These two levels of thought can occur simultaneously and may influence each other. Object-level cognition can influence meta-level cognition to the extent that people are able to *monitor* object-level processes. Furthermore, meta-level processes can influence object-level cognition by *controlling* decisions and judgments (Metcalfe & Shimamura, 1994; Nelson, 1996). However, monitoring of object-level processes or constructs may not always be possible or complete, leading to biased or inaccurate meta-level perceptions. This distinction is related to the distinctions that have been made between implicit and explicit constructs (Fazio, 1995; Kitayama & Rarasawa, 1997) and conscious and unconscious mental processes (Jacoby, Toth, & Yonelinas, 1993).

ATTITUDE STRENGTH

In this chapter, we seek to advance understanding of such distinctions with a focus on the notion of attitude strength. Considerable research has demonstrated that some attitudes are difficult to change and strongly influence thoughts and behaviors, whereas other attitudes are easy to change and have little influence. This distinction has been defined as a difference in attitude strength. Strong attitudes are those that are resistant to change, persist over time, and influence behavior and cognition (Petty & Krosnick, 1995).

Resistance. Resistance is perhaps the most studied defining feature of strong attitudes and has most often been examined by assessing attitude change or persuasion (e.g., Mutz, Sniderman, & Brody, 1996; Petty & Cacioppo, 1986). Resistance refers to the attitude's ability to withstand attack. Strong attitudes are less likely to change in response to a persuasive message or processes shown to change attitudes (e.g., listing the reasons for one's attitude). Although typically measured by assessing attitudes at two times and calculating change or by comparing a treatment and control group in an experiment, researchers have also measured meta-resistance by asking people how likely they would be to change their attitudes or by asking how much they had changed them in response to persuasion.

Impact on behavior. A second feature of strong attitudes is that they influence behavior (Boninger et al., 1995; Fazio, Chen, McDonel, & Sherman, 1982). Attitudes may influence behavior in at least two ways. First, attitudes may influence the decision of whether or not to act. Strong attitudes presumably motivate action, whereas weak attitudes do not. Second, attitudes may influence the extent to which chosen actions are attitude-consistent, such that stronger attitudes may result in more attitude-consistent behavior.

Information processing. Strong attitudes also influence cognition, such as the processing of information in one's environment. Broadly, attitude strength may influence people's motivation or interest in acquiring attitude-relevant information. Furthermore, because people have a limited capacity to attend to and remember information, we must often choose among a variety of possibilities. When cognitively busy or overloaded, the process of choosing which information to attend to and remember may happen automatically, and people may not be aware of its occurrence. Strong attitudes may also direct attention under such circumstances.

Perceptions of attitude-relevant information. Strong attitudes may also influence people's perceptions of attitude-relevant information. For example, strong attitudes may influence perceptions of the attitudes of others. The false consensus effect is the tendency for people to overestimate the proportion of others who share their opinions (Marks & Miller, 1987). The false consensus effect may occur for a number of reasons: because one's own attitude is salient when making a judgment about the attitudes of others (Marks & Miller, 1987) or is used as an anchor when judging others' attitudes (Davis, Hoch, & Ragsdale, 1986); because people selectively affiliate with others who share their opinions (Berscheid & Walster, 1978); because believing that others share one's opinion reinforces the belief that one's attitudes are correct (Marks & Miller, 1987); because we project "good qualities" (in this case our attitudes) on liked others (the evaluation principle; Sherman, Chassin, Presson, & Agostinelli, 1984); because people attribute their own attitudes to situational factors (e.g., Jones & Nisbett, 1971) and may perceive that the same situational factors would similarly lead others to have similar attitudes; or because people may interpret the attitude object differently (i.e., "differential object construal"; Gilovich,

1990), which may affect how people report their own attitudes and others'. Many of these processes may be stronger when the attitude involved is stronger.

Influence on judgments. Strong attitudes may also influence evaluations to a greater extent than do weak attitudes. For example, people evaluate candidates on the basis of many considerations, including candidates' positions on policy issues. People like a candidate to the extent that the candidate's attitude on an issue is similar to their own (Downs, 1957), consistent with the more general finding that people like similar others more than dissimilar others (Byrne, 1961, 1971). However, not every person uses every issue equally to evaluate candidates. Some issues are weighted more heavily than others (Krosnick, 1988, 1990), and attitude strength is revealed by the extent to which people use an issue to evaluate a candidate.

THE CURRENT INVESTIGATION

Research Questions

In this chapter, we pull together the ideas and literatures reviewed thus far by investigating the meta/operative distinction regarding accessibility, which is one aspect of attitudes thought to be related to their strength. Attitudinal accessibility has usually been measured operatively, but it can also be measured meta-attitudinally. OP accessibility can be defined as the speed with which an attitude can be retrieved from memory or constructed and reported, and has been measured using response latencies (Fazio, & Powell, 1997). MA accessibility can be defined as a person's subjective perception of the ease of retrieving an attitude from memory or constructing the attitude and can be measured by asking people how quickly their attitudes come to mind or how easy it is to bring their attitudes to mind (Bassili, 1996).

MA and OP: Same or different? We set out to determine if MA and OP measures of accessibility assessed a single construct or distinct MA and OP constructs. If people have access to the features of their attitudes, MA and OP measures of these features are likely to assess the same construct. Supporting this possibility is evidence that people may be able to accurately report some psychological constructs accurately (Mandler, 1975; Miller, 1962; Neisser, 1967), including their favorable or unfavorable evaluations of objects (Wilson, 1990). In addition to being able to describe the valence and extremity of the attitude itself, people may also have access to other attributes of their attitudes. If so, MA reports of attitude accessibility may reflect the same construct assessed by OP measures, and OP and MA measures of accessibility would then be strongly related.

However, there are reasons to believe MA and OP measures of accessibility may not be strongly related. Although people may have a summary evaluation stored in memory that is easily retrieved and reported, and they may be able to easily retrieve information from memory about the attitude object and construct an attitude, accurately describing attitude accessibility may be difficult. People may not store in memory a summary of the strength of the link between the attitude object and the evaluation, and may not be able to accurately monitor how long it takes them to retrieve an attitude when asked to report their attitude accessibility, since important distinctions are in terms of fractions of seconds.

Another reason why MA measures of attitude accessibility might be inaccurate involves the effects of reporting context. Many studies have shown that perceptions of physical constructs, such as weight, can be biased by context (e.g., Sherif & Hovland, 1961). The actual weight of a 10 lb. weight is the same regardless of whether it was lifted after a 30 lb. weight or after a 1 lb. weight, but the 10 lb. weight seems lighter in the first context than in the second. Similarly, perceptions of attitude accessibility and other psychological constructs may be changed by context, even when the construct itself remains unchanged.

Relying on people's perceptions of attitude accessibility also requires the assumption that people are willing to accurately report those perceptions. People may sometimes be motivated to construct favorable images of themselves for other people, sometimes via deceit. Considerable evidence has now accumulated documenting such systematic and intentional misrepresentation when answering questionnaires. For example, people are more willing to report socially embarrassing attitudes, beliefs, and behaviors when their reports are anonymous (Paulhus, 1984; Warner, 1965) and when respondents believe researchers have other access to information about the truth of their thoughts and actions (Sigall & Page, 1971). Thus, some people sometimes distort their answers to questions to present themselves as having more socially desirable attitudes, beliefs, or behavioral histories, and the same sorts of motivations could conceivably bias reports of attitude accessibility. In the research reported here, we explored the accuracy of self-reports of accessibility.

Consequences of MA and OP accessibility. The second question addressed by the current investigation is whether MA and OP measures of accessibility have independent effects on thoughts and behaviors. Even if MA measures of accessibility are not highly related to their OP counterparts, much evidence suggests that people's subjective experiences are meaningful and consequential (Fried & Aronson, 1995; Hart, 1965; Koriat, 2000; Petty & Wegener, 1993, 1995; Wegener, Kerr, Fleming, & Petty, 2000; Zanna & Cooper, 1974). If OP and MA measures of attitude accessibility assess separate constructs, and MA measures tap meaningful and consequential subjective experiences, the two types of measures may also have distinct effects on cognition and behavior.

Hypotheses

OP accessibility seems likely to have two types of influence on behavior and cognition. First, it may influence the processes by which people choose which information in their environment to attend to, particularly when people are unable or unmotivated to attend to everything in their environment. Attitude objects associated with attitudes that are high in OP accessibility may be particularly consequential when resources do not allow deliberate processing of the information in one's environment. Individuals with attitudes toward an object that are high in OP accessibility may automatically orient toward information about it.

When people choose to attend to or are exposed to attitude-relevant information not by their own choice (e.g., in situations where they cannot make choices about allocating attention), attitudes high in OP accessibility seem likely to come to mind and to influence judgment processes. As such, these attitudes may induce biased processing and discounting of attitude-inconsistent information. Similarly, individuals high in operative accessibility may discount the attitudes of others when these attitudes are inconsistent with their own.

OP accessibility may not always be consequential. Specifically, when decisions are made via careful, thoughtful deliberation, the influence of OP accessibility may be reduced or even eliminated (Fazio, 1990).

MA accessibility. The experience of ease of performing other tasks has been found to influence a variety of types of judgments (Aarts & Dijksterhuis, 1999; Dijksterhuis, Macrae, & Haddock, 1999; Haddock, Rothman, Reber, & Schwarz, 1999; Haddock, Rothman, & Schwarz, 1996; Kelley & Lindsay, 1993; Schwarz et al., 1991; Wänke, Schwarz, & Bless, 1995; Winkielman, Schwarz, & Belli, 1998). However, there is no consensus about when ease of retrieval influences judgments. Some researchers have argued that ease primarily influences judgments when motivation to engage in effortful thought is high, and others have argued the opposite. For example, Rothman and Schwarz (1998) argued that ease influences persuasion primarily under conditions of low elaboration as a cue. Similarly, Aarts and Dijksterhuis (1999) found that ease of retrieval influenced frequency estimates, but not when participants were motivated to be accurate. However, Tormala, Petty, and Briñol (2002) and Wänke and Bless (2000) found that ease of retrieving arguments influence persuasion under conditions of high elaboration.

People may use MA accessibility (the experienced ease of attitude retrieval) as information about how strong or crystallized their attitudes are. People who feel that it is difficult for them to think of their attitude may attribute that difficulty to lack of a strong attitude toward the attitude object, so they may choose not to place much weight on the object when making decisions or choosing courses of action. In addition, perceiving a lack of strong feelings toward an object may make people believe that they cannot successfully defend their attitude, so they may not invest much effort in trying to do so.

MA accessibility's influence seems likely to be moderated by two types of factors. First, a self-perception process seems likely to require at least some conscious thought, even if a high degree of motivation to think carefully is not necessary. Thus, perception of ease seems unlikely to be used as information when judgments are made automatically. Second, MA accessibility may not inform deliberate judgments if people think that their perceptions of accessibility are not diagnostic of true accessibility. For example, if a person finds it easy to retrieve an attitude but attributes that ease to some recent situational experience rather than to chronic accessibility, he or she may not use the perception of ease when deciding whether to use the attitude.

The Present Study

To explore these possibilities, we assessed the relations of MA and OP measures of attitude accessibility to a variety of behaviors and judgments that might be affected by these strength-related attitude features. Participants in our study were undergraduate students ($N = 654$) enrolled in an introductory psychology class at Ohio State University. They came to a laboratory in groups of 5 to 15 during the fall of 2000, coinciding with the 2000 presidential campaign. Each participant completed a questionnaire individually on a computer. Participants were randomly assigned to answer questions about one target issue, either abortion or capital punishment. Data on the two issues were combined in all analyses reported below.

Each questionnaire consisted of two primary sections. In the first, attention to attitude-relevant information, which is called "orienting," was measured via a procedure adapted from Roskos-Ewoldson and Fazio (1992). Participants were shown a list of nine words for 2 seconds and asked to recall as many of them as they could. Four such lists were shown to each participant. Recall of information about the target issue was a measure of whether participants noticed the information. Choices of political issues about which to learn new information were also assessed. Participants ranked pieces of information on many topics from those they would most like to learn to those they would least like to learn. Each list contained one piece of information about the target issue. Participants were also asked to evaluate the candidates running in the 2000 presidential election (George W. Bush and Al Gore).

In the second section of the study, participants answered questions about the target issue. First, they answered four questions to assess their attitudes toward the policy on 7-point rating scales. Response latencies were measured for each of the four attitude reports as an OP measure of attitude accessibility. Immediately after reporting their attitudes, participants reported the speed and ease with which their attitudes had come to mind. This was our measure of MA accessibility. Next, participants' perceptions of others' attitudes on the issue were assessed to measure the magnitude of the false consensus effect, and participants reported their perceptions of George W. Bush's and Al Gore's attitudes toward the policy. Participants reported whether they had engaged in specific activist behaviors to express their attitudes on the issue, how involved they had been in activities related to the issue generally, their interest in learning more about the issue, and their perceptions of the amount and direction of bias in media coverage of the issue.

Finally, resistance to attitude change was measured. Participants were asked how resistant they perceived their attitudes to be, which was our MA measure. OP resistance was assessed by measuring attitude change in response to a persuasive message. Participants read a counterattitudinal essay, reported their thoughts about the essay, and reported their attitudes a second time.

Analysis Strategy

Multiple measures of each construct of interest were administered, allowing us to conduct latent variable covariance structure modeling (Jöreskog & Sörbom, 1996). This approach has a number of advantages: It allowed us to test the fit of a hypothesized model to the observed data. For example, we assessed the goodness of fit of a model in which MA and OP measures of attitude accessibility are assumed to assess a single accessibility construct. We also gauged the effects of latent variables representing MA and OP accessibility on latent variables representing thoughts and actions. Using this analytic approach reduces the distorting influence of measurement error (Alwin, 1974; Jöreskog, 1974; Kenny, 1979; Widaman, 1985).

RESULTS

Relation between MA and OP measures of attitude accessibility. To examine the relation between MA and OP measures of accessibility, two models were tested using confirmatory factor analysis. First, a model in which all MA and OP measures were specified to be indicators of a single latent construct was tested. The fit of this model was assessed and compared to that of one in which the MA measures were specified to be indicators of one latent construct, the OP measures were specified to be indicators of a second latent construct, and the two latent constructs were allowed to covary. If the second model fit the data considerably better than the first model did, that would suggest that the two constructs are distinct.

Effects on thoughts and behavior. For each measure of thought or behavior, the parameters of four covariance structure models were estimated, always controlling for attitude extremity (see, e.g., Thompson, Zanna, & Griffin, 1995; Zanna & Rempel, 1988). The first model gauged the conclusions that might be drawn if MA and OP measures of accessibility were assumed to reflect a single construct, based on the assumption that MA and OP measures of accessibility are interchangeable and can therefore be combined in measuring a single latent construct.

In past studies, most researchers have used either MA *or* OP measures of accessibility. To assess whether one would draw different conclusions from using one of the two types of measures rather than the other, the parameters of two other models were estimated, in which accessibility was assessed only by MA measures or only by OP measures. Next, two latent variables indicated by MA and OP measures were used to predict the thought or behavior simultaneously in a single model, gauging the impact of each measure (MA and OP) while controlling for the other.

Model fit was assessed by three standard statistics: the ratio of the χ^2 statistic to the degrees of freedom, the root mean square error of approximation (RMSEA), and the goodness-of-fit index (GFI).

Relation between MA and OP accessibility. A confirmatory factor analysis in which all seven measures of accessibility were constrained to be indicators of a single latent factor did not fit the data well, suggesting that the seven measures of accessibility did not reflect a single latent construct. A two-factor confirmatory factor model fit the data well, and the relation between MA and OP accessibility was not significantly different from zero. These results suggest that OP accessibility and MA accessibility are two separate, *unrelated* constructs. However, even if measures of OP and MA accessibility appear to assess separate constructs, OP and MA accessibility may have the same effects on thinking and actions.

Resistance. Next, the relation of OP and MA attitude accessibility to attitude resistance was tested. Analyses predicting OP resistance indicated that MA and OP measures of accessibility simultaneously both were significant and positive predictors of resistance: Greater accessibility was associated with greater resistance. When predicting resistance measured meta-attitudinally (by asking participants how likely they thought they would be to change their attitude), MA and OP measures of accessibility both had significant, positive effects on resistance. Thus, MA and OP accessibility each predicted unique variance in both OP and MA resistance.

Activism. When the amount of specific attitude-expressive activist behaviors that people had performed was predicted, MA accessibility was unrelated to activism, but OP accessibility was significantly and negatively related to activism, such that greater accessibility was associated with *less* activism. Likewise, when predicting answers to more general questions about how involved participants had been in activities related to the issue, MA accessibility was unrelated to activism, but OP accessibility was negatively related to activism, such that higher accessibility was related to less activism.

Information processing. Neither MA nor OP accessibility was related to general expressed interest in learning attitude-relevant information, nor was either measure of accessibility related to participants' actual choices of which specific pieces of information to obtain. When predicting orienting to attitude-relevant information, OP accessibility was significantly and positively related to orienting (as in past research), but MA accessibility was not.

The false consensus effect. MA accessibility was unrelated to the magnitude of the false consensus effect, but the latter was significantly and positively predicted by OP accessibility, indicating that people with more accessible attitudes perceived that a larger percentage of others agreed with them.

Perceptions of news media bias. A measure of perceived media bias was constructed, and we explored whether accessibility moderated the relation of attitudes to this index. In fact, OP accessibility moderated the impact of attitudes on perceived media bias, but MA accessibility did not. Individuals with more OP accessible attitudes perceived the media to be more biased against their own positions than those with less OP accessible attitudes.

Candidate evaluations. To explore the impact of attitude accessibility on the ingredients of political candidate evaluations, two variables were computed. First, candidate preference was measured by subtracting participants' attitudes toward George W. Bush from their attitudes toward Al Gore. Second, an issue discrepancy variable was calculated by subtracting the absolute value of the difference between participants' position on the issue and George Bush's position on the issue from the absolute value of the difference between participants' position and Al Gore's position. Positive values on this variable meant that a participant's attitude was more similar to George Bush's than to Al Gore's. MA accessibility marginally significantly moderated this relation, but OP accessibility did not. Higher MA accessibility was associated with more use of the issue in evaluating the candidates.

DISCUSSION

Factor Structure

Our confirmatory factor analyses suggest that MA and OP measures of accessibility assess distinct constructs. A model in which MA and OP measures were specified to be indicators of a single latent factor fit the data atrociously, but a model including separate MA and OP factors fit the data well. In this model, the correlation between MA and OP accessibility was not significantly different from zero, suggesting that people may not be aware of or able to report the accessibility of their own attitudes accurately.

Impact on Thoughts and Action

OP and MA accessibility had unique effects on thinking and action. The consequences of MA and OP accessibilities were sensible and interpretable when the conceptual differences between the constructs were considered.

OP accessibility. As expected, OP accessibility led to greater resistance (both MA and OP), perhaps via biased processing, as Fazio and Williams (1986) suggested. OP accessibility also led to greater false consensus and greater perceived hostile media bias, perhaps also via biased processing of information about other's attitudes (i.e., discounting of attitudes that are inconsistent with one's own). Attitudes high in OP accessibility directed automatic information acquisition, but OP accessibility was unassociated with more deliberate information acquisition. OP accessibility did not shape the ingredients of candidate evaluations, suggesting that this process may be a more deliberate, thoughtful one.

Surprisingly, higher OP accessibility was associated with *less* attitude-expressive activism. Because activism often requires the allocation of limited resources (such as time and money), deciding to engage in such behavior seems likely to be the result of deliberate thought. As such, no association between OP accessibility and activism would be expected. But instead, we saw consistent negative associations. This finding raises a possibility that has not been considered in the literature to date: that OP accessibility may inhibit attitude-expressive behavior. A useful focus for future research will be exploring if this occurs.

MA accessibility. MA accessibility was positively associated with both MA and OP resistance, consistent with the hypothesis that individuals who believe it is easy for them to think of their attitude were motivated by this belief to defend their attitude. Additionally, MA accessibility was positively associated with using candidates' positions on an issue to evaluate them. This suggests that perceived ease of retrieval may have led people to choose to place weight on the issue. MA accessibility was not related to perceptions of hostile media bias, the false consensus effect, information seeking behavior, or activism, suggesting that attitude impact on these phenomena may happen automatically rather than deliberately.

This initial foray into MA accessibility thus provides some evidence that it is a consequential construct. However, because it is unassociated with OP accessibility, understanding the origins of MA accessibility will be an important focus for further developing this construct conceptually. Identifying the causes of MA accessibility may also help to further development of hypotheses about its nature and consequences.

This zero correlation has especially important implications for one interesting line of argument that has been put forth in the past: that attitude accessibility may be a cause of attitude importance. For example, Roese and Olson (1994) suggested that when people are asked to report the amount of personal importance they attach to an attitude, they may do so in part by noting how quickly the attitude comes to mind. "If my attitude comes immediately to mind when I search for it," people might think, "then it must be important to me. But if my attitude comes to mind only after I dredge my memory for a while, then it must not be a very important attitude to me." This perspective presumes that people have relatively weak senses of the importance they attach to attitudes and objects (e.g., Bassili, 1996) and therefore engage in self-perception-like processes (Bem, 1967, 1972) in order to resolve these ambiguities. Furthermore, this perspective presumes that people perceive the accessibility of their attitudes and use those perceptions when making some judgments.

Although Roese and Olson (1994) reported evidence that they said indicated that OP accessibility was indeed a cause of reports of attitude importance, these investigators made an accidental computational error, yielding their analyses uninformative. And when Bizer and Krosnick (2001) conducted proper tests of the hypothesis using Roese and Olson's general approach, evidence disconfirmed the claim that OP accessibility is a cause of personal importance ratings.

But perhaps it is too soon to completely reject Roese and Olson's hypothesis on the basis of that evidence. Although Bizer and Krosnick's (2001) evidence did disconfirm the claim that OP accessibility causes importance, the present study's evidence that OP and MA accessibility are completely uncorrelated with one another raises an alternative possibility: Perhaps MA accessibility is a cause of importance. If this is so, then there may be some truth to Roese and Olson's intuition, though along slightly different lines than they were thinking. Investigating this possibility could be done by manipulating MA accessibility and exploring the impact of such a manipulation on importance ratings. Our findings suggest that Roese and Olson's manipulation of OP accessibility (via repeated attitude expression) did not necessarily increase MA accessibility. So future studies might attempt to do so and then test the notion that people infer the personal importance of an attitude based partly on their perceptions of the ease with which they can retrieve that attitude.

Relation to Past Research

In contrast to past research concluding that "the distinction between operative and meta-attitude measures is more about the method of measurement than about the property being measured" (Bassili, 1996, p. 648), we found that both MA and OP measures of attitude accessibility explained unique variance in thinking and action. Thus, for attitude accessibility, the sharp empirical distinction between OP and MA measures is more about distinct constructs being measured than about the methods of measurement being different ways to tap the same construct. Unlike past work, we examined a broad array of measures of uses and impact of attitudes, and we used multiple measures of all constructs rather than a single indicator approach. So there is reason to have confidence in our conclusion in this regard.

Implications for Measurement

The finding that MA and OP accessibility are different constructs has implications for the way that strength-related attitude features, and psychological constructs in general, should be measured. Specifically, our results suggest that psychologists should be careful to choose their measures based on their conceptualizations and theories, not simply on convenience. Psychologists who rely on people's perceptions of their own psychological constructs should perhaps reconsider if they are interested in the underlying psychological constructs themselves. If however, researchers are interested in people's *perceptions* per se, MA measures are preferable. Thus, researchers who rely only on OP measures may be missing part of the picture, just as researchers who rely only on MA measures may be.

Perhaps more importantly, our research has implications for the way psychologists think about psychological constructs. Reports of people's perceptions should not necessarily be treated as interchangeable with less subjective, more direct measures of psychological constructs. In developing theories, designing studies, and interpreting results, psychologists should be careful to be consistent in how they conceptualize the psychological constructs being studied. Furthermore, combining measures that may assess different constructs may lead to faulty conclusions.

Rather than throwing out self-reports of people's perceptions as measures of personality characteristics, attitudes, thoughts, or emotions and trying to use measures that do not reflect perceptions, our research suggests that to get the full picture of how people's minds work, researchers should use both types of measures and study the independent effects of both.

Our evidence contributes to a growing literature showing that although meta-level perceptions are important for understanding people's judgments and behavior, even when they do not match their object-level counterparts (see Bless & Forgas, 2000, for a review). The importance of meta-level perceptions has been documented in a range of substantive areas, including attitudes, stereotyping, and prejudice. We found that both meta-attitudinal perceptions and operative assessments of attitude accessibility influence people's thoughts and actions. In this domain, then, attitudinal processes and perceptions of those processes appear to be equally important elements of comprehensive theory building.

REFERENCES

Aarts, H., & Dijksterhuis, A. (1999). How often did I do it? Experienced ease of retrieval and frequency estimates of past behavior. *Acta Psychologica, 103*, 77–89.

Alwin, D. F. (1974). Approaches to the interpretation of relationships in the multi-trait-multimethod matrix. In H. L. Costner (Ed.), *Sociological methodology 1973–1974* (pp. 79–105). San Francisco: Jossey-Bass.

Bargh, J. A., Chen, M., & Burrows, L. (1996). Automaticity of social behavior: Direct effects of trait construct and stereotype activation on action. *Journal of Personality and Social Psychology, 71*, 230–244.

Bassili, J. N. (1996). Meta-judgmental versus OP indexes of psychological attributes: The case of measures of attitude strength. *Journal of Personality and Social Psychology, 71*, 637–653.

Bem, D. J. (1972). Self-perception theory. In L. Berkowitz (Ed.), *Advances in Experimental Social Psychology*, (Vol. 6, pp. 1–62). New York: Academic Press.

Berscheid, E., & Walster, E. H. (1978). *Interpersonal attraction*. Reading, MA: Addison Wesley.

Bizer, G. Y., & Krosnick, J. A. (2001). Exploring the structure of strength-related attitude features: The relation between attitude importance and attitude accessibility. *Journal of Personality and Social Psychology, 81*, 566–586.

Bless, H., & Forgas, J. P. (2000). *The message within: The role of subjective experience in social cognition and behavior.* Manheim, Germany: Manheim University Press.

Boninger, D. S., Krosnick, J. A., Berent, M. K., & Fabrigar, L. R. (1995). The causes and consequences of attitude importance. In R. E. Petty and J. A. Krosnick (Eds.), *Attitude Strength: Antecedents and Consequences.* Hillsdale, NJ: Erlbaum.

Byrne, D. (1961). Interpersonal attraction and attitude similarity. *Journal of Abnormal Social Psychology, 62*, 713–715.

Byrne, D. (1971). *The attraction paradigm.* New York: Academic Press.

Comte, A. (1830–1842). *Cours de philosophie positive* (6 vols.). Paris: Bachelier.

Davis, H. L., Hoch, S. J., & Ragsdale, E. K. E. (1986). An anchoring and adjustment model of spousal predictions. *Journal of Consumer Research, 13*, 25–37.

Dijksterhuis, A., Macrae, C. N., & Haddock, G. (1999). When recollective experiences matter: Subjective ease of retrieval and stereotyping. *Personality and Social Psychology Bulletin, 25*, 760–768.

Downs, A. (1957). *An economic theory of democracy.* New York: Harper & Row.

Fazio, R. H. (1990). Multiple processes by which attitudes guide behavior: The MODE model as an integrative framework. In M. P. Zanna (Ed.), *Advances in experimental social psychology* (Vol. 23, pp. 75–109). New York: Academic Press.

Fazio, R. H. (1995). Attitudes as object-evaluation associations: Determinants, consequences, and correlates of attitude accessibility. In R. E. Petty & J. A. Krosnick (Eds.), *Attitude strength: Antecedents and consequences* (pp. 247–282). Mahwah, NJ: Erlbaum.

Fazio, R. H., Chen, J., McDonel, E. C., & Sherman, S. J. (1982). Attitude accessibility, attitude-behavior consistency, and the strength of the object-evaluation association. *Journal of Experimental Social Psychology, 18*, 339–357.

Fazio, R. H., Jackson, J. R., Dunton, B. C., & Williams, C. J. (1995). Variability in automatic activation as an unobtrusive measure of racial attitudes: A bona fide pipeline? *Journal of Personality and Social Psychology, 69*, 1013–1027.

Fazio, R. H., & Powell, M. C. (1997). On the value of knowing one's likes and dislikes: Attitude accessibility, stress, and health in college. *Psychological Science, 8*, 430–436.

Fazio, R. H., & Williams, C. J. (1986). Attitude accessibility as a moderator of the attitude-perception and attitude-behavior relations: An investigation of the 1984 presidential election. *Journal of Personality and Social Psychology, 51*, 505–514.

Fried, C. B., & Aronson, E. (1995). Hypocrisy, misattribution, and dissonance reduction. *Personality and Social Psychology Bulletin, 21*, 925–933.

Gilovich, T. (1990). Differential construal and the FCE. *Journal of Personality and Social Psychology, 59*, 623–634.

Greenwald, A. G., & Banaji, M. R. (1995). Implicit social cognition: Attitudes, self-esteem, and stereotypes. *Psychological Review, 102*, 4–27.

Greenwald, A. G., Banaji, M. R., Rudman, L. A., Farnham, S. D., Nosek, B. A., & Mellott, D. S. (2002). A unified theory of implicit attitudes, stereotypes, self-esteem, and self-concept. *Psychological Review, 109*, 3–25.

Greenwald, A. G., McGhee, D. E., & Schwartz, J. L. K. (1998). Measuring individual differences in implicit cognition: The Implicit Association Test. *Journal of Personality and Social Psychology, 74*, 1464–1480.

Haddock, G., Rothman, A. J., Reber, R., & Schwarz, N. (1999). Forming judgments of attitude certainty, intensity, and importance: The role of subjective experiences. *Personality and Social Psychology Bulletin, 25*, 771–782.

Haddock, G., Rothman, A. J., & Schwarz, N. (1996). Are (some) reports of attitude strength context dependent? *Canadian Journal of Behavioural Science, 28*, 313–316.

Hart, J. T. (1965). Memory and the feeling-of-knowing experience. *Journal of Educational Psychology, 56,* 208–216.

Jacoby, L. L., Toth, J. P., & Yonelinas, A. P. (1993). Separating conscious and unconscious influences of memory. *Journal of Experimental Psychology: General, 122,* 139–154.

Jones, E. E., & Nisbett, R. E. (1971). The actor and the observer: Divergent perceptions of the causes of behavior. In E. E. Jones, D. E. Kanouse, H. H. Kelley, R. E. Nisbett, S. Valins, & B. Weiner (Eds.), *Attribution: Perceiving the causes of behavior.* Morristown, NJ: General Learning.

Jöreskog, K. G. (1974). Analyzing psychological data by structural analysis of covariance matrices. In D. H. Krantz, R. D. Luce, R. C. Atkinson, & P. Suppes (Eds.), *Contemporary developments in mathematical psychology* (Vol. 2, pp. 1–56). San Francisco: Freeman.

Jöreskog, K. G., & Sörbom, D. (1996). *LISREL 8: User's reference guide.* Chicago: Scientific Software International.

Kelley, C. M., & Lindsay, D. S. (1993). Remembering mistaken for knowing: Ease of retrieval as a basis for confidence in answers to general knowledge volume questions. *Journal of Memory and Language, 32,* 1–24.

Kenny, D. A. (1979). *Correlation and causality.* New York: Wiley.

Kitayama, S., & Rarasawa, M. (1997). Implicit self-esteem in Japan: Name letters and birthday numbers. *Personality and Social Psychology Bulletin, 23,* 736–742.

Koriat, A. (2000). The feeling of knowing: Some metatheoretical implications for consciousness and control. *Consciousness and Cognition, 9,* 149–171.

Krosnick, J. A. (1988). The role of attitude importance in social evaluation: A study of policy preferences, presidential candidate evaluation, and voting behavior. *Journal of Personality and Social Psychology, 55,* 196–210.

Krosnick, J. A. (1990). Government policy and citizen passion: A study of issue publics in contemporary America. *Political Behavior, 12,* 59–92.

Lieberman, J. D., Solomon, S., Greenberg, J., & McGregor, H. A. (1999). A hot new way to measure aggression: Hot sauce allocation. *Aggressive Behavior, 25,* 331–348.

Likert, R. (1932). A technique for the measurement of attitudes. *Archives of Psychology, 140,* 5–53.

Mandler, G. (1975). *Mind and emotion.* New York: Wiley.

Marks, G., & Miller, N. (1987). Ten years of research on the false-consensus effect: An empirical and theoretical review. *Psychological Bulletin, 102,* 72–90.

Metcalfe, J., & Shimamura, A. P. (1994). *Metacognition: Knowing about knowing.* Cambridge, MA: MIT Press.

Miller, G. A. (1962). *Psychology: The science of mental life.* New York: Harper & Row.

Mutz, D. C., Sniderman, P. M., & Brody, R. A. (1996). *Political persuasion and attitude change.* Ann Arbor: University of Michigan Press.

Neisser, U. (1967). *Cognitive psychology.* New York: Appleton-Century-Crofts.

Nelson, T. O. (1996). Consciousness and metacognition. *American Psychologist, 51,* 102–116.

Osgood, C. E., Suci, G. J., & Tanenbaum, P. H. (1957). *The measurement of meaning.* Urbana: University of Illinois.

Paulhus, D. L. (1984). Two-component models of socially desirable responding. *Journal of Personality and Social Psychology, 46,* 598–609.

Payne, B. K., Cheng, C. M., Govorun, O., & Stewart, B. (2005). An inkblot for attitudes: Affect misattribution as implicit measurement. *Journal of Personality and Social Psychology, 89,* 277–293.

Petty, R. E., & Cacioppo, J. T. (1986). *Communication and persuasion: Central and peripheral routes to attitude change.* New York: Springer-Verlag.

Petty, R. E., & Krosnick, J. A. (1995). *Attitude strength: An overview.* Mahwah, NJ: Erlbaum.

Petty, R. E., & Wegener, D. T. (1993). Flexible correction processes in social judgment: Correcting for context-induced contrast. *Journal of Experimental Social Psychology, 29*, 137–165.

Petty, R. E., & Wegener, D. T. (1995). Flexible correction processes in social judgment: The role of naive theories in corrections for perceived bias. *Journal of Personality and Social Psychology, 68*, 36–51.

Roese, N. J., & Olson, J. M. (1994). Attitude importance as a function of repeated attitude expression. *Journal of Experimental Social Psychology, 30*, 39–51.

Roskos-Ewoldson, D. R., & Fazio, R. H. (1992). On the orienting value of attitudes: Attitude accessibility as a determinant of an object's attraction of visual attention. *Journal of Personality and Social Psychology, 63*, 198–211.

Rothman, A. J., & Schwarz, N. (1998). Constructing perceptions of vulnerability: Personal relevance and the use of experiential information in health judgments. *Personality and Social Psychology Bulletin, 24*, 1053–1064.

Schwarz, N., Bless, H., Strack, F., Klumpp, G., Rittenauer-Schatka, H., & Simons, A. (1991). Ease of retrieval as information: Another look at the availability heuristic. *Journal of Personality and Social Psychology, 61*, 195–202.

Sherif, M., & Hovland, C. I. (1961). *Social judgment: Assimilation and contrast effects in communication and attitude change*. New Haven, CT: Yale University Press.

Sherman, S. J., Chassin, L., Presson, C. C., & Agostinelli, G. (1984). The role of evaluation and similarity principles in the FCE. *Journal of Personality and Social Psychology, 47*, 1244–1262.

Sigall, H., & Page, R. (1971). Current stereotypes: A little fading, a little faking. *Journal of Personality and Social Psychology, 18*, 247–255.

Skinner, B. F. (1974). *About behaviorism*. New York: Random House.

Thompson, M. M., Zanna, M. P., & Griffin, D. W. (1995). Let's not be indifferent about (attitudinal) ambivalence. In R. E. Petty & J. A. Krosnick (Eds.), *Attitude strength: Antecedents and consequences* (pp. 361–386). Mahwah, NJ: Erlbaum.

Thoreau, H. D. (1993). *A year in Thoreau's journal: 1851*. New York: Penguin Books.

Thurstone, L. L. (1927a). A law of comparative judgment. *Psychological Review, 34*, 273–286.

Thurstone, L. L. (1927b). Psychophysical analysis. *American Journal of Psychology, 38*, 368–389.

Titchener, E. B. (1912). The schema of introspection. *American Journal of Psychology, 23*, 485–508.

Tormala, Z. L., Petty, R. E., & Briñol, P. (2002). Ease of retrieval effects in persuasion: A self-validation analysis. *Personality and Social Psychology Bulletin, 28*, 1700–1712.

Wänke, M., & Bless, H. (2000). The effects of subjective ease of retrieval on attitudinal judgments: The moderating role of processing motivation. In H. Bless & J. P. Forgas (Eds.), *The message within: The role of subjective experience in social cognition and behavior* (pp. 143–161). Philadelphia: Psychology Press.

Wänke, M., Schwarz, N., & Bless, H. (1995). The availability heuristic revisited: Experienced ease of retrieval in mundane frequency estimates. *Acta Psychologica, 89*, 83–90.

Warner, S. L. (1965). Randomized response: A survey technique for eliminating evasive answer bias. *Journal of the American Statistical Association, 60*, 63–69.

Watson, J. B. (1924). *Behaviorism*. New York: Norton.

Wegener, D. T., Kerr, N. L., Fleming, M. A., & Petty, R. E. (2000). Flexible corrections of juror judgments: Implications for jury instructions. *Psychology, Public Policy, and Law, 6*, 629–654.

Widaman, K. F. (1985). Hierarchically nested covariance structure models for multitrait–multimethod data. *Applied Psychological Measurement, 9*, 1–26.

Wilson, T. D. (1990). Self-persuasion via self-reflection. In J. Olson & M. P. Zanna (Eds.), *Self-inference processes: The Ontario symposium* (Vol. 6, pp. 43–67). Hillsdale, NJ: Erlbaum.

Winkielman, P., Schwarz, N., & Belli, R. F. (1998). The role of ease of retrieval and attribution in memory judgments: Judging your memory as worse despite recalling more events. *Psychological Science, 9,* 124–126.

Wundt, W. (1987). *Outlines of psychology* (C. H. Judd, Trans.). St. Clair Shores, MI: Scholarly Press. (Original work published 1897)

Zanna, M. P., & Cooper, J. (1974). Dissonance and the pill: An attribution approach to studying the arousal properties of dissonance. *Journal of Personality and Social Psychology, 29,* 703–709.

Zanna, M. P., & Rempel, J. K. (1988). Attitudes: A new look at an old concept. In D. Bar-Tal & A. W. Kruglanski (Eds.), *The social psychology of knowledge* (pp. 315–354). New York: Cambridge University Press.

AUTHOR NOTE

The data reported here were described in a doctoral dissertation submitted by the first author to the Ohio State University. Jon Krosnick is University Fellow at Resources for the Future. The authors would like to thank Richard Petty, Russ Fazio, and the Ohio State University Political Psychology Interest Group for their comments and suggestions. Correspondence concerning this manuscript should be addressed to Allyson L. Holbrook, Survey Research Laboratory (MC 336), University of Illinois at Chicago, Chicago, IL 60607 (e-mail: allyson@uic.edu) or Jon Krosnick, 432 McClatchy Hall, 450 Serra Mall, Stanford University, Stanford, CA 94305 (e-mail: Krosnick@stanford.edu).

8

Vicarious Cognitive Dissonance
Changing Attitudes by Experiencing Another's Pain

JOEL COOPER

Can people experience dissonance and undergo attitude change because of the actions of others? New research in the domain of cognitive dissonance suggests that the answer is yes. It has long been established that when people behave in ways that are at variance with their attitudes, they experience the unpleasant affective state of dissonance, and their attitudes change as a consequence. We now know that dissonance can also be aroused vicariously. Observers who witness others acting in a counterattitudinal manner may, under appropriate conditions, experience dissonance and be motivated to change their own attitudes.

Vicarious dissonance (Cooper & Hogg, 2007) is a novel approach at the nexus of two well-established theories in social psychology: social identity and cognitive dissonance. We propose that people experience dissonance vicariously when they observe a member of their social group behave in ways that are inconsistent with that group member's attitude. Like personal cognitive dissonance (Festinger, 1957), vicarious dissonance is experienced as an uncomfortable feeling of negative affect; it occurs when people have choices about their behavior and is heightened when behavior leads to aversive consequences. However, vicarious dissonance does not require the individual to behave inconsistently but only requires that he or she *observe* a fellow group member behaving at variance with his or her attitude. It is the ability to be motivated by the actions of a fellow group member that makes vicarious dissonance not only a fascinating phenomenon in its own right, but also makes it highly useful in creating attitude and behavior changes on a broad scale. Simply put, the counterattitudinal behavior of one member of a group has the potential to activate motivation on the part of other group members to undertake changes of their own attitudes and behaviors. In this chapter, I will present evidence that under a specified set of circumstances, this can have highly beneficial effects on health-related actions and attitudes.

FROM PERSONAL TO VICARIOUS DISSONANCE

The tenets of cognitive dissonance theory are well established in the literature. Dissonance refers to a state of discomfort that results from holding incompatible cognitions, such as smoking while aware of its adverse impact on one's health. The aversive experience of dissonance motivates efforts to reduce it (Cooper & Fazio, 1984; Harmon-Jones, Amodio, & Harmon-Jones, this volume; Losch & Cacioppo, 1990; Stone & Cooper, 2001). In a typical research study (e.g., Linder, Cooper, & Jones, 1967), participants are induced to write a statement in support of a position with which they disagree. As a result, they change their attitudes in the direction of the statement they just wrote, thereby reconciling their beliefs with their behavior and minimizing the aversiveness of the outcome. Similarly, beginning with Brehm's (1956) classic study on consumer choices, research has shown that the postdecisional consequences of making choices results in opinion change supporting the choice. Dissonance has also been shown to affect the justification of effort that has been expended in the pursuit of a goal (Aronson & Mills, 1959), which in turn has been shown to facilitate the ability of obese people to lose weight (Axsom & Cooper, 1985), of phobic participants to overcome their fears (Cooper, 1980), and of speech-anxious individuals to learn to speak more comfortably (Axsom, 1989).

No good theory remains static. Dissonance has evolved from a theory solely about cognitions in the head to a theory that is intimately involved with notions of self. One of Festinger's original and innovative insights was to conceive of the social world as a series of cognitive representations in the mind of the actor. This permitted perceptions of personal behaviors, attitudes, and emotions to coexist with perceptions of the physical and social world in determining the consonance or dissonance of a set of relationships. Aronson (1968) was perhaps the first scholar to suggest that when it comes to arousing dissonance, not all cognitions inside the head are created equal. He suggested that the special cognition of *self* must be part of the equation if dissonance is to be aroused. Similarly, Steele's (1988) theory of self-affirmation and Tesser's (1988) theory of self-evaluation maintenance placed dissonance reduction strictly in the service of protecting and enhancing the self. Stone and Cooper's (2001) "self-standards" model of dissonance, building on Cooper and Fazio's (1984) earlier "New Look" approach, strengthened the theoretical bond between dissonance and self by specifying that the self is multidimensional and that the cognitive accessibility of different aspects of the self determines how and whether a particular behavior leads to the state of cognitive dissonance

The Social Self

Recent theorizing has made clear that the self is both personal and social (Leary & Tangney, 2003; Rhodewalt & Peterson, this volume). It is about one's own personal characteristics and simultaneously about one's interconnectedness with others and with social groups (e.g., Brewer & Gardner, 1996). Because we believe the self is relevant to the dissonance process, we must broaden our understanding of dissonance to include the important aspects of self-conception based not only on individual experiences but also on our membership in social groups.

Prior research connecting the experience of cognitive dissonance to membership in social groups was sporadic at best during the formative period of dissonance research. Ironically, the first study of cognitive dissonance ever reported was the study of disconfirmed expectancies by members of a doomsday cult who believed that the world would end in a cataclysmic flood. Their reactions to the disconfirmed expectancy formed the basis of *When Prophecy Fails* (Festinger, Riecken, & Schachter, 1956). However, it would take researchers several decades to systematically vary group membership and assess the impact of participants' acting as individuals compared to their acting as members of a small group. (Cooper & Mackie, 1983; Zanna & Sande, 1987).

In the theory of vicarious dissonance, we went more to the heart of the meaning of group membership. We considered the effect of one group member's counterattitudinal advocacy on the attitudes and behaviors of other members of one's group. Social identity theory was the vehicle that helped us link the dissonant behavior of one group member with the attitudes of other members of the group. Because of the impact of social identity on members of social groups, we reasoned that dissonance aroused in one group member could cause other group members to experience dissonance vicariously and result in attitude change by the other members of the social group.

Social Identity

The theory of social identity offers a wide-ranging perspective on the relationship between collective self-conception and both group and intergroup processes (for contemporary statements see Hogg, 2005b, 2006). It incorporates Tajfel and Turner's (1979) original emphasis on intergroup relations, social comparison, and self-esteem motivation, as well as Turner and colleagues' later analysis of self-categorization and prototype–based depersonalization (Turner, Hogg, Oakes, Reicher, & Wetherell, 1987). According to social identity theory, people cognitively represent groups in terms of prototypes—that is, fuzzy sets of attributes that simultaneously capture in-group similarities and intergroup differences. These attributes include beliefs, attitudes, perceptions, feelings, intentions and behaviors—in short any and all dimensions that can be used to segment the social world into discrete categories that are distinctive and high in entitativity (Hamilton & Sherman, 1996). Prototypes describe, evaluate, and prescribe group attributes.

The process of social categorization perceptually depersonalizes other people. It transforms perceptions of other people from unique individuals into embodiments of the relevant in-group or out-group prototype. Categorization-based depersonalization underpins stereotyping and valenced perceptions of other people.

Social categorization of self operates in exactly the same way. It depersonalizes self-conception and transforms one's own perceptions, beliefs, attitudes, feelings, and behaviors to conform to the in-group prototype. Self-categorization transforms individuals into group members, individual and interpersonal self-concept into collective self-concept, personal identity into social identity, and individual behavior into group and intergroup behavior. Self-categorization generates such well-defined and heavily researched phenomena as in-group bias, intergroup discrimination, ethnocentrism, in-group cohesion and solidarity, in-group loyalty and attraction, and in-group normative attitudes, feelings, and behaviors.

Depersonalization involves assimilation of self and others to relevant prototypes. Thus, within a contextually salient group, self-categorization replaces self–other differences with in-group prototypical similarity or interchangeability. The self–other distinction is blurred into a single, collective self: Self and other are *fused* into a single entity. This fusion gives rise to *intersubjectivity*, where one experiences the other as oneself. Working from different theoretical orientations, Wright, Aron, and Tropp (2002) have also argued that self-categorization extends the self-concept to include others in the self, and research by Mackie and associates (Mackie, Maitner, & Smith, 2007) shows that self-categorization may facilitate a process whereby in-group members experience the emotions of fellow group members.

The fusing of the self with one's group and with prototypical group members requires that identification with the group be strong. The more strongly a person feels about her or his membership in the group, the more central the group is to a person's self-definition and self-concept. Fusing of self and other is heightened when the group's prototype is clear and focused and when the observed in-group member is highly prototypical of the group. Research has shown that people in groups are perceptually attuned to subtle differences among group members in how prototypical they are (e.g., Haslam, Oakes, McGarty, Turner, & Onorato, 1995)—there is a clearly perceived prototypicality gradient that engenders both rejection of marginally prototypical members who threaten group integrity and strong endorsement of highly prototypical members (Hogg, 2005a). Thus, the process of fusion of self and other members of one's group will be affected by the degree of perceived prototypicality of a specific other member, and moderated by perceived self-prototypicality.

Another aspect of social identity theory that is relevant to the theory of vicarious cognitive dissonance is its perspective on attitude change. The social influence process associated with social identity is referent informational influence (Abrams & Hogg, 1990). When people identify with a group, they learn the group's normative attitudes primarily from the behaviors of highly prototypical in-group members. It is therefore not surprising that we tend to assimilate our attitudes to group standards (Turner, 1991) or that our attitudes polarize toward positions expressed by group members (Mackie, 1986; Mackie & Cooper, 1984). In short, the behavior and attitudes of in-group members have their greatest impact on those who are highly identified with the group, and it is they who are more likely to be influenced by group norms (Terry & Hogg, 1996). A clear derivation of this fact is that people who are highly identified with their group are the ones who are most likely to experience vicarious cognitive dissonance, especially based on the behavior of prototypical group members.

The important idea drawn from social identity theory is that where common group membership is psychologically salient, social categorization of self and in-group others generates prototype-based depersonalization. Self and others are "fused" because they are viewed in terms of a common in-group prototype—others' attitudes, feelings, experiences, and behaviors can become one's own, particularly when the other is a highly prototypical member of a group with which we identify strongly. There emerges an empathic bond, an intersubjectivity, which enables one to experience the other as oneself. Not only may this protect against harming the other (cf. Galinsky & Moskowitz, 2000)—after all, the other *is* the self—but it may also allow one to vicariously experience others' thoughts and feelings, and to take the role of another in constructing a sense of who one is (see Mead, 1934).

Although social identity theory and cognitive dissonance theory developed from different traditions and perspectives, it should be noted that both literatures owe an intellectual debt to the seminal work of Fritz Heider's work on cognitive balance. From a balance theory perspective, people's representations of cognitive units are experienced as more comfortable if they are affectively balanced rather than unbalanced. Heider (1946, 1958) knew that a cognitive unit could apply broadly, but his lens was focused on the individual in his or her relationship with others. The lens of dissonance theory was more typically focused on the relationship of behavioral and attitudinal units within individuals while social identity theory focused on the relationship of units within or between groups. The theory of vicarious dissonance simply broadens the perspective of dissonance and social identity theory to allow the representations of cognitions about attitudes, behaviors, and groups to occupy the same psychological space. The simultaneous representations of cognitions about groups and individuals, each consistent with the principles of psychological balance, give rise to our predictions: People experience cognitive dissonance when a member of their in-group behaves in ways that are out of balance with their attitudes.

AN EXISTENCE PROOF FOR VICARIOUS DISSONANCE

Our initial foray to find empirical confirmation of vicarious dissonance was a study conducted at Princeton University (Norton, Monin, Cooper, & Hogg, 2003). The general idea was to have participants observe another student agreeing to write an essay that took a position that the observers thought was counterattitudinal. The question we asked was whether the participants would experience cognitive dissonance and change their own attitudes solely because of the behavior of the fellow student. From our theoretical analysis of social identity and dissonance processes we expected that the mere observation of counterattitudinal behavior would lead to attitude change in our participants, provided that the participants and the essay writer were members of the same social group and provided that the participants identified with and felt positive about being a member of their group.

The method we used for the study serves as a paradigm for much of the research we consider in this chapter, so I will present it in some detail. We created a fictitious cover story that participants found intriguing and involving. For our research purposes, the cover story created a rationale for a student to witness a fellow student agree to write a counterattitudinal message and to learn whether or not the student was a member of the participant's social group. At Princeton University, all entering undergraduate students are assigned at random to one of five residential colleges. Each student lives and eats in one of the colleges, and each college has its own social and academic activities. The student's residential college served as the crux of the in-group versus out-group manipulation because each participant believed that he or she was witnessing an interaction with a student who happened to be a fellow resident of his or her residential college (in-group member) or happened to be a resident of a different residential college (out-group member).

The students arrived for a study of "linguistic subcultures" in groups of two, although each reported to a separate room, separated by two-way mirrors. We told the students that we were interested in how people in different residential colleges come to speak in slightly different ways, learning to use slightly different inflections or terms in their spoken behavior. For example, we know that people who live in the Midwest develop a slightly different pattern of speech than people who live in South Carolina or Massachusetts. The experimenter explained that the purpose of the students' participation in the current study was to see if these speech patterns occur in microcosms—that is, small groups within a larger context. We told the students that, in this study, we wanted to see if the speech patterns of students in the different residential colleges at Princeton University were different from one another and whether we could measure them.

We explained that one of the two students, selected at random, was going to deliver a speech on a given topic and the other student was going to listen carefully, and then respond to several questions about the speaker's speech patterns. Each participant was told that he or she was the one who had been randomly picked to rate the speech, while the student in the other room was assigned to give the speech. The procedure allowed us to make the student's residential college group salient and manipulate systematically whether the speaker's residential college group was the same (in-group) or different (out-group) from the participant's. The experimenter found a pretext to turn the lights on briefly, which allowed the participants to see that there truly was another student in the other room. The illumination was kept low so that the students' identities could not be accurately discerned. What students did not realize was that each of them had been assigned the role of listener. All information about what the alleged other student said or did was manipulated by instruction or audiotape.

The experimenter left the room, ostensibly to instruct the other participant about the speech he or she was to make. During the intervening period, participants filled out various measures, including measures of how much they liked and felt identified with their residential college on a scale developed by Hogg and his associates (Hogg, Hains, & Mason, 1998). In a few minutes, the experimenter returned with a tape recording that included the completed speech and the experimenter's alleged conversation with the other student. On the tape, the experimenter explained that he was fortunate to be able to combine two studies into one. The Dean's office had asked for a study trying to assess student opinion about the possibility of raising tuition fees by a more than typical amount. Using a cover story developed by Linder, Cooper, and Jones (1967), the experimenter asked the student to write a strong and forceful speech advocating a spike in tuition fees. He explained that this would be the speech that the other subject (i.e., the real participant) would rate for its linguistic features and that it would then be sent on to the Dean's office. The experimenter also asked the alleged other student how he or she felt about raising tuition and the student responded, "Well…I'd be against it."

The participants thus had a credible, albeit fabricated, story that allowed them to overhear an in-group or an out-group member make a counterattitudinal speech on a controversial topic. The tape recorder was stopped while the writer supposedly organized his or her thoughts, and then restarted for the participant to hear the alleged speech. The speech was a relatively brief exposition on how higher tuition rates could allow the university to hire more faculty, purchase more books for the library, and so forth. Before rating the speech for its linguistic properties, participants were asked about their own attitudes toward tuition increases at the university. This served as the dependent measure of our study.

The results of the study showed clearly that observing a fellow group member behave in a counterattitudinal fashion caused the participant to change his or her attitude in the direction of the group member's counterattitudinal advocacy. As predicted by vicarious dissonance, this effect *only* occurred when the participant strongly identified with his or her group. In the absence of a strong affinity with one's group, observing an in-group or an out-group member did not affect participants' attitudes.

FOLLOWING THE RULES: VICARIOUS DISSONANCE AND THE NEW LOOK MODEL OF DISSONANCE

The next questions we asked were whether vicarious dissonance is experienced similarly to personal dissonance and whether the conditions for its arousal follow similar rules. The goal of our follow-up study (Norton et al., 2003) was to manipulate in a single experiment some of the variables that are known to affect personal cognitive dissonance and assess their impact on vicarious dissonance. From the decades of research on personal dissonance, we know that dissonance only occurs when a person is responsible (i.e., makes an act of free choice) to act in a counterattitudinal fashion (Cooper, 1971; Davis & Jones, 1960; Linder et al., 1967) and when the act has potential unwanted consequences (Cooper & Fazio, 1984; Cooper & Worchel, 1970; Scher & Cooper, 1989; Stone & Cooper, 2001). There are some models of cognitive dissonance theory that take issue with whether an unwanted consequence is a necessary condition for dissonance to occur (Beauvois & Joule, 1999; Harmon-Jones et al., this volume; Harmon-Jones, Brehm, Greenberg, Simon, & Nelson, 1996), but all agree that producing an unwanted event is, at the very least, an important cognition for the arousal of dissonance. To the extent that the changes of attitudes we found in the first two studies were based on a vicarious version of cognitive dissonance arousal, then the effect should similarly depend on the existence of choice and the potential occurrence of an unwanted consequence.

We used our familiar procedure, although this time at the University of Queensland in Australia. The attitude issue was the imposition of up-front fees (payment of tuition up-front rather than through a loan to be repaid later on), which was a very unpopular position at the time for students at universities throughout

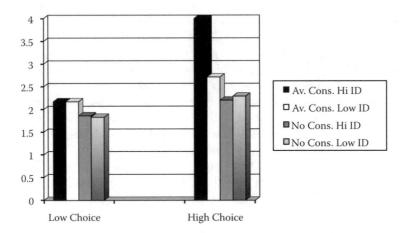

Figure 8.1. Attitude change as a function of choice, consequence, and group identification.

Australia. Not surprisingly, we requested the speechwriter in this experiment to make a strong and forceful statement supporting the collection of up-front fees. We manipulated the two crucial independent variables: choice of the speaker to make the counterattitudinal speech and whether or not the speech had the potential to lead to an aversive consequence. The participants' level of in-group identification was measured with the scale used in our previous study.

The results are depicted in Figure 8.1. For ease of presentation, we grouped the identification variable by a median split, although regression analysis confirms the results of the factorial analysis of variance. The second-order interaction supported our hypothesis. As predicted, participants changed their attitudes in the direction of the position advocated in the fellow group member's essay, provided that (1) the fellow group member had high choice to write the essay, (2) the speech had a potentially unwanted consequence, and (3) when the participants felt strongly identified with their fellow students at the University of Queensland. The first two of those variables are the ones that typically enable personal dissonance to occur (high choice and high consequences). Thus, dissonance was aroused in the observer in precisely the same conditions in which dissonance would have been experienced by the speaker—but only when the observers were highly identified with and attracted to their in-group.

We also assessed what vicarious dissonance *feels* like. We asked participants to rate their affect on scales devised by Elliot and Devine (1994) that have been used frequently in the dissonance literature. We asked them how bothered, uneasy, and uncomfortable they felt. We found no differences among conditions. However, we also asked the participants about their *vicarious affect*: "How do you think you would feel if you were in the speech writer's position?" This time, we found some fascinating effects: We obtained the very same second-order interaction that we had obtained for attitudes. Participants who were strongly identified with their group and who witnessed the counterattitudinal speech made under conditions of high choice and high unwanted consequences expressed the highest degree of vicarious negative affect. As they placed themselves in their group member's shoes, they expressed considerable discomfort.

VICARIOUS DISSONANCE AND VICARIOUS HYPOCRISY: FOCUS ON BEHAVIOR AND HEALTH

One of the intriguing methods for inducing the feeling of cognitive dissonance is to have people engage in proattitudinal, rather than counterattitudinal, advocacy. Dissonance is induced by reminding people of their past behavior that was inconsistent with their attitudes and inconsistent with their current advocacy. Known as the hypocrisy paradigm (Aronson, Fried, & Stone, 1991; Stone, Weigand, Cooper, & Aronson, 1997), this instance of dissonance is particularly useful at encouraging more attitude-consistent behaviors and for moving attitudes to more extreme proattitudinal positions. For example, Stone et al. (1997) asked university participants to make a speech to high school students urging them to use condoms each and every time they had sexual relations. Some of the participants were asked to think of times that they had had sex without using a condom. Others were not asked to think of their attitude-discrepant behavior. Later, the university participants were given the opportunity to purchase condoms. Those who had made a strong statement advocating the use of condoms and who had had their attention focused on their past behavioral inconsistency were more likely to purchase condoms than if they had not been made mindful of their past behavior. In short, becoming aware of prior behavior that was discrepant from a stated attitude causes dissonance and results in changes of behavior in the direction of the attitude.

One advantage of inducing dissonance through hypocrisy is that it enables us to influence attitudes that really matter to people (see Crano, this volume; Johnson & Boynton, this volume). When we consider attitudes in a domain such as health maintenance, we are dealing with attitudes and behaviors that affect people's daily lives, their health habits, and their well-being. If only we could influence people to adopt more positive attitudes toward health behaviors, we could use our theories of attitude change for the benefit of the individual and society. One roadblock to change is that in many critical areas of healthcare, people already hold pro-health attitudes. Those attitudes do not always predict their behaviors (Johnson & Boynton, this volume).

Hypocrisy is well suited for arousing dissonance when we want to induce behaviors that people already agree with...but do not often do. For example, encouraging people to use condoms to protect against HIV and AIDS is a position people generally agree with, but with which they do not always comply. Eating a healthy diet for weight loss and for better health is similarly endorsed by most people. Encouraging people to comply consistently is a more difficult proposition. In this research program, we wanted to turn our attention to an issue of major importance for protection against melanomas and carcinomas—that is, taking the simple precaution of applying sunscreen when exposed to the sun.

In two studies we examined whether hypocrisy can be experienced vicariously and, if so, whether it could result in the change of behaviors and behavioral

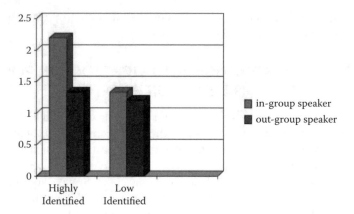

Figure 8.2.   Changes (bolstering) of attitudes toward using sunscreen.

intentions to act in ways conducive to improved health. Both studies involved the use of sunblock to protect against the risk of skin cancer. One study was conducted at the University of Queensland, located in a subtropical Australian state with a high incidence of skin cancer and where students are well aware of the need to protect against the sun. Participants overheard a fellow student from UQ agree to make a speech advocating the use of sunblock every time a person goes outdoors. In the hypocrisy condition the speaker was made mindful of the occasions in which she failed to practice what she advocated. Participants overheard the experimenter ask the speaker if she had ever gone outdoors without using sunblock. The experimenter explained that she was interested in understanding the reasons that people sometimes do not use sunblock, even though they know it is excellent protection against the risk of skin cancer. Yes, the speaker admitted, in truth she did not use sunblock on every occasion and then listed some reasonable excuses for failing to apply it. In the hypocrisy condition, then, the speaker heard a fellow group member advocate a proattitudinal position and also heard the group member become mindful of the occasions in which she had not acted in accordance with that belief. In an advocacy-only condition, the speaker agreed to make the speech favoring the use of sunscreen, but was not explicitly made mindful of the occasions in which she had not used it.

We then asked the participants about their own behavioral intentions. We asked them to respond to the statement, "I intend to start carrying sunblock with me wherever I go" on a scale ranging from 1 (*not very likely*) to 9 (*very likely*). The results showed that women participants who listened to the hypocritical speaker indicated a greater intention to carry sunblock compared to those who listened in the advocacy-only condition. As predicted, the interaction between group identification and hypocrisy was also significant. Vicarious hypocrisy occurred only for students who were highly identified with their group. The results are depicted in Figure 8.2.

A similar experiment conducted in the United States (Fernandez, Stone, Cooper, Cascio, & Hogg, 2008) included an additional factor of having an in-group versus out-group member make the prosunscreen speech. Students at the University of Arizona were asked to listen to a speech made by another student that encouraged people to use sunblock as a preventative measure for skin cancer. The participants were told that the University of Arizona was collaborating with rival university, Arizona State University, on a project to develop effective public service announcements designed to convince high school students to use sunblock as protection against skin cancer.   The experimenter explained that public service announcements had already been made by college students during the previous phase of the study, and the purpose of the current session was to offer an assessment of the messages. Participants listened to a tape recording of a female student who made a strong speech advocating the use of sunblock every day to protect against the threat of melanomas. Of course, all participants heard precisely the same speech, but the cover story allowed us to vary whether the hypocritical speechmaker was allegedly from the person's in-group (Arizona) or from the rival out-group (Arizona State). The speech concluded with the statement, "No matter how busy you think you are with school or work, you can and should always wear sunscreen to reduce your risk of cancer."

In the *target-advocacy* condition, the recording ended after the statement was complete. However, in the *target-hypocrisy* condition, the strong statement at the end of the speech laid the groundwork for demonstrating the target's inability to practice what she had preached. For participants in the target-hypocrisy condition, the tape continued with the researcher explaining that it would be helpful to know more about why college students fail to use sunblock every time they spend time in the sun. He indicated that researchers in the sunblock program had made a list of common reasons people use for not applying sunblock. The target asked to see the list and then responded, "Yeah, it's true for me. I can see some of the major reasons why I don't use sunblock regularly right here on the top. I sometimes forget it in my car, or in the house...or I'm in too much of hurry to stop and put it on before I go out." In this way, the target, who had already advocated the consistent use of sunblock whenever one goes out of doors, publicly admitted to behavior that contradicted the statement. We predicted that the participant would experience vicarious dissonance from overhearing another student confess to the hypocrisy— but only if the fellow student was from the participant's in-group. The hypocrisy of students from the rival institution, Arizona State University, should not lead to vicarious hypocrisy.

At the conclusion of the research session, participants were asked about their attitudes toward always using sunblock and the strength of their intention to use sunblock in the future. We concluded with a behavioral measure: All participants were given a coupon that they could redeem for free bottles of sunblock. All they needed to do was to send a confirmation of their desire to have the free sample to the e-mail address listed on the coupon. The e-mail address belonged to the researchers and we were able to tally the number of people who actually tried to acquire the sunblock. (And we did send them their free bottle of sunblock.)

The results of the study were exciting. As we had predicted, female participants' attitudes became more ardent that sunscreen should always be used—provided that the target speaker was from the in-group and the participant felt highly identified with that in-group. Behavior was also dramatically affected. In the condition in which the University of Arizona participant felt highly identified with her university, witnessing the in-group speaker admit to her hypocrisy resulted in 70% of the participants e-mailing their request for their complimentary sunscreen. By contrast, only 54% of the other participants bothered to reclaim their coupons. Taken together, the two studies showed that people's attitudes, behavior intentions, and actual behaviors were influenced in a positive way by the arousal of vicarious dissonance.

The Reach of Vicarious Dissonance

As several chapters in the current volume attest, there has often been a tension between theoretically generated studies of attitudes and persuasion and an interest in studying "attitudes that matter." When Festinger and Carlsmith (1959) set out to show the counterintuitive phenomenon that became known as induced compliance, they had very little interest in describing the degree of enjoyment people had about turning pegs and sorting spools. One attitude issue is often as good as any other, as long as it serves the function of assessing theoretically driven change. At the same time, however, there is a disquieting feeling that a discipline that concentrates solely on attitudes that are constructions in the laboratory or are measures of arbitrary issues may be flirting with the perception of irrelevance.

Kurt Lewin (1947) taught us that there is nothing as practical as a good theory. When working in a theoretically driven field like cognitive dissonance, there is always the hope that a full and careful understanding of the theory will allow for applications to attitudes that matter. And, indeed, examples abound in which the findings generated in the dissonance laboratory have been used for issues that matter, such as using effort justification techniques to facilitate dieting, to relieve phobias, or to reduce speech anxiety. Vicarious dissonance simultaneously allows for theory development and behavior/attitude change on issues that matter. While testing the theoretical implications of people's vicarious affective arousal on behalf of fellow in-group members, people can be cajoled to believe more strongly in the importance of good health practices and to behave more proactively to attain those goals.

CONCLUSION

In this chapter, I have considered the evidence that cognitive dissonance can be experienced vicariously. Because we are social animals and take our identity partly from our group memberships, we experience an overlap or fusion with typical members of our groups. This sows the seeds of vicarious dissonance. Our group members' discomfort becomes our discomfort; their dissonance becomes ours. We experience discomfort vicariously and change our attitudes in order to reduce it. Not only does this expand the reach of dissonance processes in understanding shifts in attitudes and behaviors, it also allows us to place dissonance at the service of promoting prosocial, proattitudinal healthy behaviors. The research discussed in this chapter represents a beginning of that effort.

REFERENCES

Abrams, D., & Hogg, M. A. (1990). Social identification, self-categorization and social influence. *European Review of Social Psychology, 1,* 195–228.

Aronson, E. (1968). Dissonance theory: Progress and problems. In R. Abelson, E. Aronson, W. McGuire, T. Newcomb, M. Rosenberg, & P. Tannenbaum (Eds.), *Theories of cognitive consistency: A sourcebook* (pp. 5–27). Chicago: Rand McNally.

Aronson, E., Fried, C., & Stone, J. (1991). Overcoming denial and increasing the intention to use condoms through the induction of hypocrisy. *American Journal of Public Health, 81,* 1636–1638.

Aronson, E., & Mills, J. (1959). The effect of severity of initiation on liking for a group. *Journal of Abnormal and Social Psychology, 59,* 177–181.

Axsom, D. (1989). Cognitive dissonance and behavior change in psychotherapy. *Journal of Experimental Social Psychology, 25,* 234–252.

Axsom, D., & Cooper, J. (1985). Cognitive dissonance and psychotherapy: The role of effort justification in inducing weight loss. *Journal of Experimental Social Psychology, 21,* 149–160.

Beauvois, J. L., & Joule, R. V. (1999). A radical point of view on dissonance theory. In E. Harmon-Jones & J. Mills (Eds.), *Cognitive dissonance: Progress on a pivotal theory in social psychology* (pp. 43–70). Washington, DC: American Psychological Association.

Brehm, J. (1956). Postdecision changes in the desirability of alternatives. *Journal of Abnormal and Social Psychology, 52,* 384–389.

Brewer, M. B., & Gardner, W. (1996). Who is this "we"? Levels of collective identity and self-representations. *Journal of Personality and Social Psychology, 71,* 83–93.

Cooper, J. (1971). Personal responsibility and dissonance: The role of foreseen consequences. *Journal of Personality and Social Psychology, 18,* 354–363.

Cooper, J. (1980). Reducing fears and increasing assertiveness: The role of dissonance reduction. *Journal of Experimental Social Psychology, 16,* 199–213.

Cooper, J., & Fazio, R. H. (1984). A new look at dissonance theory. In L. Berkowitz (Ed.), *Advances in Experimental Social Psychology* (Vol. 17, pp. 229–262). Hillsdale, NJ: Erlbaum.

Cooper, J., & Hogg, M. A. (2007). Feeling the anguish of others: A theory of vicarious dissonance. In M. P. Zanna (Ed.), *Advances in experimental social psychology* (Vol. 39, pp. 359–403). San Diego, CA: Academic Press.

Cooper, J., & Mackie, D. (1983). Cognitive dissonance in an intergroup context. *Journal of Personality and Social Psychology, 44,* 536–544.

Cooper, J., & Worchel, S. (1970). Role of undesired consequences in arousing cognitive dissonance. *Journal of Personality and Social Psychology, 16,* 199–206.

Davis, K. E., & Jones, E. E (1960). Changes in interpersonal perception as a means of reducing cognitive dissonance. *Journal of Abnormal and Social Psychology, 61,* 402–410.

Elliot, A. J., & Devine, P. G. (1994). On the motivational nature of cognitive dissonance: dissonance as psychological discomfort. *Journal of Personality and Social Psychology, 67,* 382–394.

Fernandez, N. C., Stone, J., Cooper, J., Cascio, E., & Hogg, M. A. (2008). *Vicarious hypocrisy: Bolstering attitudes to reduce dissonance after exposure to a hypocritical ingroup member.* Unpublished manuscript, University of Arizona.

Festinger, L. (1957). *A theory of cognitive dissonance.* Stanford, CA: Stanford University Press.

Festinger, L., & Carlsmith, J. M. (1959). Cognitive consequences of forced compliance. *Journal of Abnormal and Social Psychology, 58,* 203–210.

Festinger, L., Riecken, H. W., & Schachter, S. (1956). *When prophecy fails.* Minneapolis: University of Minnesota Press.

Galinsky, A. D., & Moskowitz, G. B. (2000). Perspective-taking: Decreasing stereotype expression, stereotype accessibility, and in-group favoritism. *Journal of Personality and Social Psychology, 78*, 509–530.

Hamilton, D. L., & Sherman, S. J. (1996). Perceiving persons and groups. *Psychological Review, 103*, 336–355.

Harmon-Jones, E., Brehm, J. W., Greenberg, J., Simon, L., & Nelson, D.E. (1996). Evidence that the production of aversive consequences is not necessary to create cognitive dissonance. *Journal of Personality and Social Psychology, 70*, 5–16.

Haslam, S. A., Oakes, P. J., McGarty, C., Turner, J. C., & Onorato, S. (1995). Contextual changes in the prototypicality of extreme and moderate outgroup members. *European Review of Social Psychology, 4*, 85–111.

Heider, F. (1946). Attitudes and cognitive organization. *Journal of Psychology, 21*, 107–112.

Heider, F. (1958). *The psychology of interpersonal relations*. New York: Wiley.

Hogg, M. A. (2005a). All animals are equal but some animals are more equal than others: Social identity and marginal membership. In K. D. Williams, J. P. Forgas, & W. von Hippel (Eds.), *The social outcast: Ostracism, social exclusion, rejection, and bullying* (pp. 243–261). New York: Psychology Press.

Hogg, M. A. (2005b). The social identity perspective. In S. A. Wheelan (Ed.), *The handbook of group research and practice* (pp. 133–157). Thousand Oaks, CA: Sage.

Hogg, M. A. (2006). Social identity theory. In P. J. Burke (Ed.), *Contemporary social psychological theories* (pp. 111–136). Palo Alto, CA: Stanford University Press.

Hogg, M. A., Haines, S. C., & Mason I. (1998). Identification and leadership in small groups: Salience, frame of reference, and leader stereotypicality effects on leader evaluations. *Journal of Personality and Social Psychology, 75*, 1248–1263.

Leary, M. R., & Tangney, J. P. (2003). *Handbook of self and identity*. New York: Guilford Press.

Lewin, K. (1947). Frontiers in group dynamics. *Human Relations, 1*, 5–42.

Linder, D. E., Cooper, J., & Jones, E. E. (1967). Decision freedom as a determinant of the role of incentive magnitude in attitude change. *Journal of Personality and Social Psychology, 6*, 245–254.

Losch, M. E., & Cacioppo, J. T. (1990). Cognitive dissonance may enhance sympathetic tonus, but attitudes are changed to reduce negative affect rather than arousal. *Journal of Experimental Social Psychology, 26*, 289–304.

Mackie, D. M. (1986). Social identification effects in group polarization. *Journal of Personality and Social Psychology, 50*, 720–728.

Mackie, D., & Cooper, J. (1984). Attitude polarization: The effects of group membership. *Journal of Personality and Social Psychology, 46*, 575–585.

Mackie, D. M., Maitner, A. T., & Smith, E. R. (2007). Intergroup emotions theory. In T. D. Nelson (Ed.), *Handbook of prejudice, stereotyping, and discrimination*. Mahwah, NJ: Erlbaum.

Mead, G. H. (1934). *Mind, self, and society: From the standpoint of a social behaviorist*. Chicago: University of Chicago Press.

Norton, M. I., Monin, B., Cooper, J., & Hogg, M. A. (2003). Vicarious dissonance: Attitude change from the inconsistency of others. *Journal of Personality and Social Psychology, 85*, 47–62.

Scher, S. J., & Cooper, J. (1989). Motivational basis of dissonance: The singular role of behavioral consequences. *Journal of Personality and Social Psychology, 56*, 899–906.

Steele, C. M. (1988). The psychology of self-affirmation: Sustaining the integrity of the self. In L. Berkowitz (Ed.), *Advances in Experimental Social Psychology* (Vol. 21, pp. 261–302). Hillsdale, NJ: Erlbaum.

Stone, J., & Cooper, J. (2001). A self-standards model of cognitive dissonance. *Journal of Experimental Social Psychology, 37*, 228–243.

Stone, J., Wiegand, A. W., Cooper, J., & Aronson, E. (1997). When exemplification fails: Hypocrisy and the motive for self-integrity. *Journal of Personality and Social Psychology, 72*, 54–65.

Tajfel, H., & Turner, J. C. (1979). An integrative theory of intergroup conflict. In W. G. Austin & S. Worchel (Eds.), *The social psychology of intergroup relations* (pp. 33–47). Monterey, CA: Brooks-Cole.

Terry, D. J., & Hogg, M. A. (1996). Group norms and the attitude-behavior relationship. A role for group identification. *Personality and Social Psychology Bulletin, 22*, 776-793.

Tesser, A. (1988). Toward a self-evaluation maintenance model of social behavior. In L. Berkowitz (Ed.), *Advances in Experimental Social Psychology* (Vol. 21, pp. 181–227). New York: Academic Press.

Turner, J. C. (1991). *Social influence.* Bristol, England: Open University Press.

Turner, J. C., Hogg, M. A., Oakes, P. J., Reicher, S. D., & Wetherell, M. S. (1987). *Rediscovering the social group: A self-categorization theory.* Oxford, England: Blackwell.

Turner, J. C., & Oakes, P. J. (1989). Self-categorization and social influence. In P. B. Paulus (Ed.), *The psychology of group influence* (2nd ed., pp. 233–275). Hillsdale, NJ: Erlbaum.

Wright, S. C., Aron, A., & Tropp, L. R. (2002). Including others (and groups) in the self: Self-expansion and intergroup relations. In J. P. Forgas & K. D. Williams (Eds.), *The social self: Cognitive, interpersonal, and intergroup perspectives* (pp. 343–363). New York: Psychology Press.

Zanna, M. P., & Sande, G. N. (1987). The effects of collective actions on the attitudes of individual group members: A dissonance analysis. In M. P. Zanna, J. M. Olson, & C. P. Herman (Eds.), *The Ontario symposium: Vol. 5. Social influence* (pp. 151–163). Hillsdale, NJ: Erlbaum.

9

Affective Influences on the Formation, Expression, and Change of Attitudes

JOSEPH P. FORGAS

What role do temporary mood states play in the way attitudes are formed, maintained, and changed? The study of attitudes and attitude change has been historically one of the key topics of social psychology. As historians of our discipline noted, it was the study of attitudes, an intrinsically mentalistic concept, that ultimately saved social psychology from succumbing to the more absurd excesses of doctrinaire behaviorism. The concept of attitudes is unique in that it captures the complex, multifaceted ways in which human beings are capable of symbolically synthesizing and representing their social experiences and then using such mental representations to form predispositions that guide their subsequent social behaviors. It was George Herbert Mead, who, in his symbolic interactionist theory, first highlighted the key role that mental processes play in the way representations of social experiences are formed and eventually come to regulate social behavior (Mead, 1934). However, the term *attitude* was not used by Mead. Rather, it was first introduced into the social science literature in the work of Thomas and Znaniecki (1928), who used the concept of attitudes to describe the changing patterns of cultural adaptation among Polish emigrants to the United States.

Social psychologists conceive of attitudes as individual constructs that consist of distinct cognitive, affective, and conative (behavioral) components (Eagly & Chaiken, 1993). Even though the affective dimension has always been a key feature of the attitude concept, relatively little work has been done exploring the dynamic role that fluctuating affective states and moods play in the way attitudes are generated, maintained, cognitively represented, organized, and expressed in social situations. This chapter will present a brief review of the origins of recent work on affect and attitudes, focusing especially on contemporary cognitive theories linking affect and attitudes. The main objective of the chapter is to review our empirical research demonstrating how mild temporary mood states can have a significant influence on attitudes toward the self and others, as well as intergroup attitudes. Further, research will be reviewed demonstrating that affective states can also influence processes of attitude change, especially the quality and effectiveness of persuasive messages.

AFFECT AND ATTITUDES: A BRIEF OVERVIEW

Even though affect has always been recognized as a critical part of attitudes, empirical research on its functions was rare until quite recently. How can we explain this surprising neglect? Historians of psychology such as Hilgard (1980) argued that affect has been neglected in psychology because of the discipline's traditional assumption that different components of the human mind, such as affect, cognition, and conation, can be studied in separation from each other as independent, isolated entities. After decades of the dominance of first the behaviorist, and later the cognitivist paradigm, affect has remained the most "neglected" member of the trilogy of mind, at least until recently (Hilgard, 1980).

Interestingly, research on attitudes is one of the areas in social psychology where the traditional attempt to separate affect, cognition, and conation is most problematic. Although attitude theories clearly recognize that affect is a key component of attitude, there has been disproportionate preoccupation with the study of the cognitive and conative components, to the relative neglect of affective features (Eagly & Chaiken, 1993). Just how important is affect as a component of, and as a determinant of, attitudes and attitude change?

In an influential article that augured the re-emergence of affect as a central topic for social psychologists, Zajonc (1980) argued that affective reactions often constitute a sovereign and primary reaction to social situations. In a concluding review two decades later, closing the debate on the primacy of affect, Zajonc (2000), citing a variety of studies, concluded that affect indeed functions as an independent, primary, and often dominant force in determining people's responses and dispositions to social situations. It seems that people can readily acquire an affective, evaluative attitude toward stimuli even though they may have no awareness of having encountered it before (Zajonc, 1980, 2000). Such affective reactions can be extremely enduring and may influence subsequent behaviors, even in the absence of any associated memory or beliefs (Zajonc, 2000). Such evidence suggests that affect may be not just one of the three components of attitudes—and a relatively neglected one at that—but is often the driving force behind responses to social stimuli and perhaps the primary dimension of all interpersonal behavior (Zajonc, 1980).

Such a view is also supported by evidence indicating that affect also plays a crucial role in how people organize their social experiences and how they cognitively represent their attitudes about them. The human ability to symbolically represent social events is a key requirement for orderly social behavior (Mead, 1934), and affective reactions seem to play a key role in how attitudes toward, and implicit cognitive representations about, common, recurring social experiences are organized (Forgas, 1979, 1982). It is connotative rather than denotative features, such as feelings of confidence, anxiety, intimacy, pleasure, or discomfort, that seem to be the key dimensions that define the implicit structure and complexity of people's mental representations of social episodes. It seems that social "stimuli can cohere as a category even when they have nothing in common other than the emotional responses they elicit" (Niedenthal & Halberstadt, 2000, p. 381).

Such findings suggest that affect is indeed a primary dimension of social attitudes, a conclusion that was anticipated more than 30 years ago by Pervin (1976), who argued that "what is striking is the extent to which situations are described in terms of affects (e.g., threatening, warm, interesting, dull, tense, calm, rejecting) and organized in terms of similarity of affects aroused by them" (p. 471). Thus, affect—the way we feel about situations, people, and social experiences—plays a predominant role in how attitudes about the social world are structured. In addition to influencing how attitudes are organized, affect also plays a dynamic role in how attitudes toward the self, others, and social situations are formed. Several studies show that experiencing temporary positive or negative affect feeds into the way attitudes about the social world are formed (Forgas, 2002). There is good evidence for a general affect-congruent pattern, where feeling good tends to make unrelated attitudes more positive, and feeling bad produces more negative, critical attitudes (Clore & Storbeck, 2006; Forgas, 1995a,b, 2002). Several theories seek to explain how such affect infusion into attitudes may occur.

EXPLANATIONS OF AFFECT INFUSION INTO ATTITUDES

Despite its professed lack of interest in mentalistic phenomena such as affect, *conditioning and associationist theories* were among the first to offer an explanation of how affect infusion into attitudes may occur. Watson's "little Albert" studies were among the first to show that attitudes toward a previously neutral stimulus, such as a cute animal, can be rapidly changed by associating the attitude object with intrinsically fear-arousing stimuli, such as loud noise. According to this view, all our complex affective reactions acquired throughout life—and thus all our attitudes—are constructed as a result of a complex pattern of cumulative and mostly incidental associations. This notion was experimentally confirmed in the domain of political attitudes in an intriguing experiment by Razran (1940), who found that people who were made to feel bad or good (being exposed to highly aversive smells, or receiving a free lunch) subsequently reported significantly more negative or positive attitudes toward persuasive messages incidentally associated with their manipulated feelings.

Decades later, Byrne and Clore (1970) and Clore and Byrne (1974), in conceptually similar experiments, showed that incidentally aroused affect can infuse a variety of interpersonal attitudes. For example, persons placed into aversive environments (noisy, unpleasant rooms—the unconditioned stimuli) experienced negative affect (the unconditioned response), and responded with more negative attitudes to people encountered in such situations (the conditioned response). In other words, an incidentally elicited affective reaction can be readily associated with social stimuli encountered in this situation. Thus, simple temporal and spatial contiguity is enough to link an independently elicited affective state and an incidentally encountered stimulus or person. Numerous studies demonstrated just such a conditioning effect (Gouaux, 1971; Gouaux & Summers, 1973; Griffitt, 1970).

Psychoanalytic theory also played an important role in highlighting the importance of affective phenomena, and in particular, pointing to the invasive and hard-to-control nature of affective reactions. Psychoanalytic theories suggested that affect can "take over" attitudes unless adequate psychological resources are available to control these impulses. Feshbach and Singer (1957), in an interesting early study, found that attempts to suppress affect (such as fear induced by electric shocks) increased the "pressure" for the suppressed affect to be projected to other people, and so infused unrelated attitudes. Fearful subjects were more likely to see "another person as fearful and anxious" (p. 286), especially when they were trying to suppress their fear, suggesting that "suppression of fear facilitates the tendency to project fear onto another social object" (p. 286).

COGNITIVE THEORIES OF AFFECTIVE INFLUENCES ON ATTITUDES

Ultimately, neither the psychoanalytic nor the associationist explanations offered a fully convincing theory of just how and why temporary feelings may influence attitudes. More recent cognitive, information processing theories proposed that affect has two kinds of effects on attitudes. First, affective states can have an *informational effect*, informing the *content and valence* of attitudes through one or two complementary mechanisms: memory-based processes (e.g., the affect priming model; see Bower & Forgas, 1981) or inferential processes (e.g., the affect-as-information model; see Clore et al., 2001). Second, affect can also exert a *processing effect*, influencing how information is processed.

Informational Effect

Memory-Based Mechanisms   Affect may infuse attitudes through selectively facilitating the retrieval and use of affect-congruent information from memory to be used when constructively interpreting social information. The associative network model proposed by Bower (1981) suggests that affect, cognition, and attitudes are integrally linked within an associative network of mental representations. An affective state should thus selectively and automatically prime associated ideas to be used in constructive cognitive tasks that require the active elaboration and transformation of information. There is strong evidence for mood-congruent effects on attitudes (Bower, 1981; Clark & Isen, 1982; Forgas & Bower, 1987); however, affect priming is also subject to important boundary conditions (Eich & Macauley, 2000; Forgas, 1995a). It appears that affect congruence in attitudes is most likely to occur when the affective state is strong, salient, and self-relevant and when the task calls for the active generation of information.

Inferential Mechanisms   Alternatively, rather than computing a judgment or an attitude on the basis of recalled features of a target, "individuals may...ask themselves: 'How do I feel about it?' /and/ in doing so, they may mistake feelings due to a pre-existing state as a reaction to the target" (Schwarz, 1990, p. 529). This "how-do-I-feel-about-it" heuristic suggests that affect influences attitudes because of an inferential error, as people misattribute their affective state to an attitude target. This theory makes predictions that are indistinguishable from the earlier conditioning research reported by Clore and Byrne (1974). Typically, people only seem to rely on affect as a heuristic cue when they are unfamiliar with the attitude object, they have no prior evaluations to fall back on, their personal involvement is low, and they have insufficient cognitive resources to compute a more thorough response. For example, in one study we asked close to 1,000 people who were feeling good or bad after seeing happy or sad films to complete an attitude survey on the street after leaving the movie theater (Forgas & Moylan, 1987). As they presumably had little time and little capacity to engage in elaborate processing before producing a response, they may well have relied on their temporary affect as a heuristic cue to infer a reaction. It is an important limitation of this theory that the informational value of affective states for attitudes often depends on the particular situational context (Martin, 2000).

Processing Effect

In addition to such informational effects (influencing what people think), affect may also influence the process of cognition, that is, how people think about an attitude object (Bless & Fiedler, 2006; Clark & Isen, 1982; Forgas, 2006). People experiencing positive affect appear to employ less effortful and more superficial processing strategies, reach decisions more quickly, use less information, avoid demanding, systematic thinking, and are more confident about their decisions. In contrast, negative affect seems to trigger a more effortful, systematic, analytic, and vigilant processing style (Clark & Isen, 1982; Schwarz, 1990). More recently, Bless (2000) and Fiedler (2000; Bless & Fiedler, 2006) suggested a fundamental evolutionary significance associated with positive and negative affect, triggering equally effortful but fundamentally different processing styles. Thus, positive affect generally promotes a more assimilative, schema-based, top-down processing style, where pre-existing ideas, attitudes, and representations dominate information processing. In contrast, negative affect produces a more accommodative, bottom-up, and externally focused processing strategy where attention to situational information drives thinking (Bless & Fiedler, 2006). These processing strategies can influence the way people construct attitudes and the way they produce more or less effective persuasive arguments.

Toward an Integrative Theory: The Affect Infusion Model (AIM)

Affect may thus influence both the content and the process of how people think. However, these effects are subject to important boundary conditions, and recent integrative theories such as the affect infusion model (AIM; Forgas, 2002) seek to specify the circumstances that facilitate or inhibit affect infusion. For example, affect priming is most reliably observed when cognitive tasks call for highly constructive processing that necessitates the use of memory-based information.

Similarly, the inferential model is only likely to be used when people lack the motivation, ability, or resources to deal with a task more exhaustively.

The AIM predicts that affective influences on cognition and attitudes depend on the processing styles recruited in different situations that can differ in terms of two features: the degree of effort, and the degree of openness of the information search strategy. By combining processing quantity (effort), and quality (openness, constructiveness), the model identifies four distinct processing styles: direct access processing (low effort, closed, not constructive), motivated processing (high effort, closed, not constructive), heuristic processing (low effort, open, constructive), and substantive processing (high effort, open, constructive). Affect infusion is most likely when constructive processing, such as substantive or heuristic processing, is used. In contrast, affect should not infuse thinking when motivated or direct access processing is used. The AIM also specifies a range of contextual variables related to the task, the person, and the situation that influence processing choices and thus affective influences.

EVIDENCE FOR THE ROLE OF AFFECT IN ATTITUDES

As the previous review suggests, affect plays a significant and interactive role in how we represent the social world and organize and express our attitudes toward various social objects. This section will review a range of empirical studies illustrating the multiple roles of affect in attitudes, including (a) affective influences on attitudes about the self, (b) affect and attitudes toward others, (c) affect and intergroup attitudes, and (d) the role of affect in attitude change and persuasion.

Affect and Attitudes Toward the Self

Fluctuating affective states play a particularly strong role in influencing our attitudes toward ourselves (Sedikides, 1995). Most research suggests a basic affect-congruent pattern: positive affect improves, and negative affect impairs, self-attitudes. For example, when students were asked to form attitudes about their success or failure on a recent exam, induced positive or negative mood had a significant mood-congruent influence. Those in a negative mood blamed themselves more when failing and took less credit for their successes, whereas those in a positive mood claimed credit for success but refused to accept responsibility for their failures (Forgas, Bower, & Moylan, 1990). Other studies indicate a somewhat more complex picture, suggesting that affect congruence in self-related thinking is subject to a number of boundary conditions.

Mood effects on self-judgments seem to depend on which *aspect* of the self is being judged (Sedikides, 1995). Peripheral, less important self-attitudes are much more likely to be influenced by temporary mood than are central, important self-attitudes. As central self-attitudes are what people believe is their "true" self, they are frequently affirmed. Central self-conceptions are well-rehearsed and require less online elaboration, reducing the scope for affect to infuse these attitudes. This was confirmed by Sedikides (1995), who found that temporary affect had less influence on attitude judgments related to central traits, but had a significant mood-congruent influence on attitudes related to peripheral traits. The process mediation of this effect was confirmed when it was found that encouraging people to think more extensively about peripheral self-conceptions—paradoxically—further increased the influence of mood on these judgments.

The nature of the *task* also moderates mood effects on self-attitudes (Nasby, 1994). When happy or sad participants were asked to affirm or reject the relevance of a number of characteristics to themselves, when the task involved rejection there was no mood effect. However, affirming the relevance of a feature to the self was highly mood sensitive. This pattern seems to be due to the different processing strategies that affirmative and rejection tasks require. Rejecting a feature as not relevant to the self is a short and direct process that requires little elaborate processing. Affectively primed information is thus less likely to influence such tasks. In contrast, affirming a trait as relevant to the self requires more elaborate thinking, and affectively primed information is more likely to have an impact on the outcome of such tasks, as predicted by the AIM (Forgas, 2002).

Self-esteem is another variable that moderates mood effects on self-attitudes. Low self-esteem persons generally have more uncertain and less stable self-attitudes, and affect may thus have a greater influence on their self-attitudes compared to high self-esteem individuals (Brown & Mankowski, 1993). The role of self-esteem in mediating mood effects on self-attitudes was also confirmed by Smith and Petty (1995), who found that mood had a significant influence on the quantity and quality of responses by the low, but not by the high, self-esteem group. Low self-esteem people seem to engage in more open and elaborate processing when thinking about themselves, and their current mood is thus more likely to infuse what they report (Sedikides, 1995).

Motivational factors also influence how affective states impact on self-attitudes (Sedikides, 1994). When happy, neutral, and sad persons were then asked to write self-descriptive statements, early responses showed a clear mood-congruent effect. However, with the passage of time, negative self-attitudes were spontaneously reversed, suggesting the operation of a spontaneous, automatic, motivated mood repair strategy. Such motivated "mood management" was also confirmed in a series of our experiments (Forgas, 2000). Negative mood effects on self-descriptions were spontaneously reversed with the passage of time, and people who scored high on self-esteem were better able to spontaneously reverse the negativity of their self-attitudes, while low self-esteem individuals persevered with negative self-attitudes.

Affect may also have an influence on self-related attitudes, as positive mood may also serve as a *resource* that allows people to overcome defensiveness and deal with potentially threatening information about themselves (Trope, Ferguson, & Raghunathan, 2001). Facing negative information about the self is threatening. Those in a positive mood are more able to voluntarily expose themselves to threatening but useful information about themselves. In other words, positive mood functions as a buffer, enabling people to handle the costs of receiving negative information. Thus, positive mood plays an important role in facilitating the process of acquiring relevant self-knowledge. The evidence thus suggests that affect often has a strong mood-congruent influence on self-related attitudes, but only when some degree of open and constructive processing is required, the attitudes are more likely to be peripheral rather than central, and there are no motivational forces to override affect congruence. Low self-esteem also seems to promote affect infusion into self-attitudes.

Affective Influences on Attitudes Toward Others

The attitudes we form toward other people play a crucial role in social life and are an essential symbolic guide to effective interpersonal behavior (Mead, 1934). Many of the early experiments demonstrating affective influences on attitudes focused on interpersonal attitudes, including the experiments discussed previously by Feshbach and Singer (1957), Clore and Byrne (1974), Griffitt (1970), and others, typically finding that those in a positive mood formed more lenient, positive attitudes and those feeling bad were more negative and critical in their attitudes toward others. How and why do these effects occur?

Several experiments shed light on the cognitive mechanisms responsible for affect infusion into interpersonal attitudes. Attitudes may be colored by affect because even the most basic interpretation of observed behaviors can be affectively distorted, due to greater availability and use of affectively primed information when interpreting ambiguous observed behaviors. This prediction was tested when we induced happy or sad affect in participants, and then showed them a videotape of their own recorded social interactions with a partner from the previous day (Forgas, Bower, & Krantz, 1984). Participants were simply asked to make a series of rapid, online judgments evaluating the observed behaviors of themselves and their partners. There was a significant affect infusion even into these basic, online behavior observations. Happy people saw more positive, skilled and fewer negative, unskilled behaviors both in themselves and in their partners than did sad subjects. These results establish that even the simple interpretation of directly observed interpersonal behaviors is distorted by affect, because affect priming influences the kinds of interpretations, constructs, and associations that people rely on as they form attitudes about indeterminate social behaviors. For example, the same smile that may be seen as "friendly" in a good mood may well be interpreted as "awkward" or "condescending" when the observer experiences negative affect. Subsequent experiments found that such affective distortions occur even when people are forming attitudes about familiar and well-known others, such as their intimate partners (Forgas, 1995a).

Affect priming appears to be largely responsible for these effects, according to further experiments. When we asked happy or sad people to form attitudes about other people described in terms of a number of positive and negative adjectives (Forgas & Bower, 1987), happy persons formed more positive attitudes, and sad persons did the opposite. Crucially, affect also influenced processing times. People spent longer reading, encoding, and processing affect-congruent details, but were faster in retrieving and producing affect-congruent attitudes. These processing differences support affect-priming theories. When *learning* new information, affect priming activates a richer activated knowledge base, increasing the time it should take to link new information to this more elaborate memory base. In contrast, when *producing* affect-congruent attitudes, the task is performed faster because the affect-congruent constructs are ready and primed. These results suggest that affective states infuse social attitudes because of the selective use of affectively primed information in the way social stimuli are encoded, retrieved, and interpreted.

Different processing strategies significantly influence affect infusion into attitudes, as the AIM suggests. Surprisingly, the more people need to think in order to compute an attitude, the greater the likelihood that affectively primed ideas will influence the outcome. In several studies, we manipulated the complexity of the task in order to create more or less demand for extensive, elaborate processing styles (Forgas, 1993, 1994, 1995b). It turns out that, paradoxically, when people have to form an attitude about a complex, ambiguous, or indeterminate person, couple, or event, they need to engage in longer, more elaborate and constructive processing, and affectively primed associations have a greater influence on the outcome. For example, when happy or sad participants were asked to form attitudes about more or less "typical" couples, happy participants formed more positive attitudes than did sad participants. However, mood effects were far greater when the couples were atypical and required longer and more extensive processing.

Similar results were obtained when we looked at mood effects on interpersonal attitudes (Forgas, 1992). Forming attitudes toward atypical persons took longer to process and was more influenced by affect. Do these effects also occur in realistic interpersonal attitudes? In several studies, we studied mood effects on people's attitudes of their real-life interpersonal relationships (Forgas, 1994). Partners in long-term intimate relationships also formed more mood-congruent attitudes, and these mood effects were accentuated when the events judged were complex and serious and so required more elaborate, constructive processing. It seems then that affect infusion into forming social attitudes is highly dependent on the processing strategies used. More elaborate, constructive processing increases the extent of affect infusion, by increasing the likelihood that affectively primed information will be used.

Can such affectively biased attitudes, once formed, also influence interpersonal behaviors? The links between attitudes and behavior is one of the perennial questions in attitude research (Eagly & Chaiken, 1993). If affect can influence attitudes, will it also influence subsequent social behaviors? Positive affect should, in general, prime positive information and produce more confident, friendly, and cooperative "approach" attitudes and behaviors, whereas negative affect should prime negative memories and produce avoidant, defensive, or unfriendly attitudes and behaviors. In one field study we found that affect had such an affect-congruent influence on attitudes toward, and responses to, a person who unexpectedly approached participants with an impromptu request (Forgas, 1998a). Students in a library received an unobtrusive mood induction and soon afterward were approached by another student (a confederate) who requested, either politely or impolitely, several sheets of paper needed to complete an essay. There was a clear mood-congruent pattern in attitudes toward, and behavioral responses to, the requester. Negative mood resulted in a more critical, negative attitude to the request and the requester and less compliance than did positive mood.

These results suggest that affect infusion can have a significant effect on determining attitudes and behavioral responses to people encountered in realistic everyday situations. Other experiments found mood effects on strategic inter-personal behaviors such as requesting (Forgas, 1999a, 1999b). Affective states should play a particularly important role in influencing attitudes and behaviors in elaborately planned interpersonal encounters such as negotiations and bargaining (Forgas, 1998c). We found that positive mood produced more positive and opti-mistic attitudes about the negotiation, led to more ambitious negotiating goals, and led to the formulation of more optimistic, cooperative, and integrative negotiating strategies. These findings suggest that affective state can influence the attitudes people form about novel social situations, the goals they set for themselves, and the way they behave in subsequent social encounters. These effects occur because uncertain and unpredictable social encounters, such as negotiation, call for open, constructive processing allowing affective states to selectively prime the thoughts and associations used in formulating attitudes, plans, and behaviors.

Affective Influences on Stereotyping, Prejudice, and Intergroup Attitudes

Attitudes toward members of in-groups versus out-groups are among the most important and most frequently researched topics in attitude research. Given the frequently demonstrated and almost universal tendency for people to prefer those similar to themselves and members of their own groups to dissimilar others, it has long been assumed that intergroup attitudes are particularly prone to irrational, affective distortions (Allport, 1954). Early attempts to explain the "emotional-ism" of intergroup attitudes were based on psychodynamic ideas of projection and displacement, and the frustration-aggression hypothesis. More recent work distinguished between affective states that are enduring versus short term, and affective states that are integral versus incidental to the intergroup experience (Bodenhausen, 1993; Haddock, Zanna, & Esses, 1993; Stangor, Sullivan, & Ford, 1991). Intergroup attitudes can certainly be influenced by transient, incidental moods as a result of conditioning processes (Clore & Byrne, 1974; Griffitt, 1970). If one regularly encounters members of out-groups in a particular affective state—such as fear, discomfort, disgust, or embarrassment—such cultural conditioning can result in deeply ingrained and enduring attitudes. It seems that affective biases in intergroup attitudes tend to be stronger when people are unaware of their feel-ings, are not motivated and/or lack the cognitive resources to control their biases, and have relatively little information about the target group (Bodenhausen & Moreno, 2000).

After all, contact with an out-group may often produce feelings of anxiety, uncertainty, and insecurity (Stephan & Stephan, 1996). The experience of anxiety may reduce information processing capacity and amplify reliance on stereotypes, producing a tendency to see all out-group members in stereotypic ways. In sev-eral experiments we found that trait anxiety significantly moderated the influ-ence of negative mood on intergroup judgments (Ciarrochi & Forgas, 1999). Low trait anxious Whites in the United States reacted more negatively to a threatening Black out-group when experiencing negative affect. Surprisingly, high trait anxious individuals showed the opposite pattern: They went out of their way to control their negative tendencies when feeling bad, and they produced more positive judgments. It appears that low trait anxious people processed automatically and allowed affect to influence their judgments, while high trait anxiety combined with aversive mood triggered a more controlled, motivated processing strategy designed to eliminate socially undesirable intergroup judgments.

Temporary positive affect can sometimes also improve intergroup attitudes, according to the so-called contact hypothesis (Allport, 1954; Amir, 1969; Brewer & Miller, 1996). According to this view, contact with out-group members in a positive affective state may reduce aversive feelings and improve intergroup relations. Contact episodes that generate positive feelings—such as successful cooperation— are likely to be especially effective.

Alternatively, positive affect may also promote more inclusive cognitive categorizations increasing the schema-driven, top-down processing of social information (Bless, 2000; Fiedler, 2000). This effect may improve intergroup attitudes when the categories activated are superordinate categories. However, according to some experimental studies, when group membership is of low relevance, positive mood may facilitate instead the use of in-group versus out-group categories, and intergroup discrimination may be increased rather than reduced as a result (Forgas & Fiedler, 1996).

Not all affective states have the same effects, however. For example, sadness, anger, and anxiety can have quite different consequences for intergroup attitudes, with sadness reducing, but anger and anxiety increasing, reliance on stereotyped attitudes (Bodenhausen, Sheppard, & Kramer, 1994; Keltner, Ellsworth, & Edwards, 1993).

Affect is thus likely to influence intergroup judgments both by influencing the information processing strategies used and influencing the way additional information is selected and used. As positive moods often facilitate top-down, schematic processing (Bless, 2000; Fiedler, 2000), happy persons may produce less accurate social judgments (Forgas, 1998b; Sinclair & Mark, 1995) and are more likely to rely on stereotype information than are neutral or sad persons (Bodenhausen, Kramer, & Süsser, 1994). However, negative affective states other than sadness, such as anger or anxiety, may also increase reliance on stereotyping, according to evidence from several experiments (e.g., Bodenhausen, Kramer, & Süsser, 1994). In addition to such processing effects associated with mood, affective states may also have informational effects, simply facilitating the use of mood-congruent knowledge in stereotype judgments. For example, Esses and Zanna (1995) found in several studies that negative moods increased the tendency to form negative judgments about ethnic minorities.

The final attitude may further be influenced by people's motivated tendency to *correct* what they perceive as undesirable or socially unacceptable judgments (Bodenhausen, Macrae, & Milne, 1998). This may involve a genuine attempt to correct for affective biases by either abandoning or recomputing an unacceptable judgment (Strack, 1992). There is some evidence that negative affect generally facilitates a more cautious, defensive interpersonal style (Forgas, 1999a, 1999b). Consistent with this notion, sad persons seem to be more likely to engage

in stereotype correction and are less likely to give expression to negative stereotypes in responding to others (Lambert, Khan, Lickel, & Fricke, 1997; Unkelbach,
Forgas, & Denson, 2009). Other negative affective states such as guilt also produce a motivated tendency to reduce or eliminate stereotyping, especially among
otherwise low-prejudiced persons (Devine & Monteith, 1993). It almost appears
as if negative affect sometimes functions as a warning signal, and this "alerting"
effect of negative mood is particularly strong for individuals who are habitually
anxious and score high on trait anxiety (Ciarrochi & Forgas, 1999).

It appears then that affect plays a complex and multiple role in intergroup
attitudes, prejudice, and stereotyping, potentially influencing every stage of the
stereotyping process. Most of these effects can be understood in terms of the informational and processing consequences of affect discussed previously. However,
contextual and situational factors also play a critical role in mediating these effects
(Martin, 2000). For example, the quality of the particular affective state, whether
it was directly elicited by the out-group, and individual differences such as trait
anxiety all seem to influence when and how affect will impact intergroup judgments. A comprehensive explanation of these effects will require an integrative
model, an issue that we will return to in the final section of this chapter.

The Role of Affect in Persuasion and Attitude Change

Students of rhetoric and persuasion have long assumed that the ability to induce an
emotional response in an audience is an important prerequisite for effective communication. Experimental studies also showed that induced positive affect promotes a positive response to persuasive messages (McGuire, 1985; Petty, Gleicher,
& Baker, 1991; Razran, 1940). In contrast, fear-arousing messages can also promote attitude change (Boster & Mongeau, 1984). However, this effect is under-
mined when fear triggers a defensive, self-protective reaction or a level of anxiety
and arousal that is distracting (Janis & Feshbach, 1953). In fact, fear seems most
effective when the audience believes that following the message is effective in
avoiding negative consequences.

Affect may influence the kind of information processing strategies people use
when dealing with a persuasive message (Petty et al., 1991). An affect-attitude link
can also be explained in terms of the direct "how do I feel about it?" heuristic suggested by Schwarz and Clore (1983). For example, Sinclair, Mark, and Clore (1994)
showed that college students were significantly more likely to agree with persuasive messages advocating comprehensive exams when they were interviewed on
a pleasant, sunny day rather than an unpleasant, rainy day. Such direct effects of
mood on responses are particularly likely when people are not able or willing to
engage in detailed processing.

The way the persuasive message is framed may also moderate the consequences of affect, as shown in an interesting study by Wegener, Petty, and Klein
(1994). When persuasive arguments emphasized positive outcomes, happy mood
produced more favorable responses. When the arguments pointed to the negative
consequences of *failing* to follow the recommended course, it was sad mood that
produced more favorable responses. It seems like good mood selectively primed

positive ideas that helped persuasion only when thinking about positive outcomes was helpful. When it was thinking about negative outcomes that most helped persuasion, it was bad mood that was more effective.

Affect in Dissonance-Induced Attitude Change

The experience of dissonance between attitudes and behaviors is one of the more potent mechanisms producing attitude change (Cooper & Fazio, 1984; Zanna & Cooper, 1974). Cognitive dissonance produces negative affect because discrepancy among cognitions undermines our clear and certain knowledge about the world, and thus our ability to engage in effective action (Harmon-Jones, 1999; Harmon-Jones, Brehm, Greenberg, Simon, & Nelson, 1996). However, other experiments suggest that negative affect is only triggered when consequences are "real" and there is an experience of personal responsibility (Cooper & Fazio, 1984). Qualitatively different dissonance experiences also seem to trigger qualitatively different affective reactions. Belief disconfirmation is more likely to produce anxiety, whereas post-decisional dissonance is more likely to induce regret. However, the availability of alternative attributions for aversive affect may also reduce subsequent attitude change. Generally, positive affect decreases, and negative affect increases, the dissonance experience and resulting attitude change. Once consonance is restored, affective state also tends to improve (Burris, Harmon-Jones, & Tarpley, 1997; Elliot & Devine, 1994). Thus, affective states seem to play an important role in attitude change, influencing both the way people respond to persuasive messages and the way they resolve attitude-behavior discrepancies. However, much work remains to be done in discovering the precise cognitive mechanisms responsible for these effects.

Affective Influences on the Production of Persuasive Messages

Affect may also influence the effectiveness of the persuasive messages people produce to bring about attitude change (Bohner & Schwarz, 1993). Despite much research on affective influences on responding to persuasion, there has been little work on how such messages are produced. We looked at this possibility in a series of recently published experiments (Forgas, 2007). In one experiment (Forgas, 2007, Experiment 1), participants received an audiovisual mood induction and were then asked to produce persuasive arguments for or against an increase in student fees and for or against Aboriginal land rights. They produced an average of seven arguments, and each argument was rated by two raters blind to the manipulations for overall quality, persuasiveness, level of concreteness, and valence (positive-negative). Results showed that those in a negative mood produced arguments on both issues that were of significantly higher quality and were judged to be more persuasive than the arguments produced by happy participants. This mood effect was largely due to the greater specificity and concreteness of arguments produced in a negative mood. A mediational analysis confirmed that it was mood-induced variations in argument concreteness that influenced argument quality.

In a further experiment, happy or sad participants ($N = 125$) were asked to produce persuasive arguments on two political issues: for or against Australia becoming a republic and for or against a radical right-wing party. Two raters ($r = .91$) assessed each argument in terms of (a) persuasiveness and argument quality, (b) valence (the use of positive or negative contents), and (c) self-relevance (the extent to which participants used personal, self-relevant themes). Sad mood again resulted in higher quality and more persuasive arguments, consistent with the theoretical prediction that negative mood should promote a more careful, systematic, bottom-up processing style that is more attuned to the requirements of a particular situation (Bless, 2001; Bless & Fiedler, 2006; Fiedler, 2001; Forgas, 2002).

However, do the arguments rated as "persuasive" by trained raters actually produce real attitude change in real persons? In Experiment 3 the arguments produced by happy or sad participants were presented to a naive audience of 256 undergraduate students. Their baseline attitudes on the four issues were assessed at the beginning of the term. After reading one of the pro or contra persuasive arguments on one of the issues written by one of the happy or sad participants in Experiments 1 and 2, their attitudes on all four issues was again assessed. Observed changes in attitudes in response to the persuasive arguments were assessed against the baseline measurement obtained earlier. Results showed that arguments written by negative mood participants in Experiments 1 and 2 were significantly more successful in producing a real change in attitudes than were arguments produced by happy participants. Attitudes were also more likely to change when the arguments advocated a popular rather than an unpopular position, and negative mood arguments were especially successful in producing attitude change when they advocated a popular position.

What happens when persuasive arguments are presented in an interpersonal context, as is usually the case in interactions before and during criminal and civil trials? Do people in a negative mood still produce more effective and more persuasive communications? In a further experiment (Forgas, 2007, Experiment 4) persuasive attempts by happy and sad people were directed at a "partner" to volunteer for a boring experiment using e-mail exchanges to convince them. The motivation to be persuasive was also manipulated by offering some participants a significant reward (movie passes) if their persuasive attempts were successful. Mood again had a significant effect on argument quality: People in a negative mood produced higher quality persuasive arguments than did the neutral group, who in turn did better than the positive group. However, the offer of a reward reduced mood effects on argument quality, confirming a key prediction of the AIM (Forgas, 1995a, 2002), that mood effects on information processing—and subsequent social influence strategies—are strongest in the absence of motivated processing. A mediational analysis confirmed that it was indeed mood-induced variations in accommodative processing and argument concreteness that mediated mood effects on argument quality.

These experiments extend earlier work and demonstrate the benefits of negative mood on the performance of cognitive tasks such as effective persuasion. Strategic social behaviors such as persuasive communication involve the same kinds of cognitive processes we considered earlier, so it is not surprising that more accommodative, careful processing should also improve the quality of strategic communications. Persuasive arguments produced in negative mood are not only of higher quality as judged by raters, but are also significantly more effective in producing genuine attitude change in people, largely because they contain more concrete details and more factual information (Cooper, 1932). These results are generally consistent with other studies suggesting that negative affect typically promotes a more concrete, accommodative, externally focused information processing style that also can reduce the incidence of judgmental errors and improve eye-witness memory (Forgas, 1998b; Forgas, Vargas, & Laham, 2005). This kind of concrete, accommodative thinking should also have direct benefits when it comes to the effective use of attitude change strategies, such as the production of persuasive arguments, something that happens frequently in everyday life, in organizations, in courtroom settings, and in legal work. This finding may have interesting applied implications, for example, in training participants in organizations and in the legal system to become more aware of mood effects on their strategies (Forgas & George, 2001).

CONCLUSION

The evidence reviewed in this chapter shows that mild, everyday affective states can have a highly significant influence on the way people form, maintain, and change their attitudes, and how attitudes and social information are cognitively represented and categorized (Forgas, 1979; Niedenthal & Halberstadt, 2000). Further, the experiments discussed here show that different information processing strategies play a key role in linking affect and attitudes. The multiprocess AIM (Forgas, 2002) in particular offers a simple and parsimonious explanation of when, how, and why affect infusion into attitudes is or is not likely to occur. A number of studies support the counterintuitive prediction based on the AIM that more extensive, substantive processing enhances mood-congruity effects (Forgas, 1994, 1995b; Nasby, 1994, 1996; Sedikides, 1995). Affect infusion influences not only attitudes but subsequent social behaviors as well (Forgas, 1998a, 1998b, 1999a, 1999c). In contrast, affect infusion is absent whenever a social cognitive task could be performed using a simple, well-rehearsed direct access strategy or a highly motivated strategy that offers little opportunity for primed mood-congruent information to infuse information processing (Fiedler, 1991; Forgas, 1995a). Affect infusion occurs not only in the laboratory, but also in many real-life situations, as evident in attitudes formed in intimate relationships (Forgas, 1994). Obviously considerably more research is needed before we can fully understand the multiple influences that affect has on attitudes and interpersonal behavior. Hopefully, this review will stimulate further interest in this fascinating and rapidly developing area of inquiry.

REFERENCES

Allport, G. W. (1954). *The nature of prejudice.* Reading, MA: Addison-Wesley.
Amir, Y. (1969). Contact hypothesis in ethnic relations. *Psychological Bulletin, 71,* 319–342.

Bless, H. (2000). The interplay of affect and cognition: The mediating role of general knowledge structures. In J. P. Forgas (Ed.), *Feeling and thinking: the role of affect in social cognition* (pp. 201–222). New York: Cambridge University Press.

Bless, H. (2001). Mood and the use of general knowledge structures. In L. L. Martin (Ed.), *Theories of mood and cognition: A user's guidebook* (pp. 9–26). Mahwah, NJ: Erlbaum.

Bless, H., & Fiedler, K. (2006). Mood and the regulation of information processing and behavior. In J. P. Forgas (Ed.), *Affect in social cognition and behavior* (pp. 65–84). New York: Psychology Press.

Bodenhausen, G. V. (1993). Emotions, arousal, and stereotypic judgments: A heuristic model of affect and stereotyping. In D. M. Mackie & D. L. Hamilton (Eds.), *Affect, cognition, and stereotyping* (pp. 13–37). San Diego, CA: Academic Press.

Bodenhausen, G. V., Kramer, G. P., & Süsser, K. (1994). Happiness and stereotypic thinking in social judgment. *Journal of Personality and Social Psychology, 66,* 621–632.

Bodenhausen, G. V., Macrae, C. N., & Milne, A. B. (1998). Disregarding social stereotypes: Implications for memory, judgment, and behavior. In J. M. Golding & C. M. MacLeod (Eds.), *Intentional forgetting: Interdisciplinary approaches* (pp. 349–368). Mahwah, NJ: Erlbaum.

Bodenhausen, G. V., & Moreno, K. N. (2000). How do I feel about them? The role of affective reactions in intergroup perception. In H. Bless & J. P. Forgas (Eds.), *The message within: Subjective experiences and social cognition.* (pp. 283–303). Philadelphia: Psychology Press.

Bodenhausen, G. V., Sheppard, L. A., & Kramer, G. P. (1994). Negative affect and social judgment: The differential impact of anger and sadness. *European Journal of Social Psychology, 24,* 45–62.

Bohner, G., & Schwarz, N. (1993). Mood states influence the production of persuasive arguments. *Communication Research, 20,* 696–722.

Boster, F. J., & Mongeau, P. (1984). Fear-arousing persuasive messages. In R. N. Bostrom (Ed.), *Communication yearbook* (Vol. 8, pp. 330–375). Beverly Hills, CA: Sage.

Bower, G. H. (1981). Mood and memory. *American Psychologist, 36,* 129–148.

Brewer, M. B., & Miller, N. (1996). *Intergroup relations.* Pacific Grove, CA: Brooks/Cole.

Brown, J. D., & Mankowski, T. A. (1993). Self-esteem, mood, and self-evaluation: Changes in the mood and the way you see you. *Journal of Personality and Social Psychology, 64,* 421–430.

Burris, C. T., Harmon-Jones, E., & Tarpley, W. R. (1997). "By faith alone": Religious agitation and cognitive dissonance. *Basic and Applied Social Psychology, 19,* 17–31.

Byrne, D., & Clore, G. L. (1970). A reinforcement model of evaluation responses. *Personality: An International Journal, 1,* 103–128.

Ciarrochi, J. V., & Forgas, J. P. (1999). On being tense yet tolerant: The paradoxical effects of trait anxiety and aversive mood on intergroup judgments. *Group Dynamics: Theory, Research and Practice, 3,* 227–238.

Clark, M. S., & Isen, A. M. (1982). Towards understanding the relationship between feeling states and social behavior. In A. H. Hastorf & A. M. Isen (Eds.), *Cognitive social psychology* (pp. 73–108). New York: Elsevier-North Holland.

Clore, G. L., & Byrne, D. (1974). The reinforcement affect model of attraction. In T. L. Huston (Ed.), *Foundations of interpersonal attraction* (pp. 143–170). New York: Academic Press.

Clore, G. L., & Storbeck, J. (2006). Affect as information for social judgment, behavior, and memory. In J. P. Forgas (Ed.), *Affect in social cognition and behavior* (pp. 154–178). New York: Psychology Press.

Cooper, J. B., & Fazio, R. H. (1984). A new look at dissonance theory. In L. Berkowitz (Ed.), *Advances in experimental social psychology* (Vol. 17, pp. 229–266). San Diego, CA: Academic Press.

Cooper, L. (1932). *The rhetoric of Aristotle.* New York: Appleton-Century.

Devine, P. G., & Monteith, M. J. (1993). The role of discrepancy-associated affect in prejudice reduction. In D. M. Mackie & D. L. Hamilton (Eds.), *Affect, cognition, and stereotyping: Interactive processes in group perception* (pp. 317–344). San Diego, CA: Academic Press.

Eagly, A. H., & Chaiken, S. (1993). *The psychology of attitudes.* New York: Harcourt Brace Jovanovich.

Eich, E., & Macauley, D. (2000). Fundamental factors in mood-dependent memory. In J. P. Forgas (Ed.), *Feeling and thinking: The role of affect in social cognition.* (pp. 109–130). New York: Cambridge University Press.

Elliot, A. J., & Devine, P. G. (1994). On the motivation nature of cognitive dissonance: Dissonance as psychological discomfort. *Journal of Personality and Social Psychology, 67,* 382–394.

Esses, V. M., & Zanna, M. P. (1995). Mood and the expression of ethnic stereotypes. *Journal of Personality and Social Psychology, 69,* 1052–1068.

Feshbach, S., & Singer, R. D. (1957). The effects of fear arousal and suppression of fear upon social perception. *Journal of Abnormal and Social Psychology, 55,* 283–288.

Fiedler, K. (1991). On the task, the measures and the mood in research on affect and social cognition. In J. P. Forgas (Ed.), *Emotion and social judgments* (pp. 83–104). Oxford: Pergamon.

Fiedler, K. (2000). Towards an integrative account of affect and cognition phenomena using the BIAS computer algorithm. In J. P. Forgas (Ed.), *Feeling and thinking: The role of affect in social cognition* (pp. 211–238). New York: Cambridge University Press.

Fiedler, K. (2001). Affective influences on social information processing. In J. P. Forgas (Ed.), The *handbook of affect and social cognition* (pp. 163–185). Mahwah, NJ: Erlbaum.

Forgas, J. P. (1979). *Social episodes: The study of interaction routines.* London: Academic Press.

Forgas, J. P. (1982). Episode cognition: internal representations of interaction routines. In L. Berkowitz (Ed.), *Advances in experimental social psychology* (pp. 59–104), New York: Academic Press.

Forgas, J. P. (1992). On bad mood and peculiar people: Affect and person typicality in impression formation. *Journal of Personality and Social Psychology, 62,* 863–875.

Forgas, J. P. (1993). On making sense of odd couples: Mood effects on the perception of mismatched relationships. *Personality and Social Psychology Bulletin, 19,* 59–71.

Forgas, J. P. (1994). Sad and guilty? Affective influences on the explanation of conflict episodes. *Journal of Personality and Social Psychology, 66,* 56–68.

Forgas, J. P. (1995a). Mood and judgment: The affect infusion model (AIM). *Psychological Bulletin, 117*(1), 39–66.

Forgas, J. P. (1995b). Strange couples: Mood effects on judgments and memory about prototypical and atypical targets. *Personality and Social Psychology Bulletin, 21,* 747–765.

Forgas, J. P. (1998a). Asking nicely? Mood effects on responding to more or less polite requests. *Personality and Social Psychology Bulletin, 24,* 173–185.

Forgas, J. P. (1998b). Happy and mistaken? Mood effects on the fundamental attribution error. *Journal of Personality and Social Psychology, 75,* 318–331.

Forgas, J. P. (1998c). On feeling good and getting your way: Mood effects on negotiation strategies and outcomes. *Journal of Personality and Social Psychology, 74,* 565–577.

Forgas, J. P. (1999a). Feeling and speaking: Mood effects on verbal communication strategies. *Personality and Social Psychology Bulletin, 25,* 850–863.

Forgas, J. P. (1999b). On feeling good and being rude: Affective influences on language use and request formulations. *Journal of Personality and Social Psychology, 76,* 928–939.

Forgas, J. P. (2000). Managing moods: Towards a dual-process theory of spontaneous mood regulation. *Psychological Inquiry, 11,* 172–177.

Forgas, J. P. (2002). Feeling and doing: Affective influences on interpersonal behavior. *Psychological Inquiry, 13,* 1–28.

Forgas, J. P. (Ed.). (2006). *Affect in social cognition and behavior.* New York: Psychology Press.

Forgas, J. P. (2007). When sad is better than happy: Negative affect can improve the quality and effectiveness of persuasive messages and social influence strategies. *Journal of Experimental Social Psychology, 43,* 513–528.

Forgas, J. P., & Bower, G. H. (1987). Mood effects on person perception judgements. *Journal of Personality and Social Psychology, 53,* 53–60.

Forgas, J. P., Bower, G. H., & Krantz, S. (1984). The influence of mood on perceptions of social interactions. *Journal of Experimental Social Psychology, 20,* 497–513.

Forgas, J. P., Bower, G. H., & Moylan, S. J. (1990). Praise or blame? Affective influences on attributions for achievement. *Journal of Personality and Social Psychology, 59,* 809–818.

Forgas, J. P., & Fiedler, K. (1996). Us and them: Mood effects on intergroup discrimination. *Journal of Personality and Social Psychology, 70,* 36–52.

Forgas, J. P., & George, J. M. (2001). Affective influences on judgments and behavior in organizations: An information processing perspective. *Organizational Behavior and Human Decision Processes, 86,* 3–34.

Forgas, J. P., & Moylan, S. J. (1987). After the movies: The effects of transient mood states on social judgments. *Personality and Social Psychology Bulletin, 13,* 478–489.

Forgas, J. P., Vargas, P., & Laham, S. (2005). Mood effects on eyewitness memory: Affective influences on susceptibility to misinformation. *Journal of Experimental Social Psychology, 41,* 574–588.

Gaertner, S. L., & Dovidio, J. F. (1986). The aversive form of racism. In J. F. Dovidio & S. L. Gaertner (Eds.), *Prejudice, discrimination, and racism* (pp. 91–125). San Diego, CA: Academic Press.

Gouaux, C. (1971). Induced affective states and interpersonal attraction. *Journal of Personality and Social Psychology, 20,* 37–43.

Gouaux, C., & Summers, K. (1973). Interpersonal attraction as a function of affective states and affective change. *Journal of Research in Personality, 7,* 254–260.

Griffitt, W. (1970). Environmental effects on interpersonal behavior: Ambient effective temperature and attraction. *Journal of Personality and Social Psychology, 15,* 240–244.

Haddock, G., Zanna, M. P., & Esses, V. M. (1993). Assessing the structure of prejudicial attitudes: The case of attitudes toward homosexuals. *Journal of Personality and Social Psychology, 65,* 1105–1118.

Harmon-Jones, E. (1999). Toward an understanding of the motivation underlying dissonance effects: Is the production of aversive consequences necessary? In E. Harmon-Jones & J. Mills (Eds.), *Cognitive dissonance: Progress on a pivotal theory in social psychology* (pp. 71–99). Washington, DC: American Psychological Association.

Harmon-Jones, E., Brehm, J. W., Greenberg, J., Simon, L., & Nelson, D. E. (1996). Evidence that the production of aversive consequences is not necessary to create cognitive dissonance. *Journal of Personality and Social Psychology, 70,* 5–16.

Hilgard, E. R. (1980). The trilogy of mind: Cognition, affection, and conation. *Journal of the History of the Behavioral Sciences, 16,* 107–117.

Janis, I. L., & Feshbach, S. (1953). Effects of fear-arousing communications. *Journal of Abnormal and Social Psychology, 48,* 78–92.

Keltner, D., Ellsworth, P. C., & Edwards, K. (1993). Beyond simple pessimism: Effects of sadness and anger on social judgment. *Journal of Personality and Social Psychology, 64*, 740–752.

Lambert, A. J., Khan, S. R., Lickel, B. A., & Fricke, K. (1997). Mood and the correction of positive versus negative stereotypes. *Journal of Personality and Social Psychology, 72*, 1002–1016.

Martin, L. L. (2000). Moods don't convey information: Moods in context do. In J. P. Forgas (Ed.), *Feeling and thinking: The role of affect in social cognition* (pp. 153–177). New York: Cambridge University Press.

McGuire, W. J. (1985). Attitudes and attitude change. In G. Lindzey & E. Aronson (Eds.), *The handbook of social psychology* (3rd ed., Vol. 2, pp. 233–346). New York: Random House.

Mead, G. H. (1934). *Mind, self and society.* Chicago: University of Chicago Press.

Nasby, W. (1994). Moderators of mood-congruent encoding: Self-/other-reference and affirmative/nonaffirmative judgement. *Cognition and Emotion, 8*, 259–278.

Nasby, W. (1996). Moderators of mood-congruent encoding and judgment: Evidence that elated and depressed moods implicate distinct processes. *Cognition and Emotion, 10*, 361–377.

Niedenthal, P., & Halberstadt, J. (2000). Grounding categories in emotional response. In J. P. Forgas (Ed.), *Feeling and thinking: The role of affect in social cognition* (pp. 357–386). New York: Cambridge University Press.

Pervin, L. A. (1976). A free-response description approach to the analysis of person-situation interaction. *Journal of Personality and Social Psychology, 34*, 465–474.

Petty, R. E., Gleicher, F., & Baker, S. M. (1991). Multiple roles for affect in persuasion. In J. P. Forgas (Ed.), *Emotion and social judgments* (pp. 181–200). Oxford, England: Pergamon Press.

Raghunathan, R., & Trope, Y. (1999). *Mood-as-a-resource in processing persuasive messages.* Unpublished manuscript.

Razran, G. H. S. (1940). Conditioned response changes in rating and appraising sociopolitical slogans. *Psychological Bulletin, 37*, 481.

Schwarz, N. (1990). Feelings as information: Informational and motivational functions of affective states. In E. T. Higgins & R. Sorrentino (Eds.), *Handbook of motivation and cognition: Foundations of social behaviour* (Vol. 2, pp. 527–561). New York: Guilford Press.

Schwarz, N., & Clore, G. L. (1983). Mood, misattribution and judgments of well being: Informative and directive functions of affective states. *Journal of Personality and Social Psychology, 45*, 513–523.

Sedikides, C. (1994). Incongruent effects of sad mood on self-conception valence: It's a matter of time. *European Journal of Social Psychology, 24*, 161–172.

Sedikides, C. (1995). Central and peripheral self-conceptions are differentially influenced by mood: Tests of the differential sensitivity hypothesis. *Journal of Personality and Social Psychology, 69*(4), 759–777.

Sinclair, R. C., & Mark, M. M. (1995). The effects of mood state on judgmental accuracy: Processing strategy as a mechanism. *Cognition and Emotion, 9*, 417–438.

Sinclair, R. C., Mark, M. M., & Clore, G. L. (1994). Mood related persuasion depends on (mis)attributions. *Social Cognition, 12*, 309–326.

Smith, S. M., & Petty, R. E. (1995). Personality moderators of mood congruency effects on cognition: The role of self-esteem and negative mood regulation. *Journal of Personality and Social Psychology, 68*, 1092–1107.

Stangor, C., Sullivan, L. A., & Ford, T. E. (1991). Affective and cognitive determinants of prejudice. *Social Cognition, 9*, 359–380.

Stephan, W. G., & Stephan, C. W. (1996). *Intergroup relations*. Boulder, CO: Westview Press.

Strack, F. (1992). The different routes to social judgments: Experiential versus informational strategies. In L. L. Martin & A. Tesser (Eds.), *The construction of social judgments* (pp. 249–275). Hillsdale, NJ: Erlbaum.

Thomas, W. I., & Znaniecki, F. (1928). *The Polish peasant in Europe and America*. Boston: Badger.

Trope, Y., Ferguson, M., & Raghunathan, R. (2001). Mood as a resource in processing self-relevant information. In J. P. Forgas (Ed.), *The handbook of affect and social cognition* (pp. 256–274). Mahwah, NJ: Erlbaum.

Unkelbach, C., Forgas, J. P., & Denson, T. F. (2008). The turban effect: The influence of Muslim headgear and induced affect on aggressive responses in the shooter bias paradigm. *Journal of Experimental Social Psychology, 44*, 1409–1413.

Wegener, D. T., Petty, R. E., & Klein, D. J. (1994) Effects of mood on high elaboration attitude change: The mediating role of likelihood judgments. *European Journal of Social Psychology, 24*, 25–43.

Zajonc, R. B. (1980). Feeling and thinking: Preferences need no inferences. *American Psychologist, 35*, 151–175.

Zajonc, R. B. (2000). Feeling and thinking: Closing the debate over the independence of affect. In J. P. Forgas (Ed.), *Feeling and thinking: The role of affect in social cognition* (pp. 31–58). New York: Cambridge University Press.

Zanna, M. P., & Cooper, J. (1974). Dissonance and the pill: An attribution approach to studying the arousal properties of dissonance. *Journal of Personality and Social Psychology, 29*, 703–709.

AUTHOR NOTE

This work was supported by a Professorial Fellowship from the Australian Research Council and the Research Prize by the Alexander von Humboldt Foundation to Joseph P. Forgas. Please address all correspondence in connection with this paper to Joseph P. Forgas, at the School of Psychology, University of New South Wales, Sydney 2052, Australia; e-mail jp.forgas@unsw.edu.au. For further information on this research project, see also the Web site at http://www.psy.unsw.edu.au/Users/JForgas/jforgas/.

Section III

Attitudes and Persuasion

10

Action-Based Model of Dissonance
On Cognitive Conflict and Attitude Change

EDDIE HARMON-JONES, DAVID M. AMODIO,
AND CINDY HARMON-JONES

Cognitive dissonance theory (Festinger, 1957) and its research have led to an increased understanding of attitude change processes. In this chapter, we review Festinger's original theory, review some revisions of the theory, and then describe a more recent conceptualization of dissonance, the *action-based model*. The action-based model begins with the assumption that many perceptions and cognitions automatically activate action tendencies. This assumption is consistent with several perspectives, such as William James's (1890) ideomotor conception, Gibson's (1966, 1979) ecological approach to perception, and subsequent elaborations of these basic ideas (Berkowitz, 1984; Dijksterhuis & Bargh, 2001; Fiske, 1992; McArthur & Baron, 1983; Smith & Semin, 2004). The action-based model goes further to suggest that when these "cognitions" with action implications come into conflict, a negative affective state is aroused, referred to as *dissonance*. Our model posits that dissonance affect is aroused because conflicting action-based cognitions have the potential to interfere with effective action. The organism is motivated to reduce this negative affect and ultimately reduce the "cognitive inconsistency" in order to behave effectively. This way of conceptualizing dissonance processes addresses many problems with past theories concerned with dissonance, and it suggests a framework for integrating an array of other nondissonance theories and research.

OVERVIEW OF THE THEORY OF COGNITIVE DISSONANCE

The original theory of cognitive dissonance predicted that when an individual holds two or more elements of knowledge that are relevant to each other but inconsistent with one another, a state of discomfort is created. This unpleasant state is referred to as "dissonance." According to the theory, the magnitude of dissonance in relation to a cognition can be formulated as equal to D / D + C, where D is the sum of cognitions dissonant with a particular cognition and C is the sum of cognitions consonant with that same particular cognition, with each cognition weighted for importance.

According to the original theory, dissonance motivates individuals to engage in psychological work in an effort to reduce the inconsistency between cognitions. So, if a dieter consumed a fattening meal, he would likely be in a state of dissonance. Assuming that the commitment to the diet is not as strong as the enjoyment of the food (at this moment), the theory would predict that he will reduce dissonance by adding consonant cognitions (e.g., "the meal was the best I have had in years"), subtracting dissonant cognitions (e.g., "I don't really need to be on a diet"), increasing the importance of consonant cognitions (e.g., "sensory pleasures are very important"), or decreasing the importance of dissonant cognitions (e.g., "diets are unimportant").

Researchers have most often measured dissonance reduction with attitude change. Attitude change in response to a state of dissonance is expected to be in the direction of the cognition that is most resistant to change. In laboratory tests of the theory, knowledge about recent behavior is usually assumed to be the cognition most resistant to change, perhaps because of the local focus on the situation (Ledgerwood & Trope, this volume). If one has recently performed a behavior, it is usually difficult to convince oneself that the behavior did not occur. Thus, attitudes often change to become more consistent with a recent behavioral commitment.

ALTERNATIVE THEORETICAL EXPLANATIONS

Beginning in the mid-1960s, researchers began to propose alternative explanations for dissonance effects. Whereas the original theory focused on an inconsistency between cognitions, these theories invoked higher-order, more complex processes, and changed the focus from inconsistency to the individual's self-concept and the individual's concern with harming others.

Self-Consistency

In self-consistency theory, Aronson (1969, 1999) proposed that dissonance only occurs when a person acts in a way that violates his or her self-concept, that is, when a person performs a behavior inconsistent with his or her self-view. Because most persons view themselves in a positive light, such that they are competent, rational, and moral, dissonance is experienced when a person behaves in an incompetent, irrational, or immoral way. One of the primary predictions derived from this revision is that high self-esteem individuals should respond with more dissonance reduction than low self-esteem individuals, because dissonance experiments induce individuals to act in ways discrepant from a positive self-view. Studies testing this prediction have produced mixed results: some showed that high self-esteem individuals showed greater attitude change, some showed that low self-esteem individuals showed greater attitude change, and some found no differences between self-esteem groups (see Stone, 2003, for review).

Self-Affirmation

Steele (1988) proposed that individuals possess a motive to maintain an overall self-image of moral and adaptive adequacy. He stated that dissonance-induced attitude change occurs because dissonance threatens this positive self-image. Steele proposed that instead of a motivation to reduce inconsistency, individuals are motivated to affirm the integrity of the self or maintain a "perception of global integrity, that is, of overall moral and adaptive adequacy" (Steele, Spencer, & Lynch, 1993, p. 885; see Sherman & Cohen, 2006, for a recent review). However, Simon, Greenberg, and Brehm (1995) presented evidence supporting Festinger's original theory over self-affirmation theory; they found that simply activating non-self-relevant but important concepts caused the same attitude effects as self-affirmations, and that self-affirmations caused individuals to reduce the importance of the dissonant cognitions. Other evidence has been presented that is difficult to interpret in self-affirmation theory terms, such as evidence suggesting that self-affirmations relevant to the recent dissonant act increase rather than decrease dissonance-related attitude change (Aronson, Cohen, & Nail, 1999).

Self-Standards Model

Stone and Cooper's (2003) self-standards model of dissonance posited that the self is multidimensional and that the accessibility of different aspects of the self determines how and whether a particular behavior leads to the state of cognitive dissonance (see also Cooper, this volume).

The self models of dissonance also have difficulty explaining the dissonance effects produced in rats (Lawrence & Festinger, 1962), as rats are believed to lack self-conceptions of morality, rationality, and competence. Four-year-old humans and capuchin monkeys, who also lack the complex self-concepts required by self models of dissonance, engage in dissonance reduction (Egan, Santos, & Bloom, 2007). Although self aspects appear to moderate dissonance processes, they are not necessary to cause dissonance (Harmon-Jones, 2000b; Stone & Cooper, 2003). In terms of the original theory, self-related cognitions would be expected to affect the magnitude of dissonance, because cognitions related to the self are often important to an adult human. Thus, results derived from the self models are compatible with the original theory, but the self models are unable to explain basic dissonance motivation effects concerning discrepancies that do not involve the self.

Aversive Consequences

Cooper and Fazio (1984) proposed that dissonance was not due to an inconsistency between the individual's cognitions, but rather to feeling personally responsible for producing an aversive consequence. According to the original theory of cognitive dissonance, the production of aversive consequences would be expected to increase the amount of dissonance produced because an aversive consequence in itself may be an important dissonant cognition, or it may strengthen one's behavioral commitment (see Harmon-Jones, 1999). However, the original theory would deny that an aversive consequence is *necessary* to produce dissonance.

The aversive consequences revision has been challenged by experiments that have found dissonance-related attitude change and negative affect to occur when individuals engage in counterattitudinal behaviors that do not produce aversive consequences (Harmon-Jones, 2000a; Harmon-Jones et al., 1996). McGregor, Newby-Clark, and Zanna (1999) also summarized research showing that attitudinal ambivalence research has provided evidence of dissonance-related negative affect in the absence of feeling personally responsible for producing negative consequences.

Nevertheless, some important questions regarding the basic mechanism underlying dissonance effects remained: Why does cognitive inconsistency evoke the negative motivational state? Why does this state motivate attitude change? Festinger (1957) posited no answers to these questions, but the action-based model of dissonance does (Harmon-Jones, 1999).

ACTION-BASED MODEL OF DISSONANCE: WHY DO DISSONANCE PROCESSES OCCUR?

The action-based model concurs with theorizing in other areas of psychology in proposing that perceptions and cognitions can serve as action tendencies (Berkowitz, 1984; Dijksterhuis & Bargh, 2001; Fiske, 1992; Gibson, 1979; James, 1890; McArthur & Baron, 1983; Smith & Semin, 2004). The action-based model further proposes that *dissonance between cognitions evokes a negative affective state because it has the potential to interfere with effective and unconflicted action.* In essence, discrepant cognitions create problems for the individual when those cognitions have conflicting action tendencies. Dissonance reduction brings cognitions into line with behavioral commitments, and serves the function of facilitating the execution of effective and unconflicted action (see also Jones & Gerard, 1967).

The action-based model proposes both a proximal and a distal motivation for the existence of dissonance processes. The proximal motive for reducing dissonance is to reduce or eliminate the negative emotion of dissonance. The distal motivation is the need for effective and unconflicted action.

After an individual makes a difficult decision, psychological processing should assist with the execution of the decision. The tendency of participants in dissonance research to view the chosen alternative more favorably and the rejected alternative more negatively after a decision may help the individual to follow through, to effectively carry out the actions that follow from the decision.

As an example, consider an important, effortful behavioral decision, such as beginning an exercise program. In this situation, the "actions" implied by the decision are the exercise behaviors. The benefits of exercise, from better-fitting clothes to improved long-term health, constitute consonant cognitions. The drawbacks of exercise, including the time commitment and muscle soreness, constitute dissonant cognitions. Dissonance affect comes from the conflict between the consonant and dissonant cognitions, and this unpleasant affect motivates the individual to decrease the discrepancy by bringing the cognitions in line with the behavioral commitment. The better an individual is able to reduce the number and importance of dissonant cognitions and increase the number and importance of consonant cognitions, the more likely it is that he or she will faithfully perform the actions required by the exercise program over the long-term and reap its benefits. From the action-based model perspective, what is important is not so much the discrepancy between the cognitions themselves, but rather the discrepancy between the cognitions' action tendencies. Cognitions consonant with the decision impel one to exercise, while cognitions dissonant from the decision have the opposite effect. Reducing the discrepancy by increasing consonant cognitions and/or decreasing dissonant cognitions would be expected to reduce negative affect. More importantly in our view, discrepancy reduction would also be expected to facilitate more effectively engaging in the exercise program.

As we review later, the action-based model is supported by neurophysiological research that demonstrates that dissonance arousal is associated with neural activations involved in the detection of response conflict and negative affect, whereas dissonance reduction is associated with neural activations involved with approach motivation. Other models of dissonance do not make these predictions and often instead propose that dissonance reduction is a self-protective process that should be associated with defensive motivation.

The action-based model views dissonance processes as adaptive. Of course, adaptive, functional psychological processes that are beneficial in most circumstances may not be beneficial in all circumstances. Occasionally, dissonance reduction may cause persons to maintain a prolonged commitment to a harmful chosen course of action, when it would be better to disengage. By adaptive, we mean that the process benefits the organism most of the time.

In addition, we must distinguish between dissonance motivation and dissonance reduction. The action-based model, like the original theory, proposes that cognitive discrepancy produces negative affect, and that the negative affect motivates attitude change (for review, see Forgas, this volume). However, it is possible to continue to maintain conflicting attitudes (although negative affect may persist). Furthermore, there are some situations in which individuals do disengage from harmful chosen courses of action, even though they may experience high levels of negative affect in the process.

TESTS OF THE ACTION-BASED MODEL

Action-Orientation and Spreading of Alternatives

According to the action-based model of dissonance, the postdecisional state is similar to an action-oriented state (Beckmann & Irle, 1985; Gollwitzer, 1990; Kuhl, 1984), where the individual is in a mode of "getting things done." Once a decision is made, an organism should be motivationally tuned toward enacting the decision and behaving effectively with regard to it. An implemental or action-oriented mind-set is one in which plans are made to effectively execute behaviors associated with the decision (Gollwitzer & Bayer, 1999). We suggest that this implemental or action-oriented state is similar to an approach motivational state. When a person is in an action-oriented state, implementation of decisions is enhanced (Gollwitzer & Sheeran, 2006). We suggest that these action-oriented states are similar to Jones and Gerard's (1967) concept of an unequivocal behavior orientation. Jones and Gerard's (1967) unequivocal behavior orientation was posited to be an adaptive strategy that forced the individuals to bring their relevant cognitions into harmony with each other. The unequivocal behavior orientation "represents a commitment to action in the face of uncertainty. Such a commitment involves the risks of acting inappropriately, but such risks are assumed to be less grave on the average than the risks of hesitant or conflicted action" (p. 185). Jones and Gerard further posited, "When the time comes to act, the great advantage of having a set of coherent internally consistent dispositions is that the individual is not forced to listen to the babble of competing inner forces" (p. 181).

The action-oriented state that follows decision-making is proposed to be equivalent to the state in which dissonance motivation operates and discrepancy reduction occurs (Harmon-Jones & Harmon-Jones, 2002). Thus, experimentally manipulating the degree of action-orientation experienced following a decision should affect the degree of discrepancy reduction. In one experiment, participants were asked to make either an easy decision or a difficult decision. Participants then completed a neutral questionnaire that asked them to list seven things they did in a typical day, or they completed an action-oriented questionnaire that asked them to list seven things they could do to perform well on the exercise they had chosen. Participants then reevaluated the exercises. Participants who made a difficult decision in the action-oriented condition demonstrated a greater increase in preference for the chosen over the rejected exercise (i.e., spreading of alternatives) than participants in the other three conditions.

In a second experiment, we replicated the results of the first experiment using a different manipulation of action-orientation (Harmon-Jones & Harmon-Jones, 2002). In this experiment, action-orientation was induced by asking participants to think about a project or goal that they intended to accomplish, and to list the steps they intended to use to successfully follow through with their decision (Gollwitzer, 1990). Two comparison conditions were also included, one in which participants wrote about a neutral, ordinary day and one in which participants wrote about an unresolved problem. Participants first made a difficult decision between two equally attractive research studies in which they could participate. Following the decision, participants completed the action-orientation manipulation, and then rerated their attitudes toward the research studies. Participants in the action-orientation condition engaged in more spreading of alternatives than did participants in the comparison conditions. This study provided stronger support for the action-based model because, in this case, the action-orientation induction was unrelated to the decision in the experiment.

Neural Activity Underlying Dissonance and Dissonance Reduction

The action-based model of cognitive dissonance is consistent with recent models of self-regulation, and it provides an important theoretical framework for placing neural processes in the context of motivated cognition.

Dissonance Arousal, Conflict Monitoring, and the Anterior Cingulate Cortex According the action-based model, dissonance is aroused by the activation of cognitions that interfere with goal-driven behavior. Although few studies have directly examined the process of dissonance arousal in the brain, much attention has been given to questions of how the brain processes response conflicts on tasks such as the color-naming Stroop (1935) task. For example, when completing the color-naming Stroop task, one's goal is to identify the ink color of a word stimulus, regardless of the word's meaning. However, the processing of word meaning is typically automatic, and when a word's meaning is incongruent with one's goal to judge the word's color, such as when the word *red* is presented in blue ink, there is conflict between the intended and the automatic response tendencies. In studies examining neural activity during the Stroop task, anterior cingulate cortex activity is greater during incongruent trials than congruent trials (Carter et al., 1998). Similar findings have been observed using other response-conflict tasks, such as the Eriksen flanker's task (Eriksen & Eriksen, 1974; Gehring, Goss, Coles, Meyer, & Donchin, 1993), and the Go/No-Go task (Botvinick, Nystrom, Fissel, Carter, & Cohen, 1999; Keihl, Liddle, & Hopfinger, 2001). Researchers have interpreted these findings as evidence that the anterior cingulate cortex plays a role in monitoring action tendencies for potential conflicts, so that other mechanisms may be engaged to override the unwanted tendency and to promote an effective goal-directed response (Botvinick, Braver, Barch, Carter, & Cohen, 2001). Thus, conflict monitoring represents the first component of a dual-process model of cognitive control, whereby the need for control is initially detected.

Recently, we have suggested that the anterior cingulate cortex, and its associated role in conflict monitoring, corresponds well to the process of dissonance arousal (Harmon-Jones, 2004). The conflict-monitoring account is consistent with the action-based model of dissonance, because it too focuses on conflicts between action tendencies. Amodio et al. (2004) integrated the conflict-monitoring framework with social psychological theories of self-regulation by examining conflict between automatic stereotyping tendencies and participants' goals to respond without prejudice. In this study, anterior cingulate cortex activity was monitored using an event-related potential measure referred to as the "error-related negativity" component (Gehring et al., 1993; van Veen & Carter, 2006). When participants—who reported low-prejudice attitudes—accidentally made responses that reflected the application of racial stereotypes, thus constituting a clear response conflict, the anterior cingulate cortex was activated. By comparison, anterior cingulate cortex activity was lower on other trial types that did not elicit conflicting actions.

In subsequent research, Amodio, Devine, and Harmon-Jones (2008) demonstrated that heightened anterior cingulate cortex activity associated with racially biased responses was only observed for participants with strong personal motivations to respond without prejudice. Participants without personal motivations (i.e., high-prejudice participants) did not show enhanced anterior cingulate cortex activity when their responses reflected the application of stereotypes. Thus, when participants made responses that were dissonant with their attitude-based intentions, anterior cingulate cortex activity was high. Furthermore, participants with stronger anterior cingulate cortex activity to dissonant responses were more likely to engage in controlled behavior (slower, more careful responding). These studies provided evidence for the role of the anterior cingulate cortex, and its associated conflict monitoring function, as a critical process underlying dissonance arousal and the control of action. This line of research demonstrated that high-level conflicts, the type with which dissonance theory has been most concerned, also activate the anterior cingulate cortex.

Response conflict tasks used in studies of the anterior cingulate cortex have also been found to cause increases in skin conductance, which indexes sympathetic nervous system arousal (Hajcak, McDonald, & Simons, 2003, 2004), and measures of negative affect such as the startle eyeblink response (Hajcak & Foti, 2008). Situations that typically evoke cognitive dissonance also cause increased skin conductance (Elkin & Leippe, 1986; Harmon-Jones et al., 1996; Losch & Cacioppo, 1990) and negative affect (Elliot & Devine, 1994; Harmon-Jones, 2000a; Zanna & Cooper, 1974). Taken together, these studies suggest that the anterior cingulate cortex is associated with the negative affective state of dissonance and involved in initiating dissonance-reducing action. These results showing that dissonance is associated with increased anterior cingulate cortex activation were derived from the action-based model, which suggests that dissonance results from the need for effective and unconflicted action (distal motive). This anterior cingulate cortex prediction could be viewed as compatible with the original theory of dissonance but is unlikely compatible with other versions of dissonance because of their focus on high-level self-consistencies or other non-consistency-oriented motivations (e.g., aversive consequences, self-affirmation).

Dissonance Reduction and the Prefrontal Cortex

The arousal of negative affect by cognitive discrepancy drives efforts to reduce the dissonant state. The process of cognitive discrepancy reduction can occur rapidly (e.g., before essay writing; Rabbie, Brehm, & Cohen, 1959). According to the action-based model, the process of discrepancy-reduction engages approach-oriented motivational processes, as the individual works to successfully implement the new commitment. Only the action-based model makes the prediction that discrepancy reduction following commitment to action involves approach motivational processes, which the model views as part of the distal motive of effecting unconflicted behavior. Other models of dissonance propose that dissonance reduction is motivated by a need to protect the self-image. Thus, these other models would not propose that dissonance reduction involves approach motivation, or that dissonance reduction would involve brain regions associated with translating intentions into effective action.

Recent neurocognitive models of control posit that the prefrontal cortex governs the implementation of a controlled response following the detection of conflict by the anterior cingulate cortex (Botvinick et al., 2001; Miller & Cohen, 2001). That is, as discrepancy-related activity in the anterior cingulate cortex rises, anterior cingulate cortex-to-prefrontal cortex communication increases. The prefrontal cortex plays a critical role in responding to the discrepancy by amplifying an intended response tendency to override the unintended tendency (Kerns et al., 2004). The action-based model suggests that whereas the anterior cingulate cortex is associated with dissonance arousal, regions of the prefrontal cortex are critical for dissonance reduction. The dissociation between the neural processes related to dissonance arousal and discrepancy reduction supports the idea that these two processes reflect the operation of independent underlying mechanisms. However, neurocognitive models do not clearly specify which regions of the prefrontal cortex contribute to different aspects of discrepancy reduction and action control, and they are silent on the role of motivation in the process of control.

Converging evidence from studies using a range of methods suggests that prefrontal cortex activity is lateralized on the basis of motivational direction, with the left frontal region being involved in approach motivational processes ("going toward"), and the right frontal region being involved in inhibitory or withdrawal motivational processes ("going away"). For instance, damage to the left frontal lobe causes depressive symptoms, with stronger depressive symptoms among patients with damage closer to the frontal pole (e.g., Robinson & Downhill, 1995). Given that depression relates to impaired approach-related processes, damage to brain regions involved in approach motivation would lead to depression.

Much research assessing electroencephalographic (EEG) activity has similarly found that increased left frontal cortical activation relates to state and trait approach motivation (Amodio et al., 2007; Amodio, Master, et al., 2008; Harmon-Jones & Allen, 1997, 1998; Harmon-Jones, 2003, 2004). Source localization of frontal asymmetry has demonstrated that it reflects activity in the dorsolateral prefrontal cortex (Pizzagalli, Sherwood, Henriques, & Davidson, 2005). For instance, research has related greater left frontal activity to the state engagement in approach-related responses (Amodio et al., 2007; Harmon-Jones & Sigelman, 2001) and to the accessibility of approach-related goals (Amodio, Shah, Sigelman, Brazy, & Harmon-Jones, 2004). In addition, fMRI studies have observed greater left prefrontal cortex activity during the retrieval of approach-related action words (Bunge, 2004; Petersen, Fox, Posner, Mintun, & Raichle, 1988). These findings suggest that the left prefrontal cortex is involved in the implementation of intended action and the formation (and restructuring) of goals to guide future action. They are also congruent with the action-based model's position that the discrepancy reduction process serves to promote goal-directed behavior through the restructuring of goal-relevant attitudes.

Considered as a whole, research on left prefrontal cortex function suggests that it is involved in approach motivational processes aimed at resolving inconsistency (MacDonald, Cohen, Stenger, & Carter, 2000; van Veen & Carter, 2006). Next, we describe a set of studies that have examined the role of left prefrontal cortex activity and approach motivation as they relate directly to the resolution of dissonance-arousing discrepancies. The prediction of the action-based model is that commitment to a chosen course of action should lead to an enhancement in relative left frontal cortical activity, which in turn should be associated with attitude change in support of the chosen course of action.

Induced Compliance and Relative Left Frontal Cortical Activation   In an experiment by Harmon-Jones, Gerdjikov, and Harmon-Jones (2008), participants were randomly assigned to a low- versus high-choice condition in an induced compliance paradigm. Immediately after starting to write the counterattitudinal essay (regarding a tuition increase at their university), participants' EEG activity was recorded. After essay completion, attitudes were assessed. Participants in the high-choice condition evidenced greater relative left frontal activation than individuals in the low-choice condition (Harmon-Jones, Gerdjikov, et al., 2008). Moreover, participants in the high-choice condition evidenced attitudes to be more consistent with the behavior than participants in the low-choice condition.

Neurofeedback of Relative Left Frontal Cortical Activity and Free Choice   In the previous experiment, when the psychological process (commitment to a chosen course of action) was manipulated and the proposed physiological substrate was measured (left frontal cortical activation), commitment to a chosen course of action increased relative left frontal cortical activation (Harmon-Jones, Gerdjikov, et al., 2008). To provide stronger causal inferences regarding the role of the left frontal cortical region in following through with the commitment (discrepancy reduction), it is important to manipulate the physiology (or proposed mediator) and measure the psychological outcome (Sigall & Mills, 1998; Spencer, Zanna, & Fong, 2005). Therefore, we conducted another experiment in which relative left frontal cortical activation was manipulated after dissonance was aroused to test whether a manipulated increase in relative left frontal cortical activation would increase dissonance reduction (attitude change).

To manipulate relative left frontal cortical activity, we used neurofeedback training of EEG. Neurofeedback presents the participant with real-time feedback on brainwave activity. If brainwave activity over a particular cortical region changes in the direction desired by the experiment, then the participant is given "reward" feedback; if brainwave activity does not change in the desired direction, either negative feedback or no feedback is given. Rewards can be as simple as the presentation of a tone that informs the participant that brain activity has changed in the desired way. Neurofeedback-induced changes result from operant conditioning, and these changes in EEG often occur without awareness of how the brain activity changes occurred (Kamiya, 1979; Kotchoubey, Kübler, Strehl, Flor, & Birbaumer, 2002; Siniatchkin, Kropp, & Gerber, 2000).

In past research, neurofeedback was effective at decreasing but not increasing relative left frontal activity after only 3 days of training. The decrease in relative left frontal activity brought about with this brief neurofeedback training caused less approach-related emotional responses (Allen, Harmon-Jones, & Cavender, 2001). Based on these past results, we predicted that a decrease left frontal condition would be more successful at changing brain activity than an increase left frontal condition.

Most importantly, we predicted that a decrease in relative left frontal activity would lead to a decrease in discrepancy reduction as measured by spreading of alternatives. To test these predictions, we used the decision paradigm developed by Brehm (1956). First, participants were randomly assigned to increase or decrease relative left frontal activation during two days of neurofeedback training. Then, on the third day, immediately following a difficult decision, participants received neurofeedback training in the same direction as the previous two days. Finally, attitudinal spreading of alternatives was assessed. In support of predictions, neurofeedback training caused a reduction in relative left frontal cortical activity, which caused an elimination of the familiar spreading of alternatives effect (Harmon-Jones, Harmon-Jones, Fearn, Sigelman, & Johnson, 2008). This experiment's manipulation of relative left frontal cortical activity, a presumed mediator of the effect of commitment on discrepancy reduction, provides strong support for the role of relative left frontal activity in discrepancy reduction processes.

Action-Oriented Mind-set and Relative Left Frontal Cortical Activation   A follow-up experiment (Harmon-Jones, Harmon-Jones, et al., 2008, Experiment 2) was designed to conceptually replicate the previous experiment. In this experiment, we manipulated action-oriented mental processing following a difficult decision. We expected to replicate past research in which the action-oriented mind-set increased discrepancy reduction following a decision (Harmon-Jones & Harmon-Jones, 2002). Secondly, we expected the action-oriented mind-set would increase relative left frontal cortical activity. Finally, we expected this increase in left frontal cortical activity would relate to discrepancy reduction, as assessed by spreading of alternatives.

To further extend past research, we included a condition to manipulate positive affect that was low in approach motivation (i.e., participants wrote about a time when something happened that caused them to feel very good about themselves but was not the result of their own actions). This was done to distinguish between the effects of positive affect and of approach motivation on spreading of alternatives. Past research suggested that action-oriented mind-sets increase positive affect (Taylor & Gollwitzer, 1995), but we do not predict that positive affect, itself, causes increased left frontal cortical activity or an increase in spreading of alternatives.

Results revealed that the action-oriented mind-set increased relative left frontal cortical activity and spreading of alternatives, as compared to a neutral condition and a positive affect/low-approach motivation condition. These results provide a conceptual replication of the past results by using a different operationalization of action-oriented motivational processing. Both experiments revealed that the hypothesized increase in action-oriented processing was manifested in increased relative left frontal cortical activity. Moreover, both studies revealed that relative left frontal activation correlated positively with spreading of alternatives. This correlation occurred across both conditions within the neurofeedback experiment and within the action-oriented mind-set condition of the second experiment.

Left Prefrontal Cortex Activity and Approach Motivation Following Prejudice-Related Discrepancy   Discrepancies between one's attitude and behavior are often investigated in the context of intergroup relations. For example, most White Americans today believe it is wrong to discriminate on the basis of race. But at the same time, most White Americans show evidence of automatically activated tendencies to express racial stereotypes and negative evaluations. Thus, in intergroup situations, people are often confronted with a discrepancy between their nonprejudiced beliefs and their implicit tendencies to express prejudice. This phenomenon clearly represents a case of cognitive dissonance.

To examine the roles of left prefrontal cortex activity and approach motivation in the context of prejudice, we preselected White American participants who reported holding low-prejudice attitudes in an earlier testing session (Amodio, Devine, & Harmon-Jones, 2007). Participants were told that we would examine their neural responses as they viewed pictures of White, Black, and Asian faces. Following this task, participants were given bogus feedback indicating that their neural activity revealed a strong negative emotional response toward Black faces, compared with White and Asian faces. This feedback was highly discrepant with participants' non-prejudiced beliefs and, as expected, aroused strong feelings of guilt on a self-report measure (beyond changes in other emotions), and participants were not imme-diately given an opportunity to engage in behavior that might reduce their guilt. Participants also showed a decrease in left frontal cortical activity compared with baseline levels, and the degree of this decrease was correlated with their experience of guilt. This pattern suggested that the initial arousal of guilt-related dissonance was associated with a reduction in approach-motivation tendencies. Although this study was not designed to measure changes in anterior cingulate cortex activity, the decrease in left-sided prefrontal cortex activity is consistent with the idea that dis-sonance arousal is associated with a reduction in approach motivation accompanied by an increase in behavioral inhibition (e.g., Amodio, Master, et al., 2008).

The effects of left frontal activity and approach motivation were examined in the second part of the study. After the guilt manipulation, participants were told that the study was completed, but that in the time remaining in the session, they could help us by judging some stimuli ostensibly to be used in a future experi-ment. Here, we provided an opportunity to reduce their discrepancy-related guilt. We told participants that we wanted their feedback on different magazine articles that we might have participants in a future study read. Participants read the head-lines of a series of different articles. Some headlines referred to articles associated with reducing prejudice (e.g., "Improving Your Interracial Interactions"). Others were filler headlines that were unrelated to intergroup relations (e.g. "Five Steps to a Healthier Lifestyle"). Participants viewed each title for 6 seconds while their EEGs were recorded. After viewing each title, they rated their personal desire to read the article. We found that participants who reported stronger guilty affect in response to the bogus feedback indicating their prejudiced response—an index of dissonance arousal—reported significantly stronger desire to read articles related to reducing prejudice. Induction-related feelings of guilt were unrelated to participants' desire to read the filler articles. Furthermore, stronger desire to read prejudice reduction articles was associated with greater left-sided prefrontal cortex activity, consistent with the idea that discrepancy reduction involves the engage-ment of approach-related action (i.e., associated with egalitarian behavior), which involves activity of the left prefrontal cortex. Hence, these results supported the action-based model of dissonance in the context of prejudice and feelings of guilt.

CONSIDERING THE ACTION-BASED MODEL AND OTHER MODES OF DISSONANCE REDUCTION

Would a change in action orientation and/or relative left frontal cortical activity affect discrepancy reduction in other dissonance-evoking situations? We would expect left frontal cortical activity to affect dissonance processes when dissonance is aroused by a strong commitment to behavior, which is what typically occurs in the induced compliance and free choice paradigms (e.g., Beauvois & Joule, 1996; Brehm & Cohen, 1962). In such situations, we predict that individuals are motivated to follow through with their behavioral commitment and to change their attitudes to be consistent with their behavior (Stone et al., 1997). However, in some induced compliance situations, individuals may reduce dissonance by means other than attitude change, perhaps because their commitment is not sufficiently strong (Gilbert & Ebert, 2002) or because their original attitude is highly resistant to change (Simon et al., 1995). In other dissonance paradigms, we would predict relative left frontal activation to relate to dissonance reduction to the extent that dissonance is likely to be reduced via approach motivational processes, such as changing one's attitudes to be more supportive of the recent behavioral commitment.

Changing one's cognitions to bring them in alignment with each other is one way of reducing the negative emotion of dissonance. This is the method of reducing dissonance most often measured in research. However, this is not the only way a person can deal with the emotive state of dissonance. It is also possible to trivialize the dissonant cognitions (Simon et al., 1995) or engage in reality-escaping behaviors such as drinking alcohol to reduce the negative dissonance state and the motivation to engage in discrepancy reduction (Steele, Southwick, & Critchlow, 1981). The action-based model would predict that reducing dissonance by means other than attitude change would be more likely when action was not greatly needed or when the action implications of the cognitions were low.

It is also possible to experience dissonance and not reduce it. The negative emotion of dissonance provides motivation to change one's cognitions, but this motivation may not always lead to such changes. In this situation, the cognitive discrepancy would still be present, but the negative affect would remain elevated, as seen when individuals with important cognitive discrepancies suffer low self-esteem (Major & Townsend, this volume). The action-based model predicts that if an individual experiences dissonance but does not reduce it, the effectiveness of his or her behavior related to the commitment would be hampered. The effectiveness of behavior could be hampered by hindering pursuit and acquisition of an immediate goal, or it may be hampered in more diffuse ways. These and other ways of dealing with cognitive discrepancies, and with the negative emotion of dissonance, need to be considered in future research.

The action-based model does not make the claim that dissonance reduction always occurs in the direction of a decision. Sometimes a person makes a decision, and the evidence is overwhelming that the wrong decision has been made. This information would arouse dissonance. When a person realizes that he or she has made a mistake, his or her original decision is no longer the cognition most resistant to change. Consider Leon, who chose to attend one university over another. After beginning the first semester, Leon might realize that the university he chose is completely unsuitable for him. He will likely not be able to reduce the dissonance associated with his decision; rather, the negative emotion of dissonance would likely increase. At some point, as dissonant cognitions continue to increase, he may choose to reverse his decision and look for a different university (Festinger, 1957, reports the results of such an experiment). Like the original theory of dissonance, the action-based model predicts that the direction of attitude change will be in the direction of the cognition that is most resistant to change.

CONCLUSION

The action-based model assumes that dissonance processes operate because they are functional, that is, most often useful for the organism. However, the action-based model does not claim that dissonance reduction is always functional. We think of dissonance processes as being similar to other functional, motivated behaviors such as eating. Eating is necessary for the survival of the organism; however, disordered eating can be harmful. Similarly, dissonance reduction often benefits persons by assisting them in acting on their decisions without being hampered by excess regret or conflict. However, if a person makes a poor decision and then reduces the dissonance associated with the decision, he or she will persist in acting on the decision when it might be advantageous to disengage. The action-based model proposes that dissonance reduction, while not always functional, is functional more often than not. In the majority of cases, it is advantageous for persons to reduce dissonance, and act effectively on their decisions. The dissonance-reduction mechanism functions to override continued psychological conflict that would potentially interfere with effective action.

We propose that the action-based model provides an explanation of the underlying, basic motivation behind dissonance processes. The action-based model assumes that, in most cases, dissonance processes are behaviorally adaptive. Dissonance reduction primarily functions to facilitate effective action. Organisms experience discomfort when they hold conflicting cognitions because conflicting cognitions impede effective action. This new way of thinking about dissonance processes, we hope, will stimulate research on dissonance theory and assist in connecting the large body of dissonance theory evidence with other research literatures.

REFERENCES

Allen, J. J. B., Harmon-Jones, E., & Cavender, J. (2001). Manipulation of frontal EEG asymmetry through biofeedback alters self-reported emotional responses and facial EMG. *Psychophysiology, 38,* 685–693.

Amodio, D. M., Devine, P. G., & Harmon-Jones, E. (2007). A dynamic model of guilt: Implications for motivation and self-regulation in the context of prejudice. *Psychological Science, 18,* 524–530.

Amodio, D. M., Devine, P. G., & Harmon-Jones, E. (2008). Individual differences in the regulation of intergroup bias: The role of conflict monitoring and neural signals for control. *Journal of Personality and Social Psychology, 94,* 60–74.

Amodio, D. M., Harmon-Jones E., Devine P. G., Curtin J. J., Hartley, S., & Covert, A. (2004). Neural signals for the detection of unintentional race bias. *Psychological Science, 15,* 88–93.

Amodio, D. M., Master, S. L., Yee, C. M., & Taylor, S. E. (2008). Neurocognitive components of behavioral inhibition and activation systems: Implications for theories of self-regulation. *Psychophysiology, 45,* 11–19.

Amodio, D. M., Shah, J. Y., Sigelman, J., Brazy, P. C., & Harmon-Jones, E. (2004). Implicit regulatory focus associated with resting frontal cortical asymmetry. *Journal of Experimental Social Psychology, 40,* 225–232.

Aronson, E. (1969). The theory of cognitive dissonance: A current perspective. In L. Berkowitz (Ed.), *Advances in experimental social psychology* (Vol. 4, pp. 1–34). New York: Academic Press.

Aronson, E. (1999). Dissonance, hypocrisy, and the self concept. In E. Harmon-Jones & J. Mills (Eds.), *Cognitive dissonance: Progress on a pivotal theory in social psychology* (pp. 103–126). Washington, DC: American Psychological Association.

Aronson, J., Cohen, G., & Nail, P. R. (1999). Self-affirmation theory: An update and appraisal. In E. Harmon-Jones & J. Mills (Eds.), *Cognitive dissonance: Progress on a pivotal theory in social psychology* (pp. 127–148). Washington, DC: American Psychological Association.

Beauvois, J. L., & Joule, R. V. (1996). *A radical dissonance theory.* London: Taylor & Francis.

Beckmann, J., & Irle, M. (1985). Dissonance and action control. In J. Kuhl & J. Beckmann (Eds.), *Action control: From cognition to behavior* (pp. 129–150). Berlin, Germany: Springer-Verlag.

Berkowitz, L. (1984). Some effects of thoughts on anti- and prosocial influences of media events: A cognitive-neoassociation analysis. *Psychological Bulletin, 95,* 410–427.

Botvinick, M. M., Braver, T. S., Barch, D. M., Carter, C. S., & Cohen, J. D. (2001). Conflict monitoring and cognitive control. *Psychological Review, 108,* 624–652.

Botvinick, M. M., Nystrom, L. E., Fissel, K., Carter, C. S., & Cohen, J. D. (1999). Conflict monitoring versus selection-for-action in anterior cingulate cortex. *Nature, 402,* 179–181.

Brehm, J. W. (1956). Postdecision changes in the desirability of alternatives. *Journal of Abnormal and Social Psychology, 52,* 384–389.

Brehm, J. W., & Cohen, A. R. (1962). *Explorations in cognitive dissonance.* New York: Wiley.

Bunge, S. A. (2004). How we use rules to select actions: A review of evidence from cognitive neuroscience. *Cognitive, Affective, and Behavioral Neuroscience, 4,* 564–579.

Carter, C. S., Braver, T. S., Barch, D. M., Botvinick, M. M., Noll, D., & Cohen, J. D. (1998). Anterior cingulate cortex, error detection, and the online monitoring of performance. *Science, 280,* 747–749.

Cooper, J., & Fazio, R. H. (1984). A new look at dissonance theory. In L. Berkowitz (Ed.), *Advances in experimental social psychology* (Vol. 17, pp. 229–264). Orlando, FL: Academic Press.

Dijksterhuis, A., & Bargh, J. A. (2001). The perception-behavior expressway: Automatic effects of social perception on social behavior. In M. P. Zanna (Ed.), *Advances in experimental social psychology* (Vol. 33, pp. 1–40). San Diego, CA: Academic Press.

Egan, L. C., Santos, L. R., & Bloom, P. (2007). The origins of cognitive dissonance: Evidence from children and monkeys. *Psychological Science, 18*(11), 978–983.

Elkin, R. A., & Leippe, M. R. (1986). Physiological arousal, dissonance, and attitude change: Evidence for a dissonance-arousal link and a "don't remind me" effect. *Journal of Personality and Social Psychology, 51,* 55–65.

Elliot, A. J., & Devine, P. G. (1994). On the motivation nature of cognitive dissonance: Dissonance as psychological discomfort. *Journal of Personality and Social Psychology, 67,* 382–394.

Eriksen, B. A., & Eriksen, C. W. (1974). Effects of noise letters upon the identification of a target letter in a nonsearch task. *Perception & Psychophysics, 16,* 143–149.

Festinger, L. (1957). *A theory of cognitive dissonance.* Stanford, CA: Stanford University Press.

Fiske, S. T. (1992). Thinking is for doing: Portraits of social cognition from daguerreotype to laserphoto. *Journal of Personality and Social Psychology, 63,* 877–889.

Gerhing, W. J., Goss, B., Coles, M. G. H., Meyer, D. E., & Donchin, E. (1993). A neural system for error detection and compensation. *Psychological Science, 4,* 385–390.

Gibson, J. J. (1966). *The senses considered as perceptual systems.* Boston: Houghton Mifflin.

Gibson, J. J. (1979). *The ecological approach to visual perception.* Boston: Houghton Mifflin.

Gilbert, D. T., & Ebert, J. E. J. (2002). Decisions and revisions: The affective forecasting of changeable outcomes. *Journal of Personality and Social Psychology, 82,* 503–514.

Gollwitzer, P. M. (1990). Action phases and mind-sets. In E. T. Higgins & R. M. Sorrentino (Eds.), *Handbook of motivation and cognition: Foundations of social behavior* (Vol. 2, pp. 53–92). New York: Guilford Press.

Gollwitzer, P. M., & Bayer, U. (1999). Deliberative versus implemental mindsets in the control of action. In S. Chaiken & Y. Trope (Eds.), *Dual-process theories in social psychology* (pp. 403–422). New York: Guilford Press.

Gollwitzer, P. M., & Sheeran, P. (2006). Implementation intentions and goal achievement: A meta-analysis of effects and processes. In M. P. Zanna (Ed.), *Advances in experimental social psychology* (Vol. 38, pp. 69–119). San Diego, CA: Academic Press.

Hajcak, G., & Foti, D. (2008). Errors are aversive: Defensive motivation and the error-related negativity. *Psychological Science, 19,* 103–108.

Hajcak, G., McDonald, N., & Simons, R. F. (2003). To err is autonomic: Error-related brain potentials, ANS activity, and posterror compensatory behavior. *Psychophysiology, 40,* 895–903.

Hajcak, G., McDonald, N., & Simons, R. F. (2004). Error-related psychophysiology and negative affect. *Brain and Cognition, 56,* 189–197.

Harmon-Jones, E. (1999). Toward an understanding of the motivation underlying dissonance effects: Is the production of aversive consequences necessary to cause dissonance? In E. Harmon-Jones & J. Mills (Eds.), *Cognitive dissonance: Progress on a pivotal theory in social psychology* (pp. 71–99). Washington, DC: American Psychological Association.

Harmon-Jones, E. (2000a). Cognitive dissonance and experienced negative affect: Evidence that dissonance increases experienced negative affect even in the absence of aversive consequences. *Personality and Social Psychology Bulletin, 26,* 1490–1501.

Harmon-Jones, E. (2000b). An update on dissonance theory, with a focus on the self. In A. Tesser, R. Felson, & J. Suls (Eds.). *Psychological perspectives on self and identity* (pp. 119–144). Washington, DC: American Psychological Association.

Harmon-Jones, E. (2003). Clarifying the emotive functions of asymmetrical frontal cortical activity. *Psychophysiology, 40,* 838–848.

Harmon-Jones, E. (2004). Contributions from research on anger and cognitive dissonance to understanding the motivational functions of asymmetrical frontal brain activity. *Biological Psychology, 67,* 51–76.

Harmon-Jones, E., & Allen, J. J. B. (1997). Behavioral activation sensitivity and resting frontal EEG asymmetry: Covariation of putative indicators related to risk for mood disorders. *Journal of Abnormal Psychology, 106,* 159–163.

Harmon-Jones, E., & Allen, J. J. B. (1998). Anger and prefrontal brain activity: EEG asymmetry consistent with approach motivation despite negative affective valence. *Journal of Personality and Social Psychology, 74,* 1310–1316.

Harmon-Jones, E., Brehm, J. W., Greenberg, J., Simon, L., & Nelson, D. E. (1996). Evidence that the production of aversive consequences is not necessary to create cognitive dissonance. *Journal of Personality and Social Psychology, 70,* 5–16.

Harmon-Jones, E., Gerdjikov, T., & Harmon-Jones, C. (2008). The effect of induced compliance on relative left frontal cortical activity: A test of the action-based model of dissonance. *European Journal of Social Psychology, 38,* 35–45.

Harmon-Jones, E., & Harmon-Jones, C. (2002). Testing the action-based model of cognitive dissonance: The effect of action-orientation on post-decisional attitudes. *Personality and Social Psychology Bulletin, 28,* 711–723.

Harmon-Jones, E., Harmon-Jones, C., Fearn, M., Sigelman, J. D., & Johnson, P. (2008). Action orientation, relative left frontal cortical activation, and spreading of alternatives: A test of the action-based model of dissonance. *Journal of Personality and Social Psychology, 94,* 1–15.

Harmon-Jones, E., Peterson, H., & Vaughn, K. (2003). The dissonance-inducing effects of an inconsistency between experienced empathy and knowledge of past failures to help: Support for the action-based model of dissonance. *Basic and Applied Social Psychology, 25,* 69–78.

Harmon-Jones, E., & Sigelman, J. (2001). State anger and prefrontal brain activity: Evidence that insult-related relative left-prefrontal activation is associated with experienced anger and aggression. *Journal of Personality and Social Psychology, 80,* 797–803.

James, W. (1950). *The principles of psychology.* New York: Dover. (Original work published 1890)

Jones, E. E., & Gerard, H. B. (1967). *Foundations of social psychology.* New York: Wiley.

Kamiya, J. (1979). Autoregulation of the EEG alpha rhythm: A program for the study of consciousness. In S. A. E. Peper & M. Quinn (Eds.), *Mind/body integration: Essential readings in biofeedback* (pp. 289–297). New York: Plenum Press.

Kerns, J. G., Cohen, J. D., MacDonald, A. W., Cho, R. Y., Stenger, V. A., & Carter, C. S. (2004, February 13). Anterior cingulate conflict monitoring and adjustments in control. *Science, 303,* 1023–1026.

Kiehl, K. A., Liddle, P. F., & Hopfinger, J. B. (2001). Error processing and the rostral anterior cingulate: An event-related fMRI study. *Psychophysiology, 37,* 216–223.

Kotchoubey, B., Kübler, A., Strehl, U., Flor, H., & Birbaumer, N. (2002). Can humans perceive their brain states? *Consciousness and Cognition, 11,* 98–113.

Kuhl, J. (1984). Volitional aspects of achievement motivation and learned helplessness: Toward a comprehensive theory of action-control. In B. A. Maher (Ed.), *Progress in experimental personality research* (Vol. 13, pp. 99–171). New York: Academic Press.

Lawrence, D. H., & Festinger, L. (1962). *Deterrents and reinforcement.* Stanford, CA: Stanford University Press.

Losch, M. E., & Cacioppo, J. T. (1990). Cognitive dissonance may enhance sympathetic tonus, but attitudes are changed to reduce negative affect rather than arousal. *Journal of Experimental Social Psychology, 26,* 289–304.

MacDonald, W. III, Cohen, J. D., & Stenger, V. A., & Carter, C. S. (2000). Dissociating the role of the dorsolateral prefrontal and anterior cingulate cortex in cognitive control. *Science, 288,* 1835–1838.

McArthur, L. Z., & Baron, R. M. (1983). Toward an ecological theory of social perception. *Psychological Review, 90,* 215–238.

McGregor, I., Newby-Clark, I. R., & Zanna, M. P. (1999). "Remembering" dissonance: Simultaneous accessibility of inconsistent cognitive elements moderates epistemic discomfort. In E. Harmon-Jones & J. Mills (Eds.), *Cognitive dissonance: Progress on a pivotal theory in social psychology* (pp. 325–353). Washington, DC: American Psychological Association.

Miller, E. K., & Cohen, J. D. (2001). An integrative theory of prefrontal cortex function. *Annual Review of Neuroscience, 24,* 167–202.

Petersen, S. E., Fox, P. T., Posner, M. I., Mintun, M., & Raichle, M. E. (1988). Positron emission tomographic studies of the cortical anatomy of single-word processing. *Nature, 331,* 585–589.

Pizzagalli, D. A., Sherwood, R. J., Henriques, J. B., & Davidson, R. J. (2005). Frontal brain asymmetry and reward responsiveness: A source-localization study. *Psychological Science, 16,* 805–813.

Rabbie, J. M., Brehm, J. W., & Cohen, A. R. (1959). Verbalization and reactions to cognitive dissonance. *Journal of Personality, 27,* 407–417.

Robinson, R. G., & Downhill, J. E. (1995). Lateralization of psychopathology in response to focal brain injury. In R. J. Davidson & K. Hugdahl (Eds.), *Brain asymmetry* (pp. 693–711). Cambridge, MA: MIT Press.

Sherman, D. K., & Cohen, G. L. (Eds.). (2006). The psychology of self-defense: Self-affirmation theory. In M. P. Zanna (Ed.), *Advances in experimental social psychology* (Vol. 38, pp. 183–242). San Diego, CA: Academic Press.

Sigall, H., & Mills, J. (1998). Measures of independent variables and mediators are useful in social psychology experiments: But are they necessary? *Personality and Social Psychology Review, 2,* 218–226.

Simon, L., Greenberg, J., & Brehm, J. W. (1995). Trivialization: The forgotten mode of dissonance reduction. *Journal of Personality and Social Psychology, 68,* 247–260.

Siniatchkin, M., Kropp, P., & Gerber, W.-D. (2000). Neurofeedback—The significance of reinforcement and the search for an appropriate strategy for the success of self-regulation. *Applied Psychophysiology and Biofeedback, 25,* 167–175.

Smith, E. R., & Semin, G. R. (2004). Socially situated cognition: Cognition in its social context. In M. P. Zanna (Ed.), *Advances in experimental social psychology* (Vol. 36, pp. 53–117). San Diego, CA: Academic Press.

Spencer, S. J., Zanna, M. P., & Fong, G. T. (2005). Establishing a causal chain: Why experiments are often more effective than mediational analyses in examining psychological processes. *Journal of Personality and Social Psychology, 89,* 845–851.

Steele, C. M. (1988). The psychology of self-affirmation: Sustaining the integrity of the self. In L. Berkowitz (Ed.), *Advances in experimental social psychology* (Vol. 21, pp. 261–302). San Diego, CA: Academic Press.

Steele, C. M., Southwick, L. L., & Critchlow, B. (1981). Dissonance and alcohol: Drinking your troubles away. *Journal of Personality and Social Psychology, 41,* 831–846.

Steele, C. M., Spencer, S. J., & Lynch, M. (1993). Self-image resilience and dissonance: The role of affirmational resources. *Journal of Personality and Social Psychology, 64,* 885–896.

Stone, J. (2003). Self-consistency for low self-esteem in dissonance processes: The role of self-standards. *Personality and Social Psychology Bulletin, 29,* 846–858.

Stone, J., & Cooper, J. (2003). The effect of self-attribute relevance on how self-esteem moderates attitude change in dissonance processes. *Journal of Experimental Social Psychology, 39,* 508–515.

Stone, J., Wiegand, A. W., Cooper J., & Aronson, E. (1997). When exemplification fails: Hypocrisy and the motive for self-integrity. *Journal of Personality and Social Psychology, 72,* 54–65.

Stroop, J. R. (1935). Studies of interference in serial verbal reactions. *Journal of Experimental Psychology, 18,* 643–662.

Taylor, S. E., & Gollwitzer, P. M. (1995). Effects of mindset on positive illusions. *Journal of Personality and Social Psychology, 69,* 213–226.

van Veen, V., & Carter, C. S. (2006). Conflict and cognitive control in the brain. *Current Directions in Psychological Science, 15,* 237–240.

Zanna, M. P., & Cooper, J. (1974). Dissonance and the pill: An attribution approach to studying the arousal properties of dissonance. *Journal of Personality and Social Psychology, 29,* 703–709.

ACKNOWLEDGMENTS

The work in this article was supported by a National Science Foundation Grant (BCS-9910702). Correspondence concerning this article should be addressed to Eddie Harmon-Jones, Texas A&M University, Department of Psychology, 4235 TAMU, College Station, TX 77843, or via the Internet to eddiehj@gmail.com.

11

Pragmatic Persuasion
How Communicative Processes Make Information Appear Persuasive

MICHAELA WÄNKE AND LEONIE REUTNER

There are many ways to change attitudes, as this book attests, and many involve presenting arguments (e.g., Crano, this volume; Prislin, this volume). Consequently, the impact of arguments has figured prominently in the history of attitude research where the characteristics of persuasive messages (Hovland, Janis, & Kelley, 1953) and the processes by which they affect attitudes (Chen & Chaiken, 1999; Greenwald, 1968; Kruglanski, Thompson, & Spiegel, 1999; Petty & Wegener, 1999) have been investigated (for reviews, see Bohner & Wänke, 2002; Crano & Prislin, 2006). That a convincing argument comes in handy when attempting to change attitudes is, of course, common knowledge and is practiced widely in social interaction, education, politics, marketing, and other areas. But what is a convincing argument? In logic, an argument is a set of premises and a conclusion, with the characteristic that the truth of the conclusion is supported by the premises. "You should eat vegetables (conclusion) because they contain lots of vitamins (premise)" sounds like a reasonable argument to most people, whereas "you should eat vegetables because they are green" does not. The intake of vitamins is considered beneficial by most people but the benefit of eating green food is less obvious. But note, that it is not the information per se which is convincing or not, but—as always in social psychology—what receivers make of it. For information to change a person's attitude in the desired direction, it is essential that the receiver draws the adequate inferences about its implications. The argument that vegetables contain vitamins will be lost on ignorant recipients who do not know what vitamins are. Thus, one may define information as compelling if, given the recipient's knowledge structure, this information leads the recipient to the conclusions desired by the persuader.

However, for social psychologists it will not come as a surprise that implications of the presented information may also be construed or inferred rather than being based on a priori knowledge. In this chapter we propose an intriguing twist of this assumption. Our central hypothesis is that the inferred meaning of presented information may be based on the very fact that the information is perceived to be presented in order to persuade. The ignorant receiver in our example may arrive at the conclusion that vitamins must be beneficial in some sense if they are presented as a reason to eat vegetables. Hence, paradoxically, one aspect that makes information compelling, is the fact that it is perceived as intended to be compelling. This assumption of self-generated compellingness is based on the notion of persuasion as a social exchange or communication game (McCann & Higgins, 1992) where the persuasion target expects the persuader to present valid and compelling information. After all, if persuasion represents a form of social communication, it seems only appropriate to apply some of the dynamics of social communication in order to understand the dynamics of persuasion.

THE ROLE OF CONVERSATIONAL RELEVANCE IN PERSUASION

A basic assumption in social communication is that information is not presented arbitrarily. Rather, as Sperber and Wilson (1986) put it, "communicated information comes with a guarantee of relevance" (p. vi). According to the cooperative principle (Grice, 1975), recipients in a communication may expect that all of the presented information is relevant to the accepted purpose of the communication. Such tacit assumptions about information relevance do not only govern informal conversations but have also been shown to be used as pragmatic inference rules to give meaning to newspaper headlines (Gruenfeld & Wyer, 1992), research instructions in experiments (e.g., Bless, Strack, & Schwarz, 1993), and survey questions (e.g., Schwarz, Strack, & Mai, 1991; Strack, Schwarz, & Wänke, 1991) (For a review, see Wänke, 2007). Applied to persuasion, this would suggest that recipients may expect that any information presented by the persuader is relevant to the persuader's goal and potentially supports the desired conclusion. If the obvious and accepted purpose of a communication is to persuade recipients of the benefits and advantages of a position, receivers should pragmatically interpret any statement— as obscure, incomplete, or ambiguous it may be—in favor of the argued position. The underlying inference rule is: "If a persuader presents this information in order to persuade me, then the information must potentially support the persuader's position." By "potentially supporting" we mean that the information has implications, which in principle support the goal of the persuader. This does not mean that the receiver necessarily accepts the inferred argument. Recipients may doubt the presented facts (e.g., "vegetables do not contain that many vitamins"), their implications (e.g., "vitamins are not that important for a healthy nutrition"), or refute the whole argument ("I don't want to be healthy"), and of course they may generate other counterarguments (e.g., "vegetables also contain pesticides"). Nevertheless, although the presented information may not necessarily change a target's attitude, it may well do so if the pragmatically inferred implications provide a compelling argument.

A similar thought underlies Areni's notion regarding the often-missing link between the presented information and the conclusion in an argument (Areni, 2002). Consider the following example taken from Areni (2002):

> "By combining 2 liquids that activate to form a foam, New Liquid Plumr Foaming Pipe Snake cleans your pipe walls quickly and easily." (p. 179)

Here, the conclusion "effective pipe cleaning" is supported by a single attribute (major premise) "foam." Why foam should be particularly efficient for cleaning pipes is, however, not said. The minor premise or conditional rule is missing. This missing link between the major premise and the conclusion is typical of what is known in rhetoric as an *enthymeme*. According to Aristotle an enthymeme is a *rhetorical syllogism* aimed at persuasion. It is an incomplete syllogism, as part of the argument is missing. Often the part does not need to be stated explicitly because recipients complete the missing premise from their knowledge. If recipients know, for example, that vitamins are good for them, then explicitly mentioning this fact may be omitted and stating that one should eat vegetables because they have many vitamins would suffice. But enthymemes may work even without a priori knowledge. This is where pragmatic implicatures come into play. According to the maxim of relation (Grice, 1975), one should only give information that is relevant to the point one wants to make. Presenting a premise and a conclusion that are not linked by a conditional rule would certainly violate conversational maxims. As Areni (2002) put it, "Grice's prescription dictates that presenting data conversationally implicates a conditional rule, and it is this principle that allows enthymemes to be transformed into coherent arguments" (p. 179).

Note however, that the assumption of pragmatic persuasion goes beyond the rhetoric of enthymemes. We argue that not only does presenting information and conclusions implicate a conditional rule between the presented information and the stated conclusion, but that merely presenting the information alone will implicate a relevant argument. Based on Gricean assumptions, persuasion targets may reason that if information is given it must support the intended conclusion, otherwise the persuader would not mention it. According to this pragmatic assumption, it is not necessary that the presented information hold particular implications per se. Even ambiguous and unfamiliar information may become a compelling argument if presumed to be presented with the intention to persuade.

To be clear, we do not claim that such a pragmatic interpretation is the only source from which presented information achieves meaning. Clearly, the interpretation and evaluation of the presented information are the result of whatever knowledge is activated. Most often the receiver will have a priori knowledge about the implications of the presented information (most people do believe vitamins to be healthy and pesticides to be harmful). But it is not so unusual that receivers possess insufficient knowledge to evaluate the information properly. For example, even those who believe vitamins to be healthy may lack the knowledge of whether 100 milligrams (mg) of vitamin C constitutes a high dose. If receivers do not possess a priori knowledge to make sense of the presented information, one source of influence is the context of being presented as potentially persuasive. If so, ignoramuses may be persuaded to eat vegetables by claiming a high pesticide and low vitamin content. After all, why mention it, if it is not persuasive?

The only necessary requirement for the pragmatic interpretation is that the persuasion target believes the information to be communicated with a particular persuasive intention. That is, the persuasion target needs to presume which attitude or behavior the persuader strives to produce. Most often this is the case. People often begin to exchange arguments only after they have discovered that they hold different viewpoints on an issue. In formal debates, discussants first state their positions and then present supporting arguments. In politics, it goes without saying that a candidate only presents information that promotes his or her own view and confutes the opponent's standpoint. Likewise, virtually everybody knows what goals advertising pursues. Thus, in many persuasion contexts, receivers are well aware of the persuader's intentions. We would argue that, due to a cooperative interpretation, it is exactly this knowledge of the persuasion goal that may help persuasion. Interestingly, this cooperative assumption that knowing the goal makes targets more vulnerable to persuasion is diametrically opposed to the notion that forewarning is a means to resist persuasion (Wood & Quinn, 2003) and that awareness of a persuasion intention may provoke suspicion and resistance (Hovland et al., 1953) or reactance (Brehm, 1968). We will turn to that issue later.

In sum, applying conversational norms to persuasion, we suggest that persuasion targets presume that information, which is communicated with the goal to persuade, comes with a guarantee of potential persuasiveness. Persuasion targets may therefore interpret any information presented in a persuasion context as having implications consistent with the persuasion goal. Thus, it is not only prior knowledge that makes recipients infer the desired conclusion from the presented information, but paradoxically, the knowledge of the desired conclusion may turn the presented information into a compelling argument.

EVIDENCE THAT AMBIGUOUS INFORMATION IS INTERPRETED CONSISTENT TO PERSUASION GOALS

The first hypothesis that can be derived from our assumptions is that ambiguous information should be interpreted as consistent with the persuasion goal. Before we turn specifically to the context of persuasion, it should be noted that there is ample evidence from other communication contexts that recipients of ambiguous information behave cooperatively. That is to say, they assume that the information is related to the general communication context and interpret it in this manner. For example, survey respondents report attitudes toward fictitious or highly ambiguous issues such as the Metallic Trade Act or an educational contribution (Bishop, Oldendick, Tuchfarber, & Bennett, 1980; Strack et al., 1991). Moreover and more relevantly, they do not pick their answers at random, but seem to interpret the issues as if they assumed that the context in which the question had been presented gave a relevant frame to its meaning. For example, respondents welcomed the introduction of an educational contribution when this question followed questions on student stipends, but they opposed it when the question appeared in the context of tuition fees. Thus, the notion that people assign meaning to presented information, although they have no prior knowledge about it, is not unreasonable.

Most of our studies were conducted in a marketing context, because marketing provides an obvious persuasion context where the recipients know, without any doubt, the goal of the presented information. Applied to marketing, our assumption of the persuasion paradox would imply that consumers may not prefer brands because the brands offer the ideal features but that, vice versa, consumers will start to favor particular features because they are advertised. For example, the reason consumers prefer food brands that are low in sodium might not be because they believe sodium is healthy but because they believe that whatever is highlighted to differentiate this brand from others must provide a benefit. If so however, imagine an advertising claim "contains more sodium than any other brand" or "sodium-enriched." Our assumption would predict that brands with either claim are preferred to nondistinct brands.

To test this assumption, participants were shown pictures of brands (Wänke, Reutner, & Friese, 2009). In one condition the packaging claimed the presence of a particular attribute (e.g., a body lotion "with Recitine"), and in the other condition its absence ("without Recitine"). Altogether, brands from five product categories were presented (body lotion, energy drink, yoghurt, fabric softener, condoms). Participants rated the attributes on a number of dimensions specific to the respective product category (e.g., Recitine nourishes skin, etc.). For each brand, a summary score of all dimensions was computed which reflects the favorable evaluation of the attribute. Over all four product categories, an ingredient was rated significantly more favorable when the brand claimed its presence rather than its absence. It seems that participants inferred that, if the attribute is advertised, it must have a benefit, but if its absence is claimed, the attribute must be harmful. It may sound cynical to suggest that claiming the absence of fictitious ingredients may provide a cheap marketing strategy. It is nevertheless an example how the truth can be misleading.

Examples from real life are not so far fetched even though we used fictitious attributes. The issue here is not that consumers made sense of fictitious information, but by using fictitious information we could make sure that participants had no prior knowledge and had to rely on their pragmatic inferences. But note that in marketing it is not uncommon that the advertised features are meaningless to many consumers. A sample of real package claims contains such attributes as sophorin in face cream, bisabolol in body lotion, or catachines in tea. Moreover, even if attributes are familiar, their benefit may nevertheless be obscure (e.g., caffeine in hair shampoo). A real example may further illustrate this point. One of the authors recently saw a jewelry catalogue of a mid-priced department store. The descriptions of the advertised pieces contained information about alloy and caratage and the noteworthy statement that all diamonds contained inclusions. For consumers who know that inclusions represent lower value in diamonds, the statement is important information for adequately evaluating the quality and price of the jewelry. However, consumers who are less familiar with diamonds and have no prior associations may perhaps interpret inclusions as an added benefit (as in amber) merely because they are used to advertisements highlighting favorable instead of unfavorable information.

Our first study provided evidence that ambiguous information is interpreted favorably when presented in a marketing context. Further studies with various design variations tested whether merely communicating ambiguous attributes also led to more positive attitudes and behavior in addition to favorable inferences (Wänke et al., 2009). Participants of one study were again shown brands with claims about fictitious attributes. For one condition the presence of the attribute was claimed (e.g., with Recitine), for another the absence (e.g., without Recitine), and for a control condition no claim was made. Supporting the fact that any marketing claim, whether it is the presence or absence of an attribute, can be perceived as indicating product superiority, consumers were willing to pay significantly more money when either the absence or presence of an attribute was claimed compared with a control condition. Thus, claiming, for example, "with Recitine" pushed sales prices as much as the claim "without Recitine." Apparently giving any information pays for marketers.

In another study, mainly nonfictitious attributes were used (e.g., detergent in gel form, white tea extract in face powder). Pretesting had shown, however, that these attributes were not rated particularly favorably per se. Nevertheless, replicating our main hypotheses, consumers reported more favorable attitudes, higher purchase interest, and willingness to pay when the ad claimed such an attribute relative to a control group.

One may, of course, ask whether the advantage of obscure information over no information was due to pragmatic inferences. Alternatively, research in the elaboration likelihood paradigm showed that under processing constraints, message recipients were more affected by the number of arguments than by the content of the argument (Petty & Cacioppo, 1984). Perhaps our claims caused a more favorable evaluation because participants had more information at hand and used it as a peripheral cue. In principle, one may imagine an effect of ambiguous claims by heuristic processing insofar as consumers may assume that a claim signals generally high desirability. In contrast to pragmatic inferences, however, such a heuristic process would entail more pronounced effects under processing constraints and less pronounced effects under more systematic processing. When we assessed need for cognition (NFC; Cacioppo & Petty, 1982), we did not find reduced effects for those high in NFC, who should be more likely to process more systematically. On the contrary, in line with our assumption that recipients actively draw inferences from the ambiguous claims, which in turn elicit persuasion, we found more pronounced effects for those high in NFC. Moreover, we also found that the effects of the claims on attitudes, such as product liking and purchase interest, were mediated by specific inferences.

These first studies provide support for the hypothesis that, in a marketing context, recipients of product information interpret ambiguous information favorably. Our full argument is, however, that such a pragmatic inference takes place due to a perceived persuasion goal and a cooperative interpretation. Ads and product packages are examples of communication with an obvious goal. Thus, we could well assume that our participants were aware of the persuasion goal. To further test our assumption, however, we varied the perception of the persuasion context.

THE ROLE OF THE PERCEIVED PERSUASION GOAL

Ambiguous information can only be interpreted as support for the persuasion goal if such a goal is perceived. A product attribute should be interpreted as a benefit of that brand mainly when it is *highlighted* by the marketer but not when communicated in a less blatant way, for example, in small print at the back of the package. Likewise a product attribute should be interpreted as a benefit of that brand mainly when it is highlighted by the *marketer* but not when communicated by a neutral source. Several studies tested these hypotheses (Wänke et al., 2009).

In contrast to the previous studies, we used nutritional information, more precisely the content of specific ingredients in food products, such as salt, fat, sugar, vitamins, and so on, as ambiguous product attributes. Although most consumers know about the implications of these nutrients, consumers are less educated regarding the respective amounts. Is 5 grams of salt in a package of potato chips a high or a low amount? Is 3 grams of sugar in a bottle of tomato ketchup relatively healthy or unhealthy? Again we assumed that consumers who do not possess adequate knowledge regarding what represents a high or low amount would use the way it is communicated as a cue. If advertised boldly, in terms of a persuasion claim, an attribute should be likely to represent a benefit or an advantage over competitors. However, if not perceived as meant to persuade, the same information will not benefit from the pragmatic interpretation. Indeed, consumers considered the same amount of salt, sugar, and fat as relatively lower when emphasized in an ad compared to when the same information was given in small print at the back of the package. Moreover, they evaluated the amount as more favorable and the brand as healthier compared to competitors. Apparently, it was not the actual amount of salt, sugar, or fat that produced this impression but the fact that the marketer advertised the amount in bold letters in the ad as if it were a differentiating advantage over competitors. Being presented less ostentatiously on the back of the package among other ingredients, the same amount is not perceived as intended to persuade but perhaps as required by regulations.

Similarly, when the amount of nutrients was communicated by a neutral source (in this case, the European Union food commission) rather than the marketer, the information had a less positive impact. We would also expect that when the same information is pointed out by a competitor rather than the persuader or a neutral source, it may even be interpreted as a lack of quality.

The results that the same information affects attitudes positively if recipients presume that the information is presented with the goal to induce positive attitudes compared to merely factual information support the assumption of pragmatic persuasion. Additional support regarding the role of the perceived persuasion goal comes from another study. Our assumption also predicts that consumers should not infer just any benefit from presented information but only benefits potentially relevant to consumers. They would assume that the ad or package claims are directed at *them* in order to persuade *them* and hence any information should imply benefits for *them*. For example, consumers care whether the attributes of a fabric softener make their towels fluffier and better smelling. They would not care, however, if the attribute enables an easier filling process at the plant or allows shipment in larger quantities. Given that package claims are obviously directed at consumers and not at retailers, producers, and distributors, implications of these claims should be persuasive to consumers and provide benefits to consumers. Advertising benefits relevant to other agents but irrelevant to consumers would violate the norm of relevance. To test this notion, participants saw products featuring claims for the presence or absence of a fictitious attribute. As described before, they rated the attribute on several product-relevant dimensions more favorably if a product claimed its presence compared to claiming its absence. However, all these dimensions were relevant to consumers of the product. In addition, consumers also rated the attribute on dimensions introduced as technical dimensions, which were relevant for producers, distributors, or retailers (e.g., accelerates production process). On these dimensions no difference between claiming the presence or absence of an attribute was obtained. As had been expected according to conversational norms, recipients seem to infer benefits relevant to the target of the communication and not just any benefit.

WHEN AWARENESS OF THE PERSUASION GOAL MAY BACKFIRE

The view that awareness of a persuasive intension does not hinder but facilitate persuasion may be surprising or even counterintuitive. Intuitively, one might assume that knowing or suspecting that a conversation partner aims to persuade one of something would rather elicit caution and bolster resistance. Indeed the classic persuasion literature claims that persuasion is lower when the communicator is perceived as intending to persuade (Berelson, 1950; Hovland et al., 1953; Walster & Festinger, 1962). For example, listeners who inadvertently overheard persuasive arguments against the link between smoking and cancer later reported higher agreement that this link was not proven compared to a control group and, more importantly, compared to participants who believed the arguments had been presented in order to influence them (Walster & Festinger, 1962). Likewise consumer research has found that claims from neutral sources led to more favorable brand attitudes than did advertising (Chaiken & Maheswaran, 1994). Similarly, a meta-analysis showed that forewarned message recipients were less persuaded than non-forewarned recipients (Wood & Quinn, 2003). In contrast, the pragmatic persuasion perspective predicts increased persuasion when a persuasion intention is perceived. This raises the following question: When does the awareness of persuasion foster persuasion, and when does it undermine it? Although we have no empirical evidence yet, we may nevertheless speculate about some differences in the research paradigms which perhaps may moderate the impact of being aware of a persuasion goal.

What the research we presented so far ignored is whether recipients believed the presented information in the first place. We assumed that consumers, by and large, believe objectively verifiable marketing claims (e.g., 5 grams of salt). They know that in competitive markets, lies about objectively verifiable claims would be easily detected and denounced by competitors, consumer organizations, or the media (Nelson, 1974). Although they are rather skeptical about advertising, this applies more to experience attributes (e.g., taste), which are subjective in nature, and credence attributes (e.g., reliability), which require long-term usage, than to objectively verifiable search attributes (Ford, Smith, & Swasy, 1990). In other words, the claim "brand A orange juice contains 20 mg vitamin C" raises less suspicion than the claim "brand A orange juice is healthy." In our studies only such objectively easily verifiable attributes were claimed, and we have no reason to believe that the truth of the stated claim was doubted. However, in persuasion contexts where trusting the presented information is an issue, awareness that the information is presented in order to persuade may possibly raise suspicions about its accuracy.

Note, however, that in our studies it is not the presented information per se that is assumed to influence attitudes but the inferences recipients draw from this information. Different from other studies, we did not present persuasive arguments but merely information from which participants inferred persuasive arguments themselves. As has been also shown by classic persuasion research, self-generated arguments may be more persuasive than presented ones (Janis & King, 1954; Kardes, 1988; King & Janis, 1956; Sawyer & Howard, 1991) as long as the self-generation does not feel too difficult (Wänke, Bohner, & Jurkowitsch, 1997).

Moreover, and related to their objective and factual nature, the claims we presented did not appear particularly manipulative—although the persuasion intention was clear. Recognizing a persuasive intention is a prerequisite for pragmatic persuasion, as explained before, but feeling manipulated may produce reactance (Brehm, 1968), suspicion, and caution. Some supportive evidence for the importance that persuasive information is perceived as factual and not as biased and manipulative comes from a third condition of a study mentioned before. As described, we had found that consumers rated food products as more favorable if nutrients were communicated as a marketing claim in the ad (or on the package) compared to the same information communicated by the European Union food commission. In a third condition, the information was also presented as a marketing claim in the ad but in a less factual form. For example, rather than advertising 5 grams of salt (factual marketing claim condition) the ad claimed "*only* 5 grams of salt." These claims led to significantly inferior product ratings than the factual marketing claims and had no advantage over a neutral source.

To follow that up, a new study again presented food ads with manipulative claims (e.g., "only") by the marketer in one condition and factual ones by the European Union as a neutral source in another condition. In addition, skepticism toward advertising (Obermiller & Spangenberg, 1998) was assessed, and consumers were classified according to a median split. Consumers who were low in skepticism toward advertising rated the products more favorable when the information was presented as a marketing claim despite the fact that the claim sounded somewhat manipulative. However, consumers who were high in skepticism toward advertising were rather negatively affected by the manipulative claims. In combination these two studies suggest that whereas fact-like marketing claims are interpreted as implicating product benefits, claims that may be perceived as more manipulative elicit negative reactions, at least among more distrusting persuasion targets.

TESTING THE LIMITS: ADVERTISING NEGATIVE CLAIMS

As we elaborated, how presented information is understood depends both on a priori knowledge and on the pragmatic inference that, if communicated as part of a persuasive communication, the information must be relevant and therefore imply support for the persuasion goal. The assumption that the pragmatic inference is particularly relevant when no a priori knowledge exists made us study attributes whose implications were ambiguous either because they were fictitious or because receivers lacked the knowledge to interpret their meaning. However, even in case of familiar attributes, their implications may be ambiguous. Attributes rarely imply only positive or only negative consequences. What seems positive on first glance may also entail shortcomings, and what seems negative may nevertheless involve a few benefits as well. For example, a camera that is easy to use may not prove very versatile or allow for complex applications, and vice versa, or an epilator that promises pain-free hair removal may not be very efficient in removing the hair by its roots.

In particular, with increasing knowledge and expertise, persuasion targets may see the hidden advantages and drawbacks. Whether they infer the less obvious and evaluatively opposite implication depends on the strength of the association and the amount of processing they invest. It seems plausible to assume that they would be inclined to think more elaborately about a piece of information if its surface implication disagrees with the intended purpose of the communication. A politician listing reasons not to vote for her or an ad praising the superior performance of the competitor clashes with recipients' expectations and may therefore instigate further processing. Clearly, the politician cannot mean that nor could the ad, and recipients will search for the persuasion-consistent implication of the seemingly inconsistent information. If so, even information that at surface seems unambiguously negative may induce positive attitude shifts and vice versa.

Supporting evidence that pragmatic persuasion may go beyond interpreting ambiguous information comes from research on two-sided messages. Advertising research has shown that unfavorable information may particularly enhance the product appeal compared to one-sided messages if the unfavorable information supports the implications of the favorable one (Bohner, Einwiller, Erb, & Siebler, 2003; Pechmann, 1992). For example, when ice cream was advertised as creamy *and* high in calories, it was liked better than merely described as creamy or when a negative feature was advertised that was unrelated to the positive claim of creaminess (Pechmann, 1992). Apparently, consumers knew that the creamier ice cream is, the more calories it contains and therefore concluded that if it is high in calories it is also likely to be creamy. Possibly, ad recipients' expectation that whatever is conveyed in an ad should be persuasive contributes to the effectiveness of two-sided ads. Assuming that ad information is meant to increase the appeal of the product, ad recipients may be particularly prone to interpret negative product information positively. Given that negative information in ads violates recipients' expectations, it may draw more attention and may be processed more thoroughly, which would also enable more inferences and elaborate interpretations. If, however, the unfavorable product information was encountered in a different context where recipients expect a different communication purpose, for example, in a consumer report, the unfavorable information would not be reinterpreted and may decrease a product's attractiveness.

To test this hypothesis we presented an ad for ice cream that either advertised the ice cream's creaminess or its high calorie content. In another condition the same information (creaminess or high in calories) came not from the advertiser but from a consumer Web site where consumers described their experience with products. We expected that recipients should be more likely to infer benefits from unfavorable information presented in ads compared to a neutral source as they expected persuasion in favor of the ice cream in the former case but not in the latter. The significant results confirmed these expectations. Participants expected the ice cream to be creamier when the information about many calories came from the advertiser compared to when it came from a neutral source. It should be mentioned that the reverse was true for communicating favorable information. When told that the ice cream was creamy, participants believed a neutral source more than the ad. As discussed before, the claim of creaminess represents an experience attribute, which is likely to be mistrusted. In sum, it seems that consumers distrust ad claims because they know that the ad wants to influence them. But for the same reason, they not only trust disclaimers but also infer persuasion-consistent information.

HOW DOES THE PRAGMATIC PERSUASION PERSPECTIVE FIT INTO SOCIAL PSYCHOLOGY?

Many approaches in classical persuasion focus primarily on the presented arguments and how they are perceived and processed by persuasion targets (Chaiken 1987; Greenwald, Brock, & Ostrom, 1968; Petty & Cacioppo, 1986; for a review, see Eagly & Chaiken, 1993). The pragmatic persuasion perspective complements this approach by pointing out that targets also take into account why the information was communicated. By doing so, the pragmatic persuasion perspective also complements classical attributional approaches to persuasion. Whereas these approaches emphasized the role of people's explanations for why communicators argued certain positions (for a review, see Eagly & Chaiken, 1993), the pragmatic persuasion perspective is based on people's explanations for why communicators present certain information in order to persuade targets of their position.

Another related perspective, less known in social psychology, is the persuasion knowledge model (PKM; Friestad & Wright, 1994; Kirmani & Campbell, 2009), which points out that consumers' persuasion knowledge is critical to how consumers make sense of and respond to marketing efforts. For example, when consumers believe that marketers are expending a lot of effort trying to persuade them, they infer that the marketer must have a good (high quality) product (Kirmani, 1990;

Kirmani & Wright, 1989). Like the pragmatic persuasion perspective, the PKM examines a persuasion attempt from the target's point of view. Whereas the PKM encompasses any knowledge related to persuasion strategies, the pragmatic persuasion perspective conceptualizes conversational norms as part of this knowledge. Central to both perspectives is the assumption that targets draw inferences not from communicated information alone but from "how and why" it is communicated.

The pragmatic persuasion perspective is certainly reminiscent of another well-known phenomenon in communication. As everyone knows and as it has also been shown empirically, context determines the meaning of statements. A "little rebellion" is interpreted differently when ascribed to Jefferson as opposed to Lenin (Asch, 1948; Lorge, 1936). Knowing the speaker's mind-set, listeners may conjure up an image of what he or she had in mind. Likewise in persuasion, knowing that the speaker tries to persuade one toward a particular direction lends meaning to what he or she says. The difference between the two perspectives is that the latter focuses more on the presumed goals of the communication rather than on the speaker's background. By doing so, the pragmatic persuasion perspective conceives of persuasion as social communication, in which both partners do their share to create an understanding. The active role of the persuasion target goes beyond elaborating the presented arguments or making inferences from cues (Chaiken, 1987; Petty & Cacioppo, 1986) but starts with interpreting the presented information. As in most other forms of communication, one cue for decoding and interpreting information is to determine the communicator's communicative purpose (McCann & Higgins, 1992). In essence, our perspective of persuasion as a communication game emphasizes the social processes involved in persuasion beyond the cognitive ones.

The persuasion game can become rather complicated. In a mass media setting, as advertising, consumers use their knowledge about what most consumers would probably want from a product. In our studies, 5 grams of salt was only inferred to be a small amount because recipients assumed that other consumers want low salt products and therefore advertising the salt content would have to imply a low amount. In a world of presumed salt-lovers, they would have arrived at the conclusion that 5 grams of salt must signal a high content, otherwise one would not advertise it. That is, consumers must let go of their own preferences in decoding the claim but use the presumed preference of a wider audience for interpreting what is meant. In personal interactions this game may get even more complicated as recipients base their interpretation on what they believe the persuader assumes of them and what they would find persuasive. The complexities, in particular in iterative exchanges, may give rise to misunderstandings and unsuccessful persuasion but also to finely tuned interpersonal communication.

CONCLUSION

Altogether, there is abundant evidence that persuasion targets interpret presented information as potentially supporting the persuader's goal. In turn, ambiguous information can become persuasive just because it is perceived as intended to persuade. Even negative information can then lead to positive inferences. The crucial variable determining whether information is persuasive is not its a priori implications but why recipients believe the information was communicated. Based on conversational logic, which states that presented information serves the purpose of the communication (Grice, 1975), presented information is pragmatically interpreted as potentially persuasive merely because its presumed purpose is persuasion.

The aim of this chapter was to extend current approaches to persuasion that rely mainly on cognitive processes by embedding persuasion within the context of social communication. Doing so created new research hypotheses, some of which were already tested and supported, others, which were only suggested. We hope that the pragmatic persuasion perspective will develop and instigate further research. In particular it seems worthwhile to extend applications beyond the domain of marketing. But in whichever direction future research will develop, we believe that a look at persuasion from the perspective of social communication is perhaps overdue in social psychology and will prove fruitful.

REFERENCES

Areni, C. S. (2002). The proposition-probability model of argument structure and message acceptance. *Journal of Consumer Research , 29*, 168–187.

Asch, S. (1948). The doctrine of suggestion, prestige and imitation in social psychology. *Psychological Review, 55*, 250–276.

Berelson, B. (1950). Communication and public opinion. In B. Berelson & M. Janowitz (Eds.), *Reader in public opinion and communication* (p. 458). Glencoe, IL: Free Press.

Bishop, G. F., Oldendick, R. W., Tuchfarber, A. J., & Bennett, S. E. (1980). Pseudo-opinions on public affairs. *Public Opinion Quarterly, 50*, 240–250.

Bless, H., Strack, F., & Schwarz, N. (1993). The informative functions of research procedures: bias and the logic of conversation. *European Journal of Social Psychology, 23*, 149–165.

Bohner, G., Einwiller, S., Erb, H.-P., & Siebler, F. (2003). When small means comfortable: Relations between product attributes in two-sided advertising. *Journal of Consumer Psychology, 13*, 454–463.

Bohner, G., & Wänke, M. (2002). *Attitudes and attitude change.* East Sussex, England: Psychology Press.

Brehm, J. W. (1968). Attitude change from threat to attitudinal freedom. In A. G. Greenwald, T. C. Brock, & T. M. Ostrom (Eds.), *Psychological foundations of attitudes* (pp. 277–296). San Diego, CA: Academic Press.

Cacioppo, J. T., & Petty, R. E. (1982). The need for cognition. *Journal of Personality and Social Psychology, 42*, 116–131.

Chaiken, S. (1987). The heuristic model of persuasion. In M. P. Zanna, J. M. Olson, & C. P. Herman (Eds.), *Social influence: The Ontario symposium* (Vol. 5, pp. 3–39). Hillsdale, NJ: Erlbaum.

Chaiken, S., & Maheswaran, D. (1994). Heuristic processing can bias systematic processing: Effects of source credibility, argument ambiguity, and task importance on attitude judgment. *Journal of Personality and Social Psychology, 66*, 460–473.

Chen, S., & Chaiken S. (1999). The heuristic-systematic model in its broader context. In S. Chaiken & Y. Trope (Eds.), *Dual-process theories in social psychology* (pp. 73–96). New York: Guilford Press.

Crano, W. D., & Prislin, R. (2006). Attitudes and persuasion. *Annual Review of Psychology, 57*, 345–374.

Eagly, A. H., & Chaiken, S. (1993). *The psychology of attitudes*. Fort Worth, TX: Harcourt Brace Jovanovich.

Ford, G. T., Smith, D. B., & Swasy, J. L. (1990). Consumer skepticism of advertising claims: Testing hypotheses from economics of information. *Journal of Consumer Research, 16*, 433–441.

Friestad, M., & Wright, P. (1994). The persuasion knowledge model: how people cope with persuasion attempts. *Journal of Consumer Research, 21*, 1–31.

Grice, H.-P. (1975). Logic and conversation. In P. Cole & J. L. Morgan (Eds.), *Syntax and semantics: Vol. 3. Speech acts* (pp. 41–58). New York: Academic Press.

Greenwald, A. G. (1968). Cognitive learning, cognitive response to persuasion, and attitude change. In A. G. Greenwald, T. C. Brock, & T. M. Ostrom (Eds.), *Psychological foundations of attitudes* (pp. 147–170). New York: Academic Press.

Greenwald, A. G., Brock, T. C., & Ostrom, T. M. (1968). *Psychological foundations of attitudes*. New York: Academic Press.

Gruenfeld, D. H., & Wyer, R. S. (1992). Semantics and pragmatics of social influence: How affirmations and denials affect beliefs in referent propositions. *Journal of Personality and Social Psychology, 62*, 38–49.

Hovland, C. I., Janis, I. L., & Kelley, H. H. (1953). *Communication and persuasion*. New Haven, CT: Yale University Press.

Janis, I. L., & King, B. T. (1954). The influence of role-playing on opinion change. *Journal of Abnormal and Social Psychology, 49*, 211–218.

Kardes, F. R. (1988). Spontaneous inference processes in advertising: The effects of conclusion omission and involvement on persuasion. *Journal of Consumer Research, 15*, 225–233.

King, B. T., & Janis, I. L. (1956). Comparison of the effectiveness of improvised versus non-improvised role-playing in producing opinion change. *Human Relations, 9*, 177–186.

Kirmani, A. (1990). The effect of perceived advertising costs on brand perceptions. *Journal of Consumer Research, 17*, 160–171.

Kirmani, A., & Campbell, M. C. (2009). Taking the target's perspective: The persuasion knowledge model. In M. Wänke (Ed.), *Social psychology of consumer behavior* (pp. 297–316). New York: Psychology Press.

Kirmani, A., & Wright, P. (1989). Money talks: Perceived advertising expense and expected product quality. *Journal of Consumer Research, 16*, 344–353.

Kruglanski, A. W., Thompson, E. P., & Spiegel, S. (1999). Separate or equal? Bimodal notions of persuasion and a single-process "unimodel." In S. Chaiken & Y. Trope (Eds.), *Dual-process theories in social psychology* (pp. 293–313). New York: Guilford Press.

Lorge, I. (1936). Prestige, suggestion, and attitudes. *Journal of Social Psychology, 7*, 386–402.

McCann, C. D., & Higgins, E. T. (1992). Personal and contextual factors in communication: A review of the "communication game." In G. R. Semin & K. Fiedler (Eds.), *Language, interaction and social cognition* (pp. 144–171). London: Sage.

Nelson, P. (1974). Advertising as information. *Journal of Political Economy, 82*, 729–754.

Obermiller, C., & Spangenberg, E. R. (1998). Development of a scale to measure consumer skepticism toward advertising. *Journal of Consumer Psychology, 7*, 159–186.

Pechmann, C. (1992). Predicting when two-sided ads will be more effective than one-sided ads: The role of correlational and correspondent inferences. *Journal of Marketing Research, 29*, 441–453.

Petty, R. E., & Cacioppo, J. T. (1984). The effects of involvement on responses to argument quantity and quality: Central and peripheral routes to persuasion. *Journal of Personality and Social Psychology, 46*, 69–81.

Petty, R. E., & Cacioppo, J. T. (1986). The elaboration likelihood model of persuasion. In L. Berkovitz (Ed.), *Advances in experimental social psychology* (Vol. 19, pp. 123–205). San Diego, CA: Academic Press.

Petty, R. E., & Wegener, D. T. (1999). The elaboration likelihood model: Current status and controversies. In S. Chaiken & Y. Trope (Eds.), *Dual process theories in social psychology* (pp. 41–72). New York: Guilford Press.

Sawyer, A. G., & Howard, D. J. (1991). Effects of omitting conclusions in advertisements to involved and uninvolved audiences. *Journal of Marketing Research, 28*, 467–474.

Schwarz N., Strack, F., & Mai, H. P. (1991). Assimilation and contrast effects in part-whole question sequences: A conversational logic analysis. *Public Opinion Quarterly, 55*, 3–23.

Sperber, D., & Wilson, D. (1986). *Relevance: Communication and cognition.* Cambridge, MA: Harvard University Press.

Strack, F., Schwarz, N., & Wänke, M. (1991). Semantic and pragmatic aspects of context effects in social and psychological research. *Social Cognition, 9*, 111–125.

Walster, E., & Festinger, L. (1962). The effectiveness of "overheard" persuasive communications. *Journal of Abnormal and Social Psychology, 65*, 395–402.

Wänke, M. (2007). What is said and what is meant: Conversational implicatures in natural conversations, research settings, media and advertising. In K. Fiedler (Ed.), *Social communication* (pp. 223–256). New York: Psychology Press.

Wänke, M., Bohner, G., & Jurkowitsch, A. (1997). There are many reasons to drive a BMW: Does imagined ease of argument generation influence attitudes? *Journal of Consumer Research, 24*, 170–177.

Wänke, M., Reutner, L., & Friese, M. (2009). *If they advertise it, it must be good: Favorable inferences from ambiguous attributes.* Unpublished manuscript.

Wood, W., & Quinn, J. M. (2003). Forewarned and forearmed? Two meta-analysis syntheses of forewarnings of influence appeals. *Psychological Bulletin, 129*, 119–138.

12

Persuasion After Ostracism
Need-Based Influences on Persuasion

KIPLING D. WILLIAMS, ZHANSHENG CHEN,
AND DUANE WEGENER

During the 1950s and 1960s, two independent research groups similarly proposed that attitudes can serve psychological needs and thus have motivational bases (Katz, 1960; Smith, Bruner, & White, 1956). They further identified a list of functions that attitudes may serve and tried to test these functions experimentally. Over the last half of the 20th century, although various researchers have adopted the functional approach to study persuasion (e.g., Shavitt, 1990; Smith et al., 1956; Snyder & DeBono, 1985), the sheer number of studies is rather small, especially as compared with the extensive list of studies of attitudes and persuasion using the more dominant cognitive approaches. Interestingly, functional approaches have prevailed in other areas of social psychological research. In particular, the nature and impact of several core social motives (e.g., belonging, self-esteem, control, etc.) have been studied extensively in literatures addressing self-concept and self-worth. In this research, it has been shown repeatedly that people strive to fortify unsatisfied social needs through cognitive as well as behavioral mechanisms (e.g., Baumeister & Leary, 1995; Crocker & Park, 2004; Pyszczynski, Greenberg, & Solomon, 1999; Williams, 2007). Because attitudes can serve different psychological needs, it is reasonable to expect that the effectiveness of persuasive attempts would often be influenced by individuals' social motives.

In this chapter, we adapt the functional approach to address how social motives might influence persuasion. Instead of emphasizing the various functions identified by theories in the 1950s and 1960s, we focus primarily on the fundamental social motives that have been identified in contemporary research on the self. Specifically, we incorporate the accumulated understanding of the nature of fundamental social needs, including needs for belonging, self-esteem, control, and meaningful existence and propose a need-based theory of persuasion. We hypothesize that when basic social needs are thwarted, people care more about information related to that need, and the ability to address the need through message-related thinking or behavior can influence how susceptible the person is to the persuasive attempt. In the following sections, we start by reviewing theories and research from functional approaches; then we list the core social motives and discuss the cognitive and behavioral mechanisms involved in responding to thwarted social needs. Our need-based approach to persuasion will be then introduced, accompanied by some initial evidence to support our hypothesis. Finally, we discuss the implications of our theorizing for persuasion and attitudes research in general.

FUNCTIONAL THEORIES OF PERSUASION

Theories and research adopting the functional approach started with identifying the basic functions of attitudes, and the most influential work was done by Katz and associates as well Smith and associates (see Eagly & Chaiken, 1993, for an overview). For example, Katz (1960) proposed that an attitude can serve one or more of four types of functions, including a knowledge function, a utilitarian function, an ego-defensive function, and a value-expressive function. The knowledge function helps individuals to organize and structure one's living environment; the utilitarian function aids in securing positive outcomes and preventing negative ones; the ego-defensive function helps to protect one's self-concept against various threats; and the value-expressive function assists in self-expression. Similarly, Smith and colleagues (1956) proposed an object-appraisal function, an externalization function, and a social adjustment function. The object-appraisal can be seen as a combination of Katz's knowledge function and utilitarian function; and the externalization function is very similar to Katz's ego-defensive function. Different from Katz's categories, Smith and colleagues (1956) emphasized how attitudes might affect one's relations with others, and the social adjustment function states that attitudes can serve to facilitate, maintain, or disrupt social relationships.

One key prediction of the functional approaches was that persuasive attempts are more effective when they match the functional basis of the targeted attitudes, which is known as the matching hypothesis (Eagly & Chaiken, 1993; Shavitt & Nelson, 2002). Unfortunately, few experimental studies were conducted to test these functional theories until almost 30 years after the theories were proposed. One of the obstacles for such investigation was that attitudes tend to serve more than one function, and it is challenging to experimentally manipulate or create attitudes with a single or idealized function (Eagly & Chaiken, 1993; Shavitt & Nelson, 2002). One way to solve this issue was to identify individuals for whom attitudes are more likely to serve a particular function (Shavitt & Nelson, 2002; Snyder & DeBono, 1985; 1987; 1989). Starting in the 1980s, researchers used the self-monitoring construct (Snyder, 1974) to test the matching hypothesis. According to Snyder and colleagues (Lavine & Snyder, 1996; Snyder & DeBono, 1985), high self-monitors strive to fit into social environments, and therefore should be more likely to form attitudes that serve a social adjustment function; low self-monitors, on the other hand, strive to behave in consistent with their inner beliefs and values, and are thus more likely to form attitudes that serve a value expression function.

Snyder and DeBono (1985) found that high self-monitors were more persuaded by ads that portrayed a positive image of people who used the product, but low self-monitors were more favorable toward products advertised by specifying the utility of the products. Thus, high self-monitors were more persuaded by social adjustive ads, but low self-monitors were more persuaded by ads that might be characterized as value-expressive, utilitarian, or object-appraising (see also DeBono, 1987; DeBono & Packer, 1991).

Another strategy for testing the matching hypothesis is by experimentally manipulating persuasive attempts to match or mismatch the dominant function of particular attitude objects (see Shavitt & Nelson, 2002). For example, Shavitt (1990) asked participants to read ads emphasizing the utilitarian function or social identity function of products that pretesting identified as serving primarily a utilitarian or a social identity function. For instance, coffee was identified as primarily serving a utilitarian function (and not a social identity function). When the ad for a brand of coffee was framed to emphasize the utilitarian function (e.g., to focus on the flavor and taste of coffee), it matched the expected function of the product; when the ad was framed to emphasize social identity functions (e.g., to reveal one's personality), it did not match the expected function of the product. Shavitt (1990) found that ads matching the product function led to more favorable attitudes toward the products than functionally mismatched ads.

More recently, Clary and colleagues (1998) expanded the functional approach to address matches (vs. mismatches) between motives to volunteer and outcome/benefits of volunteering. The researchers identified 6 motives underlying volunteerism, including values (similar to Katz's 1960 value-expressive function of attitudes), understanding (related to the knowledge and object appraisal functions), social (similar to the social adjustive function), career (related to Katz's utilitarian function), protective (related to the ego-defensive function or externalization concerns), and enhancement (related to the ego-defensive function). In field studies, Clary et al. (1998) found that when volunteers' perceived benefits following their volunteering experiences matched their underlying motivations, they became more satisfied with their volunteering experiences and had high levels of intentions to volunteer in the future.

Matching effects were also found when examining the relation between a store's atmosphere and product functions. For example, Schlosser (1998) proposed that store atmosphere could serve as a social identity appeal and that a pleasing atmosphere should enhance perceptions of the quality of social identity products but not utilitarian products. Two experiments supported this matching hypothesis between store atmosphere and product functions. Moreover, Schlosser (1998) found that people indicated greater intentions to purchase products when the store atmosphere matched rather than mismatched the product function.

Various persuasion mechanisms might be responsible for matching effects. Some matching effects have been attributed to relatively simple "cue effects." For example, DeBono (1987) informed high self-monitors (presumed to hold attitudes serving social-adjustive functions) or low self-monitors (presumed to hold attitudes serving value-expressive functions) that either (a) a strong majority of their peers favored institutionalization of the mentally ill or (b) favorable attitudes toward institutionalization were associated with values of being a responsible and loving person. Even when these claims were not accompanied by substantive message arguments (DeBono, 1987, Experiment 2), high self-monitors agreed more with institutionalization of the mentally ill when that policy was favored by the majority of their peers, but low self-monitors agreed more with institutionalization when that position was associated with cherished values.

In other cases, researchers have attributed matching effects to biases in more effortful information processing. For example, Lavine and Snyder (1996) found that matching effects were mediated by the favorability of cognitive responses to the persuasive message and by perceptions of message quality. That is, consistent with biases in processing when message elaboration is relatively high, low self-monitors generated more favorable thoughts and perceived messages to be of higher quality when they appealed to values rather than image. In contrast, high self-monitors generated more favorable thoughts and perceived the same messages to be of higher quality when they made an appeal to image rather than values. Similarly, Ziegler, von Schwichow, and Diehl (2005) provided research participants with a message source that matched or mismatched the attitude function. Similar to other instances of biased processing (e.g., biases based on source credibility; Chaiken & Maheswaran, 1994), participants agreed more with the ambiguous message when the source matched (vs. mismatched) attitude functions. However, the bias in processing was not observed when participants were provided with unambiguous messages. Participants agreed more with unambiguous strong arguments than unambiguous weak arguments regardless of their levels of self-monitoring.

All the previously discussed studies supported the matching hypothesis. However, it should be noted that functional matching might not always lead to greater persuasion. For instance, under conditions of relatively moderate elaboration likelihood (i.e., with neither particularly high nor low levels of processing motivation), Petty and Wegener (1998) showed that matching arguments can enhance or reduce attitude change depending on the cogency of the matched information. Petty and Wegener exposed high or low self-monitors to information pretested to be relatively strong or weak and to relate to products' image or quality (cf., Snyder & DeBono, 1985). Strong information was more persuasive than weak information, but this was especially true when the information matched rather than mismatched the presumed function served by message recipients' attitudes. Thus, functional matching increased persuasion when information was strong but decreased persuasion when information was weak. Similarly, DeBono and Harnish (1988) provided participants with a message source that was unattractive but expert or that was attractive but nonexpert. Low self-monitors processed information more extensively when the source was an expert, but high self-monitors processed information more extensively when the source was attractive. Thus, in each case, the source that matched the presumed attitude function increased processing of the message (which led to increased persuasion if message arguments were strong but to decreased persuasion if message arguments were weak). Although the reviewed studies provided important insights on the matching hypothesis, they did not directly address situations in which social needs were specifically thwarted. That is, although people differing in their self-monitoring tendencies might hold attitudes for different reasons and people might consider certain objects as most likely to serve certain functions, most contemporary studies of functional matching did not go the additional step of threatening high self-monitors' social standing, threatening low self-monitors' sense of value-expression, or threatening the extent to which the person's possessions served their dominant functions. This is a definite point of departure between contemporary research on functional approaches to persuasion and research on the self, where needs-based theories have thrived in recent years. In the following section, we modify Williams's (1997, 2007, 2009) need-threat/need-fortification framework to propose that thwarted or unsatisfied social motives can affect how people deal with persuasive attempts related (or unrelated) to those motives.

WILLIAMS'S NEED-THREAT/ NEED-FORTIFICATION FRAMEWORK

The past 20 years have seen much empirical research and theory development concerning coping with threatened social needs. The literature consistently suggests that when these social needs are thwarted, people strive to fortify the thwarted needs through cognitive and behavioral mechanisms. Interestingly, research on social exclusion/ostracism has found seemingly conflicting (i.e., prosocial vs. antisocial) reactions toward social exclusion (see Williams, 2007). Williams (1997, 2009) proposed a need-threat/need-fortification framework to explain such controversies. The key ideas of this framework are that social exclusion/ostracism threatens four fundamental needs (i.e., to belong, to maintain reasonably high self-esteem, to perceive control over one's social environment, and to perceive one's existence as meaningful) and that people engage in fortifying responses when each need is threatened. Past research indeed shows that thwarting of each need can result in efforts to replenish or rebuild one's standing on that dimension central to the sense of self.

Belonging

People desire positive and lasting relationships (Baumeister & Leary, 1995; Williams, 2001), and they strive for social connections when the belonging need is unsatisfied. Ostracized individuals have been shown to be more likely to conform to others (Williams, Cheung, & Choi, 2000) and more willing to donate money to a student organization (Carter-Sowell, Chen, & Williams, 2008). These behavioral responses may address needs for belonging, especially if conformity makes the person feel closer to the other and if donation to the student organization creates some identification on the part of the person with the organization. Most recently, it was found that individuals who were socially excluded mimic a subsequent interaction partner more than individuals who were initially included (Lakin, Chartrand, & Arkin, 2008).

People also engage in cognitive responses to fortify a threatened belonging need. For instance, Gardner, Pickett, and Brewer (2000) found that social exclusion led to enhanced memory for events related to affiliation. Further, Pickett, Gardner, and Knowles (2004) found that socially excluded individuals performed better on tasks requiring judgment of social information. Aside from these complex cognitions (e.g., memory and judgment), socially excluded individuals performed better on tasks involving early-stage perceptual processing than socially included individuals (DeWall, Maner, & Rouby, 2009). Finally, traits associated with deficits in belonging need, such as the need to belong and loneliness, each correlate similarly with cognitive performance (Pickett & Gardner, 2005).

It is important to point out that people's desire to fortify a threatened belonging need does not imply that they would seek affiliation indiscriminately. For example, although socially excluded individuals attempt to rebuild connections with others, exclusion does not make them affiliate with the perpetrators of exclusion or with novel partners with whom they do not anticipate face-to-face interaction (Maner, DeWall, Baumeister, & Schaller, 2007). Maner et al. (2007) further found that people who are more afraid of negative evaluation from others are less willing to interact with new partners in an affiliative fashion. These findings suggest that socially excluded individuals regulate their resources to maximize the chance of acceptance by others. They are less willing to spend their resources or efforts in activities that seem unlikely to improve their social inclusion status. Such regulation may even happen without cognitive awareness. For example, Lakin et al. (2008, Study 2) found that those excluded by an in-group mimic a later in-group member more than a later out-group member.

Self-Esteem

Self-esteem is the extent to which one views oneself positively or negatively. In other words, self-esteem is one's attitude toward oneself (see DeMarree, Petty, & Briñol, 2007). Of course, people prefer positive self-images, and they engage in various strategies to serve the purpose of self-enhancement when the positive images are threatened. At an individual level, when people feel badly about a misdeed or negative outcomes, they might use other positive self-concepts to affirm the self (Steele, 1988), attribute the outcomes to external instead of internal factors (Miller & Ross, 1975), or make downward comparison to maintain self-esteem (Wills, 1981). In addition, self-esteem can function as a monitoring system when people face the threat of exclusion or rejection (Leary, Tambor, Terdal, & Downs, 1995). Specifically, social exclusion threatens self-esteem, and self-esteem can provide a fast and automatic assessment of other's inclusion or exclusion intentions that helps to regulate one's attempts to enhance inclusion or avoid exclusion. At an intergroup level, according to social identity theory (Tajfel, 1982), the desire to main positive self-identity and self-image can lead to evaluations that favor one's in-groups and derogates out-groups.

Control

People need to perceive control over their social environment (Heider, 1958; Seligman, 1998), and they attempt to reclaim control cognitively (illusions of control,

Taylor & Brown, 1988) or behaviorally. Lawson Williams and Williams (1998) demonstrated that people desire higher levels of control when their perceived control is threatened. In both studies, participants were waiting with two other individuals (actually confederates) who pretended to be friends with each other or strangers to each other. While they were waiting, a seemingly spontaneous ball tossing game occurred and participants were either included or ostracized (see Williams & Sommer, 1997). Pilot-testing revealed that participants feel less in control of the social situation when seated with two individuals who are friends with each other in comparison with two individuals who are strangers. In Study 1, following the ball tossing, the participants worked with a late-arriving confederate in a "mindreading" task. The participant was given the opportunity to request the confederate turn his head as often as the participant wished, until the participant then guessed at what playing card (red or black) the confederate was looking. Control was exerted by requesting head turns. In Study 2, following the ball toss game, the participants (all females) filled out Burger's desire for control scale (Burger, 1984).

The control deprivation provided by sitting with strangers, combined with the control deprivation incurred through ostracism, should cause the most control threat. Consistent with this reasoning, in both studies, participants who were suffering the most control threat (those ostracized by confederates who were friends with each other) showed the highest amount of exerted control (Study 1) and desired control (Study 2). Thus, depriving individuals of social control, through an outgroup manipulation and an ostracism manipulation caused behaviors or intentions to reclaim control.

A more recent study does not use ostracism, but shows similar effects when one's newly acquired majority status appears precarious. Prislin, Sawicki, & Williams (2009) used a change from minority to majority paradigm (see Prislin, this volume) and found that the new majorities were more likely to abuse their new power only if they perceive that their rise to majority status is fragile or gotten by arbitrary (and therefore, not predictable) means. The abuse of power is a behavioral means to maintain control (Prislin et al., 2009).

Meaningful Existence

Over the past 20 years or so, social psychologists have extensively studied the motive to feel meaningful and significant. From the terror management perspective (Greenberg, Pyzczynski, & Solomon, 1986), the conflict between the survival instinct and the awareness of the inevitability of death produces the potential for paralyzing terror, and people tend to defend their cultural worldviews to boost their sense of being significant and meaningful. The literature shows consistently that mortality salience enhances one's liking of people whom support one's worldview but increases one's derogation toward those who challenge it. For example, research found that Christian participants in the mortality salience condition reported more fondness of a Christian target and more adverse reactions to a Jewish target (Greenberg et al., 1990). Similarly, after a mortality salience induction, American participants increased their affection for a pro-American essay author and increased their disdain for an anti-American essay author (Greenberg, Simon, Pyszczynski, Solomon, & Chatel, 1992).

A NEED-BASED THEORY OF PERSUASION AND INITIAL EVIDENCE

The preceding review shows the power of these social motives in guiding people's feelings, thinking, and behaviors. People are motivated to increase or boost their social needs via cognitive or behavioral mechanisms when these fundamental motives are threatened. Because attitudes serve social functions, it is reasonable to expect that these social needs or motives can also have important implications for attitudes and persuasion. When people's social needs (e.g., needs to belong, for self-esteem, to control, and for meaningful existence) are threatened, their response to various persuasive influences should help to fortify the thwarted needs. For example, if a persuasive attempt suggests an opportunity to form social bonds with others, socially excluded people or those with high need to belong might be more likely, at least in some circumstances, to be influenced by such an attempt than socially included people.

Indeed, the very idea that persuasion can function to facilitate the change of individuals' internal status is not new in the literature of attitude and persuasion. People holding ambivalent attitudes process proattitudinal more than counterattitudinal information in an attempt to resolve the ambivalence (Clark, Wegener, & Fabrigar, 2008). Dissonance theorists concur that people change their attitudes to reduce or eliminate the unpleasantness associated with dissonance (see Harmon-Jones, Amodio, & Harmon-Jones, this volume). Also, when people face threats to their worldviews, they usually respond by further confirming their beliefs (see Major & Townsend, this volume).

In this chapter, we primarily focus on the four basic needs discussed earlier. These needs were chosen because each of them has been shown to lead to fortifying response when it is threatened. These needs (or motives) are meant neither to be exhaustive nor exclusive. It is worthwhile to point out that these motives overlap substantially with the core social motives suggested by Fiske and colleagues (Fiske, 2002, 2004; Stevens & Fiske, 1995) that include belonging, understanding, controlling, enhancing self, and trusting.

Some Initial Data

Our initial research examined a small portion of the overall theory: susceptibility to persuasion by need-fortifying messages pretested to be reasonably cogent or strong. We asked participants to play an online ball tossing game with two other players (cf., Williams, Cheung, & Choi, 2000). During the game, participants were included (received 33% of the total tosses), partially ostracized (16%), or fully ostracized (6%). Following the ostracism manipulation, participants were presented with a message promoting senior comprehensive exams. The arguments in the message were framed so that it either fortified people's belonging need or it threatened people's belonging need. For example, an argument framed as fortifying the belonging need suggested that in order to do well on the comprehensive exams, students would need to study in groups and interact with others frequently. An argument framed as threatening people's belonging need suggested that in order to perform well on the comprehensive exams, students would have to withdraw from their social activities and study alone most of the time.

We hypothesized that ostracized participants will be more susceptible to a persuasive message if the ostracism episode held hope for future inclusion. Thus, we hypothesized that the impact of ostracism on persuasion depends on both the quantity of ostracism and the value frame of the persuasive message. If partially ostracized, reinclusion seems more achievable, but if fully ostracized reinclusion is doubtful. Furthermore, persuasion following ostracism should increase to the extent that the message itself facilitates rather than inhibits belonging goals.

We found a significant two-way interaction between the ostracism manipulation and the need-fortifying versus need-threatening arguments. That is, partially ostracized participants were more persuaded by arguments fortifying the belonging need and were less persuaded by arguments threatening the belonging need compared with included participants; however, fully ostracized participants resisted persuasion even by "matching" arguments and reacted more like the included participants (in terms of relative lack of differentiation between the need-fortifying and need-threatening arguments).

Fleshing Out the Theory

In the simplest of terms, our theory suggests that individuals are most likely to attend to features of persuasive appeals that imply fortification of fundamental needs. People are bombarded by messages constantly, so they are likely to filter out information that is not particularly relevant or pertinent. If, however, a message promises to fortify our sense of belonging, self-esteem, control, or meaningful existence, it is more likely that individuals experiencing a recent threat to one or more of those motives will attend to the persuasive features that relate to that need. Unlike previous theory and research on functional attitude bases, this tendency to selectively attend to and process message content related to *threatened* needs is crucial.

In our initial research, we used messages pretested as being reasonably cogent or strong. Thus, individuals whose needs had been threatened, by ostracism for example, should be more persuaded by such messages than individuals whose need satisfaction was relatively high (because they had been recently included). We suggest, however, that messages containing specious arguments would not be more persuasive to recently ostracized participants. We believe that thwarting or threatening of a need enhances attention and sensitivity to information perceived as related to the need. However, when message recipients are sufficiently motivated and able to think about the arguments in the persuasive message, their reactions to the message should reflect not only their level of need fulfillment but also their assessments of the merits of the claims made in the message. Therefore, if information perceived as related to the need is found to be weak and not at all compelling, the enhanced attention to this information will often decrease, rather than increase, persuasion by that message (cf., Petty & Wegener, 1998). These influences on amount of attention and processing given to need-relevant information may be most likely when motivation and ability to process the message are relatively moderate (i.e., not constrained to be extremely high or low).

However, this heightened attention or sensitivity to need-relevant features of the persuasion setting could also result in different types of persuasion outcomes at higher or lower levels of motivation and ability to think carefully about available information. When motivation or ability is lacking (and, therefore, elaboration of the persuasive message is unlikely, Petty & Cacioppo, 1986), a thwarted or threatened need may lead to selective use of available heuristics that help one to reestablish the sense of self related to the need. For example, if the source of a persuasive message is socially attractive but knows little about the topic (cf., DeBono & Harnish, 1988), then thwarting the need to belong might accentuate the likelihood of agreeing with the socially attractive source, but thwarting a need for meaningful existence might be less likely to result in agreement with the attractive (possibly "superficial") source. Instead, thwarting of a need for meaningful existence may increase the likelihood of agreeing with sources that represent a person's worldview. If the message topic itself relates to the thwarted or threatened need, then message recipients who lack motivation or ability to think may seize on any available persuasion factors that allow them to take a position that rebuilds their desired sense of self. In other words, use of persuasion heuristics may not simply serve as a simple shortcut to determining whether a given attitude is "correct" (see Petty & Cacioppo, 1986, for discussion). Heuristics or other cues may be used to serve alternative goals in the persuasion setting, such as bolstering one's wounded sense of self.

If motivation and ability to think are high (and, therefore, elaboration is likely) then motives to address thwarted or threatened needs may bias information processing in a direction that helps to address the need. These biases in processing could again involve selective use of available information or persuasion factors that help the person to develop an attitude that addresses the need. However, when biased processing is at work, thoughts about the merits of the persuasive message would be colored by the motives to address the thwarted or threatened need (instead of the more direct effects of the motives—perhaps on use of heuristics—when motivation or ability to think is lacking).

Another high-elaboration influence of thwarted needs would relate to recent research on self-validation (e.g., Petty, Briñol, & Tormala, 2002; for a review, see Briñol & Petty, 2009). That is, persuasion features that address a threatened or thwarted need might influence the confidence that message recipients have in their thoughts about the message or topic. In past research, self-validation effects have been more likely when the confidence-inducing factor is introduced after, rather than before, the message (e.g., Briñol, Petty, & Tormala, 2002) and when motivation and ability to think are high (e.g., Briñol, Petty, & Tormala, 2004). Thus, in these situations, message recipients have had thoughts about the topic before they experience confidence or doubt in those thoughts.

In some situations, learning that a particular position will help one satisfy a threatened need might boost confidence in thoughts that support that position or undermine confidence in thoughts that oppose that position. This directional difference in effects on thought confidence would diverge from previous effects in which a persuasion factor (such as a credible source or message recipient experience of happy mood or power) has similar confidence effects on all thoughts about the message (regardless of whether they are favorable or unfavorable; see Briñol & Petty, 2009). Yet, there is some precedence for this directional asymmetry. That is, Clark, Wegener, Briñol, and Petty (2009) provided research participants with information about a child's socioeconomic status (SES) after behaviors that led participants to believe that the child was relatively intelligent or unintelligent. When the SES information provided convergent support for initial perceptions, participants experienced increased confidence in their initial thoughts about the child and used those thoughts to make stronger recommendations for enrolling the child in gifted or remedial classes compared with conditions in which the SES information opposed participants' initial reactions to the child.

Threatened or thwarted social needs might be another setting in which the direction of the need creates asymmetry in which thoughts are supported or opposed by the motives involved. If, for example, a previously ostracized message recipient learns afterward that a majority of peers supports a particular position, then any thoughts the recipient had in support of that position might be bolstered by the consensus information and held with confidence, whereas any initial reactions opposing that position might be held with diminished certainty.

Boundary Conditions

Of course, this approach implies a number of boundary conditions regarding the susceptibility to persuasion of individuals with thwarted social needs. The thwarted or threatened need may influence reactions to information perceived as relevant to addressing the need, but not to other need-irrelevant information. Thus, it is reasonable to expect that socially excluded people might often be more persuaded by appeals (especially under high- or low-elaboration settings) that provide chances to improve social connections with new partners, but not by appeals unrelated to social connections or attributable to sources that would not help to address the thwarted social need. This expectation would be consistent with past findings that socially excluded individuals affiliate with partners with whom they have a chance to meet in person, but not with perpetrators of exclusion or novel partners with whom they do not anticipate to meet (Maner et al., 2007). When elaboration likelihood is more moderate, of course, the persuasive effects of the information would depend on whether the message arguments are relatively strong or weak. And, when elaboration likelihood is high but need-relevant information comes to light after the persuasive message, validation of thoughts about the message and topic would depend on the consistency of the thoughts with the persuasion features that address the social need.

Following this logic, ostracized individuals should be more susceptible to persuasion (under high or low elaboration likelihood or when strong arguments are presented with moderate elaboration likelihood) when the appeal appears associated with a larger chance of fortifying the belonging need than when it seems associated with a smaller chance. The likelihood of forming social connections could be influenced by time, distance, or other methods. It seems reasonable, for example, to expect that ostracized participants would be more sensitive to appeals that provide an opportunity to form social bonds in a near future than in a distance future. We are now collecting data to test these hypotheses.

CONCLUSION

The functional approach of persuasion has a long history in social psychological research. Theories developed in the 1950s and 1960s first recognized and emphasized that attitudes could serve social and emotional needs. Past research on persuasion has studied individual difference variables, such as self-monitoring, need for cognition, and so on. The intention of this chapter is to draw researchers' attentions to the rich literature on basic social motives, which can refocus need-based persuasion effects on thwarting or threatening core social motives. Our approach also resonates with the advocacy of viewing persuasion as a socially situated process (see Prislin, this volume). Generally, we believe that threatened social needs, including belonging, self-esteem, control, and meaningful existence can direct the attention of message recipients to information perceived as related to the threatened need. This directing of attention can influence how people respond to persuasive attempts and can ultimately increase or decrease persuasion depending on a number of additional factors, including the level of elaboration likelihood and the extent to which message recipients view information in the persuasion setting or particular attitudinal positions as helpful in addressing the thwarted social needs.

REFERENCES

Banaji, M. R., & Prentice, D. A. (1994). The self in social contexts. *Annual Review of Psychology, 45,* 297–332.

Baumeister, R. F., & Leary, M. R. (1995). The need to belong: Desire for interpersonal attachments as a fundamental human motivation. *Psychological Bulletin, 117,* 497–529.

Briñol, P., & Petty, R. E. (2009). Persuasion: Insights from the self-validation hypothesis. In M. P. Zanna (Ed.), *Advances in experimental social psychology* (Vol. 41, 69–118). New York: Elsevier.

Briñol, P., Petty, R. E., & Tormala, Z. L. (2002). *Source credibility as a determinant of self-validation effects in persuasion.* Poster session presented at the 13th general meeting of the European Association of Experimental Social Psychology, San Sebastián, Spain.

Briñol, P., Petty, R. E., & Tormala, Z. L. (2004). Self-validation of cognitive responses to advertisements. *Journal of Consumer Research, 30,* 559–573.

Burger, J. M. (1984). Desire for control, locus of control, and proneness to depression. *Journal of Personality, 52,* 71–89.

Carter-Sowell, A. R., Chen, Z., & Williams, K. D. (2008). Ostracism increases social susceptibility. *Social Influence, 3,* 143–153.

Chaiken, S., & Maheswaran, D. (1994). Heuristic processing can bias systematic processing: Effects of source credibility, argument ambiguity, and task importance on attitude judgment. *Journal of Personality and Social Psychology, 66,* 460–473.

Clark, J. K., Wegener, D. T., Briñol, P., & Petty, R. E. (2009). Discovering that the shoe fits: The self-validating role of stereotypes. *Psychological Science, 20,* 846–852.

Clark, J. K., Wegener, D. T., & Fabrigar, L. R. (2008). Attitudinal ambivalence and message-based persuasion: Motivated processing of proattitudinal information and avoidance of counterattitudinal information. *Personality and Social Psychology Bulletin, 34,* 565–577.

Clary, E. G., Snyder, M., Ridge, R. D., Copeland, J., Stukas, A. A., Haugen, J., et al. (1998). Understanding and assessing the motivations of volunteers: A functional approach. *Journal of Applied Social Psychology, 24,* 1129–1149.

Crocker, J., & Park, L. E. (2004). The costly pursuit of self-esteem. *Psychological Bulletin, 130,* 392–414.

DeBono, K. G. (1987). Investigating the social adjustive and value-expressive functions of attitudes: Implications for persuasion processes. *Journal of Personality and Social Psychology, 52,* 279–287.

DeBono, K. G., & Harnish, R. J. (1988). Source expertise, source attractiveness, and the processing of persuasive information: A functional approach. *Journal of Personality and Social Psychology, 55,* 541–546.

DeBono, K. G., & Packer, M. (1991). The effects of advertising appeal on perceptions of product quality. *Personality and Social Psychology Bulletin, 17,* 194–200.

DeMarree, K. G., Petty, R. E., & Briñol, P. (2007). Self and attitude strength parallels: Focus on accessibility. *Social and Personality Psychology Compass, 1,* 441–468.

DeWall, C. N., Maner, J. K., & Rouby, D. A. (2009). Social exclusion and early-stage interpersonal perception: Selective attention to signs of acceptance. *Journal of Personality and Social Psychology, 96,* 729–741.

Eagly, A. H., & Chaiken, S. (1993). *The psychology of attitudes.* Fort Worth, TX: Harcourt Brace Jovanovich.

Fiske, S. T. (2002). Five core social motives, plus or minus five. In S. J. Spencer, S. Fein, M. P. Zanna, & J. Olson (Eds.), *Motivated social perception: The Ontario symposium* (Vol. 9, pp. 233–246). Mahwah, NJ: Erlbaum.

Fiske, S. T. (2004). *Social beings: A core motives approach to social psychology.* New York: Wiley.

Gardner, W. L., Pickett, C. L., & Brewer, M. B. (2000). Social exclusion and selective memory: How the need to belong influences memory for social events. *Personality and Social Psychology Bulletin, 26,* 486–496.

Greenberg, J., Pyszczynski, T., & Solomon, S. (1986). The causes and consequences of the need for self-esteem: A terror management theory. In R. F. Baumeister (Ed.), *Public self and private self* (pp. 189–212). New York: Springer-Verlag.

Greenberg, J., Pyszczynski, T., Solomon, S., Rosenblatt, A., Veeder, M., Kirkland, S., & Lyon, D. (1990). Evidence for terror management theory II: The effects of mortality salience on reactions to those who threaten or bolster the cultural worldview. *Journal of Personality and Social Psychology, 58,* 308–318.

Greenberg, J., Simon, L., Pyszczynski, T., Solomon, S., & Chatel, D. (1992). Terror management and tolerance: Does mortality salience always intensify negative reactions to others who threaten one's worldview? *Journal of Personality and Social Psychology, 63,* 212–220.

Heider, F. (1958). *The psychology of interpersonal relations.* New York: Wiley.

Katz, D. (1960). The functional approach to the study of attitudes. *Public Opinion Quarterly, 24,* 163–204.

Lakin, J. L., Chartrand, T. L., & Arkin, R. M. (2008). I am too just like you: Nonconscious mimicry as an automatic behavioral response to social exclusion. *Psychological Science, 19,* 816–822.

Lavine, H., & Snyder M. (1996). Cognitive processing and functional matching effect in persuasion: The mediating role of subjective perceptions of message quality. *Journal of Experimental Social Psychology, 32,* 580–604.

Lawson Williams, H., & Williams, K. D. (1998, April). *Effects of social ostracism on desire for control.* Paper presented at the meeting of the Society for Australasian Social Psychology, Christchurch, New Zealand.

Leary, M. R., Tambor, E. S., Terdal, S. K., & Downs, D. L. (1995). Self-esteem as an interpersonal monitor: The sociometer hypothesis. *Journal of Personality and Social Psychology, 68,* 518–530.

Maner, J. K., DeWall, C. N., Baumeister, R. F., & Schaller, M. (2007). Does social exclusion motivate interpersonal reconnection? Resolving the "Porcupine Problem." *Journal of Personality and Social Psychology, 92,* 42–55.

Miller, D. T., & Ross, M. (1975). Self-serving biases in attribution of causality: Factor or fiction? *Psychological Bulletin, 82,* 313–325.

Petty, R. E., Briñol, P., & Tormala, Z. L. (2002). Thought confidence as a determinant of persuasion: The self-validation hypothesis. *Journal of Personality and Social Psychology, 82,* 722–741.

Petty, R. E., & Cacioppo, J. T. (1986). *Communication and persuasion: Central and peripheral routes to attitude change.* New York: Springer-Verlag.

Petty, R. E., & Wegener, D. T. (1998). Matching versus mismatching attitude functions: Implications for scrutiny of persuasive messages. *Personality and Social Psychology Bulletin, 24,* 227-240.

Pickett, C. L., & Gardner, W. L. (2005). The social monitoring system: Enhanced sensitivity to social cues as an adaptive response to social exclusion. In K. Williams, J. Forgas, & W. von Hippel (Eds.), *The social outcast: Ostracism, social exclusion, rejection, and bullying* (pp. 213–226). New York: Psychology Press.

Pickett, C. L., Gardner, W. L., & Knowles, M. (2004). Getting a cue: The need to belong and enhanced sensitivity to social cues. *Personality and Social Psychology Bulletin, 30,* 1095–1107.

Prislin, R., Sawicki, V., & Williams, K. D. (2009). *Only new majorities who feel no control over the shift in status are likely to abuse their power.* Unpublished manuscript, San Diego State University.

Pyszczynski, T., Greenberg, J., & Solomon, S. (1999). A dual-process model of defensive against conscious and unconscious death-related thoughts: An extension of terror management theory. *Psychological Review, 106,* 835–845.

Schlosser, A. E. (1998). Applying the functional theory of attitudes to understanding the influence of store atmosphere on store inferences. *Journal of Consumer Psychology, 7,* 345–369.

Seligman, M. E. P. (1998). *Learned optimism* (2nd ed.). New York: Simon & Schuster.

Shavitt, S. (1990). The role of attitude objects in attitude functions. *Journal of Experimental Social Psychology, 26,* 124–148.

Shavitt, S., & Nelson, M. R. (2002). The role of attitude functions in persuasion and social judgment. In J. P. Dillard & M. Pfau (Eds.), *The persuasion handbook: Theory and practice* (pp. 137–153). Thousand Oaks, CA: Sage.

Smith, M. B., Bruner, J. S., & White, R. W. (1956). *Opinions and personality.* New York: Wiley.

Snyder, M. (1974). Self-monitoring of expressive behavior. *Journal of Personality and Social Psychology, 30,* 526–537.

Snyder, M., & DeBono, K. G. (1985). Appeals to images and claims about quality: Understanding the psychology of advertising. *Journal of Personality and Social Psychology, 49,* 586–597.

Snyder, M., & DeBono, K. G. (1987). A functional approach to attitudes and persuasion. In M. P. Zanna, J. M. Olson, & C. P. Herman (Eds.), *Social influence: The Ontario symposium* (Vol. 5, pp. 107–125). Hillsdale, NJ: Erlbaum.

Snyder, M., & DeBono, K. G. (1989). Understanding the functions of attitudes: Lessons from personality and social behavior. In A. R. Pratkanis, S. J. Breckler, & A. G. Greenwald (Eds.), *Attitude structure and function* (pp. 361–381). Hillsdale, NJ: Erlbaum.

Steele, C. M. (1988). The psychology of self-affirmation: Sustaining the integrity of the self. In L. Berkowitz (Ed.), *Advances in experimental social psychology* (Vol. 21, pp. 261–302). New York: Academic Press.

Stevens, L. E., & Fiske, S. T. (1995). Motivation and cognition in social life: A social survival perspective. *Social Cognition, 13*, 189–214.

Tajfel, H. (1982). Social psychology of intergroup relations. *Annual Review of Psychology, 33*, 1–30.

Taylor, S. E., & Brown, J. D. (1988). Illusion and well-being: A social psychological perspective on mental health. *Psychological Bulletin, 103*, 193–210.

Williams, K. D. (1997). Social ostracism. In R. M. Kowalski (Ed.), *Aversive interpersonal behaviors* (pp. 133–170). New York: Plenum Press.

Williams, K. D. (2001). *Ostracism: The power of silence.* New York: Guilford Press.

Williams, K. D. (2007). Ostracism. *Annual Review of Psychology, 58*, 425–452.

Williams, K. D. (2009). Ostracism: Effects of being ignored and excluded. In M. Zanna (Ed.), *Advances in experimental social psychology* (Vol. 41, pp. 279–314). New York: Academic Press.

Williams, K. D., Cheung, C. K. T., & Choi, W. (2000). CyberOstracism: Effects of being ignored over the Internet. *Journal of Personality and Social Psychology, 79*, 748–762.

Williams, K. D., & Sommer, K. L. (1997). Social ostracism by one's coworkers: Does rejection lead to loafing or compensation? *Personality and Social Psychology Bulletin, 23*, 693–706.

Wills, T. A. (1981). Downward comparison principles in social psychology. *Psychological Bulletin, 90*, 245–271.

Ziegler, R., von Schwichow, A., & Diehl, M. (2005). Matching the message source to attitude functions: Implications for biased processing. *Journal of Experimental Social Psychology, 41*, 645–653.

13

Persuasion as Social Interaction

RADMILA PRISLIN

"Stand up! Stand up! Stand up and fight... We never give up! We never quit!" thundered presidential candidate John McCain on the eve of the 2008 U.S. presidential election. His combativeness flew in the face of the poll results. Although he was losing support during the entire month preceding the election, McCain remained determined to persuade the voters of his ultimate victory. As his numbers were declining, McCain continued talking to the voters in the hope to reverse his fortune. Addressing voters' concerns about the sinking economy, McCain proposed several promising initiatives. However, he failed to elaborate on any of them, leaving voters puzzled. Eager to present himself as an advocate for the middle class, McCain surrounded himself with middle-class faces. However, his would-be face of the middle-class America, Joe the Plumber, abandoned him shortly after joining his campaign. As if this did not give enough ammunition to the late-night comedians, McCain managed to receive a last-minute endorsement from the unpopular sitting president whom he had strategically avoided throughout the campaign. It appeared that the more he tried, the worse McCain did. In the end, he lost the election.

Of course, losing or winning an election is a complexly determined outcome. Yet, none of the many factors that may affect the outcome will matter much if a candidate lacks motivation to seek voters' support or the ability to do so. Motivation to influence and the ability to generate persuasive arguments are conditions sine qua non for persuasion to occur. What determines them? In this chapter, I will explore the possible social origins of persuasive motivation and persuasive efficacy. Specifically, I will focus on the role of social support in sustaining motivation and ability to persuade. As McCain's example illustrates, a persuader's motivation to influence may survive a decrease in social support. Persuasive efficacy, however, appears to be more sensitive to the fluctuations in social support. With his numbers declining, McCain's persuasiveness eroded to the point where many wondered what had happened to "the old" McCain. Interestingly, during the same period, his opponent's persuasiveness was on the upward trajectory. As social support for Barack Obama surged, his message became increasingly convincing, even to those who did not count themselves among his admirers. The parallel between the persuasiveness trajectory and the support trajectory is intriguing. The traditional persuasion paradigm would suggest that changes in persuasiveness likely brought about changes in social support. Yet, the opposite might have been just as true. If indeed changes in social support shaped the strength of their messages, political candidates were transformed from agents of influence to targets of influence.

Understanding agents' responsiveness to their targets' reactions requires that persuasion be conceptualized as a social interaction. When agents and targets interact, influence necessarily flows bidirectionally. As a persuasive interaction evolves, the agents' intentional attempts to alter target attitudes trigger target reactions. These, in turn, affect the agents' subsequent persuasive attempts. Over time, this reciprocal influence creates the social structure that further shapes interactions between agents and targets. Within this approach, the roles of agents and targets are relative in that they are (arbitrarily) assigned when influence is presumably initiated; however, these roles change over time as the involved parties continue to interact. The line of research presented in this chapter represents an initial step in demonstrating the relative roles of agents and targets. Specifically, studies presented here document how agents' motivation to persuade and their persuasiveness depend on the dynamics of social relationships that are created in the process of agent-target interactions.

AN (ALMOST EXCLUSIVELY) TARGET'S PERSPECTIVE IN THEORIZING AND RESEARCH ON PERSUASION

The traditional approach to persuasion has focused almost exclusively on targets of persuasion and the effects of their characteristics on persuasive outcomes. If agents' characteristics are considered at all, they are again examined from a target's perspective; that is, as moderators of a target's reactions. Yet, agents' characteristics may affect not only reactions to persuasive messages but also their production. For example, Forgas (2007) recently showed that fluctuations in agents' affective states produced marked differences in the type and quality of persuasive arguments they generated. Agents in mildly negative moods, in comparison to those in positive and neutral moods, generated more concrete persuasive arguments that proved more effective in swaying targets' attitudes.

In addition to neglecting the agent's perspective, a typical persuasion study is a one-time affair that examines targets' immediate reactions to a written message attributed to an agent (cf., Kumkale & Albaracín, 2004). The targets and the agent almost never interact. As a result, they have no opportunity to develop a socially meaningful relationship. Relational issues, if addressed at all, typically are reduced to information given to the targets to consider. Targets presumably derive their motivations for responding to persuasive appeals from the nature of their relationship with the influencing agent (Prislin & Wood, 2005).

Relational categories that may motivate targets' responses to influence were discussed within classical typologies of social influence. For example, French and

Raven (French, 1956; French & Raven, 1959) postulated five categories of social power that emerge from distinct agent-target relationships and enable an agent to influence his or her targets. Kelman's (1958) typology complements their categorization by focusing on the targets' responses. According to French and Raven, an asymmetrical relationship in which the influencing agent possesses the means to satisfy the target's hedonic needs endows the agent with reward power and the power to coerce. The target's responses, motivated by desire to obtain positive outcomes and avoid negative outcomes, represent superficial compliance with the agent's request rather than a genuine acceptance of the target's position (Kelman, 1958). The target's responses, however, may be motivated by his or her acceptance of the agent's position of authority as legitimate within socially prescribed hierarchy of roles. The resultant legitimate power afforded to the agent is similar to expert power afforded to an agent perceived as superior in knowledge. In both cases, the target responds to influence within a relationship whose asymmetry is accepted rather than imposed. In a different type of relationship in which the target identifies with the agent, the agent's standards are accepted as one's own. Identification (Kelman, 1958) and the resultant referent power afforded to the agent were later elaborated within social categorization theory that discusses influence in the group context (Turner, 1991).

In addition to these relational bases of influence, French and Raven introduced a relatively relationship-free category of influence. Informational power, based in the quality of information the agent can provide in response to the target's epistemic needs, typically results in internalization of the information-supported position (Kelman, 1958). The rich theorizing about relational bases of responding evident in these and other typologies of influence (e.g., Asch, 1952; Festinger, 1950; Kelley, 1952) was subsequently reduced to a simple dichotomy between relationship-based normative influence and message-based informational influence, with the former presumably leading to superficial conformity and the latter presumably leading to a genuine attitude change (Deutsch & Gerard, 1955). This simplified view of normative and informational influence is slowly giving way to more sophisticated analyses of relational motives (for review, see Prislin & Wood, 2005), with contemporary dual process models postulating independence between motives and responses to persuasive appeals (Albarracín, Johnson, & Zanna, 2005). The power of relational motives to generate genuine change is evident in research on vicarious dissonance (Cooper, this volume), the role of trust in persuasion (Wänke & Reutner, this volume), the attitude-behavior relationship (Johnson & Boynton, this volume), and the need-based approach to persuasion (Williams, Chen, & Wegener, this volume)

RELATIONSHIPS (SHOULD) MATTER FOR AGENTS OF INFLUENCE

If relationships inform a target's response to persuasion, it stands to reason that relationships should also inform how persuasion is practiced by an agent. However, theorizing about the importance of relational issues for agents of influence is scarce. It is mostly reduced to the issue of agents' surveillance over targets to ensure their yielding to influence (Prislin & Wood, 2005). Specifically, agents exercising reward and punishment power in the French and Raven parlance must monitor targets' responses to deliver rewards and punishments accordingly. Exercise of other types of power presumably requires little if any surveillance. Yet, it would be wrong to conclude that agents relying on other types of power to exercise influence need not be concerned with relational issues. For example, agents exercising legitimate power and expert power presumably must adhere to the mutually accepted standards of conduct to maintain the very relationship that feeds their power to influence. Similarly, an exercise of referent power would be difficult if agents were not responsive to the targets' needs. In short, relationships are just as consequential for agents of influence as they are for targets, though this is not widely acknowledged in theorizing and research on persuasion.

An agent's perspective is similarly neglected in research on the role of group membership in persuasion. The importance of group membership in persuasion is evident in elaborate theorizing and vibrant research on influence from minority and majority groups (for recent review, see Martin & Hewstone, 2008) and the role of social identity in persuasion (Turner, 1991). Numerous models of minority and majority influence have been developed exclusively from the perspective of targets of influence. They explain targets' reactions to minority or majority influence and processes underlying targets' reactions. Very little is known about how agents' minority or majority status may affect their motivation to exert influence and their influence strategies. Similarly, the social identity theory account of influence considers how the social context of groups (in-group vs. out-group) affects targets' reactions to influence (for recent review, see Smith & Hogg, 2008). It says nothing about how the same social context of groups would affect agents' influence attempts.

PERSUASION FROM AN AGENT'S PERSPECTIVE: INTERACTING WITH TARGETS OVER TIME

Conceptualizing persuasion as an interaction aimed at effecting change in the involved parties' attitudes and beliefs has several important implications. First, because an interaction is bidirectional, influence exerted in the persuasion process is also bidirectional. Just as a party initiating the process, and therefore assigned the role of an agent, influences targets, so too do targets influence the agent. At minimum, targets' reactions to the agent's persuasive attempts feed back to affect the agent's subsequent actions. Second, an interaction presumes dynamic exchanges that evolve over time. To the extent that these exchanges alter attitudes and beliefs of the involved parties, they may also change the relationships and the social context in which influence evolves. In the context of dyadic relationships, interactions may change one or both parties' understanding of the nature of their relationship and, therefore, the basis of influence. In the context of group relationships, interactions may change a party that is initially in the majority to a minority and vice versa. Also, interactions and the resultant changes over time may transform some of the interaction partners from in-group members to out-group members and vice versa. In short, when conceptualized as social interaction, persuasion—and the social context in which it evolves—become dynamic, as they typically are in real-life circumstances (Mason, Conrey, & Smith, 2007).

The field of social psychology currently lacks methodological tools and analytical techniques that would fully capture the dynamic nature of persuasion (cf., Smith & Conrey, 2007). Attempts to examine persuasion in the context of freely interacting groups are few (Stasser, Kerr, & Davis, 1989; Tindale, Davis, Vollrath, Nagao, & Hinsz, 1990), and computational simulations are still in the developmental phase (Hastie & Stasser, 2000). Nonetheless, some of the basic tenets of the dynamic approach can be tested using traditional experimental techniques. For example, reciprocity of influence may be tested under the controlled experimental conditions in which participants, acting as agents of influence, interact with confederates, acting as targets, to examine the effects of confederates' feedback on the agents' subsequent reactions (e.g., Forgas, 2007, Study 4). Using this approach, Rind and Kipnis (1999) demonstrated that participants who employed different influence techniques to secure confederates' agreement changed their self-perceptions in accordance with the technique used. Specifically, participants using rational arguments described themselves as intelligent, whereas those using authoritative influence described themselves as dominant. This research was among the first to demonstrate how an important aspect of agents' self-concept was shaped by their targets' acceptance of their advocacy.

In a rare experimental demonstration of the reciprocal effects of persuasion on attitudes, Prislin, Limbert, and Bauer (2000, Study 1) demonstrated that agents' own attitudes and meta-attitudinal characteristics were affected by their targets' reactions to their initial persuasive attempts. Specifically, in a face-to-face interaction with their targets (confederates), agents sought to win majority support for their position on an attitude issue. Sequentially elaborating their positions on various aspects of the issue, agents received feedback from targets after each of the elaborations. Initial positive (negative) feedback rendered sources successful (unsuccessful). As agents continued their persuasive attempts, subsequent feedback either reaffirmed their initial (lack of) success, or reversed it when some of the targets who initially agreed (disagreed) with them switched to disagreeing (agreeing). Although agents' initial attitudes on the issue were equivalent across experimental conditions, their postexperimental attitudes differed significantly. Agents who became decreasingly successful (successful → unsuccessful) changed their attitudes away from the position preferred by agents who remained successful throughout the interaction. Agents who became increasingly successful (unsuccessful → successful) did not change their attitudinal positions; however, they strengthened their attitudes. This was evident in a significant increase in the importance they attached to their attitudes and a widening of the latitude of attitudinal positions they found unacceptable. Additional research revealed that agents also interpreted differences in attitudinal positions as either deviance or diversity in accordance with the results of their persuasive efforts. Decreasingly successful agents interpreted attitudinal differences as diversity, whereas consistently successful agents viewed differences as deviance (Prislin, Brewer, & Wilson, 2002). This pattern of results nicely illustrates the dynamic nature of agents' reactions, which vary according to the feedback they receive from their targets.

PERSUASIVE MOTIVATION AND PERSUASIVE EFFICACY: THE EFFECT OF TARGETS' FEEDBACK

Persuasion is a motivated action aimed at influencing other people's attitudes and beliefs. Specific motives for exerting influence are many and are likely similar to those that drive responding to influence (Briñol & Petty, 2005; Prislin & Wood, 2005). Whereas persuasive attempts may be driven by many motives, they are ultimately sustained by the intensity of those motives. Thus, it is important to understand what determines the intensity of persuasive motivation. Why do some agents persist in their efforts to persuade even when they face seemingly insurmountable obstacles? For example, what sustained McCain's apparent motivation to seek voters' support even while his approval rates were continually declining?

Persuasive motivation can be understood in the context of a general theory of motivation called energization theory (Brehm & Self, 1989). According to the theory, motivation to achieve a goal originates from judgment that the goal is desirable and achievable. Such a goal motivates efforts toward its achievement. Governed by the principle of energy conservation, efforts to achieve a goal should be sufficient enough to meet the goal but minimal enough not to exceed the necessary minimum. Thus, once a goal is achieved, goal-directed efforts should subside. Efforts to achieve a goal should also subside if they prove unsuccessful over a period of time. Consistently unsuccessful efforts render the goal unfeasible and therefore not motivating irrespective of how desirable it may be (Wright & Brehm, 1989).

A generic goal desired by all agents of persuasion is to win targets' support for their attitudinal positions. When the goal is achieved, successful agents should lose their motivation to continue persuading their (already persuaded) targets. Agents should also lose their persuasive motivation if their repeated efforts to win targets' support prove unsuccessful. Consistent failure signals that it is not feasible to persuade targets and that therefore, future persuasive attempts would be futile. In short, agents consistently successful in persuading their targets, and agents consistently unsuccessful in persuading their targets, should experience a decrease in motivation to persuade over time.

Agents' success at persuading their targets, however, may vary. Over time, initially successful agents may lose support and those initially unsuccessful may eventually win their targets' support. Variable success signals to agents that their goal of persuading targets is achievable but not assured. A goal that appears to be within reach but not secured should energize further efforts toward goal achievement. Thus, both increasingly successful agents who win targets' support after initial failure, and decreasingly successful agents who lose targets' support after initial success, should show an increase in motivation to persuade over time.

The hypothesized variations in persuasive motivation are especially important because of their potential effects on persuasive efficacy. To the extent that persuasion is a motivated action, its efficacy should be determined, at least partially, by motivation to influence others. Other things being equal, the more motivated agents are to influence their targets, the more efficient they should be in their advocacy, at least up to a point. Assuming that the relationship between motivation and efficacy is curvilinear, increases in persuasive motivation should translate to increases in persuasive efficacy until motivation reaches an optimal level after which any further increase might interfere with efficacy. The latter would be a case of a persuader "too eager" to persuade to be effective.

An initial test of these hypotheses was presented to participants as a study of political campaigns (Prislin, Boyle, Farley, Jacobs, & Zandian, 2009). In each experimental session, a naive participant, who acted as a political candidate, tried to win support for his or her position on ten social issues from confederates, who acted as voters. Each time the candidate explained his or her position on an issue, the voters communicated their feedback, verbally accepting or rejecting the candidate's advocacy. On the first five issues, the candidate either received support from most of the voters to be rendered successful or was rejected by most of the voters to be rendered unsuccessful. The candidate's initially established (lack of) success was either maintained for the remaining of his or her interaction with voters (stable conditions), or was reversed when some of the voters switched from accepting (rejecting) to rejecting (accepting) the candidate's advocacy on the sixth through the tenth round (changed condition).

With participants' permission, all sessions were videotaped. The participants' behavior was later coded for indicators of persuasive motivation and efficacy. Participants' persuasive motivation was assessed by coding nonverbal behaviors that were found to be indicative of the intent to influence others (Mehrabian & Williams, 1969). Participants' persuasive efficacy was assessed by rating strength and clarity of their advocacy (Hamilton, Hunter, & Burgoon, 1990; Stiff, 1986). Both persuasive motivation and persuasive efficacy were assessed twice: after participants' initial status was established and at the end of interaction when their initial status was either upheld or reversed.

The results revealed a significant loss of persuasive motivation and the resultant decrease in persuasive efficacy in agents whose advocacy was consistently rejected (consistently unsuccessful agents). In contrast, there was a significant gain of persuasive motivation and the resultant increase in persuasive efficacy in agents whose advocacy was accepted after initial rejection (unsuccessful → successful agents). This pattern suggests that initially unsuccessful agents deliberately adjusted their subsequent advocacy according to their targets' successive feedback. They almost ceased their advocacy in response to their targets' continuing rejection but intensified it in response to their targets' increasing acceptance of their argument. This, however, did not appear to be the case for initially successful agents. Those whose advocacy was consistently successful experienced a significant motivational loss though they remained efficient in their advocacy. On the other hand, initially successful agents whose advocacy was subsequently rejected (successful → unsuccessful) maintained their motivation to persuade but became decreasingly successful at doing so. Their persuasive efficacy decreased significantly over time. They likely experienced their targets' feedback as social rejection, which was shown to impair intellectual abilities needed to persuade others (Baumeister, Twenge, & Nuss, 2002).

The possibility that increasingly unsuccessful agents experienced their targets' feedback as social rejection is suggested by previous findings about these agents' strong negative reactions toward dissenting targets (Prislin et al., 2002; Prislin & Christensen, 2005; Prislin et al., 2000). This possibility was tested directly in another study whose procedure was highly similar to the previously described study. That is, in a direct interaction with confederates, participants initially experienced either success or failure in their persuasive attempts, which was later either kept stable or reversed. Participants in the new study were asked about the extent to which their sense of rejection (vs. belongingness) changed over the course of their interactions with others (Prislin, Davenport, Michalak, Uehara, & Xi, 2009). As anticipated, increasingly unsuccessful agents (successful → unsuccessful) reported that they felt increasingly rejected by others whose behavior they found upsetting. In contrast, increasingly successful agents (unsuccessful → successful) reported that they felt increasingly accepted by others. Interestingly, they did not find others' behavior comforting as much as they found it noncommittal.

A possible constraint on the generalizability of these findings is the process of data collection. Coders of the behaviors indicating persuasive motivation and efficacy had ample time and opportunities to observe and decipher the meaning of agents' reactions. Real-life circumstances, however, rarely afford such a luxury. Ordinary persuasive interactions mostly evolve in real time, with targets assessing agents' reactions "online." Would variations in agents' reactions be evident in the course of an ongoing interaction that does not allow for a playback of agents' behavior? Answering this question was important not only to document the generalizability of the previous findings. Additionally, if variations in agents' persuasive motivation and efficacy are readily apparent to targets, they may affect targets' subsequent reactions.

To examine whether the original findings would replicate in an "online" assessment of agents' reactions, confederates in a new study had a dual task. In addition to providing feedback to naive participants as they did in the original study, they also rated the participant's persuasive motivation and efficacy twice: upon establishment of the participant's initial status (successful vs. unsuccessful) and during the final round of the participant's advocacy that either corroborated their initial status or reversed it (successful ↔ unsuccessful). The results from these "online" ratings closely matched previous findings obtained by coding persuasive motivation and efficacy from the videotaped agent-target interactions. Thus, variations in persuasive motivation and efficacy as a result of agents' (in)consistent success in the interaction with their targets appear to be readily apparent.

To examine whether variations in agents' persuasive motivation and efficacy would feed back to affect targets' reactions, participants in a new study were randomly presented with one of the four vignettes describing the patterns of variations in persuasive motivation and efficacy found in the four experimental conditions examined in the previous studies. Specifically, participants were presented with a vignette that described a political candidate as either (a) consistently winning voters' support with his strong messages but apparently showing little interest to reach voters once he won their support ("winning incumbent," who remains efficient in spite of his declining motivation), (b) losing voters' support after he initially secured it, as his messages became decreasingly convincing despite his continuing efforts to reach voters ("losing incumbent," whose efficacy is decreasing in spite of his strong motivation), (c) consistently failing to win voters' support as strength of his messages and interest in reaching voters appeared to wane ("failing opposition," whose efficacy and motivation are both in decline), or (d) increasingly gaining voters' support after initial failure, as the strength of his messages and interest in reaching voters increased ("raising opposition," whose motivation and efficacy are both improving).

Participants were asked how likely they would be to support the political candidate described in the vignette they read. Their responses indicated that the increasingly successful ("raising opposition") candidate would receive more enthusiastic support than any other, including the consistently successful ("winning incumbent") candidate. Additional analyses of participants' thought listings suggested that they admired the increasingly successful ("rising opposition") candidate. In contrast, there was little admiration for the decreasingly successful ("losing incumbent") candidate. Although the "losing incumbent" candidate was perceived as just as motivated as the "raising opposition" candidate, his lack of success appeared to portray him as desperate. His overall negative evaluation suggests that motivation in the absence of success does not impress. McCain's experience seems to reinforce this conclusion.

CONCLUSION

Persuasion conceptualized as social interaction involves bidirectional exchanges between agents and targets that extend over a period of time. In these exchanges, the motivations, cognitive abilities, and affective states of the agents (e.g., Forgas, 2007) are just as important as those of the targets. Emerging from these interactions are social relations that may define agents' and targets' positions on such important social dimensions as numerical status, power, or prestige. When successful agents secure a sufficient number of followers among their targets, they are placed in the numerical majority. This numerical supremacy may carry additional benefits of power, prestige, or both. Indeed, these benefits associated with persuasive success may be at the root of persuasive attempts. Importantly, the dynamic nature of persuasive interactions that evolve over time allows for change in social relations and the resultant social position. As successful agents become unsuccessful, and vice versa, they may experience change in their status, power, or prestige. Influence, as conceived within this framework, is symmetrical, dynamic, and relationship laden. This conceptualization resonates with a long-advocated social contextualization of attitudinal phenomena (Eagly & Chaiken, 1993) and a recent theorizing about socially situated cognition (Smith & Semin, 2004, 2007) and social influence (Mason et al., 2007).

The conceptualization of persuasion as social interaction emphasizes phenomena currently neglected in persuasion research. Most importantly, it calls attention to the agents of persuasion, who should be as sensitive to the interaction dynamics as the targets have traditionally been assumed to be. This proposition received support in a series of studies in which an agent attempted to influence multiple targets (confederates) to adopt his or her position on important social issues. As the agent advocated his or her position, targets initially provided positive feedback that cast the agent as successful (majority) or negative feedback that cast the agent as unsuccessful (minority). Subsequent feedback on the agent's continuing advocacy either kept initially established status stable or reversed it (successful ↔ unsuccessful). Our studies revealed that the social context that emerged from agent-targets interactions affected agents' attitudes. Decreasingly successful agents who failed after initial success altered their attitudes, moving them in a newly emerging normative direction. In contrast, increasingly successful agents who succeeded after initial failure strengthened their attitudes. Increased importance that they attached to their attitudes, along with a widened scope of attitudinal positions that they found objectionable, indicated that increasingly successful agents became entrenched in the position that they advocated.

Increasingly successful agents (unsuccessful → successful) also showed an increased motivation to continue their persuasive advocacy, which became progressively more efficient. Their decreasingly successful counterparts (successful → unsuccessful), however, appeared to be heading in the opposite direction. Although their persuasive motivation remained high in the aftermath of change in their status, it did not translate into persuasive efficacy. To the contrary, these agents became progressively less efficient. Taken together, these findings indicate that in the dynamic social context, an overall high level of motivation to win a persuasive argument is likely to fuel a continuing influence battle. Its outcome, however, is more likely to favor increasingly successful agents. Their increasing motivation to advocate their position and their apparent intolerance for opposite positions is likely to make them a formidable rival. Decreasingly successful agents' motivation to oppose them is likely to be short-lived unless it is translated into a different argument. For that to happen, these agents may need a temporary withdrawal from the persuasive arena to rethink their persuasive strategy.

Even if increasingly successful agents ultimately win the influence battle, they are not likely to make the attitudinal landscape completely uniform. Our results show that extended success breeds complacency. Once established, successful agents appear to lose their persuasive motivation. Although they may remain efficient in their advocacy, their apparent nonchalance is likely to be costly. It generates resentment in their targets, who may withdraw or even reverse their support. Persuasive success, therefore, may carry seeds of a failure. An important implication of this proposition is that the tremendous power of majority to persuade (for reviews, see Allen, 1965; Asch, 1956; Kruglanski & Mackie, 1990) may have a short half-life unless a challenging minority invigorates its motivation to persuade. Consistently successful agents who, by definition, are in the majority appear to need some opposition (an active minority) in order to remain successful.

Opposition or an active minority, however, may be hard to arise and even harder to sustain. Not only is being in the opposition socially costly (Prislin, in press), it is also demotivating when it comes to exerting influence. Consistently unsuccessful agents lose both their motivation and ability to persuade. Given these burdens, important questions for future research are: What motivates agents holding minority opinion to raise their voice and attempt to persuade, and what powers their argument in the face of initial failure to influence targets? Answering these questions will require a truly dynamic approach to theorizing and research on persuasion. It should capture not only agents' reactions, which were examined in this chapter, but also reactions of all participants in the persuasive interaction. Such a dynamic, temporal approach should help to explain the factors that motivate minorities to raise their voice and that ultimately determine their success or failure. It may be that circumstances that constrain one-time minority influence and facilitate one-time majority influence (Crano, 2001; Moscovici, 1980; Martin & Hewstone, 2008) evolve over time. The dynamic, temporal, relational approach that allows all interaction participants to be influenced while trying to persuade holds promise for invigorating persuasion research by opening new questions and recasting old ones.

REFERENCES

Albarracín, D., Johnson, B. T., & Zanna, M. P. (2005). *The handbook of attitudes*. Mahwah, NJ: Erlbaum.

Allen, V. L. (1965). Situational factors in conformity. In L. Berkowitz (Ed.), *Advances in experimental social psychology* (Vol. 2, pp. 133–175). San Diego, CA: Academic Press.

Asch, S. E. (1952). *Social psychology*. Englewood Cliffs, NJ: Prentice-Hall.

Asch, S. E. (1956). Studies in independence and conformity. *Psychological Monographs, 70*(416).

Baumeister, R. F., Twenge, J. M., & Nuss, C. K. (2002). Effects of social exclusion on cognitive processing: Anticipated closeness reduces intelligent thought. *Journal of Personality and Social Psychology, 83*, 817–827.

Brehm, J. W., & Self, E. A. (1989). The intensity of motivation. *Annual Review of Psychology, 40*, 109-131.

Briñol, P., & Petty, R. (2005). Individual difference in attitude change. In D. Albarracín, B. T. Johnson, & M. P. Zanna (Eds.), *The handbook of attitudes* (pp. 575–615). Mahwah, NJ: Erlbaum.

Crano, W. D. (2001). Social influence, social identity, and ingroup leniency. In C. K. W. De Dreu & N. K. De Vries (Eds.), *Group consensus and minority influence: Implications for innovation* (pp. 122–143). Oxford, England: Blackwell.

Deutsch, M., & Gerard, H. B. (1955). A study of normative and informational influences upon individual judgment. *Journal of Abnormal and Social Psychology, 51*, 629–636.

Eagly, A. H., & Chaiken, S. (1993). *The psychology of attitudes*. Fort Worth, TX: Harcourt Brace Jovanovich.

Festinger, L. (1950). Informal social communication. *Psychological Review, 57*, 271–282.

Forgas, J. P. (2007). When sad is better than happy: Negative affect can improve the quality and effectiveness of persuasive messages and social influence strategies. *Journal of Experimental Social Psychology, 43*, 513–528.

French, J. R. P., Jr. (1956). A formal theory of social power. *Psychological Review, 63*, 181–194.

French, J. R. P., Jr., & Raven, B. H. (1959). The bases of social power. In D. Cartwright (Ed.), *Studies in social power* (pp. 150–167). Ann Arbor, MI: ISR.

Hamilton, M. A., Hunter, J. E., & Burgoon, M. (1990). An empirical test of an axiomatic model of the relationship between language intensity and persuasion. *Journal of Language and Social Psychology, 9*, 235–255.

Hastie, R., & Stasser, G. (2000). Computer simulation methods for social psychology. In H. T. Reis & C. M. Judd (Eds.), *Handbook of research methods in social psychology* (pp. 85– 116). New York: Cambridge University Press.

Kelley, H. H. (1952). Two functions of reference groups. In G. E. Swanson, T. M. Newcomb, & E. L. Hartley (Eds.), *Readings in social psychology* (2nd ed., pp. 410–414). New York: Holt.

Kelman, H. C. (1958). Compliance, internalization, and identification: Three processes of attitude change. *Journal of Conflict Resolution, 2*, 51–60.

Kruglanski, A. W., & Mackie, D. M. (1990). Majority and minority influence: A judgment process analysis. In W. Stroebe & M. Hewstone (Eds.), *European review of social psychology* (Vol. 1, pp. 229–261). Chichester, England: Wiley.

Kumkale, G. T., & Albarracín, D. (2004). The sleeper effect in persuasion: A meta-analytic review. *Psychological Bulletin, 130*, 143–172.

Martin, R., & Hewstone, M. (2008). Majority vs. minority influence, message processing, and attitude change: The source-context-elaboration model. In M. P. Zanna (Ed.), *Advances in experimental social psychology* (Vol. 40, pp. 237–326). San Diego, CA: Academic Press.

Mason, W., Conrey, F. R., & Smith, E. R. (2007). Situating social influence processes: Dynamic, multidirectional flows of influence within social networks. *Personality and Social Psychology Review, 11*, 279–300.

Mehrabian, A., & Williams, M. (1969). Nonverbal concomitants of perceived and intended persuasiveness. *Journal of Personality and Social Psychology, 13*, 37–58.

Moscovici, S. (1980). Toward a theory of conversion behavior. In L. Berkowitz (Ed.), *Advances in experimental social psychology* (Vol. 13, pp. 209–239). San Diego, CA: Academic Press.

Prislin, R. (2010). Minority groups in society. In J. Levine & M. Hogg (Eds.), *Encyclopedia of group processes and intergroup relations* (pp. 562–566). Thousand Oaks, CA: Sage.

Prislin, R., Boyle, S., Farley, A., Jacobs, E., & Zandian, F. (2009). *Persuasion in the dynamic context: On being influenced while trying to persuade.* Manuscript under review.

Prislin, R., Brewer, M., & Wilson, D. J. (2002). Changing majority and minority positions within a group vs. an aggregate. *Personality and Social Psychology Bulletin, 28*, 640–647.

Prislin, R., & Christensen, P. N. (2005). Social change in the aftermath of successful minority influence. *European Review of Social Psychology, 16*, 75–111.

Prislin, R., Davenport, C., Michalak, J., Uehara, K., & Xi, Y. (2009). [Persuasion and social relations]. Unpublished raw data.

Prislin, R., Limbert, W. M., & Bauer, E. (2000). From majority to minority and vice versa: The asymmetrical effects of losing and gaining majority position within a group. *Journal of Personality and Social Psychology, 79*, 385–397.

Prislin, R., & Wood, W. (2005). Social influence: The role of consensus in attitudes and attitude change. In D. Albarracín, B. T. Johnson, & M. P. Zanna (Eds.), *The handbook of attitudes and attitude change* (pp. 671–706). Mahwah, NJ: Erlbaum.

Rind, B., & Kipnis, D. (1999). Changes in self-perceptions as a result of successfully persuading others. *Journal of Social Issues, 55*, 141–156.

Smith, E. R., & Conrey, F. R. (2007). Agent-based modeling: A new approach for theory-building in social psychology. *Personality and Social Psychology Review, 11*, 87–104.

Smith, E. R., & Semin, G. R. (2004). Socially situated cognition: Cognition in its social context. In M. P. Zanna (Ed.), *Advances in experimental social psychology,* (Vol, 36, pp. 53–117). San Diego, CA: Academic Press.

Smith, E. R., & Semin, G. R. (2007). Situated social cognition. *Current Directions in Psychological Science, 16*, 132–135.

Smith, J. R., & Hogg, M. A. (2008). Social identity and attitudes. In W. D. Crano & R. Prislin (Eds.), *Attitudes and attitude change* (337–360). New York: Psychology Press.

Stasser, G., Kerr, N. L., & Davis, J. H. (1989). Influence processes and consensus models in decision-making groups. In P. B. Paulus (Ed.), *Psychology of group influence* (pp. 279–325). Hillsdale, NJ: Erlbaum.

Stiff, J. B. (1986). Cognitive processing of persuasive message cues: A meta-analytic review of the effects of supporting information on attitudes. *Communication Monographs, 53,* 75–89.

Tindale, R. S., Davis, J. H., Vollrath, D. A., Nagao, D. H., & Hinsz, V. B. (1990). Asymmetrical social influence in freely interacting groups: A test of three models. *Journal of Personality and Social Psychology, 58,* 438–449.

Turner, J. C. (1991). *Social influence.* Pacific Grove, CA: Brooks/Cole.

Wright, R. A., & Brehm, J. W. (1989). Energization and goal attractiveness. In L. Pervin (Ed.), *Goal concepts in personality and social psychology* (pp. 169–210). Hillsdale, NJ: Erlbaum.

AUTHOR NOTE

I am grateful to Jennifer Filson for her valuable comments on an earlier version of the chapter.

Section *IV*

Applications and Implications of Attitude Research

14

Experiments as Reforms
Persuasion in the Nation's Service

WILLIAM D. CRANO

In his *Reforms as Experiments*, Campbell (1969) urged the integration of strong investigative methods with large-scale social interventions that had come on line in Lyndon Johnson's Great Society programs. His call to bring social psychology's many gifts to the society at large had been an integral feature of the field for years (Lewin et al., 1945; Lewin, Heider, & Heider, 1936), but *Reforms* reinvigorated the challenge to social psychology to become a force for progressive social change by daring its practitioners to evaluate socially relevant interventions carried out in its name. Campbell's vision, along with Michael Scriven's (1991, 1997, 2003), began the formalization of the field of evaluation research, which focuses on the empirical, scientific, controlled assessment of large-scale (and small-scale) social interventions. As almost all social interventions involve the manipulation of beliefs, attitudes, and intentions in the service of behavior change, it is fitting to consider both the application of attitude research to contemporary social problems, along with attitude assessment, as any attitude (re)adjustment worth attempting is worth evaluating. The integration of the complementary epistemological orientations of Campbell and Scriven resulted in a movement with the potential to enrich our efforts as responsible citizens and social scientists. This was a clearly a necessary move, which the field as a whole would do well to emulate. As McGuire (2003) observed, "a Mandarin stance of science for science's sake, however claimed by the high-table elite, would lose support from other segments of society, including funding agencies" (p. 135). We have seen his prediction come to pass.

THE OTHER SIDE OF REFORMS

It is a mistake to read Campbell's *Reforms* solely as a call for a more comprehensive, responsible, and systematic assessment of our ideas when they are applied to vexing social problems. It was that and much more. Not only were the denizens of Campbell's brave new experimental world to assess and evaluate the outcomes of their theory-based brainstorms, they were responsible for creating and refining in laboratory and field contexts the very theories that formed the logical bases for the interventions in the first place. Our responsibility was not only to evaluate the theories chosen to undergird the interventions mounted on behalf of society, but to create those theories and ensure they were used properly to develop and adjust the interventions that ultimately were implemented (Crano & Brewer, 2002; Shadish, Cook, & Campbell, 2002; Shadish, Cook, & Leviton, 1991).

We have not fared well on this score, not because of a lack of effort or good will, but because of the undisciplined application of ideas based more on self-perceptions of infallibility than evidence-based knowledge (see Johnson & Boynton, this volume). One area in which such failures are especially apparent is our application of knowledge amassed over years of persuasion research. Persuasion is the hallmark of social psychology (McGuire, 1986; Prislin & Crano, 2008). More than 70 years ago, Allport (1935) designated attitude as social psychology's "most distinctive and indispensible concept" (p. 784). The same may be said today. While we could trace our heritage to Aristotle (1991, 1999), whose *Rhetoric* still stands as a testament to his genius, I prefer to locate the scientific beginnings of the science of persuasion in the more prosaic confines of New Haven. It was at Yale University that Hovland set up shop after World War II, gathering the best attitude researchers of his time, whose contributions still command respect. It is arguable that much of what we do in persuasion today is shaped by what was done in Hovland's program more than a half century ago (McGuire, 1996). Not all of Hovland and company's findings have stood the test of time, but the influence of their labors remains. Most important was the way they went about the work. In one of their key monographs, Hovland and colleagues (1953) expressed their commitment to theory-guided, experimental, laboratory-based research to study basic persuasion processes (a search that Blascovich & McCall, this volume, has extended today into the virtual world). Their insistence on the primacy of theory as a guide, bolstered by a strict adherence to the logic of the experimental method, is a testament to the authors' prescience and stands in stark contrast to that which is apparent in many of our largest and most costly social intervention programs today. At the same time, the application of their work to contemporary problems was evident in their choice of topics of study. This is not to suggest that the experiment is the only road to enlightenment. Experiments do free us from a host of annoying rival alternative hypotheses, but at times their use is premature, and correlational or quasi-experimental methods are more appropriate (Crano & Brewer, 2002).

THE UNITED STATES' WAR ON DRUGS

The adherence to theory in guiding research, especially applied research, is not evident in many of our major social interventions. The National Youth Anti-Drug Media Campaign (NYAMC) provides a recent example of a program that could have had a major effect on adolescent drug involvement, but it was doomed from the start because of limitations of theory, design, and implementation. This chapter focuses on features of this uniquely American, massive, mass-mediated intervention, as it provides fertile ground for exposition of proper and improper persuasion techniques, of what was, and of what might have been.

The NYAMC was initiated in 1997 during the presidency of Bill Clinton. It was to prove the largest and costliest social intervention on drug abuse in the history of the United States. The intervention was rushed to the field in response to a reversal of the secular trend that had seen a steady and continuous decline in adolescent drug use, principally marijuana and inhalants. The goals of the campaign were to educate and thereby enable America's youth to reject illicit drugs, to delay or deter initiation (especially to marijuana and inhalants), and to persuade occasional users to bring their dalliances to an end.

These are admirable aims, but the devil is in the details, and the massive multi-billion dollar effort, mounted with the best of intentions, was star crossed from the start. The thematic emphases of the program shifted erratically over the course of the campaign. In addition to hampering the "branding" of the campaign, the erratic pattern of changes in theme and focus suggests that the NYAMC was brought to the field prematurely, an impression reinforced by a consideration of the basic design flaws that defined the fundamental fabric of the program (Crano, 2002). For example, the NYAMC failed to make use of any baseline measures, rendering impossible the assessment of change. It also failed to employ an untreated control or even a comparison group. In combination, these design decisions, based on temporal constraints and political expediency rather than scientific logic, made it extremely difficult to pinpoint the effects of the various media and messages used.

Worse than the design flaws was the effective lack of operational theory used to develop the media messages, the heart of the prevention program. The program was not devoid of theory—the NYAMC ads were structured loosely on Fishbein and colleagues' (2002) *Integrated Model of Behavior Change*, which holds that attitudes, norms, and perceived (self-) efficacy are critical variables that determine the behavioral outcomes of persuasion. The model is reasonable, grounded in considerable research, and well worth serious consideration—and it has performed well in smaller scale research (Rhodes, Stein, Fishbein, Goldstein, & Rotheram-Borus, 2007; Yzer et al., 2004; Zhao et al., 2006). However, the NYAMC honored the theory more in the breach than in practice. Operationally, theory played only a minor role in the actual development of messages. This failure of translation from theory to application was critical and laid the foundation for the intervention's ultimate failure, which can be traced to a fundamental misunderstanding, or neglect, of features inherent in any persuasive context.

Some Procedures and Results

Except for its scale, the conduct of the NYAMC was relatively straightforward. Antidrug messages were designed, pro bono, by some of the country's best marketing firms. Air time and ad space was bought, and the ads were delivered to a waiting public through a variety of media. Every year for 4 years, a large-scale evaluation was conducted on a panel of adolescents (9–18 years of age) who were randomly sampled from the population at large, thus allowing generalization of results to the nation's youth (for details, see Crano, Siegel, Alvaro, Lac, & Hemovich, 2008; Orwin et al., 2006). The evaluation data were archived in the National Survey of Parents and Youth (NSPY), the primary tool used in the evaluation of the program's effects.

The evaluation could not use a standard experimental format because of the design flaws so evident in the development of the program. Instead, program evaluators adopted a propensity-score weighted/dose response approach, which associated reported variations in ad exposure with subsequent drug attitudes, intentions, and use across the 4 yearly measurement rounds. The evaluation was a 4-year longitudinal panel design with three overlapping cohorts. Follow-up response rates after the first interview were remarkably high, ranging from 86% to 93%; respondents "aged-out" of the design when they reached age 19 (see Hornik, Jacobsohn, Orwin, Piesse, & Kalton, 2008, and Orwin, et al., 2006).

At least on one score, the NYAMC was quite successful: More than 75% of the youth surveyed reported being exposed at least weekly to a NYAMC-sponsored antidrug message, over 4 years, through various media channels. This level of exposure is rarely reached in marketing programs, and to my knowledge, never for this extended period of time, but then, most media blitzes are not budgeted in the billions of dollars either. Although coverage is a necessary condition for success of mass mediated persuasion campaigns, it is not sufficient. The more critical issue is whether the ads were persuasive. On this score, the data were considerably less accommodating.

Analyses of the panel data (see http://www.drugabuse.gov/about/organization/despr/westat/#reports and https://www.nspycenter.com/default.asp) suggested clearly that the ads did not achieve their goal to reduce and prevent drug use. Hornik et al. (2008) found that respondents' intentions to avoid marijuana were negatively associated with exposure to the campaign's antidrug ads between the first and second years. Further, perceived antimarijuana social norms appeared to be negatively affected by ad exposure on each successive measurement round. Worse yet, respondents' marijuana use intentions were significantly associated with ad exposure over the final 2 years of the campaign. The more NYAMC antidrug ads youth saw, the less they intended to avoid marijuana, the more they thought their peers used marijuana, and the stronger was their intention to use it!

WHERE DID IT GO WRONG?

It would be easy to throw stones in reaction to the outcome of this massive project. How did it happen? Who is responsible for this enormous waste of resources and opportunity? There are plenty of targets to go around, and no small supply of rocks. To build the case for a new way of approaching mediated interventions, we might consider some of the features of this program that clearly failed. Rather than lay blame, it is more productive to outline a general framework for media-based persuasion whose application might help ensure more positive results. Before doing so, however, we must reflect on one of the most significant reactions to the negative outcome of the intervention, namely the view that the mass media are ill equipped to serve as delivery vehicles for critical social interventions. In light of the many mass mediated studies that have failed to deliver (e.g., see Atkin, 2004; Brecher, 1972), this view is reasonable, but its logical implication is contrary to the many social intervention studies of this type that have succeeded (Crano & Burgoon,

2002; Derzon & Lipsey, 2002; Flay & Sobel, 1983). The mass media can deliver successful interventions—they have done so in the past. In the NYAMC, it was not the media that failed, it was the message.

Why did the campaign fail to persuade despite the barrage of copy that ensured that for 4 years, more than three quarters of the nation's youth were exposed weekly to at least one antidrug message? A review of the overall program leads to three inescapable conclusions: (a) The messages themselves were not well wrought, (b) they were not coordinated in such a way as to lead to a cumulative effect, and (c) they did not target the audience that they were designed to motivate.

Targeting

In marketing research, there is relatively widespread consensus that targeting ads to those most in need of them, or most likely to use or be swayed by them, is clearly indicated when expensive mass media are used to deliver a persuasive message (Donohew, Lorch, & Palmgreen, 1991; Noar, Zimmerman, Palmgreen, Lustria, & Horosewski, 2006; Selnow & Crano, 1987). Indeed, some communication scientists have even called for the use of tailored approaches, in which messages specifically created for *individual receivers* are produced and delivered (Rimal & Flora, 1997; Rimer & Kreuter, 2006; Suggs, 2006; Updegraff, Sherman, Luyster, & Mann, 2007). With today's technology, the capability to create messages that capitalize on each receiver's individual proclivities, needs, and personality is well within reach. The NYAMC was designed as a targeted campaign, but the targeting factor was unduly gross and changed from year to year. As such, the advantages of targeting were seriously diluted, though some of the campaign's targeting was done well. In some cases, media outlets that appealed to specific racial or ethnic groups were employed, and messages deployed accordingly. However, the lack of quality messages attenuated these potentially helpful effects.

Coordination and Accumulative Effects

A disciplined and coordinated focus on what was aired was essential, and lacking. This failure to develop cumulative program impact must be laid at the feet of the campaign organizers, whose persuasive emphases shifted from month to month, and the Partnership for a Drug Free America, the organization responsible for recruiting the marketing firms that created the ads that aired, and integrating the ads into a cumulative, coordinated, and hard hitting campaign. This failure was predestined, because in seeking the best marketing firms to contribute their services, the Partnership necessarily asked many different firms for their assistance, and many firms responded altruistically. However, there is no evidence in the ads produced to suggest that the varying contributors knew what the other firms were doing; thus, they could not coordinate efforts. Under these conditions, ad impact was not likely to cumulate, and it did not.

This failure illustrates two underlying working assumptions on which the messaging strategy was based, and which are incorrect (Crano & Prislin, 2006; Prislin & Crano, 2008). The first of these is that a single message can do the trick—that accumulation is not necessary. This might be true in the case of a message of exceptional power attacking an issue on which the receiver is not extremely self-interested, but this is not the case when discussing marijuana and inhalants with many adolescents. The somewhat paradoxical complementary position implicitly adopted is that message quality does not matter much; exposure is all important. This position represents a severe misunderstanding of the persuasion literature. Certainly exposure frequency can enhance ad evaluation (Winkielman & Cacioppo, 2001; Zajonc, 1968), but its effects are mitigated when attention is focused on the frequently occurring stimuli. Mere exposure has its greatest effects when the exposure is incidental, and the stimuli are meaningless. With meaningful stimuli, other considerations come into play, including message strength (Cacioppo & Petty, 1989). It also is true that overexposure can seriously attenuate an ad's effectiveness (Appel, 1971). The two underlying assumptions that guided the messaging strategy led to a neglect of critical persuasive factors, and an overemphasis on much less important features (Prislin, this volume).

WHAT MIGHT HAVE BEEN DONE TO IMPROVE OUTCOMES?

Targeting and Tailoring

Targeting specific subgroups with ads and via media that were maximally accessible was done well by the campaign. However, in addition to targeting, it should be apparent that message effects will differ as a function of characteristics of the receiver (Crano, Gilbert, Alvaro, & Siegel, 2008). This is reinforced in our research on marijuana and inhalant users, using data from the nationally representative sample of youth who participated in the evaluation of the NYAMC. We categorized adolescent respondents into user, vulnerable nonuser, or resolute nonuser groups (Crano, Siegel, et al., 2008). Resolute nonusers were defined as adolescents who had never used marijuana, and were adamant that they never would. Their progression to marijuana usage was retarded relative to that of vulnerable group, who also had never used at the time of the first measure, but who, unlike their resolute peers, were not absolutely insistent that they would remain abstinent (Figure 14.1). The apparently minor variation on a single response item allowed prediction of very large differences in marijuana usage over the 4 years of the NSPY. Allied research supports these results. It indicates that vulnerable and resolute nonuser groups respond very differently to different messaging formats, to strong or weak threats, to different message sources, to social versus physical threats, and to misdirection or forewarning of persuasive intent (Crano, Siegel, Alvaro, & Patel, 2007; Quinn & Wood, 2004; Ramirez et al., 2004).

Accumulation

Maintaining a consistent brand helps ensure that the effects of earlier advertising efforts will accumulate (Miller & Muir, 2004). The solution to the lack of accumulation is straightforward. Ad producers must know the general aims of

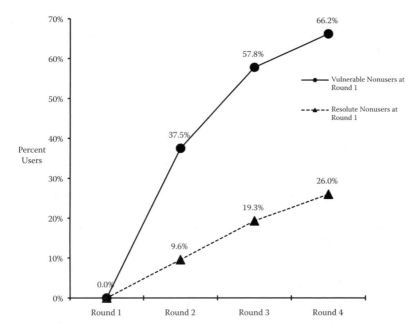

Figure 14.1.   Marijuana initiation trajectories of round 1 resolute and vulnerable nonusers across four measurement rounds (data from the National Survey of Parents and Youth; $N = 2111$).

the campaign, and also what the other ad developers on the project are doing, or have done. Loss of accumulative effect is less likely if a single marketing group is used to produce all ad copy, because the ads' originators presumably would maintain continuity of approach. This continuity is the reason that advertisers seek to establish a brand. Even if a solitary marketing company were used in the NYAMC, the factors theoretically responsible for the success (or failure) of prior ads must be considered if effects are to accumulate. The lack of this general understanding, of a theory of persuasive effects, was the root of the campaign's failure. While there are many ways to persuade, the underlying dynamics of persuasion must be attended to, and in this program they were not.

MESSAGING AND THE DYNAMICS OF ATTITUDE MODIFICATION

Attitude Formation

Any campaign that seeks to modify receivers' attitudes and subsequent intentions and behaviors must be based on a reasonable, well-researched, and empirically supported theory of attitude development or change. The differentiation between development and change has been a feature of research on attitudes for many years (Johnson & Eagly, 1989), but it has not received the attention it deserves. Recent research on evaluative conditioning (EC) promises to change this state of affairs (e.g., see Walther & Langer, 2008; Walther, Nagengast, & Trasselli, 2005). Work on EC indicates that attitudes toward unfamiliar objects can be formed via mere association between the new object and another object whose valence is established. Thus, a consistent association of a new politician with one who is nationally revered is expected to benefit the neophyte. Extrapolating from this research to marijuana prevention suggests that EC may be used with young adolescents with no history of use, and no strong attitudes toward the drug, to lessen their probability of initiation. If no strong promarijuana attitudes exist, EC may be used to fuel avoidance. The strength of these evaluatively conditioned reactions remains to be seen (Petty & Krosnick, 1995), but they should provide a useful buffer against the mindless acceptance of an offer to partake in drug use, which we have found to be strongly related to initiation. Under the appropriate conditions (e.g., when in a group of friends) merely being offered a drug is sufficient to move many young adolescents from abstinence to first use. Conceivably, this susceptibility would be lessened if an evaluatively conditioned negative response were attached to the drug.

Messaging and Attitude Change

Established beliefs are the focus of attention in attitude change contexts. Changing beliefs, rather than forming them, involves processes quite different from those encountered in EC (see Wänke & Reutner, this volume). Although some argue that EC can affect established attitudes (Walther & Langer, this volume), the more common approach involves use of meaningful communications to prompt message receivers to modify their beliefs. This message-based orientation is a common feature of almost all the major persuasion models, from Hovland et al. (1953) to today's dual (Deutsch & Strack, 2006; Petty & Cacioppo, 1996; Petty, Cacioppo, & Goldman, 1981) and single process models (Kruglanski et al., 2003; Kruglanski & Thompson, 1999). All of these models share a common and easily accepted axiom that people want to be correct in their beliefs and actions. Accordingly, they will attend to information that is presented to them, especially when the issue under consideration is of high personal relevance, or vested interest (Crano, 1995, 1997; Lehman & Crano, 2002). It is reasonable to assume that a communication contrary to the person's established beliefs on a highly vested issue will be considered and contested. Two features of this expectation deserve emphasis. First, we are concerned with issues that matter to the receivers; second, we are dealing with counterattitudinal communications, not messages that reinforce the individual's established beliefs. For too long, we have researched reactions to attitude change treatments aimed at attitudes of relatively little importance to receivers. Most theorists today argue that different cognitive routes to persuasion are traversed as a function of the extent to which the issue under contention concerns the receiver (e.g., Petty & Cacioppo, 1986).

The outcome of the contest between the advocated position proposed in the persuasive message and the target's established beliefs, termed counterargumentation (Hovland et al., 1953), determines the success or failure of the persuasion attempt (see Petty, Tormala, & Rucker, 2004). In logic, a counterargument is an objection to an objection, and this meaning conveys the sense of Hovland and colleagues' use of the term. The persuasive message must rebut a belief of the message receiver, who is expected to try to rebut the rebuttal—if the issue is sufficiently involving to the receiver to justify the effort.

Over the years, we have developed many ways of enhancing the likelihood that the advocated position will prevail over the counterargument. Presenting a message under distraction or cognitive load, linking it to a source of high credibility, reducing the apparent intent to persuade...the list of message enhancing catalysts could be extended almost indefinitely, but rather than develop a catalogue of all known persuasiveness factors, let us focus on the processes that must be involved in persuasion (McGuire, 1969). If a message is to persuade, it must, among other things, present cogent reasons that argue for its adoption. We can manipulate the factors that affect the likelihood that the requisite consideration will occur, so the presented information will be elaborated open-mindedly, but the more basic requirement is that the material conveyed actually informs the receiver about the proper position to adopt. It is not enough to tell receivers they are wrong. The effective message will tell them why they are wrong and how they can get right. If the message is devoid of this information, or if the information is generic and banal ("Just Say No"), then tactics designed to enhance message elaboration are largely irrelevant, as there is little to elaborate upon. In short, the message must convey knowledge or information and, under ideal circumstances, advice about how to overcome the identified problem. If it does not do so, we need not worry about how the information is best transmitted. Conveying knowledge is important for a number of reasons, not the least of which is the positive association between attitudes bolstered by knowledge and enhanced attitude strength (Crano & Prislin, 2006; Krosnick & Abelson, 1992; Wood, Rhodes, & Biek, 1995).

Fear. In many contexts that involve social marketing or prosocial messaging, fear-based communications are used to change attitudes and behaviors (Dillard & Anderson, 2004; Green & Witte, 2006; Ruiter, Abraham, & Kok, 2001). This tendency is related to the issues involved in social marketing, which often involve advice to avoid certain behaviors—don't use drugs, avoid fatty foods, don't smoke, and so on. Although use of fear appeals is common, there is considerable controversy regarding their utility, especially in applied mass mediated contexts (e.g., Hastings, Stead, & Webb, 2004). The controversy surrounding fear arousal is due to a somewhat myopic main effects view of how fear affects persuasion. The proper question is not whether fear appeals work, but on whom they work, and under which circumstances. Fear arousing messages can prove very effective (e.g., see Green & Witte, 2006) if they are used properly, but can backfire if the emotion aroused by the message interferes with the receiver's ability or motivation to process. Trying to scare a young adolescent about the physical dangers of inhalant abuse, for example, is ill-advised if the adolescent is an inhalant user (Crano et al., 2007). If abstinent, the fear arousing message might prove useful if the receiver is considering initiation; if the receiver is resolutely abstinent, the message probably will not hurt (but see Erceg-Hurn, 2008), but it represents a waste of scarce resources.

Violating prior experience. Another messaging difficulty that arises particularly when using fear arousing messages—but which can occur with nonemotional appeals as well—has to do with communications that promise an outcome that the receiver on the basis of prior experience or logic finds incredible (Forgas, this volume). Tormala and his colleagues have demonstrated that the very act of rejecting a persuasive message may strengthen the established attitude, and these iatrogenic responses are especially likely when the message originates from powerful or prestigious sources like the National Institute on Drug Abuse, or The Partnership for a Drug Free America (Petty, Briñol, Tormala, & Wegener, 2007; Tormala, 2008; Tormala, Clarkson, & Petty, 2006; Tormala & Petty, 2002, 2004). Prevention ads that promise extreme consequences are reasonable only if the extreme consequences are relatively immediate and their cause indisputable. If the promised consequences are exaggerated, however, the message (and its advice) will be rejected, and the established attitude will be bolstered. This is not what we want to do when creating a drug prevention campaign, but it appears exactly to be the outcome with the NYAMC and other campaigns that (mis)used fear arousing messages that flew in the face of their audience's prior experience (Erceg-Hurn, 2008).

Violating expectancies. A similar result occurs when a receiver's expectations regarding an outcome, formed on the basis of a media campaign, are violated. Skenderian and her colleagues found that respondents in the NSPY survey whose expectations regarding the dire promised consequences of marijuana use were disconfirmed formed more positive attitudes toward the drug, and stronger intentions to use it. These effects were amplified if their changed expectations were based on prior experience (Skenderian, Siegel, Crano, Alvaro, & Lac, 2008). The utility of experience-based attitudes in predicting behavior has long been recognized (Fazio & Zanna, 1978a, 1978b; Fazio, Zanna, & Cooper, 1978; Glasman & Albarracin, 2006; Prislin, 1993). The added value Skenderian et al. (2008) is the realization that experience coupled with rejection of media-based expectations may result in behavior opposite to that recommended by the mediated information. This result counsels extreme caution when promising consequences that may not ensue. Adolescents who expect that marijuana usage will result in a loss of all friends will prove very difficult targets for future antimarijuana persuasion if they find that this dire outcome does not come to pass when they use the drug. Indeed, the disconfirmation of their expectations will lead to greater resistance to subsequent antimarijuana communications and, even worse, stronger intentions to use the drug. It is conceivable that many of the iatrogenic effects found in the prevention literature arise because we have overpromised the (dire) consequences that will ensue from the receiver's not following our sage advice. If the receivers' prior experiences belie the advice, we not only have lost this battle, but have disadvantaged ourselves in future battles as well.

The obvious solution to the problem of overpromising is not to do so. The consequences of marijuana, inhalant, or other drug use are real and need not be exaggerated. Even when the consequences are real, if they are uncommon, their use in persuasive messages is likely to backfire. The rational course is to promise honestly, *and* to promise outcomes that are not easily falsifiable on the basis of incomplete information. That is, if marijuana affects ambition, it is not reasonable to promise adolescents that users will find themselves failing in school, unable to enroll in selective universities, and unable to find good jobs. On the basis of their own experience, they will reject these promises. On the other hand, the assertion that the average wage of adolescent marijuana users as adults is considerably lower than those who abstained from the drug is true may prove believable, and would be difficult to falsify unambiguously. Messages of this type should be used. They do point out the harms associated with a drug, but they cannot easily be rejected on the basis of direct experiences. Media that pose the threat that anabolic steroid abuse shrinks men's testicles, reduces sperm count, causes infertility, baldness, and development of breasts would seem to fill the bill. For most young men, these outcomes are real, they are not particularly desirable, and they are not readily falsifiable—the effects occur, but their manifestation takes time. This means that using extremely dire threats in media campaigns is not indicated, unless outcomes are immediately evident, unavoidable, terrible, and undeniably caused by the drug in question. Even in such cases, the evidence is not favorable. Erceg-Hurn's (2008) review of the Montana Meth campaign supplies a good example of the dangers of overhysterical advertising (see www.Montanameth.org).

The Montana Meth Project is an antimethamphetamine public service media campaign. Its antidrug messages are sensational and highly emotive, and its producers have claimed major successes in deterring Montana's youth from engaging in meth use. The program's claimed success had been widely trumpeted, and although none have been vetted in reputable peer-reviewed publications, the approach has been adopted in a number of other states. Unfortunately, upon close analysis, claims of campaign success do not hold up. After 6 months of exposure to the campaign, for example, Erceg-Hurn found a three-fold increase in the number of Montana teens who reported that meth use was not risky; they also were more likely to voice similar opinions regarding heroin and cocaine. Indeed, those who viewed the semi-ubiquitous ads were four times more likely to approve of regular meth use! Coupled with these findings was the result that fully half of the sample's teenagers felt the Montana Meth messages exaggerated the dangers involved with meth use. Whether or not they are correct is in some ways beside the point. The fact that half the message receivers responded negatively to the messages suggests that the messaging approach is in dire need of revision, and reinforces the point that messages must be both credible and not easily falsified. It is not yet possible to say that the Montana Meth Project has done more harm than good, but the data certainly seem to point in that unhappy direction.

A RECIPE FOR MEDIA CAMPAIGNS BASED ON FUNDAMENTAL THEORIES OF ATTITUDE STRUCTURE AND CHANGE

A working model of a framework that might prove highly useful in structuring an antidrug media campaign that has a reasonable chance of success, based on the past half century of theorizing on attitude formation and attitude change, would integrate the various rants evident throughout this chapter. A model that integrates these earlier observations requires that we first decide upon the target audience. If we are designing an antidrug media campaign, we must recognize that messages addressed to users will be different from those directed to nonusers who are considering initiation, which will differ from the messages designed to reinforce the beliefs and behaviors of resolute antidrug nonusers who will receive our message. It also must be recognized that an approach that maximizes persuasive outcomes for one group might not be maximally effective for another.

How should the messages be constructed? We have learned the importance of needs analyses when mounting any type of social intervention. In the present case, the need for the intervention is understood, just as it is understood that such an analysis will have been performed in advance of any serious campaign planning. In addition to determining the need for a program, however, when designing the intervention we also should consider a preliminary analysis that is designed to assess the target population's understandings surrounding the issue at hand. Is the audience aware of the problem? Are there strong attitudes on the critical issue, or does ambivalence reign? Answers to these questions will suggest the choice of either an attitude formation or an attitude change strategy. In the case of ill-formed beliefs, an evaluative conditioning approach may work well (see Walther & Langer, this volume). Under the circumstances described, it will prove more efficient and will enjoy a higher probability of success than an attitude change strategy, which by definition assumes that the target audience possesses attitudes in need of changing.

If formative study of the target audience suggests the existence of established beliefs about the drug in question, however, then an attitude change approach is indicated. The utility of the preliminary study is that it can, if thoughtfully designed, provide an atlas of the beliefs and allegiances that must be overcome if the program is to succeed. This information may even support an approach in which messages tailored to any number of receiver characteristics are developed. The preliminary study can allow for this level of precision, but it is costly. In either event, using tailoring or targeting, it is foolhardy to assume that certain attitudes must be changed before we are certain that they exist in our target population (Siegel, Alvaro, Patel, & Crano, 2009). And it is equally foolhardy to mount a campaign that fails to confront beliefs whose reversal might have marked effects on attitudes that are the causal agents of the behaviors we wish to modify.

The preliminary analysis is useful for yet another reason, which has to do with its potential to facilitate the evaluation of the ultimate intervention. The formative research will alert investigators to the problems that are most likely to be encountered, and this will allow them to plan accordingly. These plans, in turn, will facilitate the planning for evaluation of program outcomes, an essential condition of any serious social intervention.

Once the target audience and the targeted beliefs are defined, the next order of business is the development of a persuasive campaign. This will involve developing a series of messages that have been designed in such a way that their effect builds upon earlier effects. These messages should be identifiable as originating from a common source. This identification should proceed from the messages themselves, not merely the tagline that follows at the end of the messages. Attaching a tagline does not establish the brand—the presented messages do.

The particular messages that will be developed will differ, depending on the function of the communication, but the "rules of engagement" are similar across message types. The information presented must be credible. Credibility can be enhanced as a result of the preliminary analyses, which help identify the particular issues that are in most need of confronting. The messages should be fact-based, they should contain arguments that challenge established beliefs, and they should show why the beliefs should be changed. If a problem behavior is involved, the message must show how the problem can be avoided or alleviated. This last point is especially important if the message makes use of fear arousal. It is not sufficient merely to scare a message recipient about an object or a behavior; some way of dealing with the threat must be provided if the message is to succeed (Green & Witte, 2006). Without efficacy information, fear arousal does not provide a clear path to the proper behavior, even in receivers who have been persuaded by the message and wish to modify their actions. This is why advice such as "Just Say No" or pictures of frying eggs that suggest "This is your brain on drugs" are not likely to affect behavior. For many young adolescents offered their first marijuana joint, it is not clear how to just say no any more than it is to imagine the relevance of frying eggs to cognitive dysfunction.

CONCLUSION

In summary, the central guidance that must direct all media-based interventions is clear: The material presented must be credible, not easily falsifiable, and not inconsistent with prior experiences or behaviorally based expectations. And, it must contain clear directives to action.

Credible. In Petty and Cacioppo's (1986) terminology, we must create *strong* messages if we expect our media to have lasting effects on receivers' thoughts and eventual actions. Strong messages, which convey credible information, are supported by expert knowledge and data. If the validity of a position can be established unambiguously, it is difficult to defuse even if it is contrary to one's wishes.

Not easily falsifiable or inconsistent with prior experience/expectations. It is foolhardy to produce media that receivers know is incorrect on the basis of their own experiences, or that is easy to refute on the basis of simple observation. If a message promises a consequence that the target does not believe will transpire, it is not likely to persuade, and it will render future persuasion even more difficult. There is a tendency toward hyperbole in much of our media-based prevention. This is natural—we know what is helpful and harmful, and a bit of exaggeration may seem justified, but succumbing to this natural tendency opens the door to a host of problems, immediate and long term. The immediate problem is that the exaggerated warning contained in our message is easily falsifiable. "You say that smoking marijuana will affect my grades, but my friend John smokes all the time and he gets straight As." "You say that only 5% of my peers use inhalants—that's crazy. Almost everyone I know is a huffer." Responses such as these are the stuff of which message rejection is made. Even worse, these reactions portend enhanced resistance to future prevention messaging.

Clear directives. It is not sufficient to point to a danger to be avoided—if the message is to have the desired effect, appropriate ways to avoid the problem must be presented. This advice is standard when dealing with fear arousing appeals—providing ways of avoiding the threatened, emotionally laced outcome must be provided if the appeal is to succeed. The same advice obtains even when high fear arousal is not a part of the messaging strategy. It is not reasonable to assume that receivers will know instinctively how to avoid drug use and their attendant problems. The preventive message must provide the answer, and if it does not, it is much less likely to succeed in its mission. This advice is so obvious as to be banal, but most of the thousands of commercial ads that are immediately available in the mass media violate this obvious prescription. Mediated messages focused on prevention or positive health behaviors have an even worse hit rate. This deficiency reflects an overconcentration on flash at the expense of the mundane mechanics of persuasion.

Evaluate. Finally, none of this matters if the outcome of our efforts is not evaluated properly. Experimental and quasi-experimental designs should be built into our persuasive efforts from the very start. If we wish to have an impact, it is critical that we have a valid, data-based story to tell. Lacking that story, which is only possible through uncompromisingly stringent design and analysis, we are in the land of the poet, the priest, or the snake oil salesman. These are not necessarily badlands, but they are not fitting surroundings for a proper social scientist.

REFERENCES

Allport, G. W. (1935). Attitudes. In C. Murchison (Ed.), *Handbook of social psychology* (pp. 798–884). Worcester, MA: Clark University Press.

Appel, V. (1971). On advertising wearout. *Journal of Advertising Research, 11,* 11–13.

Aristotle. (1991). *On rhetoric: A theory of civic discourse* (G. A. Kennedy, Trans.). New York: Oxford University Press.

Aristotle. (1999). *Nichomachean ethics* (2nd ed.; T. Irwin, Trans.). Indianapolis, IN: Hackett.

Atkin, C. (2004). Promising strategies for media health campaigns. In W. D. Crano & M. Burgoon (Eds.), *Mass media and drug prevention: Classic and contemporary theories and research* (pp. 35–64). Mahwah, NJ: Erlbaum.

Brecher, E. M. (1972). *Licit and illicit drugs: The Consumers Union report on narcotics, stimulants, depressants, inhalants, hallucinogens, and marijuana—including caffeine, nicotine, and alcohol.* Boston: Little, Brown.

Cacioppo, J. T., & Petty, R. E. (1989). Effects of message repetition on argument processing, recall, and persuasion. *Basic and Applied Social Psychology, 10*(1), 3–12.

Campbell, D. T. (1969). Reforms as experiments. *American Psychologist, 24,* 409–429.

Crano, W. D. (1995). Attitude strength and vested interest. In R. E. Petty & J. A. Krosnick (Eds.), *Attitude strength: Antecedents and consequences* (pp. 131–157). Hillsdale, NJ: Erlbaum.

Crano, W. D. (1997). Vested interest, symbolic politics, and attitude-behavior consistency. *Journal of Personality and Social Psychology, 72*(3), 485–491.

Crano, W. D. (2002). Introduction. In W. D. Crano & M. Burgoon (Eds.), *Mass media and drug prevention: Classic and contemporary theories and research* (pp. 19–34). Mahwah, NJ: Erlbaum.

Crano, W. D., & Brewer, M. B. (2002). *Principles and methods of social research* (2nd ed.). Mahwah, NJ: Erlbaum.

Crano, W. D., & Burgoon, M. (2002). *Mass media and drug prevention: Classic and contemporary theories and research.* Mahwah, NJ: Erlbaum.

Crano, W. D., Gilbert, C., Alvaro, E. M., & Siegel, J. T. (2008). Enhancing prediction of inhalant abuse risk in samples of early adolescents: A secondary analysis. *Addictive Behaviors, 33*(7), 895–905.

Crano, W. D., & Prislin, R. (2006). Attitudes and persuasion. *Annual Review of Psychology, 57,* 345–374.

Crano, W. D., Siegel, J. T., Alvaro, E. M., Lac, A., & Hemovich, V. (2008). The at-risk adolescent marijuana nonuser: Expanding the standard distinction. *Prevention Science, 9*(2), 129–137.

Crano, W. D., Siegel, J. T., Alvaro, E. M., & Patel, N. M. (2007). Overcoming adolescents' resistance to anti-inhalant appeals. *Psychology of Addictive Behaviors, 21*(4), 516–524.

Derzon, J. H., & Lipsey, M. W. (2002). A meta-analysis of the effectiveness of mass-communication for changing substance-use knowledge, attitudes, and behavior. In W. D. Crano & M. Burgoon (Eds.), *Mass media and drug prevention: Classic and contemporary theories and research* (pp. 231–258). Mahwah, NJ: Erlbaum.

Deutsch, R., & Strack, F. (2006). Reflective and impulsive determinants of addictive behavior. In R. W. Wiers & A. W. Stacy (Eds.), *Handbook of implicit cognition and addiction* (pp. 45–57). Thousand Oaks, CA: Sage.

Dillard, J. P., & Anderson, J. W. (2004). The role of fear in persuasion. *Psychology & Marketing, 21*(11), 909–926.

Donohew, L., Lorch, E. P., & Palmgreen, P. (1991). Sensation seeking and targeting of televised anti-drug PSAs. In L. Donohew, H. E. Sypher, & W. J. Bukoski (Eds.), *Persuasive communication and drug abuse prevention* (pp. 209–226). Hillsdale, NJ: Erlbaum.

Erceg-Hurn, D. M. (2008). Drugs, money, and graphic ads: A critical review of the Montana Meth Project. *Prevention Science, 9,* 256–263.

Fazio, R. H., & Zanna, M. P. (1978a). Attitudinal qualities relating to the strength of the attitude-behavior relationship. *Journal of Experimental Social Psychology, 14*(4), 398–408.

Fazio, R. H., & Zanna, M. P. (1978b). On the predictive validity of attitudes: The roles of direct experience and confidence. *Journal of Personality, 46*(2), 228–243.

Fazio, R. H., Zanna, M. P., & Cooper, J. (1978). Direct experience and attitude-behavior consistency: An information processing analysis. *Personality and Social Psychology Bulletin, 4*(1), 48–51.

Fishbein, M., Cappella, J., Hornik, R., Sayeed, S., Yzer, M., & Ahern, R. K. (2002). The role of theory in developing effective antidrug public service announcements. In W. D. Crano & M. Burgoon (Eds.), *Mass media and drug prevention: Classic and contemporary theories and research* (pp. 89–117). Mahwah, NJ: Erlbaum.

Flay, B., & Sobel, J. L. (1983). The role of mass media in preventing adolescent substance abuse. In T. J. Glynn, C. G. Leukefeld, & J. P. Ludford (Eds.), *Preventing adolescent drug abuse: Intervention strategies.* Rockville, MD: NIDA.

Glasman, L. R., & Albarracin, D. (2006). Forming attitudes that predict future behavior: A meta-analysis of the attitude-behavior relation. *Psychological Bulletin, 132*(5), 778–822.

Green, E. C., & Witte, K. (2006). Can fear arousal in public health campaigns contribute to the decline of HIV prevalence? *Journal of Health Communication, 11*(3), 245–259.

Hastings, G., Stead, M., & Webb, J. (2004). Fear appeals in social marketing: Strategic and ethical reasons for concern. *Psychology & Marketing, 21,* 961–986.

Hornik, R., Jacobsohn, L., Orwin, R., Piesse, A., & Kalton, G. (2008). Effects of the national youth anti-drug media campaign on youths. *American Journal of Public Health, 98,* 2229–2236.

Hovland, C. I., Janis, I. L., & Kelley, H. H. (1953). *Communication and persuasion.* New Haven, CT: Yale University Press.

Johnson, B. T., & Eagly, A. H. (1989). Effects of involvement on persuasion: A meta-analysis. *Psychological Bulletin, 106*(2), 290–314.

Krosnick, J. A., & Abelson, R. P. (1992). The case for measuring attitude strength in surveys. In J. M. Tanur (Ed.), *Questions about questions: Inquiries into the cognitive bases of surveys* (pp. 177–203). New York: Russell Sage Foundation.

Kruglanski, A. W., Chun, W. Y., Erb, H. P., Pierro, A., Mannetti, L., & Spiegel, S. (2003). A parametric unimodel of human judgment: Integrating dual-process frameworks in social cognition from a single-mode perspective. In J. P. Forgas, K. D. Williams, & W. von Hippel (Eds.), *Social judgments: Implicit and explicit processes* (pp. 137–161). New York: Cambridge University Press.

Kruglanski, A. W., & Thompson, E. P. (1999). Persuasion by a single route: A view from the unimodel. *Psychological Inquiry, 10*(2), 83–109.

Lehman, B. J., & Crano, W. D. (2002). The pervasive effects of vested interest on attitude-criterion consistency in political judgment. *Journal of Experimental Social Psychology, 38*(2), 101–112.

Lewin, K., French, J. R. P., Jr., Hendry, C., Deets, L. E., Zander, A., Lippitt, R., et al. (1945). The practicality of democracy. In G. Murphy (Ed.), *Human nature and enduring peace: Third yearbook for the Society for the Psychological Study of Social Issues* (pp. 295–347). Boston: Houghton Mifflin.

Lewin, K., Heider, F., & Heider, G. M. (1936). *Principles of topological psychology.* New York: McGraw-Hill.

McGuire, W. J. (1969). The nature of attitudes and attitude change. In G. Lindzey & E. Aronson (Eds.), *The handbook of social psychology* (Vol. 3, pp. 136–314). Reading, MA: Addison-Wesley.

McGuire, W. J. (1986). The vicissitudes of attitudes and similar representational constructs in twentieth century psychology. *European Journal of Social Psychology, 16*(2), 89–130.

McGuire, W. J. (1996). The Yale communication and attitude-change program in the 1950s. In E. E. Dennis & E. Wartella (Eds.), *American communication research—The remembered history* (pp. 39–59). Mahwah, NJ: Erlbaum.

McGuire, W. J. (2003). Doing psychology my way. In R. J. Sternberg (Ed.), *Psychologists defying the crowd: Stories of those who battled the establishment and won* (pp. 119–137). Washington, DC: American Psychological Association.

Miller, J., & Muir, D. (2004). *The business of brands.* Hoboken, NJ: Wiley.

Noar, S. M., Zimmerman, R. S., Palmgreen, P., Lustria, M., & Horosewski, M. L. (2006). Integrating personality and psychosocial theoretical approaches to understanding safer sexual behavior: Implications for message design. *Health Communication, 19*(2), 165–174.

Orwin, R., Cadell, D., Chu, A., Kalton, G., Maklan, D., Morin, C., et al. (2006). *Evaluation of the National Youth Anti-drug Media Campaign: 2004 Report of findings.* Retrieved February, 2009, from http://nida.nih.gov/DESPR/Westat/NSPY2004Report/Vol1/Report.pdf

Petty, R. E., Briñol, P., Tormala, Z. L., & Wegener, D. T. (2007). The role of metacognition in social judgment. In A. W. Kruglanski & E. T. Higgins (Eds.), *Social psychology: Handbook of basic principles* (2nd ed., pp. 254–284). New York: Guilford Press.

Petty, R. E., & Cacioppo, J. T. (1986). *Attitude change: Central and peripheral routes to persuasion.* New York: Springer-Verlag.

Petty, R. E., & Cacioppo, J. T. (1996). *Attitudes and persuasion: Classic and contemporary approaches.* Boulder, CO: Westview Press.

Petty, R. E., Cacioppo, J. T., & Goldman, R. (1981). Personal involvement as a determinant of argument-based persuasion. *Journal of Personality and Social Psychology, 41*(5), 847–855.

Petty, R. E., & Krosnick, J. A. (1995). *Attitude strength: Antecedents and consequences.* Hillsdale, NJ: Erlbaum.

Petty, R. E., Tormala, Z. L., & Rucker, D. D. (2004). Resisting persuasion by counterarguing: An attitude strength perspective. In J. T. Jost, M. R. Banaji, & D. A. Prentice (Eds.), *Perspectivism in social psychology: The yin and yang of scientific progress* (pp. 37–51). Washington, DC: American Psychological Association.

Prislin, R. (1993). Effect of direct experience on the relative importance of attitudes, subjective norms and perceived behavioral control for prediction of intentions and behavior. *Psychology: A Journal of Human Behavior, 30*(3), 51–58.

Prislin, R., & Crano, W. D. (2008). Attitudes and attitude change: The fourth peak. In W. D. Crano & R. Prislin (Eds.), *Attitudes and attitude change* (pp. 3–15). New York: Psychology Press.

Quinn, J. M., & Wood, W. (2004). Forewarnings of influence appeals: Inducing resistance and acceptance. In E. S. Knowles & J. A. Linn (Eds.), *Resistance and persuasion* (pp. 193–213). Mahwah, NJ: Erlbaum.

Ramirez, J. R., Crano, W. D., Quist, R., Burgoon, M., Alvaro, E. M., & Grandpre, J. (2004). Acculturation, familism, parental monitoring, and knowledge as predictors of marijuana and inhalant use in adolescents. *Psychology of Addictive Behaviors, 18*(1), 3–11.

Rhodes, F., Stein, J. A., Fishbein, M., Goldstein, R. B., & Rotheram-Borus, M. J. (2007). Using theory to understand how interventions work: Project RESPECT, condom use, and the integrative model. *AIDS and Behavior, 11*(3), 393–407.

Rimal, R. N., & Flora, J. A. (1997). Interactive technology attributes in health promotion: Practical and theoretical issues. In R. L. Street, Jr., W. R. Gold, & T. R. Manning (Eds.), *Health promotion and interactive technology: Theoretical applications and future directions* (pp. 19–38). Mahwah, NJ: Erlbaum.

Rimer, B. K., & Kreuter, M. W. (2006). Advancing tailored health communication: A persuasion and message effects perspective. *Journal of Communication, 56*(1), S184–S201.

Ruiter, R. A. C., Abraham, C., & Kok, G. (2001). Scary warnings and rational precautions: A review of the psychology of fear appeals. *Psychology & Health, 16*(6), 613–630.

Scriven, M. (1991). *Evaluation thesaurus* (4th ed.). Thousand Oaks, CA: Sage.

Scriven, M. (1997). Truth and objectivity in evaluation. In E. Chelimsky & W. R. Shadish (Eds.), *Evaluation for the 21st century: A handbook* (pp. 477–500). Thousand Oaks, CA: Sage.

Scriven, M. (2003). Evaluation in the new millennium: The transdisciplinary vision. In S. I. Donaldson & M. Scriven (Eds.), *Evaluating social programs and problems: Visions for the new millennium* (pp. 19–41). Mahwah, NJ: Erlbaum.

Selnow, G. W., & Crano, W. D. (1987). *Planning, implementing, and evaluating targeted communication programs: A manual for business communicators.* New York: Quorum Books.

Shadish, W. R., Jr., Cook, T. D., & Campbell, D. T. (2002). *Experimental and quasi-experimental designs for generalized causal inference.* Boston: Houghton Mifflin.

Shadish, W. R., Jr., Cook, T. D., & Leviton, L. C. (1991). *Foundations of program evaluation: Theories of practice.* Thousand Oaks, CA: Sage.

Siegel, J. T., Alvaro, E. A., Patel, N., & Crano, W. D. (2009). "…you would probably want to do it. Cause that's what made them popular": Exploring perceptions of inhalant utility among young adolescent non-users and occasional users. *Substance Use and Misuse, 44,* 597–615.

Skenderian, J. J., Siegel, J. T., Crano, W. D., Alvaro, E. E., & Lac, A. (2008). Expectancy change and adolescents' intentions to use marijuana. *Psychology of Addictive Behaviors, 22*(4), 563–569.

Suggs, L. S. (2006). A 10-year retrospective of research in new technologies for health communication. *Journal of Health Communication, 11*(1), 61–74.

Tormala, Z. L. (2008). A new framework for resistance to persuasion: The resistance-appraisals hypothesis. In W. D. Crano & R. Prislin (Eds.), *Attitudes and attitude change* (pp. 213–234). New York: Psychology Press.

Tormala, Z. L., Clarkson, J. J., & Petty, R. E. (2006). Resisting persuasion by the skin of one's teeth: The hidden success of resisted persuasive messages. *Journal of Personality and Social Psychology, 91*(3), 423–435.

Tormala, Z. L., & Petty, R. E. (2002). What doesn't kill me makes me stronger: The effects of resisting persuasion on attitude certainty. *Journal of Personality and Social Psychology, 83*(6), 1298–1313.

Tormala, Z. L., & Petty, R. E. (2004). Resisting persuasion and attitude certainty: A meta-cognitive analysis. In E. S. Knowles & J. A. Linn (Eds.), *Resistance and persuasion* (pp. 65–82). Mahwah, NJ: Erlbaum.

Updegraff, J. A., Sherman, D. K., Luyster, F. S., & Mann, T. L. (2007). The effects of message quality and congruency on perceptions of tailored health communications. *Journal of Experimental Social Psychology, 43*(2), 249–257.

Walther, E., & Langer, T. (2008). Attitude formation and change through association: An evaluative conditioning account. In W. D. Crano & R. Prislin (Eds.), *Attitudes and attitude change* (pp. 87–110). New York: Psychology Press.

Walther, E., Nagengast, B., & Trasselli, C. (2005). Evaluative conditioning in social psychology: Facts and speculations. *Cognition & Emotion, 19*(2), 175–196.

Winkielman, P., & Cacioppo, J. T. (2001). Mind at ease puts a smile on the face: Psychophysiological evidence that processing facilitation increases positive affect. *Journal of Personality and Social Psychology, 81,* 989–1000.

Wood, W., Rhodes, N., & Biek, M. (1995). Working knowledge and attitude strength: An information-processing analysis. In R. E. Petty & J. A. Krosnick (Eds.), *Attitude strength: Antecedents and consequences* (pp. 283–313). Hillsdale, NJ: Erlbaum.

Yzer, M. C., Cappella, J. N., Fishbein, M., Hornik, R., Sayeed, S., & Ahern, R. K. (2004). The role of distal variables in behavior change: Effects of adolescents' risk for marijuana use on intention to use marijuana. *Journal of Applied Social Psychology, 34*(6), 1229–1250.

Zajonc, R. (1968). Attitudinal effects of mere exposure. *Journal of Personality and Social Psychology Monographs, 9*(2, Pt. 2), 1–27.

Zhao, X., Sayeed, S., Cappella, J., Hornik, R., Fishbein, M., & Ahern, R. K. (2006). Targeting norm-related beliefs about marijuana use in an adolescent population. *Health Communication, 19*(3), 187–196.

ACKNOWLEDGMENTS

Preparation of this research was supported by a grant from the U.S. National Institute on Drug Abuse (5R01DA020879-02). The contents of this paper are solely the responsibility of the author and do not necessarily reflect the views of the Institute.

15

Psychological Implications of Attitudes and Beliefs About Status Inequality

BRENDA MAJOR AND SARAH S. M. TOWNSEND

In virtually all societies, inequalities exist among social groups in the distribution of tangible and intangible social goods such as access to food, medical care, shelter, respect, and power. An enduring question for political philosophers, sociologists, and psychologists concerns how these inequalities are maintained and perpetuated. Shared attitudes and beliefs about why status inequalities exist (i.e., status ideologies) are an essential element of this process (Jost & Banaji, 1994; Major, 1994; Major & Schmader, 2001; Sidanius & Pratto, 1993). Status ideologies explain status differences among individuals and groups, proscribe rules for gaining status, and frequently justify the status quo (Jost & Banaji, 1994; Major, 1994). We begin this chapter by briefly reviewing research on status ideologies and discussing the role that meritocracy—the dominant status ideology in many Western capitalist societies such as the United States—plays in legitimizing inequalities in contemporary Western societies. We then discuss how endorsement or rejection of this ideology shapes people's affective and physiological reactions to disadvantage and prejudice directed against themselves or their social groups. Collectively, the research reviewed here indicates that culturally shared attitudes and beliefs about the causes of status inequality in society exert an important effect on individual psychological processes, shaping affective reactions to prejudice against one's social group, and physiological responses during interactions with members of higher status groups.

STATUS IDEOLOGIES

A status ideology is an integrated and shared system of social attitudes, beliefs, and values that describes and explains existing status differences in society and the rules or standards necessary to be a person of value and status within that society (Crandall, 1994; Jost, Burgess, & Mosso, 2001; Major, Kaiser, O'Brien, & McCoy, 2007). Thus, status ideologies are both descriptive and proscriptive. Other related terms used to describe this construct include stratification beliefs (Bobo & Hutchings, 1996), social mobility belief structures (Hogg & Abrams, 1988), hierarchy enhancing (or attenuating) myths (Sidanius & Pratto, 1993), and system-justifying beliefs (Jost & Banaji, 1994). Like the study of attitudes more generally, the concept of status ideologies attempts to capture the way in which people understand and represent their social worlds and interactions (Forgas, this volume).

Status ideologies serve several important and related psychological functions. First, they function as lay theories that individuals use for everyday sense making (Levy, Chiu, & Hong, 2006). As such, they are an important component of individuals' worldviews, operating implicitly and explicitly to guide perceptions, expectations, and interpretations of the social world (Frey & Powell, 2005; Koltko-Rivera, 2004). Second, status ideologies reduce epistemic uncertainty. By providing a coherent explanation of existing status differences in society they help to satisfy humans' need to see their world as orderly, predictable, and meaningful, thereby allowing them to function more effectively (Van den Bos & Lind, 2002). Third, by providing an understanding of how status is achieved, status ideologies also provide guidelines for how one's own status might, or might not, be improved. Thus, for example, the belief that success is based on hard work provides a road map for achieving personal success.

Status ideologies are not individually held attitudes and beliefs, but are products of the local sociocultural environment in which an individual exists (e.g., nation, region, ethnic group; Shweder, 1995). Hence, they are broadly known and often widely shared within a cultural context. Importantly, as Levy and colleagues (2006) observe, when ideologies or lay theories are shared by individuals within a particular society, they become part of that group's shared reality and worldview.

THE IDEOLOGY OF MERITOCRACY

Different cultures have different status ideologies to explain social inequality. For example, in India, a dominant status ideology is that caste determines status. In Westernized, capitalist countries such as the United States, the dominant status ideology is that merit determines status. Meritocracy is a highly individualistic status ideology, holding that any individual, regardless of group membership, can be successful if he or she works hard enough or is talented enough (Kluegel & Smith, 1986; Plaut, Markus, & Lachman, 2002). Meritocracy is often conceptualized and measured in terms of a variety of theoretically related attitudes and beliefs, such as the Protestant Work Ethic (i.e., the belief that success is based on hard work), the belief in a just world, and the belief in individual mobility (i.e., the belief that individuals can get ahead regardless of group membership; Crandall, 1994; Katz & Hass, 1988; Lerner, 1980; Major et al., 2002; Rubin & Peplau, 1975; Weber, 1905/1992). Although these beliefs are only moderately correlated with each other, collectively they form a coherent ideology in which status in society is believed to be fairly distributed, based on individual merit and hard work, and individually deserved (Crandall, 1994; Furnham & Proctor, 1989; Katz & Hass, 1988; O'Brien & Major, 2005).

Meritocracy is widely endorsed by individuals of all levels of social status in the United States (Crandall, 1994; Furnham & Proctor, 1989; Jost & Hunyady, 2002; Kluegel & Smith, 1986). Indeed, the belief that anyone can gain status through individual effort and merit is often referred to as the "American Dream." As the dominant status ideology in the United States, meritocracy is inculcated in American culture through shared stories such as Horatio Alger and The Little Engine That Could. The sheer pervasiveness of the message that anyone has the opportunity to succeed in America through hard work and talent means that most citizens are aware of the ideology of meritocracy, even if they do not personally endorse it as true. Consequently, people's thoughts, behaviors, and feelings can be influenced by this ideology whenever cues in the environment make it salient. Such cues might include, for example, motivational posters ("It's all up to you!"), advertisements (Nike's "Just do it" campaign), news stories about individuals who succeed despite adversity (Oprah Winfrey) or cultural events (e.g., the election of Barack Obama to the U.S. presidency). When meritocracy is activated, individuals construe and explain their social world in a manner consistent with this activated system of attitudes and beliefs (McCoy & Major, 2007).

An important consequence of the ideology of meritocracy is that it is status-legitimizing, that is, it helps to preserve a view of existing unequal status arrangements in society as fair, just, and deserved (Jost & Hunyady, 2002; Major, 1994; Sidanius & Pratto, 1993). Consider, for example, the belief that hard work leads to success, or the belief that people get what they deserve. These beliefs justify status inequalities by holding people responsible for their station in life and by locating the cause of their outcomes within their own efforts, merit, or deservingness. These beliefs lead to different inferences about the worth of members of social groups with different status positions. The assumption that social status is based on merit and hard work leads to the inference that individuals and groups that possess more social goods (i.e., those that are high status) must have greater inputs (e.g., intelligence, skill, persistence) and hence be more "worthy" or "meritorious" than individuals and groups with fewer social goods (i.e., those that are low status; Jost & Hunyady, 2002; Major, 1994; O'Brien & Major, 2005; Ridgeway, 2001). Indeed, research has shown that endorsing or activating meritocracy is related to an increased sense of entitlement among people from higher status groups and a decreased sense of entitlement among people from lower status groups (Major, 1994; O'Brien & Major, 2009; see also Jost & Hunyady, 2002).

Research also has shown that the more people endorse attitudes and beliefs associated with meritocracy, the more negative attitudes they hold toward members of low-status groups (Katz & Hass, 1988), the more they blame members of lower status groups for their relative disadvantage (e.g., Crandall, 1994), and the more they derogate people who blame their failures on discrimination rather than themselves (Kaiser, Dyrenforth, & Hagiwara, 2006). These inferences are often shared by members of low- as well as high-status groups. The apparent consensuality of meritocracy in Western, capitalist societies gives it social validity and increases its power to legitimize status inequality (Ridgeway, 2001; Sidanius & Pratto, 1993). The status ideology of meritocracy sustains social inequality both by altering perceptions of the treatment and social goods that members of different groups deserve, and by preventing people from realizing when they are being treated unfairly (Major, 1994).

Justice scholars have offered three major explanations for why members of low-status groups often endorse attitudes and beliefs about the social system that justify the very status hierarchy that disadvantages them. First, people have a natural tendency to assume that what "is" is what "ought" to be (Heider, 1958), a tendency known as the naturalistic fallacy (Eidelman & Crandall, 2009). Cognitive biases, such as the naturalistic fallacy and other status quo biases, lead people to assume that existing social hierarchies are good and better than any possible alternatives. Second, people from high-status groups have a vested interest in maintaining the status quo. They also have the power and means to see that beliefs that justify the status quo are prominently represented in the culture. Thus, high-status groups endorse legitimizing beliefs because they reinforce their relatively privileged position in society and low-status groups endorse legitimizing beliefs because cultural forces persuade them to do so (Sidanius & Pratto, 1993). Third, people are motivated to endorse beliefs that legitimize the status quo because of a psychological need to believe that the world (or at least the world relevant to themselves) is a just and fair place (e.g., Jost & Banaji, 1994; Jost & Hunyady, 2002; Lerner, 1980). Jost and colleagues, for example, theorize that people have a fundamental need to preserve the belief that existing social arrangements are legitimate, justifiable, and necessary. Legitimizing the social hierarchy helps individuals to maintain their belief that the world is a fair, predictable place and increases their sense of certainty, security, and control.

VARIATION IN ATTITUDES AND BELIEFS ABOUT STATUS INEQUALITY

Although meritocracy is widely known and endorsed in the United States, people differ in the strength of their endorsement of this ideology. Given the complexity of modern societies, different reference groups can be found that provide at least some degree of validation for a wide variety of attitudes and beliefs about the underlying basis and legitimacy of the status hierarchy (Anson, Pyszczynski, Solomon, & Greenberg, 2009). As a result, people may hold a status ideology that is inconsistent with the status ideology that is dominant within the culture as a whole but that is consistent with that of their reference group.

People who have repeatedly experienced a lack of contingency between their own efforts and their outcomes, or who have repeatedly witnessed this lack of contingency in the lives of others like themselves may come to reject meritocracy as a meaningful explanation of their own reality and as a basis of their value (Major et al., 2002). Members of low-status ethnic groups often are less likely to hold meritocratic attitudes than are members of high-status ethnic groups (e.g., Major et al., 2002; O'Brien & Major, 2005). Some endorse a status ideology that explains the existing status hierarchy in terms of bias, discrimination, and/or favoritism (Major & Townsend, 2010). Embracing a system-de-legitimizing ideology, such as the belief that status inequalities are due to discrimination, may be self-protective for those who frequently face devaluation. This ideology may protect personal and collective self-esteem by providing explanations other than a lack of individual effort or merit for one's own (or one's group's) position of disadvantage in society (Crocker & Major, 1989). It may also enable members of socially devalued groups to anticipate and prepare for injustice thereby lessening its sting.

REACTIONS TO DISCONFIRMATION OF ATTITUDES AND BELIEFS ABOUT STATUS

Although people generally perceive and interpret their social worlds in ways that support and confirm their status ideologies, there are occasions in which this strategy fails. Sometimes experiences or events in the world violate people's attitudes and beliefs about how the world works. How do people react when this happens? What happens, for example, when people who believe that if they work hard they will be promoted discover that promotion is instead based on family connections or denied because of the color of one's skin? What happens when people who believe that discrimination will certainly hold them back from success end up succeeding? Answering this question of how people react when their experiences are inconsistent with their status ideologies is informed by research on how people react when their experiences are inconsistent with their attitudes.

Several lines of theory and research predict that inconsistencies between one's beliefs and attitudes and one's experiences engender anxiety. For example, Heider's (1946, 1958) balance theory proposed that inconsistency, or imbalance, among attitudinal elements creates "tension" which represents a motivational force for cognitive change to restore psychological balance. Festinger (1957) described cognitive dissonance as a state of discomfort and arousal associated with any inconsistency between relevant cognitions, asserting that a motivational state of dissonance is aroused by the juxtaposition of two cognitive elements, x and y, when "not-x follows from y" (see Greenwald & Ronis, 1978, p. 13). In fact, people have even been shown to experience a state of vicarious dissonance when they witness a member of their social group behaving in a way that is counter to that group member's attitudes (Cooper, this volume).

The idea that people are motivated to maintain consistency in their beliefs about themselves and their social world also plays a central role in a variety of other psychological theories, including self-verification theory (Swann, 1992), expectancy theory (Olson, Roese, & Zanna, 1996), uncertainty management theory (Van den Bos & Lind, 2002), terror management theory (TMT; Greenberg, Solomon, & Pyszczynski, 1997), lay theories of intelligence (Plaks & Stecher, 2007), and the meaning maintenance model (Heine, Proulx, & Vohs, 2006). These theories assume that people strive to maintain consistency in their beliefs and behaviors so as to increase a sense of predictability and control. Inconsistencies disrupt a person's predictive ability and create feelings of uncertainty, thereby lessening a sense of control (Van den Bos & Lind, 2002). Dissonance between one's expectancies and one's experiences may also evoke a negative affective state because it interferes with one's ability to effectively act in the situation (Harmon-Jones, Amodio, & Harmon-Jones, this volume).

A number of studies have shown that freely behaving in a way that is inconsistent with one's attitudes leads to a state of tension or arousal. Most studies have used indirect research techniques. For example, Zanna and Cooper (1974) showed that people who freely chose to write a counterattitudinal essay did not subsequently change their attitude when given the opportunity to attribute their presumed arousal to a plausible external source, whereas those who did not have this opportunity to misattribute their arousal did change their attitude.

Inconsistency-induced arousal is not limited to contexts in which people write counterattitudinal essays. A recent set of experiments demonstrated that simply encountering an inconsistency between one's expectancies and one's experiences can be threatening, as indexed by physiological responses (Mendes, Blascovich, Hunter, Lickel, & Jost, 2007). Participants who interacted with a partner who violated stereotypical expectancies (e.g., a rich Latino American; a poor European American, or an Asian American who spoke with a southern accent) exhibited cardiovascular and behavioral responses consistent with a psychological state of threat compared to those who interacted with a more expected or typical partner.

According to Olson and colleagues (1996), disconfirmation of expectancies is unpleasant even when the experience that led to the disconfirmation is positive. They note that even when someone expects the worst but experiences the best, he or she will experience an initial negative affective reaction, even if the disconfirmation produces secondary affective reactions that are positive. In their view, disconfirmation of expectancies will generally produce initial negative affect because unpredictability and uncertainty are unpleasant, because disconfirmation can produce dissonance, and because the experience of surprise can itself be unpleasant in some circumstances. Furthermore, they observe:

> All else being equal, people will prefer to have their expectancies confirmed and are likely to experience positive affect (satisfaction, vindication) on confirmation, or perhaps reduction of negative affect (uncertainty, fear)...It is possible that the confirmation of negative expectancies, though "satisfying" in some sense, may generate aversive affect for other reasons. An individual who expects the worst and has his or her fears confirmed may feel depressed or anxious about how things turned out. Such occurrences constitute secondary affect, however, from inferences that occur after the confirmation. The initial affective response to the confirmation itself should typically be positive (based on the assumption that the desire for a stable, predictable world is primary). Moreover, even secondary negative affect will be the exception rather than the rule. (p. 226)

A recent set of studies by Plaks and Stecher (2007) illustrates how violations of one's worldview can be anxiety provoking, even when the outcome is positive. They hypothesized that people's lay theory of intelligence, that is, whether they endorse an entity (intelligence is fixed) or incremental (intelligence is malleable) theory of intelligence, shapes how they react to performance feedback. Specifically, Plaks and Stecher posited that people should be discomfited by performance outcomes that are inconsistent with their lay theory even when the performance outcome is good, noting that "entity theorists, like everyone, should experience greater overall positive affect following improved performance compared with static performance. However, the epistemic disorientation created by unanticipated success means that for entity theorists, this joy will be mingled with anxiety" (p. 670). Consistent with their predictions, when given feedback that their own performance had either declined or improved, entity theorists displayed more anxiety and greater effort to restore prediction confidence than did incremental theorists. However, when performance remained rigidly static despite a learning opportunity, incremental theorists evinced more anxiety and compensatory effort than did entity theorists.

Perhaps the clearest evidence of the strength of the desire to maintain consistency between one's attitudes and beliefs and experiences comes from self-verification theory. In a substantial body of research, Swann and his colleagues have shown that people preferentially seek information consistent with their attitudes and beliefs about themselves, regard self-consistent information as more valid, surround themselves with others who share their view of themselves, and contest others who challenge their attitudes and beliefs about themselves (see Swann, Rentfrow, & Guinn, 2003, for a review). Further, they show that this occurs even for individuals whose self-concepts are negative. Underlying this motive for self-verification, in Swann's view, is a desire for predictability and control.

WORLDVIEW VERIFICATION THEORY

We recently extended this line of thinking to attitudes and beliefs about the system (Major et al., 2007). We posited that people also seek consistency between their understanding of status relations in society and their experiences, and are discomfited by experiences that violate their status ideology, even when those experiences are positive. We termed this perspective worldview verification theory (WVT). According to WVT, the consistency (or inconsistency) between the contents of people's status ideology and their experiences determines their initial responses to those experiences. Although everyone should experience greater overall positive affect following positive outcomes compared to negative outcomes, inconsistency produces anxiety due to epistemic concerns. Thus, we hypothesized that people will experience initial anxiety (threat) when they encounter information that disconfirms their status ideology or worldview, relatively independently of the valence of the experience. Hence, like self-verification theory (Swann, 1992), cognitive dissonance theory (Festinger, 1957), and expectancy theory (Olson et al., 1996), WVT emphasizes people's desire for consistency and coherence rather than their desire for positivity.

Extending our analysis to intergroup relations, we posited that the experience of being a target of prejudice or discrimination is inconsistent with the belief that status in society is based on merit and deserved. Consequently, being a target of prejudice should be anxiety-provoking for people who endorse meritocracy, and motivate them to attempt to reaffirm the threatened worldview. In contrast, being a target of prejudice or discrimination is consistent with the status ideology of those who reject a meritocratic ideology. Consequently, being a target of prejudice should not be anxiety provoking for these individuals, because these events confirm their worldview. In its strong form, WVT predicts that people who reject meritocracy may experience a feeling akin to initial positive affect upon encountering evidence of prejudice against themselves or their group, because it is worldview affirming.

In short, WVT predicts that people who expect the system to be fair will be threatened by evidence that it is not fair, whereas people who expect that the system is unfair will be threatened by evidence that it is fair. This inconsistency may be particularly threatening or dissonance arousing because of the general nature of status ideologies. As shared attitudes about status inequality they transcend specific situations and, therefore, may function as action guides "at a distance" that abstract across the peculiarities of particular contexts and interactions and are more resistant to change (Ledgerwood & Trope, this volume).

Several studies examining the association between self-esteem and perceived discrimination provide support for WVT. Major et al. (2007; Experiment 1) examined the relationship between perceived discrimination against one's ethnic group and personal self-esteem among a sample of Latino American university students. Using decreases in self-esteem as a proxy for threat or anxiety, we predicted and found that among Latino participants who strongly embraced meritocracy beliefs, the more discrimination they perceived to exist against their ethnic group, the lower their personal self-esteem. Among Latino participants who rejected a meritocracy ideology, in contrast, the more discrimination they perceived directed against their ethnic group, the higher their personal self-esteem. Foster, Sloto, and Ruby (2006) observed a similar pattern: higher belief in meritocracy was associated with higher self-esteem among women and ethnic minorities who reported few experiences of personal discrimination but lower self-esteem among those who reported many experiences of personal discrimination.

Several experiments also provide support for WVT. Major et al. (2007; Experiment 2) examined whether endorsing a meritocracy ideology moderated the effects on self-esteem of exposure to discrimination against the in-group versus a nonself-relevant group. Latino American students who read that Latino American students from their university were victims of pervasive discrimination had lower self-esteem than the control group (students who read about prejudice against a non self-relevant group) the more they endorsed meritocracy, but higher self-esteem than the control group to the extent that they rejected this ideology. In addition, consistent with the prediction that people will attempt to reaffirm a threatened worldview, high meritocracy endorsers in the in-group prejudice condition blamed their in-group significantly more for its low status than did low endorsers in that condition, whereas high- and low-meritocracy endorsers did not differ in the extent to which they held their in-group responsible for its low status in the control condition. Foster and Tsarfati (2005) showed that women who endorsed meritocracy beliefs had lower self-esteem if they failed a test due to gender discrimination rather than due to lack of merit. In contrast, women who rejected meritocracy beliefs had higher self-esteem if they failed a test due to gender discrimination rather than due to lack of merit.

From the perspective of WVT, evidence that discrimination against one's group is rare is consistent with the worldview of individuals who believe that status is accorded on the basis of merit but disconfirms the worldview of individuals who reject a meritocracy status ideology. Hence, WVT leads to the counterintuitive prediction that individuals who reject meritocracy will have lower self-esteem if they encounter information that prejudice against their group is rare (because this violates their worldview) than if they encounter evidence that it is pervasive (because this confirms their worldview). Just the reverse should be observed among individuals who endorse meritocracy.

To test this hypothesis, we asked women to read one of two articles: one describing prejudice against women in the United States as pervasive, or one describing prejudice against women in the United States as rare (Major et al., 2007; Experiment 3). As predicted, among women who strongly endorsed meritocracy, reading that prejudice against women is pervasive decreased their self-esteem relative to reading that prejudice against women is rare. In contrast, among women who rejected meritocracy, reading that prejudice against women is pervasive increased their self-esteem relative to reading that prejudice against women is rare. This study also showed that women who strongly endorsed a meritocracy ideology were more likely to blame women for their low status when they read that sexism was pervasive rather than rare. In contrast, women who rejected meritocracy ideology were unlikely to blame women for their low status regardless of whether they read that sexism was pervasive or rare.

Recently, Kaiser and Pratt-Hyatt (2009) provided support for WVT in a different context. They showed that Whites who endorsed meritocracy beliefs expressed more negative attitudes toward strongly identified minorities relative to weakly identified minorities, whereas Whites who personally rejected meritocracy beliefs displayed the opposite pattern. Further, they showed that this occurred because Whites associated a strong minority identity with a challenge to the legitimacy of the system. This challenge to the legitimacy of the system threatened the worldview of those who endorsed meritocracy, but confirmed the worldview of those who rejected meritocracy.

IS WORLDVIEW DISCONFIRMATION THREATENING?

The idea that either the presence or the absence of prejudice can be threatening depending on a person's status ideology provides a reasonable explanation for the findings described above. However, none of these studies directly demonstrated threat, the primary psychological state assumed to be induced by worldview disconfirmation. The concept of threat is central to many psychological theories, including dissonance theory (e.g., Festinger, 1957), social identity theory (Tajfel & Turner, 1986), TMT (Greenberg et al., 1997), and stereotype threat theory (Steele & Aronson, 1995), to name just a few. Despite its ubiquity as a central theoretical construct, attempts to directly measure the psychological experience of threat via self-reports have been notoriously unsuccessful. Self-report measures of threat, including measures of affect, threat emotions, and anxiety, often fail to show predicted effects (e.g., Matheson & Cole, 2004; Steele & Aronson, 1995). People often are unable to report when they feel threatened or, for a variety of reasons, they are unwilling to do so. Furthermore, many psychological threat defenses operate unconsciously. One way researchers have attempted to address this problem is by using physiological measures. For example, several studies showed that writing a counterattitudinal essay under high-choice conditions leads not only to attitude change, but also to heightened physiological arousal, as indexed by elevated galvanic skin responses (Elkin & Leippe, 1986; Losch & Cacioppo, 1990).

According to the biopsychosocial (BPS) model of challenge and threat (Blascovich & Tomaka, 1996), psychological states of challenge and threat can be indexed by distinct patterns of cardiovascular reactivity (CVR) and hormonal responses during motivated performance situations. Based on an integration of Dienstbier's (1989) physiological toughness model and Lazarus and Folkman's (1984) appraisal theory, the BPS model relies on relative activation of the sympathetic adrenal medullary (SAM) axis and the hypothalamic pituitary adrenal cortical (HPA) axis to differentiate challenge and threat states. Challenge states (when resources are appraised as exceeding demands) are dominated by SAM activation. In contrast, threat states (when demands are appraised as exceeding resources) are dominated by HPA activation.

CV responses mediated via SAM activation are characterized by enhanced cardiac performance, particularly left ventricle contractility (VC) and cardiac output (CO), and additionally, increases in epinephrine that result in vasodilation or decreased systemic vascular resistance (total peripheral resistance; TPR). In contrast, threat is associated not only with SAM activation, but also with HPA activation, which is associated with increases in cortisol. Additionally, increases in norepinephrine in threat states inhibit vasodilation and often produce vasoconstriction (i.e., increases in TPR). Challenge is regarded as physiologically more adaptive because the body is able to utilize the increased blood flow, whereas threat is regarded as maladaptive because the body is unable to use increased blood flow due to TPR levels remaining static or increasing from baseline. Challenge and threat states are sometimes, but not always, associated with positive and negative affective states, approach and avoidance motivations, and differences in task performance and nonverbal behavior.

In a recent set of experiments we capitalized on insights from BPS theory to directly test the hypothesis that worldview disconfirmation leads to a psychological state of threat (Townsend, Major, Sawyer, & Mendes, 2009). We hypothesized that members of low-status groups would exhibit greater threat, as evidenced by their pattern of CVR (i.e., higher TPR, lower CO), when interacting with a partner who expressed attitudes that were inconsistent with their status ideology compared to when interacting with a partner who expressed attitudes that were consistent with their status ideology. Furthermore, we hypothesized that this pattern should be evident both among those who endorse meritocracy interacting with a prejudiced partner, and among those who reject meritocracy interacting with a nonprejudiced partner. To test this hypothesis, we conducted two experiments. In both experiments, members of a low-status group (Latino American women in Experiment 1, European American women in Experiment 2) interacted with a confederate who was a member of a higher status group (European American women in Experiment 1, European American men in Experiment 2). In addition, the confederate either did or did not express attitudes that were prejudiced toward the participant's ethnic or gender group. Participants' attitudes and beliefs about the system (the extent to which they believed in individual mobility and believed that status differences are legitimate) were assessed several weeks prior to the experiments. Participants' CVR was assessed while they interacted with the confederate.

Consistent with predictions from WVT, interacting with a prejudiced other induced a threat pattern of CVR among individuals who endorsed meritocracy but not among those who rejected meritocracy beliefs. Conversely, interacting with a nonprejudiced partner induced a threat pattern of CVR among individuals who rejected meritocracy but not among those who endorsed meritocracy. These findings illustrate how people's general attitudes and beliefs about status in society can influence their psychological and physiological experiences during specific intergroup interactions. Encountering prejudice in interactions with higher status out-groups is inconsistent with the status ideology of those who believe the system is based on merit, and hence elicits feelings of threat. In contrast, the absence of prejudice in interactions with higher status out-groups violates the status ideology of those who believe the system is discriminatory, causing them to experience threat.

CONCLUSION

The idea that people are motivated to maintain consistency in their attitudes and beliefs has a long tradition within social psychology. Evidence from a number of areas of research has converged to demonstrate that consistency is vital for maintaining feelings of certainty, predictability, and control, and that inconsistency is affectively negative and physiologically arousing. The research reviewed in this chapter extends prior work on the motivation for consistency in new directions. It suggests that in addition to desiring consistency between our attitudes and behaviors and in our self-views, we are also motivated to maintain consistency in our worldviews. In particular, people seek consistency between their attitudes and beliefs about status in society and their experiences, and are threatened (as indexed by lower self-esteem and patterns of cardiovascular reactivity) by experiences that disconfirm their ideas about status relations. Importantly, the threat induced by inconsistency occurs even when the experience is objectively positive (e.g., an out-group evaluator is not prejudiced). These findings illustrate why intergroup relations are so resistant to change.

REFERENCES

Anson, J., Pyszczynski, T., Solomon, S., & Greenberg, J. (2009). Political ideology in post-9/11 America: A terror management perspective on maintenance and change of the status quo. In J. T. Jost, A. C. Kay, & H. Thorisdottir (Eds.), *Social and psychological bases of ideology and system justification* (pp. 210–240). New York: Oxford University Press.

Blascovich, J., & Tomaka, J. (1996). The biopsychosocial model of arousal regulation. In M. Zanna (Ed.), *Advances in experimental social psychology* (Vol. 28, pp. 1–51). San Diego, CA: Academic Press.

Bobo, L., & Hutchings, V. L. (1996). Perceptions of racial group competition: Extending Blumer's theory of group position to a multiracial social context. *American Sociological Review, 61,* 951–972.

Crandall, C. S. (1994). Prejudice against fat people: Ideology and self-interest. *Journal of Personality and Social Psychology, 66*, 882–894.

Crocker, J., & Major, B. (1989). Social stigma and self-esteem: The self-protective properties of stigma. *Psychological Review, 96*, 608–630.

Dienstbier, R. A. (1989). Arousal and physiological toughness: Implications for mental and physical health. *Psychological Review, 96*, 84–100.

Eidelman, S., & Crandall, C. S. (2009). A psychological advantage for the status quo. In J. T. Jost, A. C. Kay, & H. Thorisdottir (Eds.), *Social and psychological bases of ideology and system justification* (pp. 85–106). New York: Oxford University Press.

Elkin, R. A., & Leippe, M. R. (1986). Physiological arousal, dissonance, and attitude change: Evidence for a dissonance-arousal link and a "don't remind me" effect. *Journal of Personality and Social Psychology, 51*, 55–65.

Festinger, L. (1957). *A theory of cognitive dissonance*. Stanford, CA: Stanford University Press.

Foster, M. D., Sloto, L., & Ruby, R. (2006). Responding to discrimination as a function of meritocracy beliefs and personal experiences: Testing the model of shattered assumptions. *Group Processes & Intergroup Relations, 9*, 401–411.

Foster, M. D., & Tsarfati, E. M. (2005). The effects of meritocracy beliefs on women's well-being after first-time gender discrimination. *Personality and Social Psychology Bulletin, 31*, 1730–1738.

Frey, R. A., & Powell, L. A. (2005). Beyond left-right ideology in the study of justice perception: Interdependent and independent distributive worldviews in Jamaica and New Zealand. *Journal of Cross-Cultural Psychology, 36*, 117–146.

Furnham, A., & Proctor, E. (1989). Belief in a just world: Review and critique of the individual difference literature. *British Journal of Social Psychology, 28*, 365–384.

Greenberg, J., Solomon, S., & Pyszczynski, T. (1997). Terror management theory of self-esteem and cultural worldviews: Empirical assessments and conceptual refinements. In M. P. Zanna (Ed.), *Advances in experimental social psychology* (Vol. 29, pp. 61–139). San Diego, CA: Academic Press.

Greenwald, A. G., & Ronis, D. L. (1978). Twenty years of cognitive dissonance: Case study in the evolution of a theory. *Psychological Review, 85*, 53–57.

Heider, F. (1946). Attitudes and cognitive organization. *Journal of Psychology, 21*, 107–112.

Heider, F. (1958). *The psychology of interpersonal relations*. Hoboken, NJ: Wiley.

Heine, S. J., Proulx, T., & Vohs, K. (2006). The meaning maintenance model: On the coherence of social motivations. *Personality and Social Psychology Review, 10*, 88–110.

Hogg, M. A., & Abrams, D. (1988). *Social identifications: A social psychology of intergroup relations and group processes*. London: Routledge.

Jost, J. T., & Banaji, M. R. (1994). The role of stereotyping in system justification and the production of false consciousness. *British Journal of Social Psychology, 33*, 1–27.

Jost, J. T., Burgess, D., & Mosso, C. O. (2001). Conflicts of legitimation among self, group, and system: The integrative potential of system justification theory. In J. T. Jost & B. Major (Eds.), *The psychology of legitimacy: Emerging perspectives on ideology, justice, and intergroup relationships* (pp. 363–388). New York: Cambridge University Press.

Jost, J. T., & Hunyady, O. (2002). The psychology of system justification and the palliative function of ideology. In W. Stroebe & M. Hewstone (Eds.), *European review of social psychology* (Vol. 13, pp. 111–153). Hove, England: Psychology Press.

Kaiser, C. R., Dyrenforth, P. S., & Hagiwara, N. (2006). Why are attributions to discrimination interpersonally costly? A test of system and group justifying motivations. *Personality and Social Psychology Bulletin, 32*, 1523–1536.

Kaiser, C. R., & Pratt-Hyatt, J. S. (2009). Distributing prejudice unequally: Do Whites direct their prejudice toward strongly identified minorities? *Journal of Personality and Social Psychology, 96*, 432–445.

Katz, I., & Hass, R. G. (1988). Racial ambivalence and American value conflict: Correlational and priming studies of dual cognitive structures. *Journal of Personality and Social Psychology, 55*, 893–905.

Kluegel, J. R., & Smith, E. R. (1986). *Beliefs about inequality: Americans' views of what is and what ought to be.* New York: Aldine de Gruyter.

Koltko-Rivera, M. E. (2004). The psychology of worldviews. *Review of General Psychology, 8*, 3–58.

Lazarus, R. S., & Folkman, S. (1984). *Stress, appraisal, and coping.* New York: Springer.

Lerner, M. J. (1980). *The belief in a just world: A fundamental delusion.* New York: Plenum Press.

Levy, S. R., Chiu, C.-y., & Hong, Y.-y. (2006). Lay theories and intergroup relations. *Group Processes & Intergroup Relations, 9*(1), 5–24.

Losch, M., & Cacioppo, J. (1990). Cognitive dissonance may enhance sympathetic tonus, but attitudes are changed to reduce negative affect rather than arousal. *Journal of Experimental Social Psychology, 26*, 289–304.

Major, B. (1994). From social inequality to personal entitlement: The role of social comparisons, legitimacy appraisals, and group membership. In M. P. Zanna (Ed.), *Advances in experimental social psychology* (Vol. 26, pp. 293–355). San Diego, CA: Academic Press.

Major, B., Gramzow, R., McCoy, S. K., Levin, S., Schmader, T., & Sidanius, J. (2002). Perceiving personal discrimination: The role of group status and status legitimizing ideology. *Journal of Personality and Social Psychology, 80*, 782–796.

Major, B., Kaiser, C. R., O'Brien, L., & McCoy, S. K. (2007). Perceived discrimination as worldview threat or worldview confirmation: Implications for self-esteem. *Journal of Personality and Social Psychology, 92*, 1068–1086.

Major, B., & Schmader, T. (2001). Legitimacy and the construal of social disadvantage. In J. Jost & B. Major (Eds.), *The psychology of legitimacy: Emerging perspectives on ideology, justice, and intergroup relationships* (pp. 176–204). New York: Cambridge University Press.

Major, B., & Townsend, S. S. M. (2010). [Correlations between status justifying beliefs and expectations of being a target of prejudice]. Unpublished raw data.

Matheson, K., & Cole, B. (2004). Coping with a threatened group identity: Psychological and neuroendocrine responses. *Journal of Experimental Social Psychology, 40*, 777–786.

McCoy, S. K., & Major, B. (2007). Priming meritocracy and the psychological justification of inequality. *Journal of Experimental Social Psychology, 43*, 341–351.

Mendes, W. B., Blascovich, J., Hunter, S., Lickel, B., & Jost, J. T. (2007). Threatened by the unexpected: Physiological responses during social interactions with expectancy-violating partners. *Journal of Personality and Social Psychology, 92*, 698–716.

O'Brien, L., & Major, B. (2005). System justifying beliefs and psychological well-being: The role of group status and identity. *Personality and Social Psychology Bulletin, 31*, 1718–1729.

O'Brien, L. T., & Major, B. (2009). The impact of group status and status-legitimizing beliefs on feelings of personal entitlement. In J. T. Jost, A. C. Kay, & H. Thorisdottir (Eds.), *Social and psychological bases of ideology and system justification.* New York: Oxford University Press.

Olson, J. M., Roese, N. J., & Zanna, M. P. (1996). Expectancies. In E. T. Higgins & A. W. Kruglanski (Eds.), *Social psychology: Handbook of basic principles* (pp. 211–238). New York: Guilford Press.

Plaks, J. E., & Stecher, K. (2007). Unexpected improvement, decline, and stasis: A prediction confidence perspective on achievement success and failure. *Journal of Personality and Social Psychology, 93*, 667–684.

Plaut, V. C., Markus, H. R., & Lachman, M. E. (2002). Place matters: Consensual features and regional variation in American well-being and self. *Journal of Personality and Social Psychology, 83,* 160–184.

Ridgeway, C. (2001). The emergence of status beliefs: From structural inequality to legitimizing ideology. In J. Jost & B. Major (Eds.), *The psychology of legitimacy: Emerging perspectives on ideology, justice, and intergroup relations* (pp. 257–277). New York: Cambridge University Press.

Rubin, Z., & Peplau, L. A. (1975). Who believes in a just world? *Journal of Social Issues, 31,* 65–89.

Shweder, R. A. (1995). Cultural psychology: What is it? In N. R. Goldberger & J. B. Veroff (Eds.), *The culture and psychology reader* (pp. 41–86). New York: New York University Press.

Sidanius, J., & Pratto, F. (1993). The inevitability of oppression and the dynamics of social dominance. In P. Sniderman & P. E. Tetlock (Eds.), *Prejudice, politics, and race in America today* (pp. 173–211). Palo Alto, CA: Stanford University Press.

Steele, C. M., & Aronson, J. (1995). Stereotype threat and the intellectual test performance of African Americans. *Journal of Personality and Social Psychology, 69,* 797–811.

Swann, W. B., Jr. (1992). Seeking truth, finding despair: Some unhappy consequences of a negative self-concept. *Current Directions in Psychological Science, 1,* 15–18.

Swann, W. B. Jr., Rentfrow, P. J., & Guinn, J. (2003). Self-verification: The search for coherence. In M. Leary & J. Tangney (Eds.), *Handbook of self and identity* (pp. 367–383). New York: Guilford Press.

Tajfel, H., & Turner, J. C. (1986). The social identity theory of inter-group behavior. In S. Worchel & L. W. Austin (Eds.), *Psychology of intergroup relations*. Chicago: Nelson-Hall.

Townsend, S. S. M., Major, B., Sawyer, P. J., & Mendes, W. B. (2010). *Can the absence of prejudice be more threatening than its presence? It depends on one's worldview.* Manuscript submitted for publication.

Van den Bos, K., & Lind, E. A. (2002). Uncertainty management by means of fairness judgments. In M. P. Zanna (Ed.), *Advances in experimental social psychology* (pp. 1–60). San Diego, CA: Academic Press.

Weber, M. (1992). *The Protestant ethic and the spirit of capitalism* (T. Parsons, Trans.). London: Routledge. (Original work published 1905)

Zanna, M., & Cooper, J. (1974). Dissonance and the pill: An attribution approach to studying the arousal properties of dissonance. *Journal of Personality and Social Psychology, 29,* 703–709.

AUTHOR NOTE

Please address all correspondence in connection with this paper to Brenda Major, at the Department of Psychology, University of California Santa Barbara, Santa Barbara, CA, 93106-9660, USA; e-mail major@psych.ucsb.edu.

16

The Self and Intergroup Attitudes
Connecting "Fragile" Personal and Collective Self-Concepts

FREDERICK RHODEWALT AND BENJAMIN PETERSON

But the truth is, is that, our challenge is to get people persuaded that we can make progress when there's not evidence of that in their daily lives...And it's not surprising then they get bitter, they cling to guns or religion or antipathy to people who aren't like them or anti-immigrant sentiment or anti-trade sentiment as a way to explain their frustrations. (Barack Obama, April 6, 2008)

In this highly publicized comment during a fundraiser early in his presidential campaign, Obama hints at a general perception that individuals who are alienated or frustrated due to their circumstances may embrace group identities and corresponding attitudes in an effort to feel better about their situation. Is this the case? If so, are certain individuals more vulnerable to frustrations that sometimes encourage hostility and antipathy toward other groups? Or, are group identities and intergroup attitudes driven by a qualitatively different process than personal goals and individual frustration? We suggest the answer is a qualified "yes" to the former question—specifically, it may be those who pursue particular self-related goals who are most likely to exemplify the kind of person described in the quote.

In this chapter, we explore how the nature of the self-concept and personal goal pursuit influence interpersonal and intergroup perceptions, both at the individual and collective levels of self-construal. More specifically, we describe what we call the "fragile" self (e.g., Rhodewalt & Peterson, 2008) and discuss its potential characteristics within both personal and group identities. We then link the defensive aspect of fragile self-concepts to attitudes toward others (and out-groups in particular), and introduce a new model of functional self-regulation through group identity and intergroup attitudes. Finally, we present new data that begin to test the general structure of the model, including the common elements of fragile personal and collective identities across two important groups (nation and religion).

Throughout this discussion of the self and intergroup attitudes, we attempt to demonstrate that identity is never a unitary construction. Just as we should avoid concentrating solely on level of personal self-esteem (i.e., is it also narcissistic or fragile?), we should also avoid concentrating solely on level of identification with a social group (i.e., what functions are served by the identity?). For example, national identity may be more or less nationalistic (e.g., Kosterman & Feshbach, 1989), while religious identity may be more or less fundamentalist (e.g., Altemeyer & Hunsberger, 1992). In the end, the important goals that are pursued and the functions that group identities come to serve for the individual, above and beyond level of self-esteem or group identification, have important implications for intergroup attitudes and relations between groups.

To illustrate this perspective, we focus in particular on goals and beliefs relevant to narcissism (Morf & Rhodewalt, 2001), such as superiority, competitiveness, entitlement, and recognition, versus more universal and adaptive motives related to acceptance, belonging, and affiliation. Our main thesis is that fragile selves, united by commonalities in content, structure, and goal-pursuit across levels, leave individuals vulnerable to self-concept threat, which may be defended against through hostile intergroup attitudes. Thus, what unites the narcissist and the nationalist, for example, is the common pursuit of superiority goals and the use of the national group to further such goals, often resulting in hostile attitudes toward other groups perceived as threatening that superiority.

THE "FRAGILE" SELF

The starting point for the model and research presented in this chapter is that the self is a construct that connects the individual to his or her social environment through motivated and strategic interpersonal behavior. We argue that much of our social behavior is in the service of *interpersonal* self-regulation (Rhodewalt & Peterson, 2008), which includes seeking and interpreting interpersonal feedback that protects and maintains desired self-conceptions and related self-esteem. It is the individual's self-concept that is being "regulated" through interactions with others, as well as the interpretation of others' reactions to them. The key question in this view involves how an individual uses the interpersonal (and even intergroup) environment to assist in the process of defining and constructing the self and affirming important beliefs and goals.

We contend that "self-regulation" processes are triggered when social cues signal that impending events are self-relevant. Far from a passive entity, the self-system works by actively operating on information received from the environment (reactive regulation), while also actively manipulating the information it is exposed to (proactive regulation). Personal motives and goals connect self-knowledge to self-regulation and direct the situations that are ultimately chosen, strategies and actions that are pursued, and standards of progress (success/failure) that are monitored (e.g., Cantor, 1990; Dweck, Higgins, & Grant-Pillow, 2003).

Thus, a central element of self-regulation is a strategic use of the social environment to garner support for one's desired self-conceptions. All people require social feedback to support their self-concept and self-esteem and, at times, actively seek such feedback. For many individuals, regulation of the self through interpersonal negotiation is adaptive (Hardin & Higgins, 1996; Leary & Baumeister, 2000; Swann, 1983), in that it builds predictability and positive social connectedness. For some, however, other people are relied on too much for self-definition, such that self-worth is defined solely by success in obtaining recognition, regard, approval, and/or acceptance (see also Crocker & Park, 2004; Deci & Ryan, 1995).

As the self becomes more fragile, such individuals rely more on social feedback to sustain their self-concepts, leaving them open to vulnerability and instability in self-esteem (Crocker & Wolfe, 2001; Kernis, 2003). Fragile self-esteem is contingent on meeting external or introjected standards, or too focused on a particular domain of importance. Fragile self-esteem is contingent on meeting external or introjected standards, or it is too focused on a particular domain of importance to the self. Although people seek affirmation on any number of characteristics and competencies, certain self-domains are more likely to impact intergroup attitudes in this process. Most relevant to the present discussion is the idea that people with fragile self-concepts often use their interpersonal relations to pursue social goals such as approval or superiority, and we have asked two central questions related to this. First, do these social goals differentially influence people's intergroup attitudes (e.g., Katz, 1960; Smith, Bruner, & White, 1956)? Second, can we identify those individuals most likely to respond to threats to the self by endorsing hostile intergroup attitudes?

The Fragile Personal Self: Narcissism

Our research suggests that individual differences in narcissism might serve as a personal marker of goals and behaviors that lead to the employment of hostile intergroup attitudes in the service of the self. Narcissists possess characteristics including (a) grandiosity, self-importance, and perceived uniqueness; (b) preoccupations with fantasies of unlimited success, wealth, beauty, and power; (c) exhibitionism and attention seeking; and (d) emotional lability in response to criticism or self-esteem threat, often manifesting in feelings of rage, shame, or humiliation (*DSM-IV-TR*, American Psychiatric Association, 2000). According to the *DSM-IV-TR*, narcissists are also prone to interpersonal difficulties likely attributable to their own interpersonal style. The *DSM-IV-TR* also specifies that narcissistic self-esteem is "almost invariably very fragile; the person may be preoccupied with how well he or she is doing and how well he or she is regarded by others" (p. 350).

The key point of our research is that it is useful to characterize narcissism as a set of processes concerned with interpersonal *self*-regulation (Morf & Rhodewalt, 2001; Rhodewalt & Peterson, 2008). There is an accumulating and broad research base supporting this model of narcissism, though most relevant to the present discussion is a set of findings that suggest that narcissists (a) have self-esteem that is positive but fragile, and more reactive to social feedback than that of less narcissistic individuals; (b) pursue social, interaction goals that involve seeking admiration and superiority as opposed to approval and acceptance; and (c) are more likely than others to respond with hostility and aggression when their selves are threatened (see Rhodewalt & Peterson, 2009, for a review).

Most pertinent to the present discussion is the fact that narcissists are not interested in just any positive feedback, but most of all feedback that *affirms* their perceived superiority. For example, on Crocker and Wolfe's (2001) Contingencies of Self-Worth Scale, the only domain on which narcissists consistently report basing their self-worth is the general domain of "competition" (Rhodewalt, Tragakis, & Peterson, 2003). Narcissists also report feeling most socially integrated when they feel admired and influential in a group (Rhodewalt, 2005).

Given this interpersonal orientation, it is not surprising that narcissism has been linked to hostility and aggression under conditions of self-threat. In general, narcissists hold negative evaluations of others, especially when those others threaten the narcissist in some way (Kernis & Sun, 1994; Morf & Rhodewalt, 1993). More to the point, Bushman and Baumeister (1998; see also Twenge & Campbell, 2003) showed that narcissists respond with greater aggression when threatened by their target. Thus, there is clear evidence that in response to threat at the interpersonal level, narcissists display greater hostility and aggression, and that such responses are linked to a desire to be viewed as superior.

The Fragile Collective Self: Nationalism and Fundamentalism

As we see through the discussion of narcissism, one example of how the self can be "fragile" is when it embodies an overriding concern with being better than other people (relative superiority, competition). Superiority goals necessitate constant vigilance in the social environment and leave the individual vulnerable to self-esteem threats, as it is difficult to always match up to others in the way one desires (while also receiving the desired public recognition for this perceived "greatness"). These threats elicit defensive self-regulatory behaviors, including hostile attitudes, derogation, and aggression.

We contend that this concern with relative superiority is not unique to the personal self. Goals involving the superiority of one's group also leave the collective self (or social identity; Tajfel & Turner, 1986) fragile and vulnerable (e.g., Brewer, 2001). For example, Brewer (1999) proposed several criteria for how "in-group love" can also breed hate and antagonism toward other groups, including perceptions of one's group as superior and sensitivity to threats from outside the group (see also Eidelson and Eidelson, 2003; Struch and Schwartz, 1989). This picture of a fragile, defensive group identity with a sense of superiority and entitlement attached to it is very similar to characteristics commonly displayed in narcissists.

How do these superiority concerns manifest themselves in important group identities? Relating specifically to the national group, a growing amount of research has focused on the distinction between patriotism and nationalism (e.g., Federico, Golec, & Dial, 2005; Kosterman & Feshbach, 1989). In terms of national loyalty, patriotism corresponds to selfless in-group love, while nationalism incorporates a selfish superiority and dominance associated with intergroup hostility (Worchel & Coutant, 1997). With regard to religious identity, there is also a history of attempts to differentiate a more secure and selfless attachment from one that is as much about the self and excluding others who are different (e.g., Allport & Ross, 1967; Batson & Burris, 1994). The most popular construct used to distinguish a defensive, fragile type of religiosity is religious fundamentalism (Altemeyer & Hunsberger, 1992, 2004). Fundamentalists may be best characterized as defensively certain about the "rightness" of their chosen religious beliefs, which may also mask (or enable) a belief in the superiority of the group with those beliefs (Peterson, 2008b). Like nationalism, fundamentalism is related to hostile attitudes toward out-groups, including other religions (Altemeyer, 2003) and those whose lifestyles may challenge the beliefs of the in-group (e.g., homosexuals; Hunsberger, 1996).

Recent research has begun to explore this connection between a fragile personal self and group identity, and its implications. For example, individuals who tend to see themselves as superior to others in general also tend to see their groups as superior to other groups (Gramzow & Gaertner, 2005; Hornsey, 2003; Stangor & Thompson, 2002). In a recent set of studies (Peterson, White, & Rhodewalt, 2008b), we found that narcissists were more likely to see an important in-group (students at their university) as more representative of an inclusive category (university students in general) relative to a rival group. This tendency toward "in-group projection" is seen as a form of collective superiority (Wenzel, Mummendey, Weber, & Waldzus, 2003). Finally, Peterson (2008c) has demonstrated that narcissism (especially entitlement) is moderately correlated with nationalism and negative attitudes toward immigrants. Weaver (2006) has even described nationalism as "national narcissism."

We argue that this evidence suggests a "transfer" of personal beliefs and goals to important group identities. If this is the case, narcissists could potentially use such identities to assist in defensive self-regulation through verification and defense of their perceived superiority, especially when threatened.

Intergroup Attitudes as Defensive Self-Regulation

This discussion of "fragile" selves—including narcissism, nationalism, and fundamentalism—emphasizes that perceived threats to the self-concept can initiate defensive response, including hostile attitudes toward, and negative evaluations of, other individuals and groups. Indeed, a growing body of research demonstrates that threats to self-esteem encourage intergroup bias and discrimination (e.g., Cialdini & Richardson, 1980; Jordan, Spencer, & Zanna, 2005; Jordan, Spencer, Zanna, Hoshino-Brown, & Correll, 2003; McGregor, Zanna, Holmes, & Spencer, 2001), as well as derogation of out-group members (e.g., Crocker, Thompson, McGraw, & Ingerman, 1987; Fein & Spencer, 1997). For example, using both real and experimentally created groups, Crocker and colleagues (1987) found that high self-esteem participants are more likely to derogate an out-group member following threat. In a similar study, Fein and Spencer (1997) demonstrated the motivational aspect of such out-group derogation, as this response was mitigated when participants were given an opportunity to self-affirm important values following the threat.

More recently, Jordan and colleagues (2005) found a subset of high self-esteem individuals who also had low implicit self-esteem (Greenwald & Banaji, 1995) to be most likely to discriminate against an out-group member following the threat (see also Kernis et al., 2005). It is noteworthy that other research has connected this combination of high explicit/low implicit self-esteem to narcissism (Jordan et al., 2003). Finally, recent research by Peterson, White, and Rhodewalt (2008a) on policy attitudes involving illegal immigration, terrorism, and same-sex marriage found hostile attitudes and support for discriminatory policy to be highly related to perceived personal threat from members of the related out-groups (illegal Mexican immigrants, Arabs/Muslims, and same-sex couples). This perceived threat also strongly correlated with both nationalism and fundamentalism, and accounted for a significant portion of the variance in the relationship between these constructs and hostile attitudes and policy support.

In sum, research suggests that the relationship between fragile selves (personal and collective) and hostile intergroup attitudes may be both mediated and moderated by threat, such that these individuals tend to perceive other groups as more threatening (mediation) and are more reactive to situational threats (moderation).

CONNECTING THE PERSONAL AND COLLECTIVE: A FUNCTIONAL MODEL OF GROUP IDENTITY AND INTERGROUP ATTITUDES

With a growing emphasis on newer "process" models of personality (e.g., Cantor, 1990; Mischel & Shoda, 1995) and the self-concept (Rhodewalt & Peterson, 2008) that emphasize goals and characteristic patterns of goal pursuit in different situations, it may be fruitful to apply such thinking to group identity as well. For example, group identities may be viewed as outlets, or "situations," in which individuals characteristically pursue goals, with differential intergroup outcomes depending on the nature of those goals. Just like any other situation, the group context can be seen as an "if...then" contingency (Mischel & Shoda, 1995) that allows full expression of personal beliefs, goals, and motives. As such, the self is dynamically involved in situations and groups we find ourselves in or choose to seek out. Many of these newer functional models of self and personality (e.g., Snyder & Cantor, 1998) emphasize the role that goals play in the expression of our personality, which is often reflected in the situations that we choose (i.e., places to live, work, socialize, and possibly groups to identify with). Thus, a group identity may serve as an affordance that is chosen and/or constructed by the individual, an outlet for self-expression and self-regulation toward important goals.

Extending the description of the fragile self outlined earlier, group identities may provide a means to address personal threats indirectly by shifting to another domain still congruent with the threatened goals and beliefs (Tesser, 2000). In other words, a group identity could facilitate defensive self-regulation and help restore self-esteem. If goals are threatened and self-esteem falls in the interpersonal domain, it may be possible to "shift" up to the collective level (to *self-categorize* in relation to an important group; e.g., Turner et al., 1994) and mount a defense in the intergroup domain (i.e., through hostile attitudes toward threatening groups). It is important that all people pursue goals interpersonally, though we often differ on the content and nature of our goals. If group identity can aid self-regulation, this would be expected regardless of the specific nature of the goals involved. People should look for groups that are consistent with their self-beliefs and goals, and construe established identities in a manner consistent with these (e.g., Swann, Polzer, Seyle, & Ko, 2004; Wright, Aron, & Tropp, 2002). Thus, the expectation is that this is a general process independent of the nature of the self-concept.

But, more interesting predictions come into play if personal goals relate to protecting a fragile self. That is because the associated goals and beliefs (i.e., grandiose, unrealistic, concerned with superiority) tend to leave the individual vulnerable to threat in the interpersonal environment. When considered in relation to the self-regulatory potential of group identities, this has several important implications beyond the general process. First, the reasons driving pursuit of a certain group identity should be similar to those beliefs and goals that cause problems interpersonally. This would not only influence the nature of group identity, but also leave it vulnerable to threats like we see with the personal identity. Second, since those with fragile selves are more vulnerable to threats that necessitate use of defensive self-regulatory strategies, they should be more likely to turn to defensive group identities and attitudes if they effectively address personal threats. Finally, the defensive identity should allow a transfer of strategies from the interpersonal domain to the intergroup domain. Thus, threats to personal superiority often associated with interpersonal aggression could translate into derogation and hostility toward a threatening out-group in a context that affords such behavior.

We offer a *functional* approach (see also Williams, Chen, & Wegener, this volume) to identify how personal goals connect to group identity and influence the nature of intragroup and intergroup behavior (Peterson, 2008b). Our functional approach calls on both classic analyses of attitude functions (Katz, 1960; Snyder & DeBono, 1989) and more recent proposals for "key" motives of group identity within the social identity approach (e.g., Baumeister & Leary, 1995; Brewer, 1991; Hogg, 2000; Swann et al., 2004; Wright et al., 2002). Katz (1960) originally proposed four main functions that attitudes may serve (instrumental-adjustive, knowledge, value-expressive, and ego-defensive), with several important qualifications: (a) A given attitude may serve different functions for different people; (b) some attitudes may serve a variety of functions for the same person; and (c) the strength of these functions tends to differ across people. More recently, researchers have made varying attempts to apply a functional logic to groups and group identities.

Some have taken a "primary" motive approach, where one particular motive is isolated as the basic and most important reason for group identity. Motives that have been proposed include self-esteem (Tajfel & Turner, 1986), self-verification (Swann et al., 2004), self-expansion (Wright et al., 2002), uncertainty reduction (Hogg, 2000), meaning and the management of existential terror (Greenberg, Solomon, & Pyszczynski, 1997), the need to belong (Leary & Baumeister, 1995), and an optimal balance between inclusion and distinctiveness (Brewer, 1991).

While all of these are important, we feel this importance varies across individuals and groups.

Others have attempted to classify types of groups according to common functions they tend to serve (Aharpour & Brown, 2002; Deaux, Reid, Mizrahi, & Cotting, 1999; Johnson et al., 2006). For example, Deaux and colleagues (1999) generated a variety of possible functions and assessed them in several known groups to compare the relative emphasis on each by type of group. They found that, on average, functions tend to vary between groups in different "clusters." Rather than arguing for one primary function regardless of group, these researchers argue that groups generally differ on the functions they serve for members. This makes sense but is akin to arguing that certain attitudes only serve certain functions. Even though a group identity may be more likely to serve a particular function on average, this overlooks the potential for individual variability within most groups on identity functions. We feel it is equally important to recognize variability within group identities that might help distinguish more adaptive loyalty from defensive forms associated with intergroup hostility.

For the purposes of this research, we developed a conception of group identity functions more in line with previous work on attitude functions. Individuals may differ in the extent to which a group identity serves any given function, and the same identity can serve different functions for different group members (and multiple functions for any one member). Consistent with our emphasis on the importance of the fragile self to intergroup processes, we also felt it was important to distinguish an identity function that would be in line with goals involving relative superiority and competition (i.e., similar to Katz's "ego-defensive" function). Certain ways of construing group identity may help such an individual feel more superior, especially if personal feelings of superiority are constantly threatened or disconfirmed. This ego-defensive function builds on what has been proposed thus far: Group identity may serve as an outlet for threatened goals and beliefs involving relative superiority when they are in need of defense or affirmation. Group identity could then be added to the "arsenal" of defensive self-regulatory strategies at the individual's disposal (Tesser, 2000).[1]

Initial evidence for a defensive identity function was provided by Peterson (2008a), who followed supporters of a university football team over the course of the season. He assessed their reasons for following the team (akin to group identity functions) prior to the season and found that those emphasizing more competitive reasons based on esteem and dominance over others were more emotionally reactive (pride, anger, shame) after wins and losses—which support or threaten this function—and also displayed more hostile attitudes toward a rival university. In contrast, those who followed the team for more social and affiliative reasons did not display such reactivity and hostility. This competitive-esteem function of the sports team appears to be fragile, and the likelihood of endorsing such group-level motives was significantly related to narcissism. We attempted to build off of these findings, applying our ideas to more consequential group identities (nation and religion) and related attitudes and using a more theory-driven tool to assess our proposed identity functions.

Further Test of the Model

Based on our previous research (Peterson & Rhodewalt, 2009), we developed a scale to measure five broad group functions: verification, certainty-meaning, expansion, social connection, and superiority (defense).[2] The Functions of Group Identity Scale is a 26-item scale comprising a list of potential psychological functions that individuals may *perceive* a group identity serving. Items were generated a priori to represent the five function categories, though subsequent factor analysis led us to combine most of the verification and certainty-meaning items into a single *verification-certainty* function. Such a pattern is consistent with Swann's (1983) conception of self-verification as a means to achieve a sense of certainty and control in one's social world. Examples of items include "support for beliefs about myself," "sense of certainty about myself and others" (*verification-certainty*); "assistance in the pursuit of personal goals," "gaining perspectives beyond my own" (*expansion*); "connections with other people," "inclusion and acceptance" (*social connection*); and "status in relation to others who are different," "sense of importance" (*superiority*). The scale was constructed such that different groups could be substituted in the instructions. The four function subscales demonstrated adequate internal consistency across both identities assessed (nation α = .87–.93; religion α = .83–.93).

We administered the Functions of Group Identity Scale in two survey studies that differed only in the group identity assessed and out-groups targeted. Participants (N = 297 in Study 1, N = 210 in Study 2) first completed several questionnaires on various personal constructs, including self-esteem, narcissism, competitiveness, need for closure, and need to belong. Then, several days later, they completed another set of questionnaires regarding their group identity, perceived identity functions, and attitudes about three relevant out-groups. For national identity (Study 1), nationalism versus patriotism (Kosterman & Feshbach, 1989) was assessed in addition to the general identity questions. For religious identity (Study 2), degree of fundamentalism (Peterson, 2008b) was also assessed. For each out-group in both studies, we assessed perceptions of threat and uncertainty in addition to attitudes to determine (a) if certain goals and identity functions were more susceptible to these factors, and (b) if they play some role in stimulating intergroup hostility.

The main purpose of this research was to gather a large amount of data in relation to two important identities and test the relationships proposed in the functional model. Thus, it was hypothesized that narcissism (due to an overriding concern with relative superiority) would connect to both national and religious identity through a defensive function that allows such individuals to feel superior through their group. Further, such an orientation to one's group identity should leave the narcissist vulnerable to threat in the intergroup arena, encouraging hostile attitudes in defense of their fragile self-concept (personal and collective). On the other hand, narcissists were not expected to pursue group identities for reasons involving social connection, though this function was predicted to be most adaptive for intergroup relations. We present the results of each study separately, focusing on the hypotheses previously presented and the connection between personal and collective fragility in each. We then briefly discuss similarities and differences in results between the two group identities.

NATIONAL IDENTITY AND
INTERGROUP ATTITUDES (STUDY 1)

Narcissism, Competitiveness, and National Identity Functions

As previous research has shown, narcissism was significantly related to competitiveness ($r = .42$). In most of the relationships that we looked at, narcissism and competitiveness predicted similar outcomes, and controlling for competitiveness often reduced narcissism's association with the outcomes of interest. Thus, narcissists' concern with relative superiority appears to account for much of the relationship between narcissism and the "fragile" identity elements and hostile intergroup attitudes. Also consistent with prior research, narcissism correlated moderately with self-esteem ($r = .35$).[3]

Given that narcissism was associated with personal superiority goals, we next examined the relations between narcissism and the four identity functions by regressing all functions simultaneously on narcissism. Only the superiority function independently predicted narcissism ($\beta = .28$), while none of the identity functions related independently to self-esteem. Replicating previous research (e.g., Peterson, 2008c), narcissism was a significant independent predictor of nationalism ($\beta = .24$), but not patriotism ($\beta = .08$). On the other hand, self-esteem was related to patriotism ($\beta = .12$), but not nationalism ($\beta = -.02$). Thus, a fragile personal self (narcissism) appears to connect to multiple aspects of a fragile national identity (superiority identity function, nationalism) as hypothesized in the functional self-regulatory model.

Narcissism and Intergroup Attitudes

We assessed hostile attitudes toward Canadians, Iranians, and illegal immigrants, as well as perceptions of threat and uncertainty from each of these groups. Unless otherwise noted, patterns were generally similar across the three out-groups. Thus, for the sake of brevity, we report on general intergroup hostility, threat, and uncertainty, based on a composite score of ratings for each group.

Narcissism independently predicted hostility toward all three out-groups ($\beta = .17$), while self-esteem tended to encourage more positive attitudes ($\beta = -.16$). Narcissists also perceived more threat ($\beta = .14$) and uncertainty ($\beta = .13$) in this intergroup context, with self-esteem negatively related to uncertainty ($\beta = -.15$) and unrelated to perceived threat. Thus, narcissists perceive more threat and uncertainty from other groups, and defend against these threats by derogating these groups. To test this idea further, we conducted a mediation analysis (Baron & Kenny, 1986) with threat and uncertainty as mediators. Only perceived threat partially mediated the relationship (Sobel $z = 2.23$, $p < .05$; Sobel, 1982), with threat remaining a significant predictor of hostility ($\beta = .45$) and narcissism's relationship attenuated ($\beta = .10$).

National Identity Functions and Intergroup Attitudes

Next, we tested relationships between national identity functions, hostile intergroup attitudes, perceived threat, and uncertainty. The superiority function consistently predicted hostility toward out-groups (β = .32), as did verification-certainty (β = .24). On the other hand, the social connection function promoted more positive intergroup attitudes (β = −.25) relative to the other three functions. Expansion did not relate to intergroup hostility.

Additionally, the superiority function related to both perceived threat (β = .26) and uncertainty (β = .22) from out-groups. Verification-certainty independently predicted only greater uncertainty (β = .35), while belonging-affiliation predicted less uncertainty (β = −.28). Testing for mediation, perceived threat (β = .48) partially mediated the relationship between superiority and intergroup hostility (Sobel z = 3.12, p < .01; superiority β = .19), while uncertainty (β = .30) partially mediated the verification-certainty and hostility relationship (Sobel z = 2.23, p < .01; verification-certainty β = .13). Thus, similar to narcissism, those who base their national identity on a defensive superiority relative to the other functions also tend to display more intergroup hostility, and this is at least in part a defense against perceived threat that such concerns leave them vulnerable to. Further, consistent with the superiority function (and narcissism), nationalism predicted intergroup hostility (β = .64), perceived threat (β = .44), and uncertainty (β = .41). Consistent with the social connection function (and self-esteem), patriotism related to more positive attitudes (β = −.25) and less uncertainty (β = −.17).

Mediating Role of the Superiority Function

Finally, we explored connections between fragile personal and collective selves by testing whether a tendency to endorse the superiority identity function by narcissists accounted for a significant portion of subsequent relationships with threat and intergroup hostility. Here, the question is whether pursuing narcissistic goals of relative superiority through national group identity (by way of related identity functions) promotes a fragile identity that is vulnerable to threat from other groups and defended against through hostile attitudes.

First, we conducted a mediation analysis predicting perceived threat by including all four identity functions in the analysis along with narcissism, self-esteem, and the other controls. The superiority function (β = .24) emerged as a significant mediator, reducing narcissism's relationship to close to zero (β = .04; Sobel z = 1.85, p = .06). Then, a similar mediation analysis was conducted predicting hostile attitudes. In support of the model, superiority (β = .27) mediated of the narcissist's hostility (see Figure 16.1), significantly attenuating the narcissism-hostility relationship (β = .10; Sobel z = 2.17, p < .05).

In summary, as predicted by our model, narcissism was related to nationalism, perceived threat in the intergroup context, and hostile intergroup attitudes, and much of this was accounted for by the tendency to pursue goals involving relative superiority through national identity. In contrast, personal self-esteem (independent of narcissism) and collective orientations involving social connection and patriotism proved more adaptive in the intergroup context. We next tested if these patterns would replicate in religious group identity.

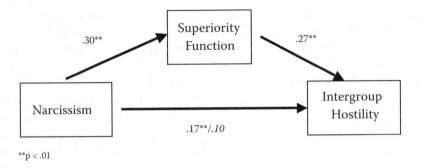

Figure 16.1. The superiority function of national identity (Study 1) as mediator of the relationship between narcissism and general hostility toward Canadians, Iranians, and illegal immigrants (composite intergroup hostility; Sobel z = 2.17, p < .05).

RELIGIOUS IDENTITY AND INTERGROUP ATTITUDES (STUDY 2)[4]

Narcissism, Competitiveness, and Religious Identity Functions

Once again, narcissism displayed a fairly strong relationship with competitiveness (r = .32). As in the national group, most of the analyses displayed similar patterns for both, and competitiveness carried some of the variance between narcissism and the identity and intergroup outcomes. As expected, narcissism and self-esteem were again moderately correlated (r = .32).

Consistent with the national identity patterns in Study 1, the only function that had a significant independent relationship with narcissism was superiority (β = .25). Somewhat surprisingly, narcissism was not related to religious fundamentalism. Thus, while narcissists within religious groups also pursue superiority goals through this identity, this does not manifest itself in a fundamentalist orientation.[5]

Narcissism and Intergroup Attitudes

Intergroup hostility, along with perceived threat and uncertainty, were assessed in the same manner as in Study 1, though this time in relation to Catholics, Muslims, and "homosexuals" as out-groups. Again, patterns were relatively consistent across the three groups, so we report relationships using a general composite of the three ratings.

Narcissism once again independently predicted hostile intergroup attitudes (β = .17), while self-esteem encouraged more positive attitudes (β = –.23). But, narcissism was not related to greater perceived threat or uncertainty in the religious intergroup context. Thus, narcissists are more hostile toward out-groups relevant to their religious identity, but this does not appear to be influenced by these precipitating factors.

Religious Identity Functions and Intergroup Attitudes

The superiority function of religious identity also consistently related to hostile attitudes about the three groups (β = .41). On the other hand, verification-certainty predicted more positive attitudes (β = −.33) relative to the other three functions, as did the social connection (β = −.18).

Additionally, superiority predicted both perceived threat (β = .27) and uncertainty (β = .31) from the out-groups. Conversely, verification-certainty independently predicted less perceived threat (β = −.25) and uncertainty (β = −.37). Uncertainty (β = .27) partially mediated the relationship between superiority and intergroup hostility (Sobel z = 3.01, p < .01; superiority-defense β = .33). Thus, as we saw with national identity, those who base their religious identity on a defensive superiority relative to other functions also tend to display more hostile attitudes toward out-groups, which in this context could be seen in part as defense against personal uncertainty. This is further evidence that group identities constructed in such a way are fragile.

Mediating Role of the Superiority-Defensive Function

As in Study 1, we attempted to connect the fragile personal self represented by narcissism to fragile religious identity by way of a superiority function and use of hostile intergroup attitudes. Here, narcissism was not related to perceived threat or uncertainty in the intergroup context. Thus, we proceeded to test the model's mediation predictions in relation to intergroup hostility. As predicted by the model, superiority-defense (β = .38) once again emerged as a significant mediator of narcissistic intergroup hostility (see Figure 16.2), reducing its effect to a level below significance (β = .09; Sobel z = 2.75, p < .01).

To recap, the results were not quite as straightforward for the functional self-regulatory model within religious identity. Narcissism was related to hostile intergroup attitudes, and much of this again was accounted for by a tendency to pursue personal goals involving relative superiority through the religious identity.

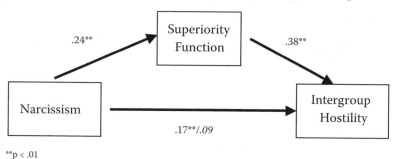

**p < .01

Figure 16.2.   The superiority function of religious identity (Study 2) as mediator of the relationship between narcissism and general hostility toward Catholics, Muslims, and "homosexuals" (composite intergroup hostility; Sobel z = 2.17, p < .05).

But, narcissism was not related to fundamentalism, and showed weak if any relationship with perceived threat or uncertainty from the out-groups.

DISCUSSION: SIMILARITIES AND DIFFERENCES IN HOW THE MODEL APPLIES TO NATIONAL IDENTITY AND RELIGIOUS IDENTITY

These initial data provided general support for the idea that (a) group identity can be differentiated according to functions it serves for the individual, with important implications for intergroup attitudes, and (b) goals that leave the self fragile at the individual/interpersonal level may also connect to similarly defensive identity functions at the collective/intergroup level. Such a defensive group identity, in turn, leaves the individual vulnerable to threat and uncertainty in the intergroup context, which is regulated in part through hostile intergroup attitudes. Several of the important patterns of relationships predicted by the model were consistent across both national identity and religious identity, with some important exceptions and differences between groups.

Although narcissism displayed low to moderate correlations with intergroup attitudes in both groups, and narcissists endorsed the superiority function of both identities, only in the national group was narcissistic intergroup hostility clearly mediated by perceived threat and/or uncertainty from other groups. The superiority function, however, did display a path through these vulnerabilities in both groups. This cycle of threat and defense (through hostile attitudes in this case) is characteristic of the fragile self, as outlined in the model we discussed earlier. Importantly, the predicted mediation model outlining narcissism's relationship to intergroup hostility through the superiority function was supported in both identities (see Figures 16.1 and 16.2).

Looking more closely at the identity functions, superiority was the least prevalent function on average in both groups, consistent with our conceptualization of it as "optional." But, superiority was clearly the most toxic and maladaptive function across both groups—it related consistently to personal narcissism, did not add anything to general group identification but rather encouraged more nationalistic/fundamentalist types of attachment, related to greater vulnerability (threat and uncertainty), and predicted more hostile intergroup attitudes. In contrast, the social connection function was a consistently more adaptive and "secure" orientation to the group—it generally related to self-esteem, patriotism, general religious identification, an absence of uncertainty and threat from other groups, and more tolerant attitudes toward others outside of one's group. Interestingly, verification-certainty showed quite different patterns between the two identities, appearing to be very important and adaptive for religious identity, while functioning more in line with superiority in relation to national identity. What we may see here is that religious identity is a more effective outlet for certainty concerns than national identity, and those who turn to the national group for certainty may be forced to look to other strategies (including out-group derogation) to establish the certainty they seek.

It is thus important to recognize the unique properties of each group, while also searching for a general process across groups. At this point, it does appear that superiority concerns are consistently toxic to intergroup relations, while concerns for social connection are more adaptive in the pursuit of group identity. While the former tends to encourage looking outward with a more comparative and competitive eye, the latter seems to encourage a more internal focus within one's own group. This is entirely consistent with conceptualizations of narcissism and secure self-esteem in the interpersonal sphere (Morf & Rhodewalt, 2001; Rhodewalt & Peterson, 2009), and is supported by prior research that attempted to look at motivations behind group identity (Peterson, 2008a).

CONCLUSION

In summary, the approach to group identity presented here is consistent with other recent attempts to move beyond a focus on degree of identification to a more fine-grained analysis of the process behind identification with groups. What is unique here is our application of models of the personal self, goals, and interpersonal self-regulation to inform this process. In other words, we believe that a focus on personal goals and a more "bottom-up" process can be fruitful to understanding intergroup attitudes alongside more predominant paradigms that focus more on how the group influences the individual in a more "top-down" process (e.g., Turner et al., 1994). Using past research and models on narcissism and the fragile personal self, we have provided some initial evidence that personal "fragility" and defensiveness can also encourage collective "fragility" and defensiveness, through the pursuit of common goals in each domain. We recognize that this only accounts for a small part of the phenomenon of interest and that a more "top-down" approach can help explain other parts where this may be found lacking.

Returning to the quote from the beginning, we are not sure whether we have captured what Obama was describing in relation to people "clinging" to religion and intergroup antipathy in reaction to personal frustration. But, we do feel that certain ways of constructing the self-concept and pursuing goals interpersonally may encourage intergroup hostility when such goals are also pursued in relation to a group identity, especially if threatened. Clearly, more targeted experimental and survey work is needed to test the predictions offered here.

END NOTES

1. The basic idea of groups serving defensive functions, especially for narcissists, is not new to clinical and psychodynamic theorizing (Freud, 1914/1953). For example, one of the main criteria for judgment of narcissistic personality disorder in the *DSM-IV-TR* (American Psychiatric Association, 2000) states that the individual "believes that he or she is 'special' and unique and can only be understood by, or associate with, other special or high-status people or institutions." The implication is that some narcissists may be motivated to join high-status groups or construe and justify groups they already belong to as superior and unique, consistent with the model being proposed here. Thus, the potential for certain individuals to perceive a group as serving an ego-defensive, superiority-promoting function may be the key connection between the fragile personal self with narcissistic goals and fragile types of group identity related

to intergroup hostility (e.g., Eidelson & Eidelson, 2003). Such a function should be highly related to prejudice, discrimination, and other forms of intergroup hostility, as well as to defensive identities such as nationalism (e.g., Kosterman & Feshbach, 1989) and religious fundamentalism (e.g., Altemeyer & Hunsberger, 1992).

2. Although an infinite number of specific functions can be delineated (e.g., Aharpour & Brown, 2002; Deaux et al., 1999), it may help to focus on primary motives that have already been identified, with the important qualification that group identities can serve different functions depending on the individual's personal goals and motives.

3. As is customary with research on narcissism (e.g., Rhodewalt & Morf, 1998), all effects that are reported here for narcissism control for this adaptive self-esteem element (with any reported self-esteem effects also free of the maladaptive narcissism element). Additional factors that were controlled for in the analyses included sex, political ideology, need for closure, and need to belong. Analyses involving only identity functions controlled for sex and political ideology only.

4. All participants in Study 2 reported a religious affiliation of some kind (all identified to a certain extent with a religious group). The vast majority of the sample (70%) reported affiliation with the dominant religion of Utah, the Church of Jesus Christ of Latter-day Saints (Mormons).

5. Part of this finding may have to do with the idea that religious fundamentalism has as much (or more) to do with a defensive certainty as superiority (e.g., Peterson, 2008b). Additionally, the predominant religious group in the sample (Mormons) tends to be somewhat more fundamentalist in their identity than those in the sample with other affiliations. This may have diminished any relationship with narcissism that may be found in general.

REFERENCES

Aharpour, S., & Brown, R. (2002). Functions of group identification: An exploratory analysis. *International Review of Social Psychology, 15*, 157–186.

Allport, G. W., & Ross, J. M. (1967). Personal religious orientation and prejudice. *Journal of Personality and Social Psychology, 5*, 432–443.

Altemeyer, B. (2003). Why do religious fundamentalists tend to be prejudiced? *International Journal for the Psychology of Religion, 13*, 17–28.

Altemeyer, B., & Hunsberger, B. (1992). Authoritarianism, religious fundamentalism, quest, and prejudice. *International Journal for the Psychology of Religion, 2*, 113–133.

Altemeyer, B., & Hunsberger, B. (2004). A revised religious fundamentalism scale: The short and sweet of it. *The International Journal for the Psychology of Religion, 14*, 47–54.

American Psychiatric Association. (2000). *Diagnostic and statistical manual of mental disorders* (4th ed., text revision; DSM-IV-TR). Washington, DC: Author.

Baron, R. M., & Kenny, D. A. (1986). The moderator-mediator variable distinction in social psychological research: Conceptual, strategic, and statistical considerations. *Journal of Personality and Social Psychology, 51*, 1173–1182.

Batson, C. D., & Burris, C. T. (1994). Personal religion: Depressant or stimulant of prejudice and discrimination? In M. P. Zanna & J. M. Olson (Eds.), *The psychology of prejudice: The Ontario symposium* (Vol. 7, pp. 149–169). Hillsdale, NJ: Erlbaum.

Baumeister, R. F., & Leary, M. R. (1995). The need to belong: Desire for interpersonal attachments as a fundamental human motivation. *Psychological Bulletin, 117*, 497–529.

Brewer, M. B. (1991). The social self: On being the same and different at the same time. *Personality and Social Psychology Bulletin, 17*, 475–482.

Brewer, M. B. (1999). The psychology of prejudice: Ingroup love or outgroup hate? *Journal of Social Issues, 55,* 429–444.

Brewer, M. B. (2001). Ingroup identification and intergroup conflict: When does ingroup love become outgroup hate? In R. D. Ashmore, L. Jussim, & D. Wilder (Eds.), *Social identity, intergroup conflict, and conflict reduction* (pp. 17–41). Oxford, England: Oxford University Press.

Bushman, B. J., & Baumeister, R. F. (1998). Threatened egotism, narcissism, self-esteem and, direct and displaced aggression: Does self-love or self-hate lead to violence? *Journal of Personality and Social Psychology, 75,* 219–229.

Cantor, N. (1990). From thought to behavior: "Having" and "doing" in the study of personality and cognition. *American Psychologist, 45,* 735–750.

Cialdini, R. B., & Richardson, K. D. (1980). Two indirect tactics of image management: Basking and blasting. *Journal of Personality and Social Psychology, 39,* 406–415.

Crocker, J., & Park, L. E. (2004). The costly pursuit of self-esteem. *Psychological Bulletin, 130,* 392–414.

Crocker, J., Thompson, L. L., McGraw, K. M., & Ingerman, C. (1987). Downward comparison, prejudice, and evaluations of others: Effects of self-esteem and threat. *Journal of Personality and Social Psychology, 52,* 907–916.

Crocker, J., & Wolfe, C. T. (2001). Contingencies of self-worth. *Psychological Review, 108,* 593–623.

Deaux, K., Reid, A., Mizrahi, K., & Cotting, D. (1999). Connecting the person to the social: The functions of social identification. In T. R. Tyler, R. M. Kramer, & O. P. John (Eds.), *The psychology of the social self* (pp. 91–113). Mahwah, NJ: Erlbaum.

Deci, E. M., & Ryan, R. M. (1995). Human autonomy: The basis of true self-esteem. In M. H. Kernis (Ed.), *Efficacy, agency, and self-esteem* (pp. 31–39). New York: Plenum Press.

Dweck, C. S., Higgins, E. T., & Grant-Pillow, H. (2003). Self-systems give unique meaning to self variables. In M. R. Leary & J. P. Tangney (Eds.), *Handbook of self and identity* (pp. 239–252). New York: Guilford Press.

Eidelson, R. J., & Eidelson, J. I. (2003). Dangerous ideas: Five beliefs that propel groups toward conflict. *American Psychologist, 58,* 182–192.

Federico, C. M., Golec, A., & Dial, J. L. (2005). The relationship between the need for closure and support for military action against Iraq: Moderating effects of national attachment. *Personality and Social Psychology Bulletin, 31,* 621–632.

Fein, S., & Spencer, S. J. (1997). Prejudice as self-image maintenance: Affirming the self through derogating others. *Journal of Personality and Social Psychology, 73,* 31–44.

Freud, S. (1953). On narcissism: An introduction. In J. Strachey (Ed. & Trans.), *The standard edition of the complete psychological works of Sigmund Freud* (Vol. 14, pp. 69–102). London: Hogarth Press. (Original work published 1914)

Gramzow, R. H., & Gaertner, L. (2005). Self-esteem and favoritism toward novel in-groups: The self as evaluative base. *Journal of Personality and Social Psychology, 88,* 801–815.

Greenberg, J., Solomon, S., & Pyszczynski, T. (1997). Terror management theory of self-esteem and cultural worldviews: Empirical assessments and conceptual refinements. In M. P. Zanna (Ed.), *Advances in experimental social psychology* (Vol. 29, pp. 61–139). New York: Academic Press.

Greenwald, A. G., & Banaji, M. R. (1995). Implicit social cognition: Attitudes, self-esteem, and stereotypes. *Psychological Review, 102,* 4–27.

Hardin, C. D., & Higgins, E. T. (1996). Shared reality: How social verification makes the subjective objective. In R. M. Sorrentino & E. T. Higgins (Eds.), *Handbook of motivation and cognition* (Vol. 3, pp. 28–84). New York: Guilford Press.

Hogg, M. A. (2000). Subjective uncertainty reduction through self-categorization: A motivational theory of social identity processes. In W. Stroebe & M. Hewstone (Eds.), *European review of social psychology* (Vol. 11, pp. 223–255). Chichester, England: Wiley.

Hornsey, M. J. (2003). Linking superiority bias in the interpersonal and intergroup domains. *Journal of Social Psychology, 143*, 479–491.

Hunsberger, B. (1996). Religious fundamentalism, right-wing authoritarianism, and hostility toward homosexuals in non-Christian religious groups. *International Journal for the Psychology of Religion, 6*, 39–49.

Johnson, A. L., Crawford, M. T., Sherman, S. J., Rutchick, A. M., Hamilton, D. L., Ferreira, M. B., et al. (2006). A functional perspective on group memberships: Differential need fulfillment in a group typology. *Journal of Experimental Social Psychology, 42*, 707–719.

Jordan, C. H., Spencer, S. J., & Zanna, M. P. (2005). Types of high self-esteem and prejudice: How implicit self-esteem relates to ethnic discrimination among high explicit self-esteem individuals. *Personality and Social Psychology Bulletin, 31*, 693–702.

Jordan, C. H., Spencer, S. J., Zanna, M. P., Hoshino-Brown, E., & Correll, J. (2003). Secure and defensive high self-esteem. *Journal of Personality and Social Psychology, 85*, 969–978.

Katz, D. (1960). The functional approach to the study of attitudes. *Public Opinion Quarterly, 24*, 163–204.

Kernis, M. H. (2003). Toward a conceptualization of optimal self-esteem. *Psychological Inquiry, 14*, 1–26.

Kernis, M. H., Abend, T. A., Goldman, B. M., Shrira, I., Paradise, A. N., & Hampton, C. (2005). Self-serving responses arising from discrepancies between explicit and implicit self-esteem. *Self and Identity, 4*, 311–330.

Kernis, M. H., & Sun, C.-R. (1994). Narcissism and reactions to interpersonal feedback. *Journal of Research in Personality, 28*, 4–13.

Kosterman, R., & Feshbach, S. (1989). Toward a measure of patriotic and nationalistic attitudes. *Political Psychology, 10*, 257–274.

Leary, M. R., & Baumeister, R. F. (2000). The nature and function of self-esteem: Sociometer theory. In M. P. Zanna (Ed.), *Advances in experimental social psychology* (Vol. 32, pp. 1–62). New York: Academic Press.

McGregor, I., Zanna, M. P., Holmes, J. G., & Spencer, S. J. (2001). Compensatory conviction in the face of personal uncertainty: Going to extremes and being oneself. *Journal of Personality and Social Psychology, 80*, 472–488.

Mischel, W., & Shoda, Y. (1995). A cognitive-affective system theory of personality: Reconceptualizing situations, dispositions, dynamics, and invariance in personality structure. *Psychological Review, 102*, 246–268.

Morf, C. C., & Rhodewalt, F. (1993). Narcissism and self-evaluation maintenance: Explorations in object relations. *Personality and Social Psychology Bulletin, 19*, 668–676.

Morf, C. C., & Rhodewalt, F. (2001). Unraveling the paradoxes of narcissism: A dynamic self-regulatory processing model. *Psychological Inquiry, 12*, 177–196.

Obama, B. (2008). *Transcript of Obama's remarks at San Francisco fundraiser Sunday*. Downloaded September 17, 2008, from http://thepage.time.com/transcript-of-obamas-remarks-at-san-francisco-fundraiser-sunday

Peterson, B. (2008a). *Fragile selves and "fair-weather" fans? Functions of sports team identification and reactions to wins and losses over time*. Manuscript in preparation, University of Utah.

Peterson, B. (2008b). *Goals and groups: Testing a functional (defensive) self-regulatory model of group identity*. Unpublished doctoral dissertation, University of Utah.

Peterson, B. (2008c). *Nationalism and anti-immigrant sentiment: Testing a model of the "fragile" collective self.* Manuscript in preparation, University of Utah.

Peterson, B., & Rhodewalt, F. (2009). *Group identity in the service of defensive self-regulation? Testing a functional self-regulatory model of group identity.* Manuscript in preparation, University of Utah.

Peterson, B., White, P. W., & Rhodewalt, F. (2008a). *Defensive national and religious identification: Relation to intergroup emotions and policy support involving threatening social issues.* Manuscript in preparation, University of Utah.

Peterson, B., White, P. W., & Rhodewalt, F. (2008b). *Personal and collective superiority: Narcissism, ingroup projection, and intergroup hostility.* Manuscript in preparation, University of Utah.

Rhodewalt, F. (2005). [Narcissism, social interaction, and self-esteem: The meaning of social inclusion]. Unpublished raw data, University of Utah.

Rhodewalt, F., & Morf, C. C. (1998). On self-aggrandizement and anger: A temporal analysis of narcissism and affective reactions to success and failure. *Journal of Personality and Social Psychology, 74,* 672–685.

Rhodewalt, F., & Peterson, B. (2008). The self and social behavior: The fragile self and interpersonal self-regulation. In F. Rhodewalt (Ed.), *Personality and social behavior* (pp. 49–78). New York: Psychology Press.

Rhodewalt, F., & Peterson, B. (2009). Narcissism. In M. R. Leary & R. H. Hoyle (Eds.), *Handbook of individual differences in social behavior* (pp. 547–560). New York: Guilford Press.

Rhodewalt, F., Tragakis, M., & Peterson, B. (2003). [Narcissism and contingencies of self-worth]. Unpublished raw data, University of Utah.

Smith, M. B., Bruner, J. S., & White, R. W. (1956). *Opinions and personality.* Oxford, England: John Wiley & Sons.

Snyder, M., & Cantor, N. (1998). Understanding personality and social behavior: A functionalist strategy. In D. T. Gilbert, S. T. Fiske, & G. Lindzey (Eds.), *The handbook of social psychology* (Vol. 1, pp. 635–679).

Snyder, M., & DeBono, K. G. (1989). Understanding the functions of attitudes: Lessons from personality and social psychology. In A. R. Pratkanis, S. J. Breckler, & A. G. Greenwald (Eds.), *Attitude structure and function* (pp. 339–360). Hillsdale, NJ: Erlbaum.

Sobel, M. E. (1982). Asymptotic intervals for indirect effects in structural equations models. In S. Leinhart (Ed.), *Sociological methodology 1982* (pp. 290–312). San Francisco: Jossey-Bass.

Stangor, C., & Thompson, E. P. (2002). Needs for cognitive economy and self-enhancement as unique predictors of intergroup attitudes. *European Journal of Social Psychology, 32,* 563–575.

Struch, N., & Schwartz, S. H. (1989). Intergroup aggression: Its predictors and distinctiveness from in-group bias. *Journal of Personality and Social Psychology, 56,* 364–373.

Swann, W. B., Jr. (1983). Self-verification: Bringing social reality into harmony with the self. In J. Suls & A. G. Greenwald (Eds.), *Social psychological perspectives on the self* (Vol. 2, pp. 33–66). Hillsdale, NJ: Erlbaum.

Swann, W. B., Jr., Polzer, J. T., Seyle, D. C., & Ko, S. J. (2004). Finding value in diversity: Verification of personal and social self-views in diverse groups. *Academy of Management Review, 29,* 9–27.

Tajfel, H., & Turner, J. C. (1986). The social identity theory of intergroup behavior. In S. Worchel & W. G. Austin (Eds.), *Psychology of intergroup relations* (pp. 7–24). Chicago: Nelson-Hall.

Tesser, A. (2000). On the confluence of self-esteem maintenance mechanisms. *Personality and Social Psychology Review, 4,* 290–299.

Turner, J. C., Oakes, P. J., Haslam, S. A., & McGarty, C. A. (1994). Self and collective: Cognition and social context. *Personality and Social Psychology Bulletin, 20,* 454–463.

Twenge, J. M., & Campbell, W. K. (2003). "Isn't it fun to get the respect that we're going to deserve?" Narcissism, social rejection, and aggression. *Personality and Social Psychology Bulletin, 29,* 261–272.

Weaver, E. B. (2006). *National narcissism: The intersection of the nationalist cult and gender in Hungary.* Oxford, England: Peter Lang.

Wenzel, M., Mummendey, A., Weber, U., & Waldzus, S. (2003). The ingroup as *pars pro toto*: From the ingroup onto the inclusive category as a precursor to social discrimination. *Personality and Social Psychology Bulletin, 29,* 461–473.

Worchel, S., & Coutant, D. (1997). The tangled web of loyalty: Nationalism, patriotism, and ethnocentrism. In D. Bar-Tal & E. Staub (Eds.), *Patriotism in the lives of individuals and nations* (pp. 190–210). Chicago: Nelson-Hall.

Wright, S. C., Aron, A., & Tropp, L. R. (2002). Including others (and groups) in the self: Self-expansion and intergroup relations. In J. P. Forgas & K. D. Williams (Eds.), *The social self: Cognitive, interpersonal, and intergroup perspectives* (pp. 343–364). New York: Psychology Press.

17

Attitudes in Virtual Reality

JIM BLASCOVICH AND CADE MCCALL

Rapid and continuing enhancements of digital virtual reality technologies have important implications for research. These advancements provide behavioral scientists, including social psychologists, with continually improving and increasingly powerful digital technology-based media research and measurement tools, especially so for experimentation. These tools increase the power and reach of social psychology's empirical methods, bolstering both the internal and ecological validity of our experiments and quasi experiments (Blascovich et al., 2002; Loomis, Blascovich, & Beall, 1999).

Additionally, open-to-the-public digital virtual venues, such as Facebook©, MySpace©, Second Life©, as well as private ones, provide new "worlds" for everyday social interactions. An ever-growing and substantial proportion of the world's population is spending more and more time interacting with each other online and digitally, thereby creating increasingly important societal venues about which relatively little has been studied and little is known by social psychologists and other scientists (but see Boellstorff, 2008, for an exception). Hence, knowledge of social influence and social interaction processes within digital virtual worlds is relatively scarce, resulting not only in meager understanding of increasingly important social milieus but also providing a new challenge regarding the generalizability of research results.

In this chapter, the substantive focus is on the operation and measurement of attitudes and persuasion. Although attitudes toward virtual reality or any of its many ramifications will not be discussed, this chapter may help shape or change attitudes toward virtual reality technologies among attitude researchers.

WHAT IS VIRTUAL REALITY?

Scholars have debated the nature of reality for ages. The study of the nature of reality can be divided analogously to the way philosophers of mind and others divide the study of consciousness into "hard" and "simple" consciousness problems (Chalmers, 1995; i.e., "What is consciousness?" and "What are the types of consciousness?" respectively). Consequently, one might label the question "What is reality?" as the "hard" or difficult problem and the question "What are the types of reality?" as the "simple" problem. However, as implied in this chapter, it is not clear which question is really the more difficult one.

In contrast to the continuing struggle and debate among interested scholars over the hard consciousness problem, many scholars from many fields concerned with the question "What is reality?" agree that what people think of as reality is a hallucination; that is, a cognitive construction. Together with religious gurus and mystics, philosophers (Huxley, 1954/2004) and experimental psychologists (e.g., Shepard, 1984) maintain that perceptions are invariably idiosyncratic hallucinations, albeit often assumed and treated as collective. Perceptions can be thought of as hallucinations in at least two ways. The first is that what people perceive via input from the senses are impoverished and mentally constructed representations of external environments. The second is that people perceive things that arguably do not exist in external environments.

Philosophers of mind and psychologists do not appear to be struggling as much with the simple consciousness problem and describe a tripartite division of consciousness into unconscious, conscious, and metaconscious categories (Schooler, 2002). The same is not true for those distinguishing among levels of reality. Hence, slower progress has been made by scholars, including virtual reality researchers, regarding the problem "What are the categories of reality?" or "What is real?" Problematically, simply asking the question "What is real?" relies upon the assumption that there are things that are not real or what some would label "virtual."

Like people who claim not to know anything about art but know what they like, many people who don't know metaphysics "know" what is real and what is not (or "virtual"). Or, do they? Is the real world what people think it is? The answer is "no" if they think it is some stable objective external reality that they see, hear, touch, smell, and taste. The answer is "yes" if they realize that the real world is only a cognitive construction.

Our position is that perceptions (i.e., hallucinations) of environments are categorized as "real" or "virtual" on the basis of what we invoke and label as the principle of *psychological relativity* (Blascovich & Bailenson, in press; Laming, 2003). Analogously to Einstein's theory of special relativity regarding time and space, psychological relativity theory states that what is mentally processed (i.e., perceived or thought of) as real and what is mentally processed (and thought of) as not real (i.e., virtual) depends on one's point of view. People contrast a particular "grounded reality"—what they believe to be the natural or physical world—with other realities they perceive that at times they believe to be imaginary or "virtual" worlds. However, what is thought to be grounded reality and what is thought to be virtual reality is often muddled or even reversed. Novelists and screen writers illustrate the relativity of virtual to grounded reality quite well in novels like *Snow Crash* (Stephenson, 1992) and *Neuromancer* (Gibson, 1984) and in movies like *The Matrix* and *The Truman Show*.

However, one need not rely solely on science fiction examples. Humans have the same experience as "Neo" or "Truman" every day. For example, during dreams, sleeping humans are often convinced that their dream worlds *are* their grounded realities, sometimes pleasurably, sometimes unpleasurably. Only when sleepers awaken are they upset or relieved that it wasn't so. As another example, consider religious beliefs. More than 75% of the earth's people report a belief in a "supreme being" of some type (Gallup International, 2009). Religious people profess that they believe the physical world itself to be a virtual world created by this supreme being. Furthermore, the physical world is described in some testaments as a sort of testing ground to triage individuals for placement after death in absolute or grounded reality of one sort (e.g., heaven) or another (e.g., hell).

Humans are clearly neurophysiologically wired to travel mentally back and forth between grounded and virtual realities as well as among virtual realities themselves. Humans not only dream during sleep, they (day) dream while awake. Human minds wander often and effortlessly from grounded reality (e.g., Klinger, 1978; Smallwood & Schooler, 2006) to somewhere else. Mind wandering likely serves some adaptive function but discussion of what function is not in the scope of this chapter. Furthermore, although enjoying endogenous capabilities to do so, humans have developed media tools, starting with language-based storytelling, to graphic arts, to theater, to manuscripts and printed books, to photographs and movies, to radio and television, and most recently to digital media, that augment their human ability to travel mentally between their grounded and virtual realities.

The most sophisticated current version of the latter—digital immersive virtual environment technology (IVET)—allows people to relatively easily and inexpensively put themselves or others in "The Matrix," so to speak, for a variety of purposes. One purpose, as social psychologists espouse, has been to experimentally manipulate or observe social influence processes and social interactions within those contexts. This is not a new idea. Rather, it is an old one combined with a newer and more powerful technology than was available when social psychologists had to construct experimental scenarios (i.e., virtual environments) with words (e.g., the ubiquitous vignette) instead of graphics, with actors (e.g., confederates) rather than digital agents, or with hardware (e.g., the prison of Haney, Banks, & Zimbardo, 1973) rather than software.

In sum, the rapid and continuing advancements of digital virtual reality technologies have important implications for social psychology on two major fronts. First, these technological advances continue to provide investigators with new media technology-based laboratory research tools that increase the power of our empirical methods with regard to both internal and external validity concerns. Second, these advances are creating new highly populated three-dimensional "worlds" (e.g., Second Life©, World of Warcraft©) for social interactions. Data reveal that an ever increasing and already substantial proportion of the world's population is spending more and more time interacting with each other via digital virtual reality media technology. At the time of this writing nearly one quarter of the world's population (approximately 1.6 out of 6.7 billion; Internet World Statistics, 2009) are networked via the Internet. Consequently, digital virtual realities are becoming more and more important social venues in raising external validity concerns because what is generalizable in the physical world might not be in digital virtual ones.

Strong arguments can be made that if the "situation" in Lewin's "person x situation topology" (Lewin, Heider, & Heider, 1936) is a virtual one, the operation of fundamental social influence processes, including attitudinal ones, needs to be examined more closely. Virtual environment technology, in particular, provides people concerned with attitudes (e.g., researchers, marketers, politicians) with increases in power not only to assess attitudes unobtrusively but to change them covertly.

VIRTUAL REALITY TECHNOLOGY

Throughout human history, people have developed technologies to help their minds travel between grounded and virtual realities. These mind-augmenting technologies include ones that stimulate virtual experiences biologically, such as pharmacological agents ranging from mind-expanding herbal (e.g., cannabis) and plant (e.g., peyote) extracts to mind-altering manufactured drugs like lysergic acid diethylamide (LSD) and chlorpromazine (Thorazine). Importantly, for our purposes here, these technologies also include a long history of ever improved media communication tools that operate exogenously.

Over the millennia, humans have developed communication media tools to facilitate social interaction via shared symbols and meaning. These tools have also expanded the communicative reach of individuals both in space (i.e., to geographically distant others) and in time (i.e., to future generations). Perhaps the first such media tools supporting mental virtual experiences was storytelling, invoking in listeners a semantic framework facilitating a more or less common mental experience. The first physical evidence of mediated communication comes from bone carvings and cave paintings, emerging as far back as 45,000 B.C. (Fang, 2008). These early graphic representations were followed by increasingly elaborate means of representation. Playwrights combined storytelling and graphic representations via human actions and scenery to form theater. Language recorded via hieroglyphics and later alphabet-based words led to manuscripts and eventually, with the invention of movable type, to mass-produced printed books. Nearly two centuries ago, still photography arrived, followed a century later by motion pictures. By the late 1800s, the "domestication" of electricity led to startlingly more powerful media, including the telegraph and the telephone. Invention of the vacuum tube led to the invention of radio, television, and the first computers. Later, invention of the transistor and other solid state devices led to the miniaturization of computers and the multitude of digital media tools humans have at their disposal today.

All of these technological advances in communicative media augment the inherent human propensity to travel someplace other than grounded reality. They are the psychological analog of the evolution of the wheel.

In some cases, communicative media themselves are invisible to social interactions. Consider the telephone. If one asks a friend, "Who are you talking to on the telephone?" he might reply, "A friend." Technically, this answer is incorrect. Indeed, most people forget that the voice they hear on a phone is not actually another person's voice. Rather, today, it is a continuously digitally tracked and rendered facsimile of that voice. The fidelity of the auditory renderings is usually good enough so that we never think that we are interacting with an auditory avatar of the person with whom we are speaking rather than the person himself or herself. Digital immersive video technology is beginning to provide levels of visual fidelity akin to the fidelity of the telephone, and social interactions in digital virtual worlds will soon be as "real" as telephone conversations are today.

In sum, reality experiences are psychologically constructed with people frequently "traveling back and forth" mentally between their grounded and virtual worlds. Humans have augmented their endogenous capabilities to do so via dreams and daydreams with the invention of communication media tools. The latter systems have increasingly become an important part of the topology in the Lewinian person/environment model (Lewin et al., 1936) of social interactional and social influence processes. Later in the chapter, we examine the significance of digital virtual reality technology for attitudinal processes and measurement while reviewing pioneering work in this area.

THE CONCEPT OF ATTITUDE

The concept of attitude has an interesting etymological history. It has been and is used both as a psychological and a positional (i.e., navigational) term in a somewhat related way. Modern usage of the term *attitude* stems from the 17th-century Italian term *attitudine*, meaning disposition (in the physical sense) or posture. In the 18th century, attitude took on its psychological meaning as "a posture of the body supposed to imply some mental state." A century later it took on its association with emotion and beliefs as "settled behavior reflecting feeling or opinion" (cf. Harper, 2001). In the 19th century, Darwin introduced the notion that attitudes are embodied in movement and expressions (Darwin, 1873). In the 20th century, Hall (1963) introduced the notion of *proxemics* (the study of personal space and distances), relating proxemic behavioral movements to constructs such as attitudes, especially ones involving affect or liking. Because a survey of definitions of attitudes is not our main purpose here, and at the risk of oversimplification and without prejudice toward other definitions, we adopt Fazio's (1990) general definition of attitudes; that is, the association between an object and its evaluation, where "object" refers to perceived objects or abstractions.

This chapter contains the first aggregation, albeit nonexhaustive, of studies involving attitude research in virtual reality of which we are aware. Here, we describe our own and others' research involving attitudinal processes in virtual environments. The foci here include implicit (e.g., proxemic and physiological) and explicit (e.g., self-report) attitude measurements and the implicit manipulation of attitudes within digital immersive virtual environments.

ATTITUDE ASSESSMENT

Social psychologists and others have a long history of interest in the study and measurement of attitudes. Indeed, many self-report questionnaire and scaling techniques were originally developed to assess attitudes, including classic techniques originally described by Thurstone (1928), Guttman (1954), Likert (1932), and Osgood, Suci, and Tannenbaum (1957). However, even as these techniques were being developed, the accuracy of self-report-based techniques became suspect when attitude-behavior discrepancies appeared, particularly regarding attitudes toward minority racial groups (e.g., LaPierre, 1934). By the 1980s, implicit physiological measures of attitudes, at least insofar as the association of attitudinal objects with affect, were validated (e.g., Cacioppo, Petty, Losch, & Kim, 1986). The interplay between the automatic activation of attitudes and conscious control was examined (cf. Devine, 1989), and implicit attitudinal measurement techniques (e.g., Nosek, Greenwald, & Banaji, 2007; see Wittenbrink & Schwarz, 2007, for others) were added to the attitude measurement armamentarium.

MEASURING ATTITUDES IN VIRTUAL REALITY

Implicit proxemic indicators (e.g., interpersonal distance, personal space, head orientation) of attitudes preceded the appearance of implicit measures based on the relationship between associations of objects and evaluations and response times by more than two decades (Hall, 1963). However, difficulties with the recording and scoring of proxemic measures in even the simplest physical experimental venues proved impractical for most researchers.

However, digital IVET has ameliorated this problem. More specifically, as Blascovich et al. (2002) illustrate, sophisticated three-dimensional digital virtual reality systems allow people wearing a head-mounted display device to move within a digital world in correspondence with their movements in the physical world in which the equipment is located. For example, they can move toward, away from, or around virtual objects, including other digitally represented "people." The technology to do so necessitates that all spatial relationships and movements of both animate and inanimate objects be tracked (and rendered) in real time very precisely (i.e., spatial accuracy within a millimeter and temporal accuracy within 40 milliseconds). Consequently, a plethora of highly accurate spatial-temporal measures (e.g., interpersonal distance, velocities, accelerations, decelerations, etc.) are automatically scored or easily calculable and available online to investigators (see Blascovich et al., 2002, for a review). We and others have found such proxemic measures exquisitely sensitive to object-evaluation associations; that is, attitudes. Additionally, the use of digital IVET does not preclude implicit peripheral neurophysiological measures, including ones associated with attitude assessment. We describe examples of these later.

Finally, digital IVET does not exclude subjective, self-report types of attitude assessments. Indeed, experience time sampling measures are particularly appropriate using digital IVET, as research participants can be placed in ecologically realistic virtual environments for relatively long periods of time. In fact, the researcher can structure immersive virtual environments to include specified social circumstances, which might be hit or miss in naturalistic field studies, thereby assuring the occurrence of circumstances of interest. Hence, research participants can be prompted at precisely identified occurrences of specific contexts. For example, participants can be signaled via a semitransparent open-ended question or Likert-type scale to which they can respond vocally or gesturally (e.g., pointing to a scale point).

VIRTUAL REALITY–BASED ATTITUDINAL STUDIES INVOLVING IMPLICIT MEASURES

We turn now to a review of several research studies conducted in our own and others' immersive virtual environment–based laboratories. This review is divided into two sections: studies aimed primarily at attitude assessment and studies aimed primarily at attitude manipulation. Within the first of these sections, we describe studies involving implicit (i.e., proxemic and physiological) attitudinal measures and operationalizations. Although there are also many studies in which explicit, self-report measures are utilized, such studies tend to be associated more with implicit attitude manipulation and are reviewed in the second section.

Proxemic Assessments of Attitude

Our initial forays into empirical work involving digital IVET involved implicit measures of people's associations of sentience or "humanness" with the depiction of human-like representations. In virtual reality terminology, digital representations of humans typically take one of two forms: avatar or agent. *Avatar* is defined as the digital representation of an actual human being, typically in real time, and *agent* is defined as the digital representation of a computer algorithm (i.e., a sort of artificial intelligence), typically, operating in real time (Bailenson & Blascovich, 2004). Although representations in either case can be other than visual (e.g., auditory), here the focus is on visual or graphic representations.

Bailenson, Blascovich, Beall, and Loomis (2003). Based on Blascovich et al.'s (2003) model of social influence within immersive virtual environments, these researchers focused on the association of sentience and digital human-like representations. More specifically, they investigated whether such associations would vary as a function of two factors: first, whether the digital human-like representations were believed to be avatars or agents by participants, and second, as a function of whether or not the digital human-like representations exhibited human-like nonverbal (i.e., movement) behaviors. Interpersonal distance served as the primary proxemic implicit measure of the association between sentience and the digital human-like representations.

The avatar/agent manipulation was accomplished by informing the participants that the digital representations that they would see in the virtual world were either actual online digital representations of actual humans or of agents. They hypothesized that research participants would be more likely to respect the personal space bubble (cf. Sommer & Becker, 1969) of avatars (i.e., online representations they thought were actual humans), independently of their human-like movements, but would respect the personal space bubble of agents as a function of the realism of their human-like movements and nonverbal signals. In the first experiment, participants in an immersive virtual environment approached standing virtual human representations that varied in their movements, including those associated with gaze. In the second experiment, the virtual human representations approached standing participants.

The results of the first experiment revealed that as participants walked toward the digital human representations, they maintained patterns of interpersonal space around those they thought to be avatars quite similarly to the patterns reported in human studies in the past. However, participants respected the personal space bubble of digital human representations they thought to be agents only if the agents displayed naturalistic mutual gaze behavior. The results of the second study, in which the digital human representations approached stationary participants, indicated that participants were more avoidant of the agent than avatars in terms of personal space. Moreover, their degree of avoidance correlated with the strength of their emotional reaction for both agents and avatars. Together these results point to the naturalistic quality and operation of proxemics when others in digital immersive virtual environments are avatars. However, agentic (i.e., algorithmic) behavioral attributions complicate the picture requiring naturalistic communicative, in this case nonverbal gaze, behavior to produce the same effect.

Most importantly, these studies suggested strongly that proxemic data collected in digital immersive virtual environments could be used to assess attitudes. Next we review several examples of such use.

McCall, Blascovich, Young, and Persky (2009). These researchers utilized implicit proxemic indexes to assess prejudice and overt aggression toward Black and White male agents in a digital immersive virtual environment. The experiment consisted of two tasks performed by participants in an immersive virtual environment. In the first, participants were instructed, similarly to the proxemic study described previously, to approach and walk around each of two agents with whom they would subsequently engage in a gun fight. The gun fight was the second task. The two conditions in the experiment were based on the apparent race of the agents, Black or White.

During the first task, the interpersonal distance that participants maintained from the agents as well as the degree of gaze avoidance participants exhibited while approaching the agents were recorded. During the second task, participants and agents engaged in shooting and hiding behaviors (behind virtual barriers) in the immersive virtual shooting room. Participants were given points for successfully hitting the agent targets and lost points when they were hit by the agents' gunshots.

Results indicated that both the interpersonal distance participants maintained between themselves and agents as well as the degree of gaze White agents. McCall et al. interpreted the interpersonal distance and gaze avoidance behaviors in the first task as proxemic indicators of racial attitudes, ones consistent with their subsequent discriminatory shooting behavior.

Dotsch and Wigboldus (2008). These researchers also examined intergroup attitudes using IVET and proxemic behaviors. More specifically, they examined the relationship between participants' implicit negative associations toward Moroccans and participants' subsequent proxemic behaviors around them. Native Dutch participants were immersed in a digital virtual environment in which they encountered digital avatars with either White or Moroccan facial features. Participants maintained greater interpersonal distance when approaching Moroccan as opposed to White avatars. Participants' implicit negative associations with Moroccans moderated both effects. Dotsch and Wigboldus concluded that their data indicate that prejudiced implicit associations may lead to unintentional, impulsive discriminatory behavior.

Gillath, McCall, Shaver, and Blascovich (2008). This research team examined participants' proxemic behaviors as they walked up and down a virtual street full of shops and populated with human-appearing agents, some of which were apparently in need of help. Participants' proxemic behaviors (interpersonal distance and gaze avoidance) toward virtual agents in apparent need of help were negatively (i.e., closer distances and less gaze avoidance) related to their preassessed dispositional degree of compassion and tendency to experience personal distress. No relationship was found between interpersonal distance and gaze avoidance toward virtual agents without need of help.

Physiological Assessments of Attitude

Blascovich, Hurst, and McCall (reported in Blascovich & Bailenson, 2009). These investigators examined stigma in an immersive virtual environment. On the basis of Blascovich's biopsychosocial model of challenge and threat (Blascovich & Mendes, 2000; Blascovich & Tomaka, 1996), numerous studies employing implicit peripheral neurophysiological markers (e.g., Blascovich, Mendes, Hunter, Lickel, & Kowai-Bell, 2001) demonstrate that when an individual interacts with a stigmatized other, even cooperatively, that individual is threatened, as evidenced by the threat pattern of cardiovascular responses (i.e., increased heart rate and increased ventricular contractility coupled with little change in cardiac output and increases in total peripheral resistance). In this study, it was reasoned that if the threat response to stigma is automatic, then participants should exhibit cardiovascular responses indicative of threat when they interact with stigmatized avatars (digital representations) representing people who were not themselves stigmatized physically.

The experiment consisted of two parts. During the first part, female research participants met a same-sex participant (actually a confederate) physically when they arrived at the lab. The confederate either physically bore a facial stigma (i.e., a "port wine" facial birthmark) or did not. In the second part, the participant and the confederate entered a shared digital immersive virtual environment where they sat at the same virtual game table and played a cooperative word-finding game. The experimental manipulation was whether or not the confederate's avatar bore the facial birthmark in the virtual world independently of whether she bore it in the physical world. Hence a classic 2 × 2 design was utilized.

The results indicated that during the first minute of game play in the immersive virtual environment, participants were threatened (as indicated by the threat pattern of cardiovascular responses) only if the confederate bore the birthmark physically, independently of whether she bore it in the immersive virtual environment. Importantly, by the fourth minute of game play, participants became threatened only if the avatar bore the birthmark in the virtual environment, independently of whether she bore it physically, and became challenged if she did not bear it virtually.

These data not only demonstrate the feasibility of peripheral neurophysiological assessment of attitudes in immersive virtual environments, but provide an important demonstration of the utility of assessing changes in attitudes implicitly over time. Interestingly, the change in attitude had to have been somehow caused by the increasingly compelling nature of the virtual experience over time and clearly points toward automatic processes at play.

Attitude Manipulation Involving Implicit Processes

As social psychologists know, there are many routes to attitude change or persuasion. Some are explicit and both persuader and target are aware of the attempt. But others factors are hidden, as Vance Packard (1957) pointed out many years ago. Debate has waxed and waned over the efficacy of so-called persuasive subliminal or unreportable messages (auditory and visual) over the years, but the current zeitgeist suggests that such techniques work. Like other media, digital virtual technology can easily accommodate such techniques.

However, there are implicit techniques that are unique to digital virtual technology, especially the immersive variety. These techniques are labeled "transformed social interactions" or "TSIs" (Bailenson, Beall, Blascovich, Loomis, & Turk, 2005). The power of TSIs rests on unique aspects of the technology. As described previously, all movements, speech, and so forth, must be tracked with a high degree of precision by various devices so that they can be rendered quickly and accurately in immersive virtual environments.

However, it is not necessary that the computer be programmed to veridically render movements, images, or both. Rather, algorithms can be added to alter the renderings. For example, when a person being tracked looks left, the computer can transpose the rendering so that his avatar looks right. When a person being tracked is sitting, the computer can render the avatar to be standing. Furthermore, the graphic representations of an individual's avatar need not be the one he has chosen or of which he is aware. Individuals' avatar movements can be rendered in ways that take account of others' movements and behaviors, as well as their preferences, so that an individual's avatar appears differently to different others in the virtual environment. Hence, people's avatars can become chameleons taking on nonverbal attributes for different interactants.

Combined with what social psychologists and others know about attitude change and persuasion, the TSI capabilities of digital virtual reality technology advances a potentially powerful set of implicit persuasive applications. Do they work? In a word, "yes."

Bailenson, Beall, Loomis, Blascovich, and Turk (2004). These investigators examined augmented or nonzero sum gaze, a TSI in which a selected participant's head and eye movements are transformed by an algorithm that renders his or her avatar's gaze directly and simultaneously at the eyes of multiple others' avatars whose own head and eye movements are being rendered veridically in terms of the movement of the person they represent. Hence, each of the others perceives that the transformed interactant (i.e., the avatar) is gazing back only at him or her. In the reported study, a presenter read a persuasive passage to two listeners under various transformed gaze conditions, including augmented gaze. Consistent with the argument that women are more sensitive to nonverbal behaviors of others than are men, the results showed that women agreed with a persuasive message more during augmented gaze than during other gaze conditions.

Guadagno, Blascovich, Bailenson, and McCall (2007). These researchers examined whether persuasive messages could be delivered effectively by known agents (i.e., computer simulations). More specifically, they investigated whether participant attitudes would change toward positions advocated by an in-group member even if the latter was known to be an embodied agent (again, a humanlike representation of a computer algorithm). In their first study, immersed participants listened to a persuasive communication from what they thought to be an avatar of another student. The latter was actually an embodied agent (again, a computer-controlled digital representation of a human), whose apparent gender was manipulated.

The results revealed an in-group favoritism effect such that there was more persuasion when the communication was delivered by a same-gendered virtual human representation. In Study 2, the investigators manipulated gender of the digital representation, communicative movement realism, and agency; that is, whether the digital representation was believed by participants to be an actual avatar or an agent. Specifically, virtual human representations high in communicative realism were more persuasive and, as in the first study, this effect was moderated by the gender match of the virtual human and the research participant. Agency was not a significant factor.

Yee and Bailenson (2006). These investigators argued that immersive virtual environments literally provide people the opportunity to take the perspective of another person and, hopefully, reduce any negative stereotypes they may have toward that person or his or her group. In this study, Yee and Bailenson manipulated embodied perspective-taking by assigning elderly or younger avatars to participants. Their results indicated that negative stereotyping of the elderly was significantly reduced among participants who were given elderly-looking avatars compared to those who were given younger-looking avatars.

Bailenson and Yee (2005). In this study, participants interacted with an embodied agent in immersive virtual reality who verbally delivered a persuasive argument. The mimicry behaviors of the agent were manipulated such that the agent either was animated via mimicry of actual participants' head movements (at a 4-second delay) or was animated via mimicry of a prerecorded participant. Agents mimicking the actual participant with whom they were interacting were more persuasive and received more positive trait ratings than those mimicking a yoked participant. Participants were unable to explicitly detect the mimicry. Of note, this was the first research to demonstrate mimicry effects with a nonhuman, nonverbal mimicker, a confirmation of the automaticity of such effects.

Bailenson and Yee (2007). These investigators examined mimicry in a nonvisual domain. More specifically, they investigated mimicry involving physical touch (i.e., haptics) by utilizing a mechanical force-feedback "handshaking" device and assessing the effects of such mimicry on participants' attitudes toward a partner. In this study, each of a pair of same-sex participants shook hands with a force-feedback joystick that recorded their hand movements. Subsequently, the two participants then greeted one another via a virtual "handshake" mediated by the force-feedback device. In each dyad, one participant received the other participant's virtual hand-shake. The other participant received his or her own virtual handshake back under the guise that it was the other person's handshake. Results demonstrated three effects. First, within participants, the position, angle, speed, and acceleration of their hand movements were highly correlated. Second, handshaking characteristics differed in predictable ways by gender. Third, and most importantly, there was an interaction between gender and mimicry, such that male participants liked people who mimicked their handshakes more than female participants did.

Yee, Bailenson, and Ducheneaut (2009). This team examined self-percep-tion effects on individuals using IVET, labeling such effects in virtual reality as "Proteus" effects. In previous work, the investigators demonstrated that partici-pants who were randomly assigned taller avatars acted more aggressively than did participants randomly assigned shorter avatars. In this investigation, the researchers examined Proteus effects in the online community Second Life©. In their first study, they found that both an avatar's height and attractiveness in an online game were significant predictors of their performance. In a second study, they found that behavioral changes stemming from the virtual environment transferred to subse-quent face-to-face interactions.

Fox and Bailenson (2009). These investigators also examined modeling and self-perception theory, this time examining the effects of self-modeling on change in attitudes toward healthy behaviors. In the first study, participants were randomly assigned to one of three conditions: vicarious reinforcement, in which participants watch their avatar gain or lose weight as the participants' physically exercised; no vicarious reinforcement, in which their avatar did not gain or lose weight as they exercised; and a condition with no avatar. Later, in a voluntary phase, par-ticipants in the vicarious reinforcement condition performed significantly more exercise than those in the other conditions.

In the second study, the investigators manipulated contingency; that is, reward (weight loss) versus punishment (weight gain). They also manipulated model iden-tity; that is, whether participants watched a virtual representation of themselves (VRS) or a virtual representation of an other (VRO). Results indicated that partici-pants planned to exercise significantly more when they viewed the virtual repre-sentation of themselves, regardless of whether reward or punishment was shown.

In a third study, participants watched a VRS running on a treadmill, a VRO running, or a VRS loitering. Postexperimental surveys indicated that participants in the VRS-Running condition reported significantly higher levels of exercise than those in other conditions.

CONCLUSION

Digital immersive virtual environment technology (IVET) arrived on the scene in social psychology as a research tool in the decade before the turn of the millennium. Its empirical value stems from natural human propensities for "psychological travel" or mind wandering abetted by a long history of media technologies to do so. Utilizing this technology, a relatively small but growing cadre of social psychological researchers have focused primarily on examining social influence and social interactional processes within ecologically realistic environments. More recently, researchers have begun to examine so-called transformed social interactions (TSIs) that the technology affords within the contexts of attitudes and persuasion. The results of their pioneering studies demonstrate the sensitivity of IVET-based unobtrusive or implicit assessments of attitudes as well as implicit, unreportable manipulations that lead to attitude change or persuasion with success.

REFERENCES

Bailenson, J. N., Beall, A. C., Blascovich, J., Loomis, J., & Turk, M. (2005). Transformed social interaction, augmented gaze, and social influence in immersive virtual environments. *Human Communication Research*, *31*, 511–537.

Bailenson, J. N., Beall, A. C., Loomis, J., Blascovich, J., & Turk, M. (2004). Transformed social interaction: Decoupling representation from behavior and form in collaborative virtual environments. *PRESENCE: Teleoperators and Virtual Environments*, *13*(4), 428–441.

Bailenson, J. N., & Blascovich, J. (2004). Avatars. In W. S. Bainbridge (Ed.), *Encyclopedia of human-computer interaction* (pp. 64–68). Great Barrington, MA: Berkshire.

Bailenson, J. N., Blascovich, J., Beall, A. C., & Loomis, J. M. (2003). Interpersonal distance in immersive virtual environments. *Personality and Social Psychology Bulletin, 29*, 1–15.

Bailenson, J. N., & Yee, N. (2005). Digital chameleons: Automatic assimilation of nonverbal gestures in immersive virtual environments. *Psychological Science*, *16*, 814–819.

Bailenson, J. N., & Yee, N. (2007). Virtual interpersonal touch: Haptic interaction and copresence in collaborative virtual environments. *International Journal of Multimedia Tools and Applications*, *37*(1), 5–14.

Blascovich, J. (2008). *Challenge and threat* (pp. 431–446). In A. J. Elliot (Ed.) Handbook of approach and avoidance motivation. New York: Erlbaum.

Blascovich, J., & Bailenson, J. N. (in press). *More human than human: How virtual reality is changing human existence.* New York: Morrow.

Blascovich J., Hurst J., & McCall, C. (2009). *Virtual stigma and the clash of consciousness.* Manuscript under review.

Blascovich, J., Loomis, J., Beall, A. C., Swinth, K. R., Hoyt, C. L., & Bailenson, J. N. (2002). Immersive virtual environment technology as a methodological tool for social psychology. *Psychological Inquiry, 2*, 103–124.

Blascovich, J., & Mendes, W. B. (2000). Challenge and threat appraisals: The role of affective cues. In J. Forgas (Ed.), *Feeling and thinking: The role of affect in social cognition* (pp. 59–82). Cambridge, England: Cambridge University Press.

Blascovich, J., Mendes, W. B., Hunter, S. B., & Lickel, B., & Kowai-Bell, N. (2001). Perceiver threat in social interactions with stigmatized others. *Journal of Personality and Social Psychology, 80*, 253–267.

Blascovich, J., & Tomaka, J. (1996). The biopsychosocial model of arousal regulation. In M. Zanna (Ed.), *Advances in experimental social psychology* (Vol. 28, pp. 1–51). New York: Academic Press.

Boellstorff, T. (2008). *Coming of age in Second Life: An anthropologist explores the virtually human*. Princeton, NJ: Princeton University Press.

Cacioppo, J. T., Petty, R. E., Losch, M. E., & Kim, H. S. (1986). Electromyographic activity over facial muscle regions can differentiate the valence and intensity of affective reactions. *Journal of Personality and Social Psychology, 50*(2), 260–268.

Chalmers, D. (1995). Facing up to the problem of consciousness. *Journal of Consciousness Studies, 2,* 200–219.

Darwin, C. (1873). *The expression of emotions in man and animals.* New York: Appleton.

Devine, P. (1989). Stereotypes and prejudice: Their automatic and controlled components. *Journal of Personality and Social Psychology, 56,* 5–18.

Dotsch, R., & Wigboldus, D. H. J. (2008). Virtual prejudice. *Journal of Experimental Social Psychology, 44*(4), 1194–1198.

Fang, I. (2008). *Alphabet to Internet: Mediated communication in our lives.* St. Paul, MN: Rada Press.

Fazio, R. (1990). Multiple processes by which attitudes guide behavior. *Advances in Experimental Social Psychology, 23,* 75–109.

Fox, J., & Bailenson, J. N. (2009). Virtual self-modeling: The effects of vicarious reinforcement and identification on exercise behaviors. *Media Psychology, 12,* 1–25.

Gallup International. (2009). *Religion in the world at the end of the millennium.* Retrieved January 15, 2010, from http://www.gallup-international.com/ContentFiles/millennium15.asp

Gibson, W. (1984). *Neuromancer.* New York: Ace Books.

Gillath, O., McCall, C., Shaver, P., & Blascovich J. B. (2008). Reactions to a needy virtual person: Using an immersive virtual environment to measure prosocial tendencies. *Media Psychology, 11,* 259–282.

Guadagno, R. E., Blascovich, J., Bailenson, J. N., & McCall, C. (2007). Virtual humans and persuasion: The effects of agency and behavioral realism. *Media Psychology, 10,* 1–22.

Guttman, L. (1954). *The principal components of scalable attitudes.* New York: Free Press.

Hall, E. T. (1963). A system for the notation of proxemic behavior. *American Anthropologist, 65,* 1003–1026.

Haney, C., Banks, C., & Zimbardo, P. (1973). Interpersonal dynamics in a simulated prison. *International Journal of Criminology & Penology, 1,* 69–97.

Harper, D. (2001). *Attitude.* Retrieved February 12, 2009, from *Online Etymology Dictionary* Web site: www.etymonline.com

Huxley, A. (2004). *The doors of perception.* New York: HarperCollins. (Original work published 1954)

Internet World Statistics. (2009). *Internet usage statistics: The Internet big picture.* Retrieved February 12, 2009, from Internet World Statistics Web site: http://www.internetworldstats.com/stats.htm

Klinger, E. (1978). Modes of normal conscious flow. In K. S. Pope & J. L. Singer (Eds.), *The stream of consciousness.* New York: Plenum Press.

Laming, D. (2003). Psychological relativity. *Behavioral and Brain Sciences, 26,* 416–417.

LaPierre, R. (1934). Attitudes vs. actions. *Social Forces, 13,* 230–237.

Lewin, K., Heider, F., & Heider, G. (1936). *Principles of topological psychology.* New York: McGraw-Hill.

Likert, R. (1932). A technique for the measurement of attitudes. *Archives of Psychology, 22,* 55.

Loomis, J. M., Blascovich, J., & Beall, A. C. (1999). Immersive virtual environments as a basic research tool in psychology. *Behavior Research Methods, Instruments, & Computers, 31,* 557–564.

McCall, C., Blascovich, J., Young, A., & Persky, S. (2009). Using immersive virtual environments to measure proxemic behavior and to predict aggression. *Social Influence, 4,* 138–154.

Nosek, B. A., Greenwald, A. G., & Banaji, M. R. (2007). The implicit association test at age 7: A methodological and conceptual review. In J. A. Bargh (Ed.), *Social psychology and the unconscious: The automaticity of higher mental processes* (pp. 265–292). New York: Psychology Press.

Osgood, C. E., Suci, G. J., & Tannenbaum, P. H. (1957). *The measurement of meaning.* Champaign: University of Illinois Press.

Packard, V. (1957). *The hidden persuaders.* New York: McKay.

Schooler, J. W. (2002). Re-representing consciousness: Dissociations between experience and meta-consciousness. *Trends in Cognitive Sciences, 6,* 339–344.

Shepard, R. (1984). Ecological constraints on internal representation: Resonant kinematics of perceiving, imaging, thinking and dreaming. *Psychological Review, 91,* 417–447.

Smallwood, J., & Schooler, J. W. (2006). The restless mind. *Psychological Bulletin, 132,* 946–958.

Sommer, R., & Becker, F. D. (1969). Territorial defense and the good neighbor. *Journal of Personality and Social Psychology, 11,* 85–92.

Stephenson, N. (1992). *Snow crash.* New York: Bantam Dell.

Thurstone, L. L. (1928). Attitudes can be measured. *American Journal of Sociology, 33,* 529–554.

Wittenbrink, B., & Schwarz, N. (2007). *Implicit measures of attitudes.* New York: Guilford Press.

Yee, N., & Bailenson, J. N. (2006). Walk a mile in digital shoes: The impact of embodied perspective-taking on the reduction of negative stereotyping in immersive virtual environments. *Proceedings of PRESENCE 2006: The 9th Annual International Workshop on Presence.* August 24–26, Cleveland, Ohio, USA.

Yee, N., Bailenson, J. N., & Ducheneaut, N. (2009). The Proteus effect: Implications of transformed digital self-representation on online and offline behavior. *Communication Research, 36,* 285–312.

Index